Biblical Narrative and the Death of the Rhapsode

Indiana Studies in Biblical Literature
Herbert Marks, general editor

Biblical Narrative and the Death of the Rhapsode

Robert S. Kawashima

INDIANA UNIVERSITY PRESS
BLOOMINGTON AND INDIANAPOLIS

Publication of this book is made possible in part
by generous support from the Koret Foundation.

Chapter 2 was originally published in *Prooftexts* 21 (2001): 158–78;
publisher, Indiana University Press.

An abridged version of chapter 6 previously appeared as: "Verbal Medium
and Narrative Art in Homer and the Bible," *Philosophy and Literature* 28 (2004):
103–17; publisher, The Johns Hopkins University Press.

This book is a publication of

Indiana University Press
601 North Morton Street
Bloomington, IN 47404-3797 USA

http://iupress.indiana.edu
Telephone orders　800-842-6796
Fax orders　812-855-7931
Orders by e-mail　iuporder@indiana.edu

© 2004 by Robert S. Kawashima

The paper used in this publication meets the minimum requirements of
American National Standard for Information Sciences—Permanence of Paper
for Printed Library Materials, ANSI Z39.48-1984.

Manufactured in the United States of America

Library of Congress Cataloging-in-Publication Data

Kawashima, Robert S., date
Biblical narrative and the death of the rhapsode / Robert S. Kawashima.
p. cm. — (Indiana studies in biblical literature)
Includes bibliographical references and index.
ISBN 0-253-34477-8 (cloth : alk. paper)
1. Narration in the Bible. 2. Bible—Criticism, Narrative.
I. Title. II. Series.
BS521.7.K38 2004
221.6'6—dc22   2004009431
1 2 3 4 5   09 08 07 06 05 04

Entia non sunt multiplicanda praeter necessitatem.
—Occam

Sire, je n'ai pas eu besoin de cette hypothèse.
—Laplace

I wish to propose for the reader's favourable consideration a doctrine which may, I fear, appear wildly paradoxical and subversive. The doctrine in question is this: that it is undesirable to believe a proposition when there is no ground whatever for supposing it true. I must, of course, admit that if such an opinion became common it would completely transform our social life and our political system; since both are at present faultless, this must weigh against it.

Bertrand Russell, *Skeptical Essays,* I

CONTENTS

ACKNOWLEDGMENTS

This book originated in my encounter with Ann Banfield's groundbreaking work *Unspeakable Sentences.* In this remarkable study she characterized the language of the novel in terms of two syntactic features: the narrative preterite (*passé simple*) and the representation of consciousness (*style indirect libre*), neither of which appears in the spoken language. She also raised the historical thesis, first proposed by Walter Benjamin and others, linking the rise of the novel to the decline of the epic art of storytelling. While pondering these ideas, it occurred to me—much to my surprise—that similar arguments could be made for biblical narrative. My initial, tentative exploration of this hypothesis (which has since become chapters 3 and 4 of this book) convinced me in a preliminary way that one could indeed describe the syntax of biblical narrative in much the same terms as that of the novel, and that this had implications for the origins of the Bible's narrative art. I saw here the makings of an interesting project, but it would need to be extended and refined. I next reexamined Robert Alter's now classic studies *The Art of Biblical Narrative* and *The Art of Biblical Poetry,* both of which had already played a crucial role in my academic formation, inspiring me, in particular, to take a specifically literary approach to the Bible. The question before me now was whether the Bible itself provided clues to its own literary origins. It did, in fact, in archaic biblical poetry. Professor Alter had, of course, already written eloquently on both biblical poetry and narrative, as well as on the differences between the two. In light of my nascent project, however, it dawned on me that in certain cases (such as Judges 4 and 5) these differences took on the form of a historical process that further corroborated my thesis. (The literary-historical analysis that grew out of this realization would eventually become chapter 2 of the present study.) I owe a scholarly and intellectual debt to both Robert Alter and Ann Banfield that cannot adequately be registered by mere documentation. I therefore wish to take this opportunity to offer my thanks here as well.

My debts do not end there. Ronald Hendel, Chana Kronfeld, and William Propp all read the entire manuscript and encouraged me during various stages of its development. Ariel Bloch, Cynthia Miller, and

Michael O'Connor generously read and commented on the book's linguistic arguments. Edward Greenstein kindly provided me with advance copies of relevant forthcoming work. Richard Friedman read parts of the manuscript and gave me the opportunity to present some of my ideas to his colleagues and students at the University of California, San Diego. It was Mark Griffith who first introduced me as a graduate student to Homer and Homer criticism (in particular, to Zielinski's law, which eventually found its way into chapter 5). Michael Nagler provided sage counsel regarding Homer, and Thomas Rosenmeyer read and commented on chapter 6. I have presented several chapters of this book before a number of professional societies, including the Society of Biblical Literature (2000 and 2001), the Association of Literary Scholars and Critics (2001), the Modern Language Association (2002), and the Society for the Study of Narrative Literature (2003). I would like to thank the various parties involved in helping me formulate my ideas more clearly.

Various revisions of the present study were undertaken while I was a Faculty Fellow at the University of California, Berkeley (2001–2003). Final preparation of the manuscript was completed during my first year as a Dorot Assistant Professor / Faculty Fellow at New York University's Skirball Department of Hebrew and Judaic Studies. I am grateful to both institutions for facilitating my work on this book in the form of a reduced teaching load. Finally, I would like to thank the Koret Foundation for its generous financial support, making possible the publication of this book through its Jewish Studies Publications Program.

I dedicate this book to my sister, my mother, and the memory of my father.

ABBREVIATIONS

AB	Anchor Bible
ANET	Pritchard, Ancient Near Eastern Texts Relating to the Old Testament
BASOR	Bulletin of the American Schools of Oriental Research
BDB	Brown, Driver, and Briggs, *A Hebrew and English Lexicon of the Old Testament*
Bib	Biblica
BibOr	Bibliotheca Orientalis
CTA	Herdner, Corpus des tablettes en cunéiformes alphabétiques
CBQ	Catholic Biblical Quarterly
GKC	Gesenius-Kautzsch-Cowley, *Gesenius' Hebrew Grammar*
HTR	Harvard Theological Review
IOS	Israel Oriental Studies
JBL	Journal of Biblical Literature
Joüon-Muraoka	A Grammar of Biblical Hebrew
JSOT	Journal for the Study of the Old Testament
KAI	Donner and Röllig, Kanaanäische und aramäische Inschriften
MT	Masoretic Text
NRSV	New Revised Standard Version
OED	Oxford English Dictionary
OS	Oudtestamentische Studiën
PTL	Poetics and Theory of Literature
UF	Ugarit Forschungen
VT	Vetus Testamentum
Waltke-O'Connor	An Introduction to Biblical Hebrew Syntax
ZAH	Zeitschrift für Althebraistik
ZAW	Zeitschrift für die Alttestamentliche Wissenschaft

*Biblical Narrative and the
Death of the Rhapsode*

•1•

INTRODUCTION: THE NOVELTY OF BIBLICAL NARRATIVE

Above all I should have to be on my guard against those phrases
which are chosen rather by the lips than by the mind, those hu-
morous phrases such as we utter in conversation . . . whereas
real books should be the offspring not of daylight and casual
talk but of darkness and silence.
　　—Marcel Proust, *Time Regained* (*In Search of Lost Time*)

The storyteller takes what he tells from experience—his own or
that reported by others. And he in turn makes it the experience
of those who are listening to his tale. The novelist has isolated
himself. The birthplace of the novel is the solitary individual.
　　　　　　—Walter Benjamin, "The Storyteller"

[T]he origin of the words drama, epic, and lyric suggests that
the central principle of genre is simple enough. The basis of
generic distinctions in literature appears to be the radical of
presentation. Words may be acted in front of a spectator; they
may be spoken in front of a listener; they may be sung or
chanted; or they may be written for a reader. Criticism, we note
resignedly in passing, has no word for the individual member
of an author's audience, and the word "audience" itself does
not really cover all genres, as it is slightly illogical to describe
the readers of a book as an audience. The basis of generic criticism in any case is rhetorical, in the sense that the genre is de-
termined by the conditions established between the poet and
his public.
　　　　　　—Northrop Frye, *Anatomy of Criticism*

If . . . to write is to pass from "I" to "he," but if "he" when substi-
tuted for "I" does not simply designate another me . . . what remains to be discovered is what is at stake when writing responds
to the demands of this uncharacterizable "he." In the narrative
form, we hear . . . something indeterminate speaking, something that the evolution of this form outlines, isolates, so that it
gradually becomes manifest, though in a deceptive way. The

1

> "he" is the unlighted occurrence of what takes place when one
> tells a story. The distant epic narrator recounts exploits that
> happened and that he seems to be reproducing, whether or
> not he witnessed them. But the narrator is not a historian. His
> song is the domain where the event that takes place there
> comes to speech, in the presence of a memory. . . . The myste-
> rious "he" of the epic institution very quickly divides: the "he"
> becomes the impersonal coherence of a *story* . . . ; the *story*
> stands by itself, preformed in the thought of a demiurge, and
> since it exists on its own, there is nothing left to do but tell it.
> —Maurice Blanchot, "The Narrative Voice"

The Rhapsode and the Scribe

Plato's *Ion* begins with the eponymous rhapsode, who has just arrived
from a competition where he took first prize for his performance of
Homer, crossing paths with Socrates. The philosopher immediately engages him in a discussion of his craft, professing, in his characteristically
ironic fashion, envy of the rhapsode's art:

> For that it befits your art [*tę technę*] for the body to be always
> adorned and for you to appear as beautiful as possible, and that, at
> the same time, it is necessary to be busy with many good poets and
> above all with Homer, the best and most divine of the poets, and
> to learn his thought thoroughly, not just his words, is enviable. Be-
> cause one could never be a good rhapsode [*rhapsǫdos*] if he did
> not understand the things said [*legomena*] by the poet. The rhap-
> sode must be the interpreter [*hermēnea*] of the thought of the poet
> to the listeners [*akouousi*], but to do this finely is impossible for
> the one who does not recognize what the poet means. All these
> things, then, deserve to be envied. (530b–c)[1]

Socrates, however, feels anything but envy for this ancient celebrity. As
becomes clear in the course of the dialogue, both the glamor of his life-
style and his supposed role as "interpreter" actually reflect the vacuous if
dramatic nature of his so-called art.[2] For Socrates argues that Ion performs not by "art" (*technē*) at all, which would entail *technical* knowledge
(*epistēmē*, 536c), but by a "divine power" (*theia . . . dynamis*, 533d),
namely, the Muse who "inspires" (*entheous*, 533e) or by whom one is "possessed" (*katechetai*, 536a). He compares the ecstatic Ion to a mere link in
a chain of metal rings dangling from a magnet (535e–536d). Within this

image, Ion, a derivative figure at some remove from the great ur-Singer, occupies a humble position in the middle of this line of epic inspiration, mediating the power of Homer (top link) and his Muse (magnet) to the rhapsode's contemporary audience (bottom link). One sees evidence of this field of force in the impact of performance upon Ion himself: "When I speak of something pitiful, my eyes fill with tears, and when of something frightening or terrible, my hair stands on end from fear and my heart leaps" (535d). Pointing out the irrational nature of such emotion, Socrates then asks Ion whether his inspired madness does not also infect his audience. He replies: "Indeed I do know it very finely. For I look down on them each time from the platform above as they are crying, casting terrible looks and following with astonishment the things said" (535e). In fact, as a paid performer Ion's livelihood depends on it.

On the other side of the Mediterranean, at about the same time that Socrates questions Ion, we find an analogous though radically different figure in the Hebrew tradition, Ezra the scribe. As part of an effort to re-establish the Jewish community in Judah following the Babylonian captivity, Ezra in effect publishes a document referred to as "the Book of the Law of Moses"—most likely the Pentateuch, which he himself may very well have redacted[3]—by reading it aloud in public.

> And the seventh month arrived, the Israelites being in their towns, and all the people gathered as one man in the square that is in front of the Water Gate. And they told Ezra the scribe [*hassōpēr*] to bring the Book [*sēper*] of the Law of Moses which God had commanded Israel. And Ezra the priest brought the law before the congregation, from man to woman and all who could listen with understanding [*mēbîn*]. And he read [*wayyiqrāʾ*] from it before the square that is in front of the Water Gate from dawn to midday, in the presence of the men and the women and those who could understand [*wĕhammĕbînîm*], the ears of all the people being turned toward the Book of the Law. And Ezra the scribe stood on a wooden platform which had been made for this purpose. . . . And Ezra the scribe opened the Book in the eyes of all the people, for he was standing above all the people, and as he opened it all the people stood. And . . . the Levites were helping the people understand [*mēbînîm*] the Law, and the people were standing in their place. And so they read [*wayyiqrĕʾû*] from the Book, from the Law of God, interpreted [*mĕpōrāš*], and were giving the sense [*śekel*], and the people understood [*wayyābînû*] the reading [*miqrāʾ*].
> (Neh. 7:72b–8:8)

In this passage Ezra has none of his Greek counterpart's charisma. He neither competes nor performs professionally. To be sure, he is a public figure, but as priest and scribe he is an academic recluse at heart, "fluent [*māhîr*] in the Law of Moses" (Ezra 7:6), one must assume, thanks only to countless hours spent in cloistered study. His performance reflects the nature of his vocation, for the narrative shows no interest in his dramatic interpretation. Although Ezra, like Ion, occupies center stage, all eyes and even ears are in fact directed toward the Book (Neh. 8:2, 3). In this respect Ezra merely actualizes the reading of the written word in a world in which both literacy and the materials used in manuscript production are relatively scarce.[4] While the Levites interpret, they do so not through theatrical gesture and intonation but by explaining obscurities and/or translating the Hebrew original into Aramaic.[5] Interpretation here is didactic, not dramatic. Thus, the emotional response of this audience (Neh. 8:9), unlike that of the rhapsode's, comes not from the power of Ezra's voice but from their sense of moral failure as revealed through the recitation of the Book of the Law (Nehemiah 9).

Ezra and Ion, whom one might take as emblematic figures of their respective narrative traditions, help bring into focus the contrast I would like to trace in the following study: the art of biblical narrative versus that of epic. On the one hand, we have Ion, the embodiment of dramatic performance and of memory. In Ezra, on the other hand, we see the reclusive scribe (*sōpēr*), who relies not on memory but on the book (*sēper*) and who appears in public merely to promulgate the written word. This contrast, however, describes not merely a conceptual dichotomy between two modes of narrative art and its transmission but, in the case of the ancient Near East, a historical development as well, specifically helping to solve a problem in the history of Israelite literature and religion that I will refer to as the "novelty" of biblical narrative.[6]

The Novelty of Biblical Narrative

Scholars have long noted that the prose narratives of the Hebrew Bible present us with something decisively new and unprecedented in ancient literature.[7] Long before Herodotus and even Homer, Israelite writers practiced a conspicuously innovative narrative art, anticipating in striking ways the modern novelist's craft. In spite of the undeniable linguistic tradition that runs from biblical literature back to its closest known antecedent, the Ugaritic narrative poems, there are substantive differences between the two corpora, raising important questions. Why does biblical narrative seem so new, so different in antiquity? What factors in ancient Israel contributed to this artistic achievement?

Gerhard von Rad, for instance, can only express a certain wonder at the sudden appearance of "historical writing"—namely, the so-called Succession Narrative recounting David's reign—in ancient Israel: "We cannot trace the origins of ancient Israelite historical writing. At a particular point in time it is there, and already we have it in its fully developed form. We can, however, trace the predisposing factors which made such an achievement possible to this people."[8] Unable to account for the origins and development of historical narrative in the Bible, to provide history with a history, he shrewdly turns to the task of imagining the cultural conditions needed for such a novel literary achievement: "Only in Solomon's era did the new order, which began in the time of David, develop its cultural potential to touch every facet of human existence. . . . A new life opened up, culturally much more broadly based than that which had been possible only a generation earlier. . . . In short, the time of Solomon was a period of 'enlightenment,' of a sharp break with the ancient patriarchal code of living" (203).

For von Rad's views on biblical literary history one must turn to comments he makes with respect to the narratives of the so-called Yahwist in his penetrating form-critical analysis of the Hexateuch.[9] As with the Succession Narrative, J, too, is "redolent of the untrammeled days of Solomon" (69). Here, however, he attempts to trace "the main stages by which traditions originally bound up with the cultus reached the literary form they have in the work of the Yahwist," concluding: "The materials have been 'historicised': their inner content has actually been removed bodily from its narrow sacral context into the freer atmosphere of common history" (68). In other words, various "cultic legends" (nonhistorical narratives whose original *Sitze-im-Leben* are to be found in pre-monarchic cultic ceremonies) evolved through a process of "historicization" into those "history-like" prose narratives characteristic of J[10]—a process related, no doubt, to the very impulse to write history. Von Rad thereby joins the history of literature to the history of religion, albeit through form criticism's crude understanding of the relation of form to function. One should note, furthermore, that his is a decidedly Israelite reconstruction, positing only that portion of the biblical text's prehistory internal to the Israelite cult. While he does allude briefly to "the problem of the more or less immediate literary antecedents on which the Yahwist may have drawn," at this point he considers it "altogether an open question," though he immediately, if cautiously, adds: "Since the discoveries of Ras Shamra [Ugarit] there is less reason than ever to doubt the possibility or indeed the probability that such literary models were available as separate entities" (64).

In fact, not long after these remarks were first published in 1938, Umberto Cassuto asserted what von Rad had only suggested, namely, that an uninterrupted poetic tradition flows from Ugarit to Israel. Not unlike von Rad, he marvels at what he calls "the earliest stages of Biblical literature": "[T]hey present us with perfected, refined compositions that attest to a long-standing artistic tradition, as though they were preceded by a developmental process over many centuries."[11] But Cassuto, taking advantage of the recently discovered Ugaritic tablets from Ras Shamra, finds that Canaanite literature shares with the Bible a repertoire of "fixed idioms and expressions." He therefore reasons that the biblical writers must have inherited a "linguistic tradition" that had been perfected centuries earlier by their Canaanite predecessors, concluding in no uncertain terms: "Biblical literature is nothing but a continuation of the Canaanite literature that preceded it" (17).

Both Cassuto and von Rad link the distinctive character of biblical narrative to developments within its content—literary history as thematic evolution. Von Rad, while practicing *form* criticism, actually has little to say by way of formal developments, speaking instead of "cultic material" whose outward form survives intact in J but whose "inner content" has been "historicised"—presumably by rejecting the cyclical patterns of myth.[12] Focusing on the Yahwist's work of historicization, he mentions "the problem of the more or less immediate literary antecedents on which the Yahwist may have drawn"—a question of form as well as of content—only in passing, presumably because he did not think a comparison of biblical narrative with its "literary models" would shed light on his understanding of J.[13] Cassuto, too, blinded by the very brilliance of his analysis of the linguistic tradition underlying biblical and Canaanite literature and focusing solely on the level of repeated word-pairs and phrases, can see only formal conservatism alongside the Bible's thematic innovation, "a literature new in truth, in its content and spirit, but a continuation of the old in its forms— new wine, so to speak, in an old flagon."[14] While such a distinction appeals to intuitions many of us share regarding the apparent contrast between the Bible and epic or myth—which I myself invoked earlier in my opening remarks—it is not enough to point out this distinction within their respective thematic concerns. For the Bible, however venerable its underlying tradition, is new in *form* as well as in *content*. In attributing the Bible's novelty solely to its thematization of history, both these scholars overlook the remarkable formal developments taking place in biblical narrative and their implications for literary history.

In this respect, Frank Moore Cross's reconstruction of the epic traditions of early Israel represents an important advance in our understanding of the relationship of biblical narrative (specifically of J and E, the "epic sources") to antecedent oral traditions.[15] In effect, he revisits von Rad's "Problem of the Hexateuch," now with full cognizance of the Ugaritic discoveries von Rad had not taken account of—specifically citing the studies by Cassuto, mentioned earlier—and substitutes for form criticism the oral-formulaic theory developed in Homeric studies by Milman Parry and Albert Lord. He can thus maintain a certain continuity between biblical narrative and epic: "I prefer to speak of J and E as variant forms of an older, largely poetic epic cycle, and hence to term JE 'epic sources.' . . . There are compelling reasons . . . to postulate that the Hebrew epic continued in the tradition of the older Canaanite epic singers" (20). At the same time, however, he can perceive the formal transformation that occurs between oral poetry and written prose: "We possess lyric poems with strong narrative content in the Song of the Sea (Exodus 15) and the Song of Deborah (Judges 5). In both instances we possess side by side prose narrative accounts (Exodus 14 and Judges 4), and in both instances the poetry is earlier, the prose secondary and derivative. We see the process of prosaizing poetic composition before our eyes" (21). Echoing von Rad's earlier study, he speculates as to J's pre-literary history:

> The Yahwist's work, unlike much of the lore he draws upon, is somewhat removed from direct cultic interest. He has transformed cultically formed tradition and poetry into "history" and prose. . . . We must suppose that the Yahwist turns epic materials into his prose work at a time when Israel's cultic institutions, notably the festivals of the league, in which the epic events were recited and enacted, had fallen into desuetude, and epic tradition thus loosened from its primary setting and function. (29)[16]

Like von Rad before him, Cross relates the rise of Israel's innovative narrative art to the "desuetude" of an older epic tradition and its related cultic institutions. Unfortunately he makes only scattered, if insightful, remarks concerning the defining characteristics of this novel narrative form.

Literary studies, meanwhile, have posited an analogous dichotomy in their analyses of the formal aesthetic dimension of biblical narrative. In the opening chapter of his magisterial survey of Western literature Erich Auerbach makes a number of suggestive observations regarding the contrastive styles of Homer and the Bible.[17] On the one hand we have the "Homeric style," whose "basic impulse . . . [is] to represent phenomena in a fully externalized form" (6), all of which consequently "takes place in the foreground" (7). The style of biblical narrative, on the other hand, "an equally ancient and equally epic style from a different world of forms" (7), gives rise to the opposite effect: "the externalization of only so much of the phenomena as is necessary for the purpose of the narrative, all else left in obscurity" (11), so that this narrative world, as he famously observes, is "fraught with background" (12). In effect, the contrasts he so brilliantly illuminates between Homer and the Bible, which we might take as the dual foundations of the Western literary tradition, help to differentiate between two fundamental narrative modes—not premised, one might add, on any direct historical relationship.

Robert Alter in effect continues this line of thought in his classic study of biblical narrative, making the double-edged argument that these ancient narratives surprisingly find their best analogue in what we call "prose fiction," and that they constitute a "sacred history" which should be understood against the background of the poetic narratives of ancient Near Eastern epic, in which "humanity [is] locked into a set of fixed hierarchies in [a] mythological world-view."[18] In a series of characteristically illuminating readings, he analyzes a number of narrative techniques crucial to biblical narrative, demonstrating throughout how "the flexibility of the prose medium enables the writer to introduce psychological distinctions, dialectical reversals of thematic direction, that would not have been feasible in the verse narratives of the ancient Near East."[19] Style, however, constitutes a merely implicit aspect of his study.[20]

David Damrosch, for his part, argues against what he sees as the scholarly acceptance of an overly simplistic distinction between the historical sense of the Bible and the purportedly primitive, mythic consciousness of the rest of the ancient Near East by drawing upon recent work on Mesopotamian historiography. He observes that an incipient historical sense informs the mythic themes in such epics, such that "no sharp division can be drawn between the divinely ordered world of nature and a separate, secular world of human historical activity. . . . Consequently, Mesopotamian literature collapses the sort of distinction made . . . between epic and history."[21] Similarly, Gerald K. Gresseth, working in the field of classics, provides a fruitful comparison of *Gilgamesh* and Homer and suggests that both evince a "new view of man" and offer a "first glimpse of the idea of humanity as something separate and apart, neither god nor animal."[22] Regardless of whether one finds such objections convincing, the palpable differences between the Bible and epic remain, waiting to be explained. That the presence of a certain historical consciousness may not adequately account for these only makes the question of form even more compelling.

Well aware of this fact, Damrosch looks for the origins of biblical narrative in the transformations of genre, arguing that the Bible's "historical prose" flows out of the literary confluence of the two dominant genres of the ancient Near East: poetic epic and prose chronicle.[23] While in principle a valuable contribution in and of itself, Damrosch's study does not in the end provide a satisfying solution to the enigma of, in his own words, "the manifest superiority of biblical narrative over the historical prose of neighboring countries."[24] As Edward Greenstein, in his sympathetic and insightful review of *The Narrative Covenant*, observes: Damrosch has "unnecessarily boxed himself in by confining his genealogy to genres and their mergers."[25] Greenstein shrewdly proposes instead that we investigate certain stylistic innovations of biblical narrative, such as "a switch from first person to third person narration" and "transformations of oral into written composition."[26] One returns, in other words, to Alter's thesis that modern prose fiction—writing par excellence, which is, as we will see, marked precisely by its use of the third person—provides the best rubric for interpreting biblical narrative, and to Cross's thesis that in Israel an epic oral tradition has given way to a literary one.

This brief survey of scholarship provides enough background for the arguments I will make here. Both philological and literary studies have posited a dichotomy between biblical narrative and epic. I propose that one can account for these two narrative modes with reference to the different aesthetic possibilities available to oral tradition and literature. It is no coincidence that philologists successfully analyzed the Pentateuch (as well as other books of the Bible) into divers sources. As a result, the "documentary hypothesis," that great achievement of nineteenth-century philology that created the modern discipline of biblical studies, taught us to perceive behind the Pentateuch the long history of composition and redaction that its narratives and laws have undergone *qua* text. Tellingly, the *Iliad* and the *Odyssey* did not succumb to the same sort of analysis. While various regional and historical dialects of Greek could be detected in Homer's poetic language, these did not provide the means to dissolve the epics into discrete sources and strata. Rather, the "Homeric question" found a different solution entirely in the work of Milman Parry and (his student) Albert Lord. Through the comparative study of Homeric epic with then living South Slavic oral traditions, they revealed Homer to be a singer who "improvised" his tales in an oral performance. Homer's formulaic style, the apparent product of a venerable oral tradition similar to those they observed first-hand in their fieldwork, provided the epic singer with a language suited to the needs of oral performance unaided by writing.

Similarly, as I have noted in passing, scholars have found evidence in both Ugaritic and early biblical poetry of an oral-formulaic tradition analogous to that proposed for Homer by Parry and Lord. In this case syntactic parallelism and those traditional word-pairs analyzed by Cassuto functioned much like the oral formula did for Homer. In light of linguistic and literary theories of narrative—and of the modern novel in particular—I will argue that biblical narrative is the result of a specifically written verbal art that one should counterpose to the oral verbal art of epic.[27] Not unlike Walter Benjamin, who perceived in "the rise of the novel at the beginning of modern times" a "symptom of . . . the decline of storytelling,"[28] I propose that the novelistic art of biblical narrative similarly results from decline of the epic arts in ancient Israel. In this view Homer and the Bible become exemplary instances of oral and written verbal art. Thus, beyond my strictly historical thesis, my study has more general theoretical implications for the study of narrative, literature, and oral tradition inasmuch as it explores, on a broadly comparative level, the distinctive features of oral and written verbal art.

Oral and Written Verbal Art

My hypothesis thus raises the question of medium in the verbal arts. While infrequently addressed, it is not a new problem. Proust, for instance, likened the achievement of Flaubert's "grammatical genius" to "what certain painters were in the history of art who changed the pigments."[29] Within this analogy, Flaubert's celebrated style, "the entirely new and personal use that he made of the past definite, the past indefinite, the present participle and certain pronouns and prepositions," constitutes in effect a technological advance, a milestone in the history of the novel, "renew[ing] our vision of things almost as much as Kant, with his Categories."[30] Throughout this study I similarly treat writing as a type of technological development, a new verbal medium possessing—like any medium in any art—its own distinctive though not necessarily superior set of inherent possibilities. Specifically, the relationship between speaker and speech is different from that between writer and writing. On the one hand, this difference is linguistic. While the speaker is present in language through various grammatical features of speech, the writer, in the course of literary history, is marked by an increasing absence from the language of the novel. It was this process that interested Roland Barthes in *Writing Degree Zero*,[31] and which eventually led him to make his infamous (because misunderstood) announcement of the "death of the author" apropos of the novel.[32] Biblical narrative, as I will argue, similarly marks the death of the rhapsode. On the other hand, this difference resides in the simple fact that writing allows an author to edit, to rewrite, whereas speech exists instantaneously and irrevocably in the act of its utterance. The ability to manipulate language and, more generally, narrative form gives rise in written narratives to techniques foreign to the traditional, improvisational art of epic, techniques premised on the impulse to innovate. Barthes recognizes this aspect of writing in what he calls the "Freedom" of the writer: "True, I can today select such and such mode of writing, and in so doing assert my freedom, aspire to the freshness of novelty or to a tradition; but it is impossible to develop it within duration without gradually becoming a prisoner of someone else's words and even of my own."[33] The fate of writing is the necessity of this freedom. Consequently, if the performance and reception of orally composed epics require the singer's adherence to the generative rules of tradition, the biblical writers demonstrate the telling freedom to break such rules.

It is for such reasons that French literary theory was for a time keenly interested in the problem of *écriture*. Theorists such as Barthes, Blanchot, and Foucault, to name a few, recognized in writing a set of inherent possibilities and problems that the novel in particular explored and resolved.[34] Strictly speaking, the very concept of "literature," etymologically related to "letter" and historically connected to the notion of belles lettres, derives from this medium. More often than not, however, literary theory, when it has bothered to define its object of study—namely, literature—has paid little if any attention to the question of verbal medium, as though "literary" were simply a synonym for "artistic." Attempts to define literary language and literary technique have therefore merely tended to distinguish between prosaic and poetic uses of language, thereby ignoring those features that characterize oral versus written aesthetic uses of language.

In this study I will make use of a number of theories of verbal arts in such a way as to take account of the question of verbal medium. In order to give a preliminary sense of what is at stake in the distinction between the spoken and written word, I will introduce the key linguistic and literary analyses of the language of narrative in order to provide the initial framework for the argument behind this book. Here I will give only minimal descriptions of each, however, since I will engage in more detailed discussions, as needed, in subsequent chapters.

My survey begins with Emile Benveniste's groundbreaking essay "The Correlations of Tense in the French Verb."[35] Observing that French has two preterites—the perfect or *passé composé* belonging to the spoken language, the aorist or *passé simple* restricted to the written—Benveniste posits two "distinct and complementary" systems in language corresponding to these two preterites, *discours* (discourse) and *histoire* (narration), respectively, thereby allowing for a style peculiar to writing.[36] Though Benveniste limited his study to the consideration of historical narratives (suggested by the term *histoire*), Käte Hamburger argued for an analogous dichotomy in her attempt to articulate the "logic of literature."[37] On the basis of the noteworthy behavior of the "epic preterite"—for my purposes, the co-occurrence of present and future temporal deictics with the preterite typical of *erlebte Rede* (or *style indirect libre*)[38]—she distinguishes between *die Aussage* (statement) system of language, which she attributes to a speaking subject, and *das fiktionale Erzählen* (fictional narration), which she claims has no narrator.[39] Thus, for Hamburger, too, there exist written narratives that do not presuppose the underlying speech act of a putative narrator.

Not surprisingly, Benveniste and Hamburger have been variously misread or unread. For their notion of a narrative without a narrator, given current orthodoxy, seems counterintuitive, running contrary as it does to the regnant view, which starts from the axiom that a story must be told by a narrator, be it effaced, omniscient, or otherwise nonhuman.[40] It remained for S.-Y. Kuroda to confront the foundations of narrative theory head on and question the axiomatic status of the narrator, while at the same time bringing the framework of generative linguistics to bear on the problem. On the basis of syntactic constructions in Japanese, he posits the existence of two distinct styles or modes of language use, "reportive" and "non-reportive," analogous to the linguistic dichotomies proposed by Benveniste and Hamburger.[41] Reportive style assumes a communicative function for language: a speaker conveying information to a hearer. As I have already observed, it has tacitly become the universal paradigm for all language use. Non-reportive style, he suggests, has no speaker but is merely written. For instance, for a certain class of sensation words a native Japanese speaker *expresses* his or her own subjective state through an adjective but uses a corresponding verb to *indicate* another's state: (1) *"Watasi wa atui"* ("I am hot"); (2) *"Anata wa atugatte iru"* ("You are hot"); (3) *"John wa atugatte iru"* ("John is hot"). Japanese grammar, in other words, makes an epistemological distinction between subjective and objective knowledge.[42] He then goes on to observe that while a sentence using the adjective form with the third person, such as **Mary wa atukatta* (Mary was hot), is unacceptable in the spoken language, it can appear in what he calls non-reportive style—novels written in the third person, for example. Even within non-reportive style, however, this construction in the third person cannot co-occur with particles signaling the first person—for example, the particle *yo*, which means something like "I am telling you." Thus, such a construction within a non-reportive text cannot be understood in a linguistically meaningful sense as a narrator's *indication* of a character's subjective state. He suggests instead that it is the direct *expression* of a third-person subjectivity not *reported* by any narrator though nonetheless linguistically *represented*. On the basis of such linguistic evidence he rejects the "communicational theory of narrative," which defines narrative as the speech act of a narrator, in favor of a "poetic" one, presupposing only the activity of the writer.[43]

Ann Banfield in a sense synthesizes these studies in her groundbreaking linguistic analyses of the language of fiction.[44] Analogous to Benveniste and Hamburger, she posits two linguistic styles: narration (141–80) and communication (111–39).[45] However, while both Benveniste and Hamburger banish the first (and second) person from narration, Banfield adduces ample evidence to the contrary, namely, narratives written in the first person that make use of the *passé simple*, on the one hand (149), and the epic preterite of *erlebte Rede*, on the other (94–95) — Proust's *In Search of Lost Time* being the paradigmatic example here.[46] What distinguishes communication from narration, then, is the presence of the second person. In communication, a speaker ("I") addresses a hearer ("you"); narration, however, as a noncommunicative style, addresses no one in particular.[47] Thus, Proust's audience is a community of anonymous readers, while his narrator, Marcel, has no interlocutor.[48] Banfield further observes that while Benveniste's *histoire* and Hamburger's epic preterite (interpreted strictly as a defining characteristic of *erlebte Rede*) seem related to each other as noncommunicative styles, they in fact have a complementary distribution. Concluding that the style of narration comprises both, she consequently defines it through its use of two (as she calls them) "unspeakable sentences": the sentence of "pure narration" corresponding to *histoire* and the sentence of "represented consciousness" corresponding to the epic preterite. She continues Kuroda's explicit arguments against the "communicational theory of narrative," inasmuch as, working within the framework of generative linguistics, she uses the adjective "unspeakable" to refer to the fact that these two sentences are rejected by native speakers as grammatical constructions *in the spoken language*. In other words, narration has no narrator.

The style of literary narrative takes on its proper significance when considered against the background of the oral-formulaic theory developed to account for the style of the Homeric epics. For the groundbreaking work of Milman Parry and Albert Lord simultaneously, if implicitly, called attention to the peculiar condition of the written text.[49] Parry, as is well known, posited a theory of traditional composition based on the artful use of formulae: "a group of words which is regularly employed under the same metrical conditions to express a given essential idea."[50] Along with this notion of the formula, he posited the principle of "thrift," which seeks to minimize redundancy in the singer's repertoire of traditional formulae: "The thrift of a system lies in the degree in which it is free of phrases which, having the same metrical value and expressing the same idea, could replace one another."[51] Both these principles of Homer's style, as Parry eventually came to see, enabled the epic singer (*aoidos*) to compose his narrative orally within an improvisational performance.[52] But a style consisting of non-overlapping formulae, it seems to me, will not allow the development of the type of linguistic dualism that characterizes literary prose narratives. For this streamlined conventional style requires that Homer and his characters speak the same heroic language. The language of oral-traditional epic is coterminous with the singer's speech.[53] I suggest that various differences between epic and the novel can be traced back to this fundamental difference in language and style.

The Death of the Rhapsode

These narrative theories, illuminating Homer on the one hand and Joyce on the other, prove equally instructive for the problem I have referred to as the novelty of biblical narrative. In the present study I will continue that tradition in biblical criticism that perceives a radical break between the Bible and epic by arguing that the Bible's novelty results from a shift from the medium of the spoken to the written word. In exploiting this new medium, the biblical writers developed a literary sense of prose style and of formal technique surprisingly akin to that of the modern novelist. The tradition has faded and the rhapsode has died. In ancient Israel one must reckon instead with the author and his text.

In support of my claim, I will offer detailed analyses, in light of various theories of narrative art, of the language and technique of biblical narrative, demonstrating precisely how biblical narrative anticipates the modern novel. In chapters 3 and 4 I focus on the question of language, demonstrating the existence in biblical prose of versions of both of Banfield's "unspeakable sentences": "pure narration" and "represented consciousness." In chapters 5 and 6 I turn to the problem of technique, contrasting the aesthetic principles underlying two formal aspects of epic and biblical narrative: temporal structure and type-scenes. In the conclusion I finally relate the art of biblical narrative to Israelite religious thought and situate these within intellectual history through an initial excavation into the "archaeology" of ancient Israelite knowledge. I specifically argue that underlying the "Mosaic revolution" of Israel's incipient monotheism is what Foucault would call an "episteme." Monotheism's epistemic break, then, would account for the frequently noted dichotomy between biblical religion and the "pagan" religions of Mesopotamia, Canaan, and, one might add, archaic Greece, providing an appropriate backdrop to Israel's remarkable literary achievement.

While this study focuses primarily on biblical narrative, the epics of Ugarit and Homer will accompany us throughout the following chapters. Homer's superlative epic art will serve here as an exemplary achievement of oral tradition. By demonstrating the possibilities of this medium, Homer will help bring into focus various grammatical and narratological features of biblical narrative as literature. Conversely, in support of my strictly historical thesis, the Ugaritic epics figure as a synecdoche for the pre-biblical Canaanite narrative tradition, a trope fully justified by Cassuto's work, mentioned earlier, on the conventional word-pairs found in both Ugaritic and biblical poetry. The very existence of these word-pairs, shared by poetic traditions separated by several centuries, would seem to indicate the widespread and continuous existence of some sort of Canaanite poetic tradition preceding biblical narrative. In fact, in recent decades several scholars, working from the Parry-Lord hypothesis of Homeric scholarship, have persuasively argued that Ugaritic and early biblical poetry stem from a type of oral-formulaic tradition, thus refining Cassuto's original discovery.[54] According to this theory, as noted earlier, poetic parallelism functions as a type of metrical constraint, while the conventional word-pairs (Cassuto's "linguistic tradition") provide the formulaic building blocks of biblical and Ugaritic poetry. One should admit that these word-pairs, as Cassuto correctly noted, appear in biblical *prose* as well as *poetry*—which helps explain Cassuto's disregard for this fundamental generic distinction. But these are merely survivals of an obsolescent tradition that has long since fallen silent. It is between the song of poetry and the silence of prose that one finds the origins of biblical narrative.

Now the Bible provides occasional glimpses of its own origins, making possible a type of preliminary experiment with which to test my hypothesis. In the following chapter, therefore, I begin my study by examining one of the narrative situations in which we see, in Cross's words, "the process of prosaizing poetic composition before our eyes":[55] Judges 4 and 5 will illustrate the transition from oral poetry to literary prose *within* the biblical corpus itself.

Before proceeding to the next chapter, I should emphasize at the outset the role theory plays throughout this book. It will not provide a "method" to be "applied" but rather a hypothesis to be tested against the evidence of biblical prose. I have aimed not at producing results by inputting data into a critical apparatus but at discovering some truth about biblical narrative and of narrative more generally. If the resemblances thus discovered between the Bible and the novel will surprise some, these are evidence not of uncanny prescience on the part of the biblical writers, nor of my modernist bias inventing a contemporary (anachronistic) approach to biblical narrative, but of "the real" within language and narrative form. I take up, in other words, the position of philosophical realism toward my object of study. But if my study is therefore "empirical," proposing falsifiable hypotheses—that is, propositions to be scrutinized in light of the evidence—it is not "empiricist." For an empirical theory (as opposed to an empiricist description) requires a certain critical distance from mere data, namely, that abstraction or idealization known as "evidence." This is the significance of Chomsky's distinction between "competence" and "performance," and of Saussure's analogous but nonidentical distinction between *langue* and *parole*. In both versions of linguistics, the former was to serve as evidence to be explained to the exclusion of the latter. I similarly propose to account only for certain formal aspects of narrative, to the neglect of that welter of "pragmatic" details one could endlessly describe. My epistemological ideal, in other words, has not been to "complicate" or to "nuance" my descriptions. Rather, my goal throughout has been to devise the most "precise" and "elegant" theory possible, to find the simplest solution with the greatest explanatory power—a version, if you will, of "Occam's razor."

For this very reason, to compare biblical narrative with the modern novel or, for that matter, to speak of Homer and the Bible in the same breath is not, as some might suppose, to commit the sin of anachronism or, more generally, to transgress the proper limits of comparative analysis.[56] It is, instead, to recognize the formal underpinnings of narrative, a dimension of verbal art unaffected by the vagaries of historical accidence, unaware of the realm of the "culturally constructed." Thus, if Homer and the Bible have no direct historical connection, what Auerbach—to take one prominent example—suggests in his analysis (indeed, in the whole of *Mimesis*) is that the limitless variety of narratives we encounter in various cultures throughout history all derive from a surprisingly limited number of formal narrative possibilities.[57] If he himself does not give a systematic account of the *principia* of these underlying resources, what is surprising, given the almost universal celebration of Auerbach's study, is how infrequently this aspect of narrative has been addressed since the publication of *Mimesis* half a century ago.

•2•

FROM SONG TO STORY: THE GENESIS OF NARRATIVE IN JUDGES 4 AND 5

I have described earlier the very special manner which Bergotte had, when he spoke, of choosing and pronouncing his words. Morel, who for a long time had been in the habit of meeting him at the Saint-Loups', had at that period done "imitations" of him, in which he exactly mimicked his voice, using just the words that Bergotte would have chosen. And now that he had taken to writing, Morel used to transcribe passages of "spoken Bergotte," but without first transposing them in the way which would have turned them into "written Bergotte." Not many people having known Bergotte as a talker, the tone of his voice was not recognised, since it differed from the style of his pen.

—Marcel Proust, *Time Regained* (*In Search of Lost Time*)

The earliest symptom of a process whose end is the decline of storytelling is the rise of the novel at the beginning of modern times. What distinguishes the novel from the story (and from the epic in the narrower sense) is its essential dependence on the book. The dissemination of the novel became possible only with the invention of printing. What can be handed on orally, the wealth of the epic, is of a different kind from what constitutes the stock in trade of the novel.

—Walter Benjamin, "The Storyteller"

For behind that half-page we are to imagine a writer racking his brains for a plausible way to get the story started; we are to imagine the fussing over point of view; the agonizing over probabilities . . . ; the wrestling with the sequence in which the characters are to be named, described, and set talking. We are to fancy (to transpose into modern terms) Jamesian beginnings, Faulknerian beginnings; the 500-word draft crumpled in a melodrama of despair; the 8,000-word draft composed, pruned, retouched, ripped up; the half-written circuitous opening, with its easy meditations on chance and destiny, never completed; the dismal brooding; and the joy.

Hugh Kenner, *The Stoic Comedians*

17

On the Origins of Biblical Narrative

Ever since the publication of Albert B. Lord's book *The Singer of Tales*, his classic comparative study of Homeric and Serbo-Croatian oral epic, various attempts have been made to apply his theories not only to biblical poetry but to biblical narrative as well.[1] More recent literary studies by Robert Alter, Adele Berlin, and Meir Sternberg,[2] however, have seriously called into question whether one can understand the minute articulations of biblical prose as remaining, in any meaningful or functional way, part of an oral tradition—though some biblical poetry admittedly does evince signs of oral composition and may well originate in an oral-formulaic tradition.[3] Meanwhile a related debate has developed around the notion of a conjectured ancient Israelite epic. Frank Moore Cross, for one, has not hesitated to speak of the Bible in terms of "epic": "In the case of the Epic materials . . . we are inclined to reconstruct a long and rich poetic epic of the era of the league, underlying JE."[4] While Shemaryahu Talmon (among others) has questioned the applicability of such a term to biblical literature, he mainly objects to the broader cultural connotations that adhere to the idea of "epic."[5] Thus, even when criticizing what he sees as the extravagances of Lord's comparative method, he does not attack the heart of Lord's theory, namely, the dynamics of oral-formulaic composition.[6] Even if, for the sake of argument, one brackets the term "epic," the possibility Cross raises of an ancient Israelite oral tradition remains.[7] Inasmuch as the Ugaritic narrative poems and the Bible's own earliest poetry—compositions exhibiting signs of oral-formulaic composition—provide us with our best glimpse into Israel's pre-biblical narrative traditions, biblical prose narrative most likely originated in and grew out of these and/or similar traditions, whence Cross's notion of "epic sources": "J and E as variant forms of an older, largely poetic epic cycle."[8]

For this reason the prose story in Judges 4 and its "synoptic parallel" in Judges 5, the Song of Deborah, provide an interesting test case.[9] One can observe in synchronic fashion the consequences following upon the biblical composer's choice of either a prose or poetic medium. Furthermore, since Judges 5 is almost certainly the earlier text, the differences between the song and the prose story may well provide a glimpse into the diachronic development of biblical literature.[10] In an instructive series of studies—part of his important and growing oeuvre on Israelite history and historiography—Baruch Halpern capitalizes on this very aspect of the situation: "The differences between SongDeb and Judges 4 offer a rare opportunity to study in a controlled setting one of the central questions in biblical studies generally: How did the Israelite historian deal with his sources? How did the Israelite 'redactor' approach his inherited materials? The query has relevance both to the process of editorial assembly and to modern source-criticism."[11] He goes on to argue, through a penetrating comparison of the two parallel accounts, that a later prose writer composed Judges 4 on the basis of the Song of Deborah. In fact, this writer's antiquarian interest as demonstrated in his conservative use of his source leads Halpern to identify him as a "historian."

While I subscribe to Halpern's bold conclusion and the arguments he bases it on, I believe he paints an incomplete and therefore distorted picture of our prose writer, whose literary activity is not fully accounted for by the historian's recovery of the past. As will become clear, by emphasizing solely that recuperative task of the historian, he reduces the writer to a "resourceful" but accident-prone tradent who constructs his story only through a series of misprisions: "These traditions grew by feeding on themselves. But insofar as the exegesis produced developments unforeseen by earlier authors, it represented misinterpretation of the sources" ("Doctrine," 55). Strictly speaking Halpern may be right, but he nonetheless neglects the more *deliberately* creative, artistic aspect of the writer's activity by assuming—in spite of or perhaps because of recent work on the rhetoric of history—that the impulse to write history is mutually exclusive with the impulse to write fiction. While scholars such as Hayden White have cogently argued that the medium of language unavoidably infects all attempts to recount the past with formal rhetorical and poetic structures, his work might be (and typically is) seen to take the next, not logically necessary, step of denying as impossible or irrelevant the aims of "realism."[12] Part of the importance of Halpern's work is precisely his defense of the possibility of a meaningful correspondence between a narrative and something that one might call "the real" in the past. It only remains to reconcile the antiquarian's search for "the real" in the past with the novelist's fictive, literary imagination. Thus, while I retrace some of Halpern's arguments and accept the overall correctness of his claims, in my own analysis of Judges 4 and 5 I will pose a different, if complementary, set of literary questions. What did the switch in literary medium entail? What is the relationship of prose narrative to oral tradition? What did the writer create in addition to, or even because of, what he failed to re-create? Specifically, I will argue that between Judges 5 and Judges 4 a crucial transition takes place from oral tradition to literature, a transition that provides us with a glimpse into the origins of biblical narrative.[13]

Before rehearsing Halpern's case, however, I would like to make some very general observations about our text as a whole. Taken by itself, the song fails to provide a full, explicit narrative account of the related events.

Without the story to prop it up, much of the song's underlying fabula would be lost. In an instructive contrast, the story stands quite well on its own, the song merely providing an effective but unnecessary complement. One must attribute this contrast partly to the fact that the poem is not, after all, a genuine narrative so much as a lyric evocation of a set of "heroic" events.[14] In addition to this observation of genre, however, one must also consider the logical structure of the poem, which presupposes a great deal of knowledge. That modern readers often harmonize the two accounts, specifically using the story to fill in the song's gaps, only confirms this judgment. In fact, this circumstance may be one indication of the song's oral-traditional origins and of the story's literary one. Consider the following observation made by David E. Bynum—an active scholar in folklore studies and former curator of the Milman Parry Collection at Harvard University—with respect to another set of narratives in Judges:

> One obvious historical fact is that the four Samson stories are not epic, ballad, or folktale. They are patently annalistic. . . . Whatever traces of oral traditional diction might subsist in them have therefore surely entered the Hebrew text through the agency of a literary retailer rather than by dictation from an oral traditional *raconteur*. I come to this opinion not via narrow stylistic evaluation of the presence or absence of a certain kind of formulary diction in the Hebrew text (which I cannot read), but on quite different and equally valid grounds. There simply are not a sufficient number of impenetrable obscurities in the Samson stories which only other texts of other narratives in the same oral tradition could explain. Such obscurities are a hallmark everywhere of true oral traditional dictated narratives. But the Samson stories as we have them have been systematically cleansed of such obscurities. That is what literary retailers of oral traditional tales have always done, and for obvious reasons.[15]

In other words, in seeking to identify oral-traditional "texts," one might look for a "formulary diction," that trait that Albert B. Lord and his teacher Milman Parry employed to identify the Homeric epics as oral-traditional narratives; or one might look for a preponderance of obscurities, a type of dense allusivity that necessitates the external clarification of an oral-traditional context. The prose story of Judges 4 betrays no sense of a formulaic diction; neither does it present the contemporary audience with especially difficult obscurities. Conversely, the Song of Deborah exhibits both the formulaic diction and that general sense of opacity typical of oral-traditional tales.[16] In fact, one does find in the Bible prose specimens of those opaque narratives that Bynum mentions: brief, tantalizingly vague episodes often noteworthy precisely for their fairy-tale quality. I am thinking especially of Exod 4:24–26, the so-called Bridegroom of Blood pericope, and Gen. 32:22–32, Jacob's famous wrestling match.[17] Perhaps it was precisely the folkloric quality of the episode in Genesis that led Roland Barthes to use a Proppian actantial analysis in his suggestive if idiosyncratic reading of Jacob's divine encounter.[18]

Halpern's "First Historian"

Let us return to Halpern's arguments. Given the fundamental agreement (along with a few striking differences) between the story and song in Judges 4 and 5, the question of their relationship naturally arises. Are they independent, reflecting variant traditions? Does the song depend on the story or vice versa? Halpern argues for the last option by analyzing two major differences: the number of tribes involved in battle and the details surrounding Sisera's death at Jael's hands. In both cases one can easily imagine the story misconstruing the song, while the converse strains credibility.

The story makes entirely clear that only two tribes participate in the battle against Sisera: Naphtali and Zebulun (4:6, 11). But the song's roster in 5:14–18, following the traditional—and, according to Halpern, conservative—reading, points to the participation of six tribes, namely, Ephraim, Benjamin, Machir, and Issachar in addition to Naphtali and Zebulun. He in fact argues, without emendation, that one can construe these difficult verses (the details of which need not concern us here) such that all ten tribes mentioned participate in battle, thus adding Reuben, Gilead, Dan, and Asher to the list, with only Meroz being singled out for censure in verse 23 ("Israelite Historian," 381–86). In any case, something like the "plain sense" of the song would indicate the involvement of six to ten tribes in battle. One could argue, though, in hyperliteral fashion, that only 5:18 indicates express military fighting on the part of any Israelites: "Zebulun, a people who scorned death, / And Naphtali, on the heights of the field"—precisely the tribes found in the story. This has led Halpern to make the compelling claim that "the historian in Jud 4:6, 11 [through a misconstrual of his evidence] has reified the reference" ("Israelite Historian," 390).

Halpern perceives a similar hermeneutic process behind the accounts of Sisera's death ("Israelite Historian," 388–90). Concerning his demise, the story again provides a clearer account than does the poem. After her hapless victim has fallen asleep under a blanket, Jael grabs her implements, "the hammer" (*hammaqqebet*) and "the tent peg" (*yĕtad hāʾōhel*), carefully takes aim, and pierces his skull with a lethal two-handed blow (4:21).[19] The song, however, permits two interpretations. Keeping in mind the prose version of the story, one might assume that Jael again takes a peg (*yātēd*) in one hand, a workman's hammer (*halmût ʿămēlîm*) in the other, and thus delivers a similar blow to Sisera's head (5:26). This seems doubtful, however, inasmuch as he is apparently standing (and not lying down) at the fatal moment (5:27). Are we to imagine him posing for her as she carefully takes aim? Halpern therefore claims that when read on its own, the song speaks of an entirely different sequence of events. While Sisera was taking his drink, "Jael crept up behind and, with the proverbial blunt instrument, bludgeoned him to death" ("Israelite Historian," 389). In this case, he observes, the peg itself serves as the lethal tool, 5:26 constituting a synonymous rather than narrative-incremental parallelism,[20] and 5:27 describes Sisera's subsequent fall to the ground, presumably from a standing position. Most likely, then, the writer misinterpreted the parallelism, thereby creating Jael's heavy-handed attack.

If Bynum is correct, the poem's elusive sense betrays something of its oral-traditional origins. At least for those of us coming after the tradition, it simply does not provide a clear narrative sequence—witness the evident difficulties our prose writer faced in making sense of this song. In spite of such difficulties, however, I find Halpern's reconstruction of the poem's narrative compelling. One should note that a heavy, metal tent peg (cf. Exod. 27:19 and 38:20) could very well have served as a makeshift weapon. Furthermore, we are in no position to determine the precise referent of this one and only occurrence of *halmût*—neither does the better-attested verb *hālam* suggest the action specifically of a hammer.[21] Having the morphology of an abstract noun (*-ût*)—relatively infrequent in pre-exilic Hebrew—it may mean nothing more specific than "hitting tool." Meanwhile, the root is entirely absent in Judges 4, which perhaps already indicates its relative obscurity, *hammaqqebet* (4:21) thus being an interpretive gloss on the prose writer's part.[22]

According to Halpern, the writer repeats this performance in the same passage with regard to the drink: "[T]he couplet, 'Water he asked; milk she provided,' read as poetry, carries no implication of a specific request or of a specific libation. It means, 'Sisera requested and received a drink'" ("Israelite Historian," 389). The writer, however, again takes the song at its word, this time resulting in Jael's ostensibly lavish hospitality. Thus, in 4:19 Sisera asks merely for water, while Jael gives him milk instead. Note, however, that the writer is not so beholden to his source that he cannot let go of certain details, namely, the "curds" (*ḥemʾâ*) and the "lordly bowl" (*sēpel ʾaddîrîm*) in 5:25.

As with the tribal roster, so with the murder scene: the prose historian misreads the song and this, in turn, leads to accidental narrative developments. Moreover, as Halpern argues at length, these accidental developments necessitate further developments (see "Sisera," 82–89) — having Sisera fall asleep under a blanket, for example, in order to make Jael's two-handed attack plausible. As a result, one can, through a combination of direct and indirect means, account for the story's details almost entirely in terms of the song. Conversely, it would take excessive ingenuity (and credulity) to imagine the song depending on the story in the same way. Thus, Halpern's theory displays both admirable economy and explanatory power, which, in turn, obviates assigning independent traditions to the two accounts.[23] Following his argument to a point, then, I would suggest that the song contains the primitive narrative kernel out of which the prose story develops. By its very nature the song apparently assumes a certain oral-traditional narrative context that would have provided the information — now lost — needed to fill in its present gaps. The narrative context we now possess, however, betrays the interpretive impulse of a later writer; it does not provide the authentic setting of living tradition.

The Genesis of Narrative

As I have suggested, Halpern presents a limiting, and therefore misleading, view of the writer's activity. By focusing solely on the task of reconstructing past events, he ignores the issue of how these events are caught in a web of human designs. He is not unaware of the writer's imaginative art, but he tries to purge as much of it as possible from this historical narrative:

> There *is* art in the presentation, as there is in Carlyle. . . . Still, the main lines of the reconstruction, the main interest of the author, were antiquarian in nature. Again, characterization is not thrust forward; the tension in the plot does not approach that of Pentateuchal narratives; the dialogue is never out of hand, the reportage — unlike that of SDeb (esp. vv. 28–30), which is not historiographic in intent — never includes symbolic or trivial detail. There is none of the elaboration that one expects from a romance. All the evidence, thus, comes down on the side of the prose's historical character. ("Sisera," 96)[24]

I do not mean to impugn the biblical writer's "historiographic" intent, but, as Halpern would surely agree, imagination must come into play in any historical narrative that rises above mere chronicle.[25] Thus, demonstrating how Jael's clumsy two-handed attack in Judges 4 results from the writer's misreading the poem, while important, does not account for its secondary life in the story, its new narrative significance. And so with the milk. "Read as poetry," 5:25 does not merely signify that "Sisera requested and received a drink" ("Israelite Historian," 389). Rather, the poetic intensification from "water" to "milk" to "ghee" and the climactic specification of the "lordly bowl" evoke a heroic act that resonates with the "epic" tenor of the song. The writer may misunderstand his source, but in the process of writing he also deliberately marshals this same act of hospitality to a strikingly different end within the story, namely, to signify Jael's motherly doting over her guest, which sets the stage for Sisera's death. The writer creates a trickster from the poet's aggressor. Returning to the murder, one now sees that whatever Jael's "absurd" ("Israelite Historian," 388) strategy may lack in a certain verisimilitude is fully compensated for by its literary effect, for, I finally note, Sisera's boyish retreat to Jael's maternal shade ingeniously complements Barak's timid stand under Deborah's protective wing.

Such observations, in other words, open up into the realm of characterization. Here even Halpern allows for the writer's "art": "Art plays a role in the choice of words and names and even in the largely implicit characterizations" ("Sisera," 97). Thus, "there are claims in the prose, of course, that were not entirely demanded by the reconstruction: the dialogue, generally; Jael's premeditation" ("Sisera," 96). Note how Jael's premeditation raises the question of inner motive, while dialogue functions as an important means of characterization in biblical narrative. Even as he admits the invention of dialogue, however, he attempts to suppress the role of the literary imagination: "At least, the dialogue between them is invented out of hand. All of these supplementary details, however trivial, serve a single end. They actualize, they help to convey the reconstruction on which the historian has decided. Again, they are functional, and not at all fancifully creative" ("Israelite Historian," 396). Nonetheless, while the writer may stay within the bounds of what he deems historical fact, to "actualize" and "convey" a historical "reconstruction" is, I suggest, to exercise, albeit on a limited scale, the imaginative impulse of fiction. For, close as this prose writer sticks to his source, the poem has nothing to say about motive, character, and dialogue.

Thus, as I have already suggested, one should not view our writer merely as a resourceful but misguided tradent. For he exploited and developed his source with great literary finesse, and I think we detect in the process of his creativity what Frank Kermode calls the "necessities of up-springing."[26] In a splendid chapter from *The Genesis of Secrecy*, he uses this idea, borrowed from Henry James, to analyze the passion narratives of each New Testament gospel with a view to tracing the way in which character springs up from the necessities of plot through a type of midrashic interpretive dialectic:

> The matter of this chapter is really quite simple. Of an agent there is nothing to be said except that he performs a function: Betrayal, Judgment. When the agent becomes a kind of person, all is changed. It takes very little to make a character: a few indications of idiosyncracy, of deviation from type, are enough, for our practiced eyes will make up the larger patterns of which such indications can be read as parts.
>
> The key to all this development—from fable to written story, from story to character, from character to more story—is interpretation.[27]

In the texts he considers, a plot function, Betrayal, takes on a proper name, Judas, and in the process of fleshing out this name, the evangelists create narrative: Judas's early career as one of the twelve; his conversation with the temple authorities and the thirty pieces of silver; various legends about his death, and so forth.

Returning to our text, let me begin with a consideration of its dramatis personae. In the song Deborah and Barak, although already distinguished with proper names, have barely risen above that primitive stage of plot function. They apparently lead the troops into battle (5:12, 15), but the battle scene itself consists primarily of a theophany.[28] It is God's meteorological/cosmological minions that spell certain doom for the enemy (vv. 20, 21)—apparently rain falls from heaven leading to the torrent of the wadi Kishon. God's storm-cloud march from his mountain abode in fact anticipates this outcome, for as God goes forth from Seir and Edom, the earth and mountains quake (from thunder?) and the clouds of heaven already begin pouring forth rain (vv. 4, 5). Not surprisingly, then, the obviously later Psalm 83 (apparently alluding to an already edited collection of judge stories) again links this and other battles to God's storm.

> Deal with them as with Midian,
> As with Sisera and Yabin in the torrent of Kishon. (v. 10)
> Thus pursue them with your tempest [*bĕsaʿărekā*]
> And with your storm [*bĕsûfātĕkā*] terrify them. (v. 16)[29]

This distribution of roles suggests that Deborah and Barak play the Helper to God's Hero, though, interestingly enough, Jael, "most blessed among women" (5:24), has her own scene in which she plays the unrivaled mortal heroine. Within the song's ranks a hierarchy takes shape. Barak (not to mention Shamgar) falls to the bottom of the ranks, beneath Jael's heroism and Deborah's leadership.[30]

Moreover, if we peer beneath the song's surface, we find that their primitive "functions" are still thinly veiled beneath their names, which by all appearances had symbolic significance in the underlying tradition; recall that Deborah means "bee," Barak "lightning," and Jael "mountain goat."[31] Both Deborah and Barak, I would suggest, originated as aspects of God's theophanic terror.[32] Consider, first, that stinging insects appear several times as God's weapons or agents with respect to the conquest.[33] Thus, while sealing the covenant at Sinai, God makes the following promise: "My terror [*ʾêmātî*] I will send before you, and I will discomfit [*wĕhammōtî*] all the people whom you come against, and I will make all your enemies turn their backs to you, and I will send the wasp [*haṣṣirʿâ*] before you and drive out the Hivites and the Canaanites and the Hittites from your presence" (Exod. 23:27, 28; see also the very similar formulations in Deut. 7:20, 23 and Josh. 24:12). The parallelistic syntax of this passage makes the wasp a veritable synonym for God's terror, which is not so surprising when one recalls that the Exodus story itself relates how God revealed himself to the Egyptians through various pests and natural disasters. Admittedly, these verses all speak of the wasp, but the bee works to similar effect: "And the Amorites who lived in that hill country went out against you and pursued you as the bees [*haddĕbōrîm*] do and crushed you from Seir till Hormah" (Deut. 1:44; see also Isa. 7:18). Lightning, of course, derives directly from the imagery of the storm theophany. In battle it specifically functions as part of God's arsenal: "And he sent forth his arrows and scattered them, / And a multitude of lightning bolts [*ûbĕrāqîm rāb*], and discomfited them [*wayhummēm*]" (Ps. 18:15 = 2 Sam. 22:15; see also the almost identical formulation in Ps. 144:6).[34] In a neat symmetry, meteorological cease-fire provides the sign of God's postdiluvian peace treaty with the earth: the rain-bow (Gen. 9:12, 13). It is especially striking that lightning and wasps/bees both revolve around the notion of divine discomfiture (*hmm*), for while this root does not appear explicitly within the song, it resurfaces (not coincidentally) in the story. In a sense, these two theophanic elements are eventually wed within the story through Deborah and her husband, Lappidoth ("torches" or "lightning"). Consider the burning mount of Exod. 20:18: "And all the people were perceiving the thunder [*haqqôllōt*] and the lightning [*hallappîdîm*] . . . and the smoking [ʿāšēn] mountain." God's appearance to Abram in Gen. 15:17 also imbues this "torch" with a revelatory aspect: "and here was a smoking [ʿāšān] oven and a flaming torch [lappîd] that passed between these pieces." I would suggest that this narrative datum is a remnant of the tradition, an indication of Deborah's original function. Some commentators have suggested—perhaps correctly—that Barak and Lappidoth are, in fact, one and the same, that in the tradition Deborah and Barak were husband and wife.[35] What seems more to the point in such an event, however, is that this marriage reifies something even further back in the tradition: the proximity of Deborah and Barak's original narrative roles.

Jael, too, would seem to be related to battle imagery, though not specifically to the theophany. Here one should first recall that in archaic poems such as Genesis 49 and Deuteronomy 33 animals serve as symbols of martial strength and prowess. It need not surprise us if names such as Jael (and, later in Judges, Oreb and Zeeb) originated from a type of oral-traditional military bestiary. Consider, for instance, Gen. 49:21: "Naphtali is a doe [ʾayyālâ] sent forth"—coincidentally, one of the key tribes in our text. Keeping in mind that ʾayyālâ appears in parallelism with yāʿēl/yaʿălâ in Job 39:1 and Prov. 5:19, Psalm 18 (= 2 Samuel 22) proves particularly instructive:

> He makes my feet [raglay] like does' [ʾayyālôt] [feet],
> And upon my high places he sets me.
> He trains my hands for battle
> So that my arms can bend a bow of bronze. (vv. 34, 35)
> I pursued my enemies and overtook them,
> And I did not turn back until they were annihilated.
> I shattered them [ʾemḥāṣēm] so that they could not rise,
> They fell [yippēlû] beneath my feet [raglāy]. (vv. 38, 39; see
>   also Hab. 3:19)

Recall that in our song Jael shatters (māḥăṣâ) Sisera's skull so that he falls (nāpal) between her feet (raglêhā) (5:26, 27).[36] Surely this is no coincidence, though neither would I identify it as an allusion. Rather, we witness the workings of (oral) traditional imagery and phraseology, here a conventional image of the surefooted warrior.

These primitive plot functions match the poem's skeletal plot structure, its impressionistic treatment of events. As noted earlier, the poem lacks a certain narrative continuity. Divided into poetic verses, the song, even when representing a temporal flow, creates the effect of a sequence of discrete scenes/moments, though each moment is evoked with a poetic intensity often enhanced through the artful use of parallelism. The story may lack the dramatic gesture of the poetic line, but it creates a much smoother narrative flow. Though no less sparse, its sequence of *waw*-consecutives seems to guarantee a minimal sense of continuity or at least creates the illusion of continuous flow, whereas in the poem the assurance of narrative continuity from one verse to the next is lacking. Thus, toward the poem's beginning one catches a glimpse of God proceeding to battle from Seir and Edom (5:4, 5). However, addressed in the second person to God—"when you came out . . . when you marched forth" (v. 4)—not even these lines constitute a directly represented narrative event. The song next continues with additional exclamations and tribal apostrophes (vv. 6–18) before finally turning to the battle's narrative. Three verses describe three "events" with only a modicum of human agency and a vague sense of the temporal/causal relationship among them: enemy kings approach in battle (v. 19); the stars fight from heaven (v. 20); the torrent of Kishon sweeps them (presumably the enemy) away (v. 21). Next one hears the galloping of horses (v. 22), which only later one might surmise as Sisera's hasty retreat (not on foot this time); then, without further ado, one finds oneself with Sisera in Jael's tent (vv. 24–27). In contrast, the story, while just as brief, provides a spare though sufficient and logically continuous sequence of events: Deborah's prophetic instigation (4:6ff.); Barak mustering the troops (v. 10); Sisera's countermove (v. 12f.); the battle (vv. 14ff.); Sisera's strictly earthbound flight (vv. 15b, 17); his final encounter with Jael (vv. 18–21), and so forth. Turning again to the murder scene, one notes how the song describes first the provision of drink, next Jael's hands reaching for the instruments of death, and finally the fatal blow. In principle, one cannot determine precisely what length of time elapses between each frame. Within its original oral context, he might have fallen asleep between verses 25 and 26, as he does in the story—though we would still have to contend with his subsequent fall to the ground. For this reason one should not place too much confidence in the "straightforward" sense of the poem. Yair Zakovitch has even attempted to reconstruct a suppressed story of seduction and betrayal.[37] Without necessarily endorsing his interpretation, one can still admit that it is in the nature of this traditional poem bereft of the tradition to tolerate radically different interpretations.

As one moves into the story, all is changed. The ties of tradition weaken as the writer, intent on creating a self-standing prose version, reworks not the tradition itself but the song, presumably fixed by now in written form[38]—further uprooting his story, as it were, from any contact with living tradition. Indeed, in light of the evident difficulties the writer encountered in trying to make sense of the song, it most likely comes to him as a mere remnant of a now lost tradition. Let us imagine him at his task.[39] He finds in the poem the most basic form of plot: conflict, specifically an ancient battle between Sisera and Israel. As for players, he finds four human characters: Jael, the heroine; Sisera, her victim; Deborah, whom he takes to be the song's lyric subject; and Barak. But how is it that Deborah usurps Barak's place, coming to sing the victory song in his stead? (Think, for instance, of David in 1 Samuel 22 or of Moses, who outsings Miriam in Exodus 15.) And how comes it that the enemy Sisera falls into Jael's hands, so that a woman steals Barak's thunder? Perhaps, the writer reasons, it was Deborah and not Barak who presided as judge over Israel—although such information is lacking in the song. To account further for Barak's lackluster role, he also imagines him as a diffident, almost unwilling, military commander. (Primitive plot and agent beget character.) Deborah, then, must have provided the impetus for battle; she was a prophetess whose oracular command set Barak in motion. But Barak, no longer just an agent but a person, questions her prophetic authority, so that in order to persuade him to act, she must vouchsafe the authenticity of her oracular word by physically accompanying her protégé into battle. (Character begets dialogue—almost entirely absent in the song and yet the primary means of conveying character in biblical narrative.) But for this assurance Barak must pay a price: his honor shall go to a woman. (And dialogue finally begets more plot.)

Meanwhile, the writer, in the process of developing his human characters, decides that God should be less visible in the story, likely because of the unavoidable tension that would exist between mortal and divine heroes.[40] While the Bible's historiosophical sense of dual causality is well known, it typically resolves into two separate planes of action. Thus, the song's account proper of the battle features supernatural activity accompanied by obligatory but ineffectual human agents (5:19-21), whereas Jael deals with her prey without a hint of divine intervention (5:24-27). The writer, for his part, also represents this dual causality, but he limits God's involvement within the story's version of the battle to a single verb: "And the Lord *discomfited* [*wayyāhom*] Sisera and all the chariots and all the army *with the edge of the sword* before Barak" (4:15, emphasis added). Note the quick and seamless transition from divine to human agency. As we have already seen, *hmm* is often associated with manifestations of divine terror,[41] and this heaven-sent act still proves, at least on one level, decisive for the battle. The writer nevertheless suppresses the external aspect of the song's theophany, and in so doing he makes room, as it were, for the Israelite sword. One should not forget, of course, that this verb also helps signal an allusion to the Reed Sea:[42]

And at the morning watch God looked upon the Egyptian camp
from the pillar of fire and cloud and discomfited [*wayyāhom*] the
Egyptian camp, and he caused the wheels of their chariots to turn
and caused them to drive with difficulty. And Egypt said, "Let me
flee from Israel, for the Lord is fighting for them against Egypt."
. . . And the sea returned at daybreak to its normal state while
Egypt was fleeing into it, and the Lord shook off Egypt into the
sea. (Exod. 14:24, 25, 27b)

In fact, I would suggest that Exodus 14 functions as a prooftext of sorts.
After all, the song's account of the battle is, to say the very least, vague. In
the song Sisera's chariots are never mentioned in the actual battle; they
appear in the song only once, in the nervous exclamation made by his
mother (5:28). The song's battle is more explicitly miraculous; the storm-
swollen Kishon selectively sweeps away precisely the enemy and not the
Israelites, so that it really makes no difference how Sisera's troops were
equipped. So what actually happened? The writer decides to develop the
chariot motif, turning it into the means of Canaanite domination (4:3),
but also of their eventual downfall. In his story the chariots become a liability within the battlefield's topography—the meteorological situation is
unspecified—and the allusion to Exodus interprets this liability as God's
mĕhûmâ, a divinely inflicted reversal of fortune that makes the chariots
vulnerable to attack. The precise details are still vague since Barak must
pursue the chariots in 4:16, but Sisera nonetheless likes his chances better on foot, and his mounted army meanwhile succumbs to the Israelite
onslaught.

We come now to Jael, the poet's central heroine, whose sudden appearance in the song and equally sudden attack raise several questions.
How and why did Sisera come to Jael? What relationship did they have?
How did she succeed in killing him with her bizarre, that is to say, apparently two-handed attack?[43] The writer begins to answer these questions by
creating Sisera's descent from the chariot and cowardly flight to Jael's tent
(4:15), for, he explains, there was a treaty between his king and her husband (v. 17).[44] Perhaps with an eye to symmetry, the writer next matches
Deborah as mother figure of the timid Barak with Jael's doting over Sisera,
inventing more dialogue and developing further the satiric characterization of Israel's enemy. Thus Jael, perceiving Sisera's sense of panic, speaks
soothing words and persuades him to take shelter with her. He replies by
meekly requesting a drink as she tucks him into bed. The dialogue ends
with his implicit denial of his own manhood: "If a man comes and asks
you, 'Is there a man here?' you will say, 'No' " (v. 20).[45] Perhaps the mater-

nal theme sprang up through a metonymic development of the milk proffered in the song; perhaps Sisera's anxious mother (5:28–30) also helped
inspire this theme. One should note as well the song's declaration in 5:7:
"Until you arose, Deborah, / Until you arose, a mother [ʾēm] in Israel."
Now Heinz-Dieter Neef assures us that ʾēm here means "adviser, helper"—
consider Joseph's status as "father" (ʾāb) to Pharaoh (Gen. 45:8)[46]—which
corresponds to her description in the story (4:4–6). But perhaps the writer
also seized upon the literal sense of "mother" in developing his heroines
vis-à-vis his antiheroes. Indeed, the combined image of mother's milk
seems to inform the infamous murder scene. Let us say the writer
(mis)understood the poem such that Jael makes an awkward two-handed
attack against Sisera. He justifies this attack and reinforces the emergent
relationship between Sisera and Jael by devising the blanket scene. At the
same time, he further develops the motif of milk. Giving milk here, however, no longer constitutes the grand gesture of the heroic past but symbol-
izes instead Jael's seemingly maternal care and perhaps—as a soporific—
also functions as part of her strategy for putting the restless child to
sleep.[47] In any case, I think one can see how even the story's innovations
may have sprouted from seeds already planted in the song.

Finally, I wish to consider the conclusion of the story over against that
of the song. The song ends, of course, with a brilliantly effective scene in
which Sisera's mother sits by the window, anxiously awaiting her son's return (5:28–30). Let me first propose that Barak's arrival at Jael's tent, a type
of recognition scene in which he verifies the enemy's death (4:22), nicely
substitutes for Sisera's mother's implicit, if partially repressed, recognition
of her son's death.[48] Furthermore, Neef makes the helpful suggestion that
the writer omits the mother's scene to avoid the difficulties of incorporat-
ing her character into the story, which would only spoil the otherwise neat
balance among the four characters.[49] Indeed, in order to account for Jael,
he has had to add at least two anticipatory comments within the story (4:11
and 17 dealing with her husband, Heber the Kenite); he perhaps even
wrote a third, which in the edited text eventually became 1:16, a remark
about Hobab the Qenite, which helps set up Heber's subsequent appearance. To justify the inclusion of the mother, then, the writer would likely
have had to invent an early scene involving Sisera's home and family; he
might even have felt compelled to invent some means of sending news of
Sisera's death back to his mother. It is instructive that the poet, in his treatment both of Jael and of Sisera's mother, can do without such background
explanations; he is unfettered by the responsibility, keenly felt by the prose
writer, of creating a sense of narrative wholeness. Concluding the story
with Barak, however, is both economical and ingenious in its own right. It

closes the circle of prophecy and fulfillment as the would-be hero sees with his own eyes Sisera's corpse, killed at the hands of the woman Jael: "[A]nd here was Sisera, fallen, dead, and the tent peg in his temple" (4:22). In that moment, shrewdly captured in a represented perception—a species of free indirect style—Barak recognizes the story's true heroine and the authenticity of Deborah's oracular word: "I will surely go with you, nevertheless, the honor shall not be yours on the path that you are taking, for it is into the hand of a woman that the Lord will sell Sisera" (4:9).

What does this process tell us about biblical literature? Whether or not the Song of Deborah is itself an orally composed poem, we have seen how its sketchy fabula and primitive agents presume the milieu of living tradition. The story is another matter entirely. As the reworking of a now fixed poem, the story exists in at least one degree of separation from tradition. Its prose has supplanted formulaic diction; its plot has grown into a self-sufficient wholeness. Finally, I think we see, above all, how folkloric agents become literary characters by shedding the necessities of function and taking on lives and personalities of their own.

From Fable to Novel

To conclude the present analysis, therefore, I would like to comment on why, precisely, the Bible's sense of character makes its narratives seem so literary, and in this sense post-traditional. The answer may be found in the competing theories of the relation of plot to character, the very issue Kermode uses to set the terms of his argument: "The relation between what is now called character and what is now called plot has been a subject of interest since Aristotle . . . gave it his attention in the *Poetics*. My discussion begins not with Aristotle, but with a more recent theorist and practitioner, Henry James."[50] While James's notion of "upspringing," as we have seen, gives precedence to character, Aristotle's position represents the opposing view: "For Aristotle the fable came first, and character (*ēthos*, admittedly not perfectly translated by 'character') followed; though this does not mean character is without importance, only that it lacks autonomy, could never originate a narrative."[51]

Regarding these rival theories, Kermode tries to sidestep the controversy altogether, suggesting that "it would be absurd to ask whether James or Aristotle is closer to the truth."[52] His defensive maneuver, however, obscures an important point. For one should keep in mind that while both Aristotle and James may speak in a prescriptive mode, each really seeks, in his own way, to account for a particular practice. Aristotle, on the one hand, writes about Greek tragedy, where the plots and dramatis personae are inherited from the tradition; in this case plot quite literally precedes any sense of character as it might be fleshed out onstage.[53] Similarly, Vladimir Propp, whom we might characterize as a modern proponent of the Aristotelian position, provides an analysis of the Russian folktale, where, once again, emphasis falls upon traditional plots and functions.[54] James, on the other hand, belongs to and writes about a radically different period in literary history—what Kermode refers to as "a late moment in the history of narrative,"[55] namely, modernism. It is the very moment in which E. M. Forster makes his famous, rather Jamesian, pronouncement regarding "round" versus "flat" characters: "The test of a round character is whether it is capable of surprising in a convincing way. If it never surprises, it is flat. If it does not convince, it is a flat pretending to be round. It has the incalculability of life about it—life within the pages of a book."[56] For such novelists, writing "novels that had lost any obvious connection with primitive fable,"[57] the tradition had long since vanished. It cannot provide them, at least in any straightforward manner, with a plot. And if such a novelist were to excavate the tradition for a fable, he would feel compelled to place it, as it were, in quotation marks in order to indicate the obligatory ironic distance—whence Joyce's *Ulysses*—or else appear naive, quaint, and outdated. In other words, a temporal as well as a conceptual gap separates Aristotle from James, and in order to bridge this gap one needs to construct a literary history that traces the transformation of fable into novel, of oral tradition into literature.

Kermode, however implicitly, does precisely this by basing a Jamesian analysis on a Proppian foundation through a diachronic projection. Carefully distancing himself from the "neo-Formalists," who "speak of a *fabula* underlying a narrative without committing themselves to the view that this fable had independent prior existence" and thus make it into "a methodological fiction merely, used to help us understand the 'narrativity' of the story we are considering,"[58] he equates instead the gospel's underlying fabula with early Christian traditions: "Let us then presuppose a *fabula*, progressively interpreted: first by Mark, then by Matthew and Luke using Mark, and by John, who perhaps used a not dissimilar but not identical original."[59] He constructs, in other words, a history that traces the evolution of what are, in effect, fables about Jesus into gospels. He can do so because the gospels— especially the synoptics—betray, like Judges 4 and 5, an identifiable line of literary dependence. Written mere decades after the events they in some way reflect, the gospels, like Judges 4, are in the very process of creating characters from agents that served the plot of pre-biblical tradition.[60] Aristotle thus gives way to James.

For this reason character—at least the type that can generate narrative out of the sheer force of its own interiority—is, as Kermode remarks, "an aspect of narrative which must in some sense always be secondary." For, he continues, "Turgenev and James are talking about the kind of novel—made possible by the existence of a great many other novels, novels that had lost any obvious connection with primitive fable—of which it was possible to say that the narrative was generated by character, by an image *en disponibilité*, in which there was no anterior 'plot' but only a germ out of which one generated an 'affair.' "[61]

Though it remains a mere suggestion in his argument, I think writing is crucial to this mode of characterization.[62] For it is the written story, loosed from the fetters of tradition, which allows for the transformation of agent into character. One should recall that the very notion of literature presupposes a culture of letters. Meanwhile, the Parry-Lord hypothesis marked a great milestone in Homer studies precisely because it restored to those epics their distinctiveness as a nonliterary, that is, oral-traditional, art.[63] Thus, while relatively undeveloped, one already sees in Barak and Deborah, in Jael and Sisera, the ability to lead one's life rather than merely follow it. Biblical narrative comes after Benjamin's storyteller, after the epic rhapsode. Homer, conversely, *is* the storyteller, the singer of tales. Thus, for all his vividness, we in a sense know Odysseus only as the man who lived through his adventures. It remains for a Euripides, *writing* several centuries later, to give such a character his post-traditional, literary existence. One might say, then, that the biblical writer, by composing imaginative stories that derive from rather than determine character, invented literature.

•3•

NARRATION AND DISCOURSE: THE LINGUISTIC DUALISM OF BIBLICAL NARRATIVE AND ITS LITERARY CONSEQUENCES

The free intellect will see as God might see, without a *here* and *now* . . . in the sole and exclusive desire of knowledge—knowledge as impersonal, as purely contemplative, as it is possible for man to attain.

—Bertrand Russell, *Problems of Philosophy*

Positions in time, as time appears to us prima facie, are distinguished in two ways. Each position is Earlier than some and Later than some of the other positions. . . .

In the second place, each position is either Past, Present, or Future. The distinctions of the former class are permanent, while those of the latter are not. If *M* is ever earlier than *N*, it is always earlier. But an event, which is now present, was future, and will be past.

—J. M. E. McTaggart, "The Unreality of Time"

Obsolete in spoken French, the preterite, which is the cornerstone of Narration, always signifies the presence of Art; it is a part of a ritual of Letters. Its function is no longer that of a tense. The part it plays is to reduce reality to a point of time, and to abstract, from the depth of a multiplicity of experiences, a pure verbal act, freed from the existential roots of knowledge, and directed towards a logical link with other acts, other processes, a general movement of the world: it aims at maintaining a hierarchy in the realm of facts. Through the preterite, the verb implicitly belongs with a causal chain, it partakes of a set of related and orientated actions, it functions as the algebraic sign of an intention. Allowing as it does an ambiguity between temporality and causality, it calls for a sequence of events, that is, for an intelligible Narrative.

—Roland Barthes, *Writing Degree Zero*

The Spoken and the Written Word

"Shibboleth," one of the few Hebrew words to enter the English language, refers in its original context to the mispronunciation of some sound or word. It takes for granted, in other words, a norm which certain linguistic performances fall short of, as when a foreigner presumes to speak a community's native tongue. Consider the etymological ur-story in Judges: "And Gilead seized the passages of the Jordan before Ephraim. And it was that whenever an Ephraimite fugitive would say, 'Let me pass!' the men of Gilead would say to him, 'Are you an Ephraimite?' And he would say, 'No.' And they would say to him, 'Please say *šibbōlet.*' But he would say '*sibbōlet,*' for he was unable to pronounce it thus" (Judg. 12:5, 6). Here, Cisjordanian Israelites betray themselves to their Transjordanian compatriots through their inability to produce the authorized reading of *šibbōlet,* hence its alternate meaning in English as a test for demonstrating or betraying one's true identity—national, regional, and so forth.

Now it turns out that in the entire Bible we find *sibbōlet* only this once, whereas *šibbōlet* appears some eighteen times, indicating that the former was a deviant spelling, tolerated here only for mimetic effect, the very effect underlying that form of narration the Russian formalists call *skaz.*[1] Cisjordanian and Transjordanian tribes, in other words, shared a common spelling for this fateful word, and an apparently Gileadite writer—at least he wrote from the Gileadites' perspective, whose pronunciation is rendered according to conventional orthography—when confronted with this situation had to exploit the resources of the alphabet in order to imitate Ephraimite speech.[2] This narrative thus turns on a writerly effect, something for the eye as well as the ear. The text had become a sufficiently established medium so that a spelling, a permutation of letters, could achieve a reality that could be played against—defamiliarized, to borrow yet again from the Russian formalists.[3] As a result, a dualism opens up on the page between a written word and a transcribed sound—analogous to the topic of this chapter, the dualism between written narration and spoken discourse.

The story itself takes place in a world after Babel and its "singular words" (*dĕbārîm ʾăḥādîm,* Gen. 11:1), a dialogic world, in Bahktinian terms. Taking this analogy further, one should also place it after the epic, whose "unitary language," Bakhtin claims, precedes the novel's heteroglossia. For, as is well known, all of Homer's characters, Barbarians included, speak Greek, specifically that monologic amalgam known as Homeric Greek. So while Odysseus may fool the Cyclops into calling him "Nobody," a witticism presuming a common tongue, one should not expect to find a shibboleth in his arsenal of tricks.

I therefore take this story as one indication of the break that separates biblical prose narrative from oral-formulaic epic verse. In positing this stylistic break, I am primarily concerned to trace the disappearance of the speaking subject from the language of narration. If one hears in epic the voice of the singer, the accents of any speaking voice are conspicuously absent in biblical narration. As a consequence of this absence, one can observe a rift within biblical narrative between the language of narration and the language of discourse (the directly quoted speech of the Bible's characters). Where the singer's voice once animated the totality of a consequently monistic world a dualism now enters the prose of the Bible, dividing its narrative world into subjective and objective facts.[4]

In naming the terms of this proposed dualism "narration" and "discourse," I allude, of course, to Benveniste's famous distinction, based on the preterites in French, between *histoire* and *discours*.[5] In his seminal essay "The Correlations of Tense in the French Verb" he explains the apparent redundancy of the two tenses in French used to relate past events: the perfect (*passé composé*) and the aorist (*passé simple*). He writes of the aorist:

> The *historical* utterance, today reserved to the written language, characterizes the narration of past events. These three terms, "narration," "event," and "past," are of equal importance. Events that took place at *a certain moment of time* are presented *without any intervention of the speaker* in the narration. (206; emphasis added)

The perfect, on the other hand,

> creates a living connection between the past event and *the present* in which its evocation takes place. It is the tense for the one who relates the facts as a witness, as a participant; it is thus also the tense that will be chosen by whoever wishes to make the reported event ring vividly in our ears and to link it to the present. Like the present, the perfect belongs to the linguistic system of discourse, for the temporal location of the perfect is the *moment of the discourse* while the location of the aorist is the *moment of the event.* (210; emphasis added)

Benveniste's distinction has particular force in French because the aorist is a strictly literary tense, not normally appearing in the spoken language, where it is felt by native speakers to be "ungrammatical"—whence Banfield's notion of an "unspeakable sentence." More fundamental than this division of labor between the spoken and the written language, however, are the two modes he posits whereby language refers to a past. Recall that Benveniste presents this essay under the section of his book entitled "*L'homme dans la langue*": "[H]ere it is the mark of man upon language, defined by the linguistic forms of 'subjectivity' and the categories of person, pronouns, and tense" (viii). On the one hand, then, the perfect tense bears the "mark of man" in that it presupposes a "present," namely, the "moment of discourse," from which privileged point in time the speaker refers to an event in his "subjective past" (214). The aorist, on the other hand, simply refers to a "certain moment of time," that is, the "moment of the event." Or, as he later states: "As a matter of fact, there is no longer even a narrator. The events are set forth chronologically, as they occurred. No one speaks here; the events seem to narrate themselves" (208). In other words, the aorist (and narration in general) is, linguistically speaking, deictic-less and thus subject-less, that is, objective.

Benveniste's notion of a non-deictic "past tense" is counterintuitive (and thus little understood) inasmuch as tense seems inherently deictic — past, present, future with respect to the moment of speech ("now"). Hans Reichenbach's classic account of tense, for instance, which continues to provide the framework for many current theories, defines each and every tense with respect to an underlying speech-act, so that a non-deictic preterite is simply inconceivable within his system.[6] As early as 1913, however, Bertrand Russell had recognized the possibility of a non-deictic preterite:

> European languages are absolutely destitute of means of speaking of an event without indicating its temporal relation to the speaker; I believe Hebrew and Chinese are preferable in this respect, but unfortunately I was never taught either. There can be no doubt that the philosophy of time has suffered very seriously from this gross incapacity of the languages spoken by western philosophers, since there is no way of expressing the eternity of the *fact* as opposed to the transiency of the *event*.[7]

What he laments in European languages, namely, that seemingly unavoidable "temporal relation" between the speaker and what he calls the "transiency of the event," is none other than deixis, which by definition has to do with the linguistic or grammatical markers of the speaker and the moment of speech: "this," "here," "now," and so forth. The possibility he hopes for in the case of Hebrew and Chinese, on the other hand, is the existence of a non-deictic preterite that would establish "the eternity of the fact," namely, a fact without "temporal relation to the speaker."

These two versions of the past tense correspond to two ways of conceiving of time. Thus, Russell—building on McTaggart's famous study "The Unreality of Time"—elsewhere distinguishes between "physical time" ("the time which arises through relations of object and object," namely, "simultaneity and succession") and "mental time" (that "time which arises through relations of subject and object").[8] Mental time has to do with the subjective perception of events, where the subject's location in time and space ("here" and "now") constitutes the deictic center with respect to which events are situated, namely, in the past, present, or future—not coincidentally the traditional designations of the verb tenses. Since this subject moves constantly through time, the coordinates of mental time likewise constantly shift—whence Roman Jakobson's "shifters," his preferred designation for deictics. What now lies in the future will eventually be present and then recede into the past. Russell captures this quality of mental time by speaking (in the passage quoted earlier) of the "transiency of the event." Physical time, conversely, describes permanent relationships between objects; it is "objective" in that the subject has been factored out of consideration. Rather than locate events deictically with respect to the "now" of the speaker, physical time depends on non-deictic temporal markers—dates, for example. Dates—unlike temporal adverbs such as today, tomorrow, and yesterday—are definite descriptions, that is, their reference does not shift: January 1, 2001, has and always will refer to the same day, and its temporal relation to another date—say, January 2, 2001—will likewise always be the same, namely, "earlier than"—whence Russell's reference to the "eternity of the fact."

In this chapter I will argue that the same dualism divides the language of biblical narrative. First, it is a question of the place of deixis in the verbal system of Biblical Hebrew, specifically with respect to its two forms of the past tense: the perfect (qatal) and the consecutive (wayyiqtol).[9] Biblical Hebrew, I propose, is analogous to French, qatal and wayyiqtol corresponding to the *passé composé* and the *passé simple*, respectively. Thus, while the perfect locates events deictically with respect to the speaker, the consecutive co-occurs with non-deictic temporal markers.[10] In fact, it has been proposed that the consecutive or wayyiqtol, like the *passé simple*, was actually a strictly literary tense—though this is now a difficult hypothesis to corroborate. Regardless of how one answers this strictly historical question regarding spoken pre-exilic Hebrew—a question to which I will return—one sees within biblical narrative a telling correlation of the perfect and consecutive to direct discourse and narration, respectively. Second, one finds a number of "expressive constructions," grammatical forms that entail reference to a speaker. They are "linguistic forms of 'subjectivity'" that register the "mark of man upon language." In biblical narrative, then, they are restricted to the quoted speech of characters, and they co-occur exclusively with the perfect. In conclusion, I will draw out the consequences of this linguistic dualism for the Bible's narrative art by contrasting it to the linguistic monism of epic.

The Dual Past of Biblical Narrative

A number of scholars have analyzed the distribution of the perfect and consecutive in terms that, at first glance, seem equivalent to Benveniste's. Hans Jacob Polotsky was apparently the first to offer explicit evidence for the opposition between the perfect and consecutive as belonging, respectively, to the "*besprochene*" and "*erzählte Welt*" (commentated versus narrated world): "[T]he change from a link in the narrative chain into a piece of direct speech involves the replacement of the sequential narrative verb-form by a verb-form suitable for 'besprochene Welt', a retrospective tense, a Perfect."[11] By adopting the terms "*besprochene*" and "*erzählte Welt*," however, Polotsky invokes what he considers "*the* book on this topic," namely, Harald Weinrich's *Tempus*[12]—which, at least to his mind, has presumably supplanted Benveniste's earlier study of tense. Other similar studies of Biblical Hebrew likewise trace their lineage to Weinrich with little or no attention paid to Benveniste.[13]

Because of Weinrich's pervasive influence, which I believe has consequences beyond notational variance, I find it necessary to devote a few remarks to *Tempus*, although a detailed engagement is far beyond the scope of the present study. One might start with comments he makes in an introductory chapter on Käte Hamburger's *Logik der Dichtung*.[14] He praises her for parting company, at least in the case of the "epic preterite," from those who view verb-forms (*Tempora*) as tenses (*Zeitformen*), but faults her for not going far enough: "Not only the 'epic preterite' . . . has those qualities described by Käte Hamburger, but the verb-forms altogether have functions as signals, which cannot be adequately described as information about time."[15] None of the verb-forms indicate tense; they convey instead the text's linguistic attitude or tone (*Sprechhaltung*). As he explains further on, the speaker (*Sprecher*) indicates through verb-forms a certain attitude (*Haltung*) in order to signal to the hearer (*Hörer*) what sort of understanding or interpretation (*Rezeption*) a text should be given: commenting (*besprechende*) verb-forms signal tension (*Gespanntheit*), narrating (*erzählende*) verb-forms signal repose (*Entspanntheit*).[16] In other words, he posits for both narrative and commentary an underlying communication-act between speaker and hearer—whence the terms listed just above—distinguishing between the two only through the vague notion of "attitude," and thus effectively obscuring, if not totally losing sight of, the theoretical-linguistic implications of Benveniste's theory.[17]

The weakness of Weinrich's study partly derives from his commitment to a taxonomic, descriptive structural linguistics he calls *Textlinguistik*. Thus, having identified "texts" as either "narrative" or "comment," he goes on to subcategorize sentences among one of three *Sprechperspektiven* (linguistic perspectives) —recovered information, degree-zero, and anticipated information—and then, within the sentence, to distribute individual verb-clauses to either linguistic foreground or background. To be sure, he provides a number of intriguing observations, but he fails to construct a unifying theory to marshal these into anything more than a descriptive taxonomy. In his discussion of Benveniste's study of tense in the French verbal system, for instance, Weinrich takes particular interest in the possibility of describing the combinatory possibilities of different syntactical categories, such as tense and person—again, a merely taxonomic project—but he makes no mention of what Benveniste considered the theoretical import of his analysis: *l'homme dans la langue*.[18]

Unfortunately, this same weakness afflicts the various attempts, referred to earlier, to apply Weinrich's schemata to Biblical Hebrew. To be sure, these studies provide some helpful data, but one must look elsewhere for a proper theory turning such data into evidence. Precisely for this reason I return here to Benveniste in hopes of recovering what I consider the real import of his groundbreaking study, namely, the dualism attainable in language between objective and subjective linguistic forms. I will now trace this same dualism within the verbal system of Biblical Hebrew by arguing that the consecutive and perfect correspond, respectively, to the aorist and perfect of French.

As I already had occasion to note, the French aorist sets forth a simple chronology, as if the events narrated themselves. In Biblical Hebrew the very form of the *waw*-consecutive, which preserves an obsolete preterite (**yaqtul*) attached to the prefixal conjunction *waw-* ("and"),[19] suggests this same succession.[20] On occasion biblical narrative capitalizes on this aspect of the tense, using a pure succession of consecutives to turn a character into a blur of sequential acts. Thus, an unreflective Esau is all action as he sells his birthright to his brother Jacob for some stew:

wayyōʾkal wayyēšt wayyāqom wayyēlak wayyibez ʿēsāw ʾet habbĕkōrâ
(Gen. 25:34)

And he ate and drank and rose and left, and Esau despised the birthright.

Five consecutives denoting five discrete, consecutive events (though perhaps one can interpret the fifth as summarizing the preceding four).[21]

Various scholars, furthermore, have discerned a pattern in the distribution of tenses analogous to the verbal system of French. Mark S. Smith notes: "The range of verbal forms utilized regularly in direct discourse exceeds the range exhibited in classical prose narrative. While the *waw*-consecutive constituted the main narrative style to express successive action, direct discourse uses forms in addition to the *waw*-consecutive forms . . . sometimes even for narration."[22] As noted earlier, Polotsky demonstrated that events recounted in narration with the consecutive are often retold by characters in the perfect, an insight adopted and expanded in Niccacci's study.[23] Here are two examples taken from the latter's discussion:

> *wayyillāḥem yôʾāb běrabbat běnê ʿammôn wayyilkōd ʾet ʿîr hammēlûkâ* (2 Sam. 12:26)

> And Joab fought against Rabbah of the sons of Ammon, and he captured the royal city.

> *wayyišlaḥ yôʾāb malʾākîm ʾel dāwid wayyōʾmer nilḥamtî běrabbâ gam lākadtî ʾet ʿîr hammāyim* (2 Sam. 12:27)

> And Joab sent messengers to David and he said, "I have fought against Rabbah. Indeed, I have captured the City of Waters."

> *wayyiqšōr ʿālāyw ʿabdô zimrî śar maḥăṣît hārākeb. . . . wayyābōʾ zimrî wayyakkēhû waymîtēhû* (1 Kings 16:9, 10)

> And his servant Zimri, chief of half the chariots, conspired against him [king Elah of Israel]. . . . And Zimri came and struck him and killed him.

> *wayyišmaʿ hāʿām haḥōnîm lēʾmōr qāšar zimrî wěgam hikkâ ʾet hammelek* (1 Kings 16:16)

> And the people who were camped heard, "Zimri has conspired against, and, indeed, he has struck the King."

As I have attempted to make clear in the English translation, a change in tense indicates a grammatical distinction between narration and (direct) discourse. This common procedure—Niccacci lists some two dozen examples—reflects a discernible pattern in the use of the preterites.

As I discuss further in later sections in this chapter, one might also note here the differences—other than that of tense—between these examples of narration and discourse. In my first example Joab (David's general) reports to David that he has attacked "Rabbah," choosing to omit "of the children of Ammon," which he considered unnecessary in speaking to David. Furthermore, as I shall argue at length, his declaration that he has "indeed" (*gam*, literally "also") captured the city carries an expressive force. In fact, he refers specifically to "the City of Waters,"[24] choosing an apparently more colorful designation of "the royal city" (thus my rendering it as a proper name) as he goes on to taunt his king: "And now, gather the rest of the people and camp against the city and capture it, lest I myself capture the city and it be called by my name" (v. 28). Here Joab refers explicitly to his subjective location in time and space, implicit throughout his report to David, through the deictic, "and now" (*wĕ'attâ*). Note a similar effect in the second example. The account in direct discourse again sorts through the facts of narration. It need not rehearse Zimri's profession for those who know his post well enough, and rather than repeat the blow-by-blow account of his coup—and he conspired and went and struck and killed him—it selects two essential events, again presenting the second with the expressive force of *wĕgam* ("and, indeed"). Note, further, that even the anonymous whispers of gossip do not presume to refer to the king by name, as does the narration proper—"Elah the son of Baasha" (1 Kings 16:8). Pragmatic and syntactic considerations, in other words, indicate a subjective coloring in discourse absent from the objectivity of narration.[25]

Having established the distribution of the perfect and the consecutive in a preliminary way—I will discuss apparent problems with this distribution shortly—I would next like to point out the temporal markers that co-occur with each. A narrative sequence in narration sometimes indicates time through a clause-initial adverbial temporal phrase followed by a sequence of consecutive verbs. In these cases the adverbial phrase, as a definite temporal description, functions like a date, that is, a non-deictic indication of time.

bĕyôm ʿăśôt yhwh ʾĕlōhîm ʾereṣ wĕšāmāyim . . . wayyîṣer yhwh ʾĕlōhîm hāʾādām (Gen. 2:4b, 7)

When the Lord God made earth and heaven . . . and the Lord God formed the man

More frequently one finds the alternate but analogous construction *wayhî* ("And it was"), the consecutive form of *hāyâ*, followed by some sort of non-deictic temporal adverbial phrase.

*wayhî kî-hēḥēl hā'ādām lārōb ʿal-pěnê hā'ădāmâ . . . wayyirʾû běnê-
hā'ĕlōhîm 'et-běnôt hā'ādām* (Gen. 6:1–2)

And it was when the human began to multiply on the face of the
earth . . . And the sons of God saw the daughters of the human . . .

wayhî bayyôm haššěbîʿî wayyāmot hayyāled (2 Sam. 12:18)

And it was during the seventh day, and the child died.

This construction apparently became the conventional opening to a
book, as in Josh. 1:1, Judg. 1:1, and Ruth 1:1, so that the consecutive itself
eventually came to characterize the incipit of a narration.

wayhî 'aḥărê môt yěhôšuaʿ (Judg. 1:1)

And it was after the death of Joshua . . .

The exclusive use of these objective temporal markers with the consecutive in narration indicates that it corresponds to a non-deictic conception
of time. It recounts events that take place, to borrow Benveniste's phrase,
"at a certain moment of time . . . without any intervention of the speaker."
In a sense, the ubiquity of that temporal adverbial phrase based on the
consecutive *wayhî* takes the non-deictic character of this tense to its logical
conclusion.

The perfect in direct speech, conversely, refers to the past from the
present, the moment of discourse. Thus, in the examples of quoted
speech discussed earlier, observe how the perfect appears in clause-initial
position, before the subject and unaccompanied by any temporal adverbial phrase: "I have fought" (2 Sam. 12:27); "Zimri has conspired" (1
Kings 16:16).[26] Instead, the pragmatic situation within the narrative world
provides a present from which an event in a past shared by speaker and
hearer is available through deictic retrospection. Furthermore, as I have
already suggested, speakers often make explicit reference to the pragmatic situation, the moment of discourse, through temporal deictics,
whose distribution thus further corroborates my theory regarding the
temporal relation signified by the perfect over against the consecutive.
For the temporal adverb *ʿattâ* ("now") occurs in discourse, not narration,
and in conjunction with the perfect, not the consecutive.[27]

wayyēlek bilʿām ʿim śārê bālāq (Num. 22:35)

And Balaam went with the leaders of Balak.

hinnēh bāʾtî ʾēlêkā ʿattâ (Num. 22:38)

"Look, I have come to you now."

wayyēʾānĕḥû bĕnê yiśrāʾēl min hāʿăbōdâ wayyizʿāqû wattaʿal šawʿātām ʾel hāʾĕlōhîm min hāʿăbōdâ wayyišmaʿ ʾĕlōhîm ʾet naʾăqātām wayyizkōr ʾĕlōhîm ʾet bĕrîtô ʾet ʾabrāhām ʾet yiṣḥāq wĕʾet yaʿăqōb wayyarʾ ʾĕlōhîm ʾet bĕnê yiśrāʾēl wayyēdaʿ ʾĕlōhîm (Exod. 2:23–25)

And the children of Israel sighed from their labor and cried out. And their groaning from their labor rose up to God. And God heard their clamor, and God remembered his covenant with Abraham, with Isaac, and with Jacob. And God looked upon the children of Israel, and God understood.

rāʾōh rāʾîtî ʾet ʿŏnî ʿammî ʾăšer bĕmiṣrāyim wĕʾet ṣaʿăqātām šāmaʿtî mippĕnê nōgĕśāyw kî yādaʿtî ʾet makʾōbāyw. . . . wĕʾattâ hinnēh ṣaʿăqat bĕnê yiśrāʾēl bāʾâ ʾēlāy wĕgam rāʾîtî ʾet hallaḥaṣ ʾăšer miṣrayim lōḥăṣîm ʾōtām (Exod. 3:7, 9)

I have certainly seen the misery of my people who are in Egypt, and their outcry against their taskmasters have I heard. Indeed, I know their sufferings. . . . And now, look, the outcry of the children of Israel has come to me, and indeed, I have seen the oppression which Egypt inflicts on them.

In both of these examples, a character with firsthand knowledge of a certain event or situation reports it to others using the "tense of the witness." This use of deictics thus marks the connection of the perfect to the "now" of the speaker. The corresponding sentence of narration demonstrates, in marked contrast, the non-deictic temporal value of the consecutive.

Expressivity in Biblical Narrative

One discovers further corroboration of the grammatical dualism between narration and discourse in the distribution of a number of "expressive" constructions in Biblical Hebrew which, though used regularly in speech, do not appear in narration, or appear in narration with a different syntactical function. Like the adverbial "now," they are deictic inasmuch as they are predicated on the presence of a speaker, and as such they co-occur with the perfect, not the consecutive. They do not, however, indicate the speaker's position in time and space, but rather his or her subjective attitude toward some perceived fact in the narrative world.

I borrow the notion of "expressivity" from Banfield, who, on the basis of generative linguistic studies of various formal aspects of subjectivity in language, posits a class of syntactic elements and constructions (Expressions) whose full interpretation requires reference to a speaker.[28] Consider, for example, those adjectives Banfield names "evaluative"—Jean-Claude Milner's "*adjectifs de qualité.*"[29] Typically an adjective describes some attribute of the noun it modifies—for example, "the old woman." Milner calls such an adjective "classifiant" because it posits a class of women, namely, those who are old. One grammatical test for identifying a classifiant adjective is therefore the ability to paraphrase it with a corresponding subordinate clause: "the woman who is old." Conversely, certain adjectives in particular syntactical constructions take on expressive force as an "evaluative" or "non-classifiant" adjective. Thus, in an exclamation such as "Poor woman!," the speaker does not classify her according to her economic standing but rather expresses a subjective attitude toward her. The paraphrase test confirms the changed nature of the adjective in this construction: *"Woman who is poor!" does not paraphrase "Poor woman!" In fact, this last example, by extension, points to another formal linguistic feature of expressions, namely, their non-embeddability, that is, they do not appear in subordinate clauses—hence the unacceptability of *"He said that poor woman!" Even when such a construction is found in narration rather than discourse, its proper interpretation still requires reference to a subjective point of view: "Poor Aunt Julia! She, too, would soon be a shade with the shade of Patrick Morkan and his horse."[30] In this passage of "represented thought" (also known as "free indirect style")—the subject of the next chapter—the exclamation (and following sentence) is assigned to the private perspective of Gabriel, the protagonist of Joyce's short story "The Dead."

In studies of Biblical Hebrew one finds a category roughly analogous to "expressivity," namely, "emphasis." But as Takamitsu Muraoka observes in his important study of the topic, it has been grossly overused, further obscuring what was already a vague, ill-defined concept.[31] What is needed is a revision of the notion of emphasis that analyzes it into subcategories, where each subcategory, identified on linguistic grounds, would be more narrowly and precisely defined. One such subcategory, I suggest, is the notion of expressivity.[32] Muraoka himself seems to recognize an expressive dimension in emphasis when he refers to the "psychological aspects of speech acts" (xiii), which I take to be equivalent to the subjectivity of the speaker. In fact, he glosses this "factor of psychology in emphatic expressions" as "an outflow and discharge of inner intensified emotion" (xiv), suggesting in particular the inflections of the human voice. If Muraoka helps clarify the notion of emphasis, his definition nevertheless does not move beyond the semantic level. This is not to say that he does not take syntax into consideration, but his definition as such makes no reference to formal grammatical considerations. For instance, Muraoka occasionally notes the uneven distribution of various constructions between "narrative" and "conversation," but he does not *explain* this distribution.[33] In what follows, I will account for this distribution as evidence for the dualism of narration and discourse, marshaling evidence that goes beyond interpretive intuition, such as the restriction of these expressive constructions to direct discourse, their co-occurrence with the perfect but not the consecutive, and their absence from indirect discourse (that is, their non-embeddability).

gam[34]

As Muraoka himself writes of this particle: "There is no denying that there are found cases in which the particle *gam* can be only inadequately and awkwardly rendered 'also'" (143). While the particle "almost always retains its additive force" (146), he adduces numerous examples where it gives in addition "an exaggerated, aggravated or extreme case" (143). As my theory would predict, all such examples come from discourse. Furthermore, when it does carry expressive force, *gam* precedes the verb, causing the now expected switch in tense. The following two examples make this expressive force particularly clear. (I have provided parallels of narration to help bring the effect into focus.)

> *wayyimʿālû běnê yiśrāʾēl maʿal baḥērem wayyiqqaḥ ʿākān . . . min haḥērem wayyiḥarʾap yhwh bibnê yiśrāʾēl* (Josh. 7:1; cf. Josh. 6:18)

And the Israelites committed a trespass against the devoted things. And Achan took . . . from the devoted things. And the anger of the Lord burned against the Israelites.

> *ḥāṭāʾ yiśrāʾēl wěgam ʿāběrû ʾet běrîtî ʾăšer ṣiwwîtî ʾôtām wěgam lāqěḥû min haḥērem wěgam gānēbû wěgam kiḥāšû wěgam śāmû biklêhem* (Josh. 7:11)

Israel has sinned. And indeed, they have transgressed my covenant, which I enjoined upon them. And indeed, they have taken from the devoted things, and indeed, they have stolen, and indeed, they have acted falsely, and indeed, they have put it amongst their own things.

wayyillāḥămû pĕlištîm wayyinnāgep yiśrā'ēl wayyānusû 'îš lĕ'ōhālāyw
wattĕhî hammakkâ gĕdôlâ mĕ'ōd wayippōl miyyiśrā'ēl šĕlōšîm 'elep
raglî wa'ărôn 'ēlōhîm nilqāḥ ûšĕnê bĕnê 'ēlî mētû ḥopnî ûpînĕḥās (1
Sam. 4:10, 11)

And the Philistines fought, and Israel was defeated, and they fled,
each man to his tent, and the slaughter was very great. And thirty
thousand foot soldiers fell from amongst Israel, while the ark of
God was taken and both of Eli's sons died, Hophni and Phinehas.

nās yiśrā'ēl lipnê pĕlištîm wĕgam maggēpâ gĕdôlâ hāyĕtâ bā'ām wĕgam
šĕnê bānêkā mētû ḥopnî ûpînĕḥās wa'ărôn hā'ēlōhîm nilqāḥâ (1
Sam. 4:17)[35]

Israel has fled before the Philistines. And indeed, there was a
great slaughter amongst the people. And indeed, both of your
sons have died, and the ark of God has been taken.

As I try to indicate with my translation, I believe *gam* functions here as a
speaker-oriented adverbial, a type of adverbial that modifies an entire sentence and is semantically predicated on the speaker of the sentence.[36] In
both examples the repetition of the adverbial foregrounds the expressive
aspect of these grim reports.

In direct discourse word order helps determine what the adverbial
modifies, and thus whether it carries expressive force.

lĕ'abdĕkā lĕya'ăqōb minḥâ hî' šĕlûḥâ la'dōnî lĕ'ēśāw wĕhinnēh-gam hû'
'aḥārênû (Gen. 32:19)

They are your servant's, Jacob's. They are a gift sent to my lord, to
Esau, and look, also he is behind us.

yāda'tî kî dabbēr yĕdabbēr hû' wĕgam hinnēh-hû' yōṣē' liqrā'tekā (Exod.
4:14)

I know that [Aaron] can speak well. And indeed, look, he is coming out toward you.

The force of *gam* in Gen. 32:19 is ambiguous. The adverbial appears in initial position—in this regard, the exclamation *hinnēh* does not count as
part of the sentence—but it is immediately followed by the noun, which it
might "modify": "He also is behind us." In Exod. 4:14, however, the adverbial, now separated by the exclamation, can no longer "modify" the subject but must modify the sentence itself. One does find *gam* in narration,

but it always attaches to a noun, whether subject or object, and carries a merely additive force.[37]

wayyāmûtû gam šĕnêhem maḥlôn wĕkilyôn (Ruth 1:5)[38]

And the two of them also died, Mahlon and Chilion.

Finally, the following example provides an instructive contrast between indirect style and the expressive force of *gam*.

wattōʾmerʾel hāʾănāšîm yādaʿtî kî nātan yhwh lākemʾet hāʾāreṣ wĕkî nāpĕlâ ʾêmatkem ʿālênû wĕkî nāmōgû kol yōšĕbê hāʾāreṣ mippĕnêkem (Josh. 2:9)

And she said to the men, "I know that the Lord has given you the land, and that terror of you has fallen upon us, and that all the inhabitants of the land melt before you."

wayyōʾmĕrû ʾel yĕhôšuaʿ kî nātan yhwh bĕyādēnû ʾet kol hāʾāreṣ wĕgam nāmōgû kol yōšĕbê hāʾāreṣ mippānênû (Josh. 2:24)

And they said to Joshua, "Truly, the Lord has given all the land into our hands, and indeed, all the inhabitants of the land have melted before us."

In fact, one almost never finds an embedded sentence-initial *gam*, suggesting that as an expressive element it is non-embeddable.[39]

ʾak

Like *gam*, *ʾak* is an adverbial, but it carries the opposite semantic value, the restrictive force of "just, only" as opposed to the additive force of "also." Like *gam*, in discourse it often, though not necessarily, functions as a speaker-oriented adverbial, in such cases carrying much the same expressive force as *gam* in its function as a speaker-oriented adverbial. Muraoka divides occurrences of *ʾak* neatly into two categories: "It is widely admitted that the particle *ʾax* has two different, but internally related (so it seems to me) functions, asseverative-emphatic and restrictive-adversative" (129).[40] The former, of course, generally corresponds to what I would call its expressive function as a speaker-oriented adverbial. Muraoka this time notes appropriately that "it is entirely understandable that the asseverative-emphatic use is especially frequent in colloquial or spoken language, although not exclusively so" (130). I am not sure what he means by his final, qualifying phrase since all of his examples, at any rate, are taken from direct discourse — or poetry, which in this regard amounts to the same thing.[41]

Strikingly, the particle occurs sixty-eight times in direct discourse in our narratives but only thirteen times in narration. These latter instances, save one, do not function as a speaker-oriented adverbial.

wayyimmāḥû min hāʾāreṣ wayyiššāʾer ʾak nōaḥ waʾăšer ʾittô battēbâ (Gen. 7:23)

And they were wiped away from the earth, and just Noah was left, and those with him in the ark.

wayyaʿaś yhwh tĕšûʿâ gĕdôlâ bayyôm hahûʾ wĕhāʿām yāšubû ʾaḥārāyw ʾak lĕpaššēṭ (2 Sam. 23:10)

And the Lord wrought a great triumph that day, but the people were coming back just to strip [corpses].[42]

Here one sees the adverbial's "restrictive" sense. They appear in non-initial position and therefore do not require a change in the tense of the clause's main verb; the switch in tense and word order in 2 Sam. 23:10b does not result from the adverbial's presence. Likewise in two other cases, where it takes on a temporal aspect.

wayhî ʾak yāṣōʾ yāṣāʾ yaʿăqōb mēʾēt pĕnê yiṣḥāq ʾābîw wĕʿēśāw ʾāḥîw bāʾ miṣṣêdô (Gen. 27:30)

And it was when Jacob had just come out from his father's presence, and Esau his brother came from his hunting.

wayyābōʾ gidʿôn . . . ʾak hāqēm hēqîmû ʾet haššōmĕrîm wayyitqĕʿû baššôpārôt (Judg. 7:19)

And Gideon came . . . when they had just set up the watchers. And they blew the trumpets.

In both examples, note how the adverbial co-occurs with the infinitive absolute construction, which here brings into focus the precise time of the verb's action. (I discuss this construction at greater length later in this chapter.)[43] In the majority of its occurrences in narration (eight out of thirteen), *ʾak* functions as a disjunctive conjunction, something like "but" or "however."[44]

ʾak habbāmôt lōʾ sārû ʿôd hāʿām mĕzabbĕḥîm ûmĕqaṭṭĕrîm babbāmôt (1 Kings 22:44)[45]

But [Jehoshaphat] did not take away the high places. Still the people would sacrifice and burn incense on the high places.

>*ak lōʾ sārû mēḥaṭṭʾ ôt bêt yārobʿām ʾăšer heḥĕṭî ʾet yiśrāʾēl* (2 Kings 13:6)

But they did not turn aside from the sins of the house of Jeroboam which he had caused Israel to sin.

We find only one expressive instance of ʾ*ak* in narration.

>*ak ʿal pî yhwh hāyĕtâ bîhûdâ lĕhāsîr mēʿal pānāyw bĕḥaṭṭōʾt mĕnaššeh kĕkōl ʾăšer ʿāśâ* (2 Kings 24:3)

Surely, this happened to Judah at the mouth of the Lord to take them away from his presence for the sins of Manasseh, according to all that he did.

But this verse is clearly an example of "authorial intrusion," and so it merely corroborates my hypothesis that expressivity is a feature of discourse. In other words, the Deuteronomist momentarily intrudes into historical narration in order to provide one of his well-known theological comments on history.[46]

But for this one example, ʾ*ak* carries expressive force only in direct discourse. In all such examples it takes initial position, almost like an exclamation.

>*ăḥōtî hîʾ* (Gen. 26:7)

She is my sister.

>*ak hinnēh ʾištēkā hîʾ* (v. 9)

But surely, look, she is your wife.

This pair of examples brings into focus the contrast between Isaac's simple statement and Abimelech's irritated exclamation shortly thereafter. Even in examples without contrastive parallels, however, the expressive quality of the speaker-oriented adverbial is clear enough.

>*ak ṭārōp ṭōrāp* (Gen. 44:28; cf. Judg. 20:39)

But surely he has, indeed, been torn apart.

>*ak laššeqer šāmartî ʾet kol ʾăšer lāzeh . . .* (1 Sam. 25:21)

But surely in vain have I protected everything that belongs to this one . . .

In these examples, first Jacob vividly recalls, years after the fact, his terrible declaration of Joseph's death, and then David bitterly reflects on Nabal's galling lack of hospitality. As has come to be expected, expressive reporting of the past uses the perfect rather than consecutive due to the verb's displacement from clause-initial position. The following pair of sentences points again to the contrast between the expressive construction and indirect style.

wayhî kir'ôt śārê hārekeb kî lō' melek yiśrā'ēl hû' (1 Kings 22:33)

And it was when the captains of the chariots saw that he was not the King of Israel . . .

'ak melek yiśrā'ēl hû' (1 Kings 22:32; cf. 1 Sam. 16:6)

But surely he is the King of Israel.

In fact, we find not a single attestation of *'ak* in indirect discourse, suggesting that it, like *gam*, is non-embeddable.

Infinitive Absolute

One expressive construction involves the infinitive absolute in what Muraoka calls a "paronomastic construction," that is, when the infinitive absolute co-occurs with a finite form of the same verb. In Muraoka's view of this construction's effect, "very often the emphasis is not placed upon the verbal action itself, but upon a modality, which is thus reinforced. One can discern various modalities or nuances" (86). He then lists these "modalities": (1) affirmation; (2) pressing request; (3) absolute obligation; (4) opposition or antithesis; (5) condition; (6) intensification of the verbal idea itself; (7) rhetorical question; (8) and, finally, common to all instances of the construction is its drawing attention to the verbal idea itself through the abstraction of the infinitival form (disconnected from person, tense, etc.) (86–88). To cite a few examples, Gen. 2:17 ("for in the day you eat from it you shall *surely die*" [*môt tāmût*, literally something like "dying, you will die"]) is an affirmation; Num. 11:15 ("If you are going to treat me thus, please *kill me at once*" [*horgēnî . . . hārōg*]) a pressing request. Note, however, that were one to remove the infinitive absolute from these two examples, one would still have an affirmation and request, respectively. In other words, the infinitive does not signify by its presence an affirmation or request per se, merely adding a certain expressivity to what is already an affirmation or a request. Muraoka's modes therefore amount to little more than an inventory of the types of sentences the construction regularly appears in.

Rather than focus on such nuances, I think the substantive distinction to be made is between expressive and non-expressive instances of the construction. Expressive uses of the construction, according to my theory, would only occur in discourse. Not coincidentally, most of Muraoka's modes logically entail a speech-act, and as he himself observes: "[T]he repetitive inf. construction is mostly employed in lively (and often with strong emotional colouring) conversation *and* legal texts. In other words, one only rarely meets with it in simple narrative" (89);[47] like poetry, legal texts are always staged as direct discourse. What one does meet with in narration, I predict, will be non-expressive. The question then becomes why the infinitive absolute construction should carry expressive force in some cases, but not in others. I believe we have here, as with *gam*, an adverbial that changes function depending on its grammatical relationship to the sentence.[48] When it attaches to the verb phrase, it functions as a "manner adverbial," describing the manner of the action—what Muraoka refers to as "intensification of the verbal idea as such" (6).[49] When the adverbial attaches to the sentence itself, conversely, it becomes what I have called a speaker-oriented adverbial, relating to the subjective attitude of the speaker rather than to the action he or she reports.[50]

For my purposes I will limit this discussion to the occurrences of the construction with a preterite. One finds that of sixty-nine occurrences of this construction, only nine appear in narration; as expected, it functions expressively only in direct speech.[51] In light of the analogy I have drawn between the infinitive absolute and *gam*, the following example is instructive.

wayyō'mer yhwh rā'ōh rā'îtî 'et 'ŏnî 'ammî . . . wĕgam rā'îtî 'et hallaḥaṣ (Exod. 3:7–9)

And the Lord said, "I have certainly seen the misery of my people . . . and indeed, I have seen [their] oppression."

In the same breath, God *expresses*, through two analogous grammatical constructions, his concern for his people. I next provide several contrasting pairs of examples to highlight the distinction between narration and discourse.

wayyāqom mōšeh wayyôši'ān wayyašq 'et ṣō'nām (Exod. 2:17)

And Moses arose and saved them and watered their sheep.

ʾîš miṣrî hiṣṣîlānû miyyad hārōʿîm wĕgam dālōh dālâ lānû wayyašq ʾet haṣṣōʾn (2:19)

An Egyptian man delivered us from the hand of the shepherds, and indeed, he actually drew water for us and watered the sheep.

wayyišlaḥ malʾākîm ʾel bilʿām (Num. 22:5, see also v. 15)

And [Balak] sent messengers to Balaam.

wayyōʾmer bālāq ʾel bilʿām hălōʾ šālōaḥ šālaḥtî ʾēlêkā liqrōʾ lāk (22:37)

And [Balak] said to Balaam, "Did I not certainly send after you to summon you?"

Again, repetition in certain examples helps bring out its expressive force.

wĕʿattâ hăṭôb ṭôb ʾattâ mibbālāq ben ṣippôr melek môʾāb hărôb rāb ʿim yiśrāʾēl ʾim nilḥōm nilḥam bām (Judg. 11:25)

And now, are you actually better than Balak son of Zippor, King of Moab? Did he actually contend with Israel? Did he actually fight against them?

wayyaʿan kol ʾîš yĕhûdâ ʿal ʾîš yiśrāʾēl kî qārôb hammelek ʾēlay wĕlāmmâ zeh ḥārâ lĕkā ʿal haddābār hazzeh heʾākôl ʾākalnû min hammelek ʾim niśśēʾt niśśāʾ lānû (2 Sam. 19:43)

And each person of Judah answered the people of Israel, "Because the King is close kin to us. And why are you angry about this matter? Have we actually eaten at the King's expense? Has [anything] actually been taken for us?"[52]

In the first example Jephthah taunts a would-be foe. In the second Judah fights with Israel for the King's favor; narration correspondingly reports that they spoke more harshly (wayyiqeš) than the Northern tribes (19:44). As an expressive construction, then, it not coincidentally becomes linked to oral storytelling in the phrase hāyōh hāyâ, meaning something like: "Once upon a time there was . . ." One may catch a glimpse of this at the beginning of this biblical folktale:[53]

hālôk hālĕkû hāʿēṣîm limšōaḥ ʿălêhem melek (Judg. 9:8)

Once, the trees went to anoint a king over themselves.

Finally, the infinitive construction does not appear in a subordinate clause with expressive force.

wayyōʾmer ʾābîhā ʾāmōr ʾāmartî kî śānōʾ śēnēʾtāh (Judg. 15:2)

And her father said, "Actually, I said/thought [to myself] that you had completely rejected her."

higgadtî lākem hayyôm kî ʾābōd tōʾbēdûn (Deut. 30:18)

I [hereby] declare to you today that, certainly, you will perish.

Judg. 15:2 contains two instances of the construction. As my translation indicates, the first functions expressively ("Actually, I thought"), while the second, embedded infinitive functions as a manner adverbial ("completely hated/rejected"). In the latter example the infinitive carries expressive force, but , as the commas indicate, it is a parenthetical attaching to the quoting speaker, not the quoted speaker.[54] This sampling gives a sense of this construction's expressive force. I do not claim that all occurrences in discourse function as a speaker-oriented adverbial, but merely that this function is limited to discourse.

Finally, in the nine examples I have found thus far of the infinitive absolute construction in narration, it never carries expressive force. Here are two representative examples.

wayyiqqaḥ mōšeh ʾet ʿaṣmôt yôsēp ʿimmô kî hašbēaʿ hišbîaʿ ʾet bĕnê yiśrāʾēl lēʾmōr pāqōd yipqōd ʾĕlōhîm ʾetkem . . . (Exod. 13:19)[55]

And Moses took the bones of Joseph with him, for he had made the sons of Israel solemnly swear saying, "God will surely visit you . . ."

wayyābōʾ gidʿôn ûmēʾâ ʾîš ʾăšer ʾittô biqṣēh hammaḥăneh rōʾš hāʾašmōret hattîkônâ ʾak hāqēm hēqîmû ʾet haššōmĕrîm (Judg. 7:19)[56]

And Gideon came, and one hundred men who were with him, to the edge of the camp at the beginning of the middle watch, right when they had just set up the watchmen.

Admittedly I must appeal to their interpretive sense, but I would argue that all such instances of the infinitive absolute prefer a reading as a (non-expressive) manner adverbial. For while authorial intrusions are not unheard of in biblical narrative, I think rendering any of these infinitives as a speaker-oriented adverbial would create a jarring effect. Thus, to my mind it makes little sense to translate Exod. 13:19 as "Joseph *surely made the sons of Israel swear"—and so with the other examples. Finally, in Judg. 7:19 (and Gen. 27:30) the infinitive functions temporally in conjunction with another adverbial, *ʾak* ("just"), and as I noted earlier in my discussion of *ʾak*, this use of the infinitive focuses entirely on the action, precisely locating the time of the action's completion. It does not have any expressive force.

hinnēh

Since I devote the next chapter entirely to *hinnēh*, I will keep my remarks here to a bare minimum. According to Muraoka, it is an "emphatic particle": "[A]s the time-honoured English translation 'Behold!' or 'Lo!' might suggest, the primary function of these particles lies in indicating that the speaker or the writer wants to draw the special attention of the hearer or the reader respectively to a fact or object which can be said to be important, new, unexpected, etc." (138). In fact, as these translations suggest, *hinnēh* typically functions as an exclamation or interjection. I will provide here several examples from direct discourse. (Consideration of its well-known function in narration must await the next chapter.)

> *wayyirʾehā yěhûdâ wayyaḥšěbehā lězônâ . . . wayyābōʾ ʾēlêhā wattahar lô* (Gen. 38:15–18)

And Judah saw her and thought her to be a prostitute . . . and he went into her and she conceived by him.

> *zānĕtâ tāmār kallātekā wĕgam hinnēh hārâ liznûnîm* (Gen. 38:24)

Tamar your daughter-in-law has prostituted herself, and indeed, look, she has conceived by her prostitution.

> *waʾădōnîyāhû yārēʾ mippěnê šělōmōh wayyāqom wayyēlek wayyahăzēq bĕqarnôt hammizbēaḥ* (1 Kings 1:50)

Now Adonijah was afraid of Solomon, and he got up and went and grasped the horns of the altar.

> *hinnēh ʾădōnîyāhû yārēʾ ʾet hammelek šělōmōh wĕhinnēh ʾāḥaz bĕqarnôt hammizbēaḥ* (1:51)

Look, Adonijah is afraid of the King, Solomon, and look, he has grabbed the horns of the altar.

In such examples, the speaker, as Muraoka observes, draws attention to a statement by introducing it with the exclamation.

Co-occurrence of Deictics and Expressive Constructions

These three forms of expressivity all limit themselves to direct discourse. They constitute what Benveniste would call "linguistic forms of subjectivity," "marks" of the speaker in his or her utterance. While I could discuss other expressive and deictic constructions, these suffice to demonstrate the deictic dimension of the perfect tense lacking in the consecutive. In fact, the deictic "now" (ʿattâ) along with these expressive constructions constitute a mutually corroborating set of evidence. For one finds numerous examples in which two or more of them appear together in quoted speech.

ʾak hinnēh ʾištĕkā hîʾ (Gen. 26:9)

Surely, look, she is your wife.

kî ʿattâ šālaḥtî ʾet yādî wāʾak ʾôtĕkā wĕʾet ʿammĕkā baddāber wat-tikkāḥēd min hāʾāreṣ (Exod. 9:15)

For now had I sent my hand and, indeed, [struck] you and your people, and you would have been cut off from the earth.

ʾak niggôp niggāp hûʾ lĕpānênû kammilḥāmâ hāriʾšōnâ (Judg. 20:39)

Surely, [Israel] has, indeed, been defeated before us as in the first battle.

ʾet bĕkōrātî lāqāḥ wĕhinnēh ʿattâ lāqaḥ birkātî (Gen. 27:36)

He has taken my birthright, and, look, now he has taken my blessing.

wĕʿattâ hinnēh yādaʿtî kî mālōk timlôk wĕqāmâ bĕyādĕkā mamleket yiśrāʾēl (1 Sam. 24:21)

And now, look, I know that, certainly, you will become king and the kingdom of Israel will be established in your hand.

zānĕtâ tāmār kallātekā wĕgam hinnēh hārâ liznûnîm (Gen. 38:24)

Tamar has played the harlot, and indeed, look, she is pregnant by her harlotry.

wĕʿattâ hinnēh ṣaʿăqat bĕnê yiśrāʾēl bāʾâ ʾēlāy wĕgam rāʾîtî ʾet hallaḥaṣ ʾăšer miṣrayim lōḥăṣîm ʾōtām (Exod. 3:9)

And now, look, the outcry of the children of Israel has come to

me, and indeed, I have seen the oppression which Egypt is inflict-
ing upon them.

meh ʿāśîtā lî lāqōb ʾōyĕbay lĕqaḥtîkā wĕhinnēh bēraktā bārēk (Num.
23:11; cf. 24:10)

What have you done to me? I brought you to curse my enemy,
and, look, you have actually blessed them!

*ʾîš miṣrî hiṣṣîlānû miyyad hārōʿîm wĕgam dālōh dālâ lānû wayyašq ʾet
haṣṣōʾn* (Exod. 2:19)

An Egyptian man saved us from the hand of the shepherds, and
indeed, he actually drew water for us and watered the sheep.

wĕʿattâ hālōk hālaktā kî niksōp niksaptâ lĕbêt ʾābîkā (Gen. 31:30)

And now, you surely went because you longed greatly after your
father's house.

In each of these examples the temporal deictic and expressive elements
all evoke a speaker in the moment of discourse. Their co-occurrence
foregrounds their deictic, expressive force, thus strengthening my overall account of expressivity in Biblical Hebrew. All this is meant to suggest
that the consecutive is used to narrate objectively (without the presence
of a speaker) a sequence of events, while the perfect is used precisely by a
speaker, whose presence takes on linguistic form: not only in the temporal relationship between speaker and event signified by the perfect tense
but in various deictics and expressive elements.[57]

The Dual Tense Sequence in Biblical Narrative

We are now in a position to analyze the distribution of the perfect and
the consecutive more precisely. One need not read far in biblical narrative to find the consecutive in discourse and the perfect in narration — apparent counterevidence to my theory. Such examples led Muraoka, in a
searching review of Niccacci's *Syntax of the Verb*, to characterize the latter's general description of tense distribution as an "oversimplifica-
tion."[58] While Muraoka is right to raise such objections, they are, in fact,
not hard to answer. As I will demonstrate, the perfect occurs in narration
in an entirely predictable fashion, namely, according to the demands of
word order; and in these cases it does not function as a deictic preterite.

Similarly, the consecutive can appear in discourse, but due to the consecutive's syntactical restrictions (analyzed earlier), it requires the suppression of all grammatical traces of the speaker's subjectivity.

The Perfect in Narration

I will deal first with the problem of the perfect in narration. Joüon-Muraoka gives the traditional view of its role in narration: "Usually a narrative begins with a qatal (historic perfect) and continues with a wayyiqtol, which is followed, if need be, by other wayyiqtols, the series of which is never broken without some particular reason."[59] In most such examples, however, the perfect does not mark the true beginning of an actual narrative but is rather already a break in a preceding sequence of consecutives, often signifying the pluperfect.[60]

> *wĕhā'ādām yāda' 'et ḥawwâ 'ištô wattahar wattēled 'et qayin* . . . (Gen. 4:1)

> Now the man knew Eve his wife. And she conceived and bore Cain . . .

Although both Joüon-Muraoka and GKC cite this verse as an example of the perfect beginning a narrative sequence,[61] this verse clearly continues the events of the preceding one, so that the perfect actually interrupts a chain of consecutives: "And [God] drove out [*waygāreš*] the man and placed [*wayyaškēn*] to the east of the garden the cherubs and the flaming sword . . ." (3:24). Thus, one can explain the switch from consecutive to perfect (and from verb-subject to subject-verb word order) as a transition in the narrative, a relative beginning analogous to a paragraph break.

   In fact, with all appearances of the perfect in narration, one must keep in mind that word order and tense go hand in hand. The addition of an adverbial phrase, for example, displaces the verb from primary position, requiring, in turn, the use of the perfect.

> *ûbĕ'arba' 'eśrēh šānâ bā' kĕdorlā'ōmer* . . . *wayyakkû 'et rĕpā'îm* (Gen. 14:5)

> And in the 14th year Chedorlaomer came . . . and struck the Rephaites.

Similarly, a number of basic grammatical constructions and literary effects in Biblical Hebrew require the switching of word order and tense, including the pairing of simultaneous, symmetrical events and mere negation.

wayyiqrā° °ēlōhîm lā°ôr yôm wĕlaḥōšek qārā° lāylâ (Gen. 1:5; symmetry)

And God called the light "day" and the dark he called "night."

wayyiša° yhwh °el hebel wĕ°el minḥātô wĕ°el qayin wĕ°el minḥātô lō° šā°â (Gen. 4:4, 5; negation and symmetry)

And the Lord regarded Abel and his offering, but Cain and his offering he did not regard.

Only occasionally does the perfect actually begin a discrete narrative sequence, and then only after an introductory adverbial phrase providing an objectively defined temporal framework—in stark contrast, one should recall, to the perfect in discourse, where characters can take for granted a shared pragmatic situation.

bĕrē°šît bārā° °ēlōhîm °ēt haššāmayim wĕ°ēt hā°āreṣ. . . . wayyō°mer °ēlōhîm yĕhî °ôr (Gen. 1:1, 3)[62]

In the Beginning, God created the heavens and the earth. . . . And God said, "Let there be light."

bayyāmîm hāhēm ḥālâ ḥizqîyāhû lāmût wayyābō° °ēlāyw yĕša°yāhû . . . (2 Kings 20:1)[63]

In those days, Hezekiah became sick to the point of dying, and Isaiah came to him . . .

Thus, even in these instances—and they are few—the perfect in narration again results from word order, namely, its non-initial sentence position (see also Gen. 14:5 above). As I demonstrated earlier, narration more frequently establishes the temporal framework through a consecutive construction, *wayhî b-* ("And it was in/during"), which not coincidentally avoids the perfect altogether precisely by placing the verb before the adverbial phrase—additional evidence that the perfect is not characteristic of narration as such. In all of these examples, then, the perfect finds its way into narration only through an accident of syntax, through a failure to meet the consecutive's strict demands on word order. The perfect has no inherent or essential connection to narration.

Furthermore, in terms of the temporal relationships involved, the perfect in narration does not locate an event deictically with respect to a speaker's present, as does the perfect in discourse. Rather, it either refers to a point in time simultaneous with (Gen. 1:5) or antecedent to (the pluperfect; see chapter 5) the narrative sequence;[64] or in those rare instances when it begins the narrative sequence it relies on a definite temporal description (2 Kings 20:1).[65] It behaves, in other words, like Benveniste's aorist. It need not concern us that the perfect in Biblical Hebrew, unlike its French counterpart, fulfills two fundamentally different roles—perhaps unavoidable in a language with few verb forms. The simple past in English, for example, serves double duty.

It rained yesterday.
On 1 January 2000, it rained.

The first sentence belongs to discourse inasmuch as the speaker describes an event in his subjective past, namely, yesterday's weather. The second, however, reads like a sentence of narration, whether historical or fictional, for regardless of when it is read or written, the moment of the event is well defined and constant, which is to say, this past does not define itself with respect to a present.[66] And so with the perfect in Biblical Hebrew.

The Consecutive in Discourse

I now turn to the consecutive in discourse. Following Niccacci and Polotsky, I distinguished between narration and discourse, at least initially, on the basis of examples where an event recounted with the consecutive is reported by a character in direct speech with the perfect. Muraoka, however, objects to such evidence:

> Furthermore, one wonders what of substance would be gained by excluding from a discussion in this regard innumerable examples of *discorso narrativo* such as Jdg 6.8f. /ʾānōḫi heʿēleti ʾetḫem mimmiṣrayim wāʾōṣiʾ . . . /. These reinforce Joüon's conviction, *pace* N[iccacci], that WAYYIQTOL is essentially a continuative, i.e. non-initial tense form, even synchronically speaking. An apparent opposition as in 2Sm 12.26 /wayyillāḥem yōʾāv . . . wayyilkōd/ (narrative) and vs. 27 /nilḥamti . . . gam lāḥadti/ (discourse) does not support the thesis that WAYYIQTOL is characteristic of narrative and QATAL of discourse. But for /gam/ we would have found /wāʾelkōd/ or /wāʾelkdā/, just as in Jdg 6.8f. quoted above, and one can hardly claim that in reporting a past event in direct speech the use of /gam/ is obligatory.[67]

In identifying the consecutive as a continuative, non-initial tense form, Muraoka means to suggest that it occurs with equal appropriateness in discourse as well as narration, as long as it *continues* a verbal sequence. As he correctly observes, in an example such as 1 Sam. 12:26 and 27, *gam* ("also") interrupts what would have been a verbal sequence, thus inducing a switch in word order and tense where otherwise one would have found the consecutive. We are now in a position to recognize, however, that the appearance of *gam* is no mere accident. It never interrupts a chain of verbs in narration but only in direct discourse, and in the latter case, as I had occasion to remark earlier, it typically carries an "expressive" force. If *gam* is not "obligatory" in direct speech, it is entirely characteristic of speech as speech.

Furthermore, even the numerous examples of narrative discourse (*discorso narrativo*) — namely, narration contained within direct speech — that Muraoka refers to do not constitute counterevidence to my thesis. Consider the particularly lengthy example in Judg. 11:15–23:

> *kōh ʾāmar yiptāḥ lōʾ lāqaḥ yiśrāʾēl ʾet ʾereṣ môʾāb wĕ et ʾereṣ bĕnê ʿammôn kî baʿălôtām mimmiṣrāyim wayyēlek yiśrāʾēl . . . wayyābōʾ . . . wayišlaḥ. . . . wayyîrĕšû ʾēt kol gĕbûl hāʾĕmōrî mēʾarnôn wĕ ad hayyabbōq ûmin hammidbār wĕ ad hayyardēn wĕ attâ . . .*

> Thus says Jephthah, "Israel has not taken the land of Moab and the land of the Ammonites, for, when they came up out of Egypt, Israel went . . . and came . . . and sent. . . . And they occupied all the Emorite borders, from the Arnon to the Jabbok, and from the wilderness to the Jordan. And now . . ."

What is of interest here is Jephthah's actual message, the quotation within the quotation. I thus bracket out the formulaic introduction ("Thus says . . ."), which belongs to the messenger. The message proper simply begins (as my account of discourse given earlier would predict) with an assertion in the perfect without any linguistic context ("Israel has not taken"), which is provided by the pragmatic situation. Jephthah supports this assertion, however, with what I can only characterize as narration — the narrative sequence following "for" (v. 16). Similar to narration attributable directly to the biblical writer, it begins with an adverbial clause ("when they came up"), followed by a chain of consecutives. This example of quoted narration would seem to contradict my claim. Note, however, that Jephthah leaves not a trace of his subjectivity in this portion of the message: no first- or second-person pronouns, no deictics, no expressive constructions. Indeed, the circumstances require that he give as objective an account as possible, and in any case he could not possibly have witnessed these events, which took place before his birth. Not coincidentally, then, this narration takes the form of a history—which, as Barthes observed, is "that time when we were not born"[68]—and is embedded in a formal, ritualized use of language at some remove from quotidian speech forms. Furthermore, note how Jephthah, having thus temporarily effaced himself, must eventually reassert the moment of discourse, at which point he once again becomes linguistically present in his speech: "and now" (*wĕʿattâ,* Judg. 11:23). I concede, then, that a speaker in the Bible can use the consecutive, but only by ceasing to speak, as it were, with his or her own voice—and biblical characters rarely do so for more than a sentence or two.[69] I thus conclude that the consecutive is a merely occasional intruder into discourse. Discourse qua discourse is characterized by the perfect, the precise mirror image of narration.

Linguistic Register

Before concluding this chapter, I should like to consider the overall register of Biblical Hebrew prose. I begin with Alter's recent instructive account of the style of biblical narrative. Based on the widespread recognition of the Bible's remarkably restricted lexicon, he first suggests that "the Hebrew of the Bible is a conventionally delimited language. . . . [I]t was understood by writers and their audiences, at least in the case of narrative, that only certain words were appropriate for the literary rendering of events."[70] Meanwhile, although rabbinic Hebrew, which emerged shortly before the common era, shows a great deal of linguistic borrowing from Aramaic, Greek, and Latin, it also uses indisputably Hebrew words which nevertheless do not appear in the Bible itself. For this reason, as Alter points out, Abba Ben-David suggests that rabbinic Hebrew developed from a vernacular that was contemporaneous with Classical Biblical Hebrew but avoided by the biblical writers.[71] Alter aptly observes: "This makes particular sense if one keeps in mind that the early rabbis were anxious to draw a line between their own 'Oral Torah' and the written Torah they were expounding."

It is worth pausing for a moment over this shuttling back and forth in biblical and post-biblical Israel between what Northrop Frye would call oral and written "radicals of presentation."[72] On the one hand, it would seem the biblical writers distinguished their sacred history from an older, oral tradition through the fashioning of a literary prose style. On the other hand, once this canon was closed, Jewish culture returned to an oral mode of discourse. In fact, an analogous gesture takes place within the Pentateuch and the Former Prophets. Deuteronomy, as the "second law," not coincidentally takes the form of an extended speech delivered by Moses, even in its narrative retellings of those events already recounted in the Tetrateuch. Similarly, the Deuteronomistic editor(s) of Deuteronomy-Kings, following the Deuteronomic writer's lead, avoids freely composing new narrative, restricting himself to merely adding theologically motivated editorial commentary, which (as I pointed out earlier) takes the form of authorial intrusion. Furthermore, he has a well-known penchant for placing speeches into the mouths of significant personages at crucial historical junctures, such as Samuel's in 1 Samuel 12 and Solomon's in 1 Kings 8.[73] It would appear, then, that once certain classical sources had established themselves, their immediate literary successors were loathe to add to them directly, only commenting on them in the mode of speech.[74]

Returning to biblical narrative, one should recall that Banfield proffered that style of storytelling the Russian formalists called *skaz* as an instance of first-person narrative given in the mode of discourse: "In the formalist conception, a tale in skaz is not really accurately labelled 'oral.' Rather, it is a written (literary) imitation of a discourse. . . . The fictional storyteller or letter writer addresses the tale to some audience, whose presence is linguistically reflected in the tale itself."[75] The conspicuous imitation of a vernacular, in other words, implies an audience listening to the oral performance signified by the text's marked pronunciation. I would suggest that the style of biblical prose, as a radical anti-vernacular—which should be distinguished as well from those conventionally fixed oral-formulaic "vernaculars" of epic singers—helps produce the inverse effect, the unspoken style of narration. For the ancient Israelite audience, reading or even listening to a recitation of the Bible, would immediately perceive in its register what Blanchot refers to as "the narrative voice."[76]

Generally this elevated style comprises both narration and discourse, as reported speech in biblical narrative in many respects does not reflect the vernacular of ancient Israel. Characters in the Bible generally speak Classical Biblical Hebrew, observing, for instance, the same restriction of vocabulary observable throughout biblical narration proper. Nonetheless, in this section I would like to point out various ways in which quoted speech seems to approach what was presumably the spoken register of Biblical Hebrew, reinforcing the dichotomy I have been describing between narration and discourse.

I begin with an observation so obvious it is often overlooked. Biblical narration is a supremely syndetic style. Its ubiquitous *waw* marks off periods of prose, establishing, as Gabriel Josipovici rightly perceived, its distinctive, ineluctable "rhythm."[77] For, as we have had ample opportunity to observe, the typical narrative sequence begins with *wayhî* and proceeds with a stately sequence of consecutives, occasionally interrupted, and then only by a clause beginning in *waw*.[78] Quoted speech, conversely, almost always begins *without* the conjunction; indeed, it often proceeds asyndetically from sentence to sentence. Since Israelites surely did not feel compelled to begin every single statement with "and," reported speech in the Bible, in this respect, no doubt approximates a syntactic pattern of the spoken language.

wayhî kî zāqēn yiṣḥāq wattikhênā ʿênāyw mērēʾôt (Gen. 27:1)

And it was that Isaac was old and his eyes were dimmed from seeing.

hinnēh nāʾ zāqantî lōʾ yādaʿtî yôm môtî (Gen. 27:2)

Look, please. I am old. I do not know the day of my death.

wayyōʾmer lô hinnēh nāʾ ʾîš ʾĕlōhîm bāʿîr hazzōʾt wĕhāʾîš nikbād kol ʾăšer yĕdabbēr bôʾ yābôʾ ʿattâ nēlākâ šam ʾûlay yaggîd lānû ʾet darkēnû ʾăšer hālaknû ʿālêhā wayyōʾmer šāʾûl lĕnaʿărô wĕhinnēh nēlēk ûmah nābîʾ lāʾîš (1 Sam. 9:6, 7)

And [Saul's servant] said to him, "Look, please, a man of God is in this city, and the man is honored. All that he says certainly comes to pass. Now, let us go there. Perhaps he will tell us about our way, by which we have gone." And Saul said, "And look, we will come, but what will we bring to the man?"

In fact, as this last example demonstrates, precisely the quoted speech beginning with *waw* is linguistically marked. In such cases the obtrusive conjunction seems to indicate the speaker's irritation or impatient disagreement as he responds to—perhaps interrupts—his interlocutor.[79]

The occasional use of unconverted *wĕqāṭal*—instances where *wĕ* does not "convert" the perfect tense into the future but simply functions as a conjunction—gives us another glimpse into the spoken language. For as Mark Smith aptly observes: "[F]orms other than the *waw*-consecutive may have expressed succession in the spoken language."[80] Joüon-Muraoka similarly remarks: "Another point which ought to be borne in mind is that the typical [Biblical Hebrew] tense system must be considered primarily a feature of a well-established literary idiom. The day-to-day prose form, let alone the spoken idiom, was most likely somewhat different, as evidenced by Arad inscriptions, e.g. Inscription no. 16 (from around 600 B.C.E.): lines 3f. [*kṣʾ ty mbytk wšlḥty ʾt h(k)sp*] *as I left your house, I sent the money*."[81] Not coincidentally, then, in its discussion of "copulative *waw* + suffix conjugation," the examples Waltke-O'Connor adduces are taken from direct discourse, suggesting that it mimics the spoken language.[82]

hētel bî wěhehĕlip ʾet maśkurtî (Gen. 31:7)

He has cheated me and changed my wages.

waʾ ănî zāqantî wāśabtî (1 Sam. 12:2)

And I, I am old and gray.

By this point it need hardly be added that in narration one would expect each clause to begin with the consecutive, or, if the perfect is used, in the form *wě*-X-perfect. For instance, one would rewrite Gen. 31:7 in the classical style as *wayhattēl bô wě ʾet maśkurtô hehĕlip* (cf. Gen. 1:5a).[83]

Note, furthermore, how the switch from consecutive to perfect usually results in chiastic syntax (here, in my hypothetical rewriting of Gen. 31:7, verb-object, object-verb) inasmuch as another part of speech (usually a noun or an object) displaces the second verb. It seems to me, then, that the syntax of classical narration puts unrealistic demands on actual speakers. For surely speakers, ancient and modern, do not normally speak in chiasms. Similarly, one imagines that in the chaotic flow of unrehearsed speech Israelite speakers would avoid saying the marked form of the conjunction *wa-*, which requires the immediate use of the consecutive imperfect with its strict word order, in favor of the unmarked *wě-*, which holds out various options as to what will come next: subject, object, verb, and so forth. It seems entirely plausible, then, that the unconverted *wěqāṭal* characterized daily speech, while the consecutive was restricted to more formal, premeditated uses of language — perhaps strictly literary contexts. Although the Hebrew tense of narration, unlike its French counterpart, does appear in direct discourse in the Bible, one must keep in mind that at least the diction of biblical prose does not generally seem to reflect the vernacular. Perhaps direct discourse in the Bible does not entirely reflect vernacular syntax and grammar either.[84] Late biblical texts, apparently approaching rabbinic Hebrew, introduce new words, phrases, and syntactical constructions that may signal the growing influence of a spoken vernacular. In fact, one sees the *waw*-consecutive fading into obsolescence in Late Biblical Hebrew. If these linguistic changes indicate a turn toward the vernacular rather than the diachronic evolution of Classical Biblical Hebrew itself, the very disappearance of the consecutive may provide further evidence for its being a strictly literary tense.[85]

It is particularly instructive, because remarkable, that in spite of its conspicuously restricted lexicon, biblical prose contains a great many diglossia. The biblical writers had multiple lexical options for a number of basic concepts, and they knew how to manipulate these for various effects. Occasionally a colloquialism enters biblical prose; in these cases its effect as such is highlighted—for modern readers, perhaps, only becomes visible— in its encounter with a near-synonymous term. Esau's fateful exchange with Jacob is no doubt the most famous example.

> *wĕyaʿăqōb nātan lĕʾēśāw leḥem ûnĕzîd ʿădāśîm wayyōʾkal wayyēšt . . .* (Gen. 25:34)

And Jacob gave Esau bread and lentil stew. And Esau ate and drank . . .

> *halʿîṭēnî nāʾ min hāʾādōm hāʾādōm hazzeh* (Gen. 25:30)

Please feed me some of this red red.

Esau's use of a term unattested in the rest of the biblical corpus, but which in rabbinic literature properly refers to animals swallowing down their feed—compare German *füttern*—betrays both something of his character and his ravenous hunger.[86] Ben-David suggests that a number of diglossia (*kefilut*) may have the same effect.

> *waʾădōnîyāhû yārēʾ mippĕnê šĕlōmōh wayyāqom wayyēlek wayyaḥăzēq bĕqarnôt hammizbēaḥ* (1 Kings 1:50)

Now Adonijah was afraid of Solomon, and he got up and went and grasped the horns of the altar.

> *hinnēh ʾădōnîyāhû yārēʾ ʾet hammelek šĕlōmōh wĕhinnēh ʾāḥaz bĕqarnôt hammizbēaḥ* (1:51)

Look, Adonijah is afraid of the King, Solomon, and look, he has grabbed the horns of the altar.

Here *ʾāḥaz*, the verb later used by the rabbis, represents the vernacular over against the literary stratum reflected by *heḥĕzîq*.[87] Though I do not have the space to analyze the precise nuances of the following examples of synonyms, I would suggest that they produce a similar effect:

> *wayyābōʾû hārōʿîm waygārĕšûm wayyāqom mōšeh wayyōšiʿān wayyašq ʾet ṣōʾnām* (Exod. 2:17)

And the shepherds came and drove them away. And Moses arose and delivered them and watered their flock.

wattō'marnā 'îš miṣrî hiṣṣîlānû miyyad hārō'îm wĕgam dālōh dālâ lānû wayyašq 'et haṣṣō'n (Exod. 2:19)

And they said, "An Egyptian man saved us from the hand of the shepherds, and indeed, he actually drew water for us and watered the flock."

wayhî bayyāmîm hārabbîm hāhēm wayyāmot melek miṣrayim wayyē'ānĕḥû bĕnê yiśrā'ēl min hā'ăbōdâ wayyiz'āqû watta'al šaw'ātām 'el hā'ĕlō-hîm min hā'ăbōdâ wayyišma' 'ĕlōhîm 'et na'ăqātām (Exod. 2:23–24)

And it was during those many days, and the king of Egypt died. And the Israelites groaned from their slavery, and they cried out, and out of their slavery their plea went up to God. And God heard their moaning.

wayyō'mer yhwh rā'ōh rā'îtî 'et 'ŏnî 'ammî 'ăšer bĕmiṣrāyim wĕ'et ṣa'ăqātām šāma'tî mippĕnê nōgĕśāyw kî yāda'tî 'et mak'ōbāyw. . . . wĕ'attâ hinnēh ṣa'ăqat bĕnê yiśrā'ēl bā'â 'ēlāy wĕgam rā'îtî 'et hallaḥaṣ 'ăšer miṣrayim lōḥăṣîm 'ōtām (Exod. 3:7, 9)

And the Lord said, "I have certainly seen the affliction of my people in Egypt, and I have heard their outcry from their masters, for I know their sufferings. . . . And now, look, the outcry of the Israelites has come up to me, and indeed, I have seen the oppression with which Egypt oppresses them."

wayyim'ălû bĕnê yiśrā'ēl ma'al baḥērem wayyiqqaḥ 'ākān . . . min haḥērem wayyiḥar 'ap yhwh bibnê yiśrā'ēl (Josh. 7:1; cf. Josh. 6:18)

And the Israelites committed a trespass against the devoted things. And Achan took . . . from the devoted things. And the anger of the Lord burned against the Israelites.

ḥāṭā' yiśrā'ēl wĕgam 'ābĕrû 'et bĕrîtî 'ăšer ṣiwwîtî 'ôtām wĕgam lāqĕḥû min haḥērem wĕgam gānĕbû wĕgam kiḥāšû wĕgam śāmû biklêhem (Josh. 7:11)

Israel has sinned. And indeed, they have transgressed my covenant, which I enjoined upon them. And indeed, they have taken from the devoted things, and indeed, they have stolen, and indeed, they have acted falsely, and indeed, they have put it amongst their own things.

wayyillāḥămû pĕlištîm wayyinnāgep yiśrā'ēl wayyānusû 'îš lĕ'ōhālāyw wattĕhî hammakkâ gĕdôlâ mĕ'ōd wayippōl miyyiśrā'ēl šĕlōšîm 'elep raglî waʾ ărôn ʾĕlōhîm nilqāḥ ûšĕnê bĕnê ʿēlî mētû ḥopnî ûpînĕḥās (1 Sam. 4:10, 11)

And the Philistines fought, and Israel was defeated, and they fled, each man to his tent, and the slaughter was very great. And thirty thousand foot soldiers fell from amongst Israel, while the ark of God was taken and both of Eli's sons died, Hophni and Phinehas.

nās yiśrāʾēl lipnê pĕlištîm wĕgam maggēpâ gĕdôlâ hāyĕtâ bāʿām wĕgam šĕnê bānêkā mētû ḥopnî ûpînĕḥās waʾ ărôn hāʾĕlōhîm nilqāḥâ (1 Sam. 4:17)

Israel has fled before the Philistines. And indeed, there was a great massacre among the people. And indeed, both of your sons have died, and the ark of God has been taken.

ûpĕlištîm nilḥāmîm bĕyiśrāʾēl wayyānusû ʾanšê yiśrāʾēl mippĕnê pĕlištîm wayyippĕlû ḥălālîm bĕhar haggilbōaʿ (1 Sam. 31:1)

And meanwhile the Philistines were fighting against Israel, and the men of Israel fled from the Philistines and the slain fell on Mount Gilboa.

wayyōʾmer ʾăšer nās hāʿām min hammilḥāmâ wĕgam harbēh nāpal min hāʿām wayyāmutû wĕgam šāʾûl wîhônātān bĕnô mētû (2 Sam. 1:4)

And he said, "The army has fled from the battle, and indeed, many from the army have fallen and died, and also, Saul and Jonathan his son have died."

Languages possess few if any sets of perfectly synonymous words since each inevitably follows its own path through linguistic history. Thus, even if these examples do not reflect the play of a specifically colloquial term against a literary one, the collision of competing words—which are, more-over, distributed between narration and direct discourse—still contributes to the entrance into biblical narrative of multiple voices, or heteroglossia, as Bakhtin would say. The "narrative voice" becomes one among many. And this, as we will now see, is contrary to the spirit of oral-traditional epic.

Epic Monism

I began this chapter by noting that biblical narrative is, as Bakhtin would say, "dialogic," an assertion subsequently corroborated by my analysis of the linguistic dualism of biblical narrative. The language of epic, conversely, is "monologic." Thus, in his essay "Discourse in the Novel" Bakhtin posits a conceptual and historical dichotomy between the two great narrative genres, the epic and the novel.[88] On the one hand, he characterizes the novel as "multiform in style and variform in speech and voice" (261), comprising various "compositional-stylistic unities": authorial narration; forms of everyday, oral narration (*skaz*); semiliterary forms (letter, diary, etc.); extra-artistic authorial speech (moral, philosophical, etc.); and the individualized speech of characters. It is through these "compositional unities . . . [that] heteroglossia can enter the novel" (263). The "majority of poetic genres," on the other hand, are characterized by "the unity of the language system" and, as a result, by the "unity of the poet's individuality as reflected in his language and speech" (264). His theory takes on historical shape inasmuch as the epic's monologism eventually evolves into the dialogism of the novel. In light of the present study, however, one might link the linguistic unity of poetic genres specifically to the oral tradition and the novel's heteroglossia to writing. By thus detaching his theory from certain historical particulars—ancient Greek epic and the modern novel—one can restore to biblical narrative its rightful place in literary history. For one can trace a similar evolution from ancient Near Eastern epic to biblical prose narrative.

Bakhtin's notion of a unitary language finds its equivalent in the work of Milman Parry and his successors, who argue that Homeric style reflects an oral-formulaic tradition. Parry, one recalls, defines the formula as "a group of words which is regularly employed under the same metrical conditions to express a given essential idea."[89] I would suggest that these regularly employed formulas under the constraint of metrical convenience constitute Bakhtin's unitary language, which in turn evokes a monistic world consisting of a set of "essential ideas." Consider the use of one type of formula, the epithet. As is well known, the names of Homeric characters typically appear alongside conventional epithets. Such epithets not only endow the hero with a certain stability of person or role but also suggest the uniform evaluation of each character within heroic culture. The narrator may at one moment refer to Agamemnon as "wide-ruling" (*euru kreiōn*, *Iliad* 1.102) or simply "powerful/ruling" (*kreiōn*, 1.130). What is interesting is that a wrathful Achilles, even while crying to his mother for justice, refers to Agamemnon in those very terms (*euru kreiōn*, 1.355). Even now, he does not—indeed, cannot—question Agamemnon's status except, perhaps, his claim of being "best of the Achaeans."

Adam Parry (Milman Parry's son) draws similar conclusions from his father's work in an essay entitled "The Language of Achilles": "The formulaic character of Homer's language means that everything in the world is regularly presented as all men (all men within the poem, that is) commonly perceive it. The style of Homer emphasizes constantly the accepted attitude toward each thing in the world, and this makes for a great unity of experience."[90] He points to the famous speech by Sarpedon as a succinct statement of the heroic ethos, which I quote here at length from Richmond Lattimore's translation:[91]

> Glaukos, why is it you and I are honoured before others
>   [*tetimēmestha malista*]
> with pride of place , the choice meats and the filled wine
>   cups . . . ?
> . . . .
> Therefore it is our duty [*chrē*] in the forefront of the
>   Lykians
> to take our stand, and bear our part of the blazing of battle,
> so that a man of the close-armoured Lykians may say of us:
> "Indeed, these are no ignoble men [*ou man akleees*] who are
>   lords of Lykia, . . ."
> . . . .
> Man, supposing you and I, escaping this battle,
> would be able to live on forever, ageless, immortal,
> so neither would I myself go on fighting in the foremost
> nor would I urge you into the fighting where men win glory
>   [*kudianeiran*].
> But now, seeing that the spirits of death stand close about
>   us
> in their thousands, no man can turn aside nor escape
>   them,
> let us go on and win glory [*euchus*] for ourselves, or yield it
>   to others. (XII.310–28)

In this closed circle of cause and effect, the tokens of honor (pride of place, choice meats, etc.) demand (*chrē*) of the hero that he fight and win honor (*timē, kudos, kleos,* etc.). Note, in particular, how Sarpedon can only evaluate himself by imagining what a third party would think of his conduct: "so that a man . . . may say of us." As A. Parry suggests, the common dualisms between speech and reality, speech and action, and speech and thought do not obtain in the Homeric world—that monistic world of essential ideas[92]—with one notable exception: Achilles. In his account the estranged Achilles does not accept the "common language" and thus

inhabits the margins of heroic culture. But even he must express his other-
ness through that same language: "Homer, in fact, has no language, no
terms, in which to express this kind of basic disillusionment with society
and the external world. The reason lies in the nature of epic verse. . . . Neither Homer, then, in his own person as narrator, nor the characters he
dramatizes, can speak any language other than the one which reflects the
assumptions of heroic society."[93] If one thus finds a monologic language
in Homer, then what one finds reflected in this language is not the "unity
of the poet's individuality" but—adjusting slightly Bakhtin's formulation
—the unity of the oral tradition.

For this reason, when characters recall events from their past that
Homer has already narrated, they do so using more or less the same language. One does not find the linguistic dualism discoverable in biblical
narrative, for the aorist serves as the primary narrative tense regardless of
who tells the story.[94] Thus one can compare Homer's third-person report
of Odysseus's much-delayed departure from Calypso's Island for the Phaiakians' (books 5 and 6) and Odysseus's first-person account of the same
events (7.240–97).[95] Consider these excerpts from Odysseus's tale of his
final approach to the Phaiakians:

> Seventeen days I sailed, making my way over the water,
> and on the eighteenth day there showed [*ephanē*, aor] the
>   shadowy mountains
> of your own country . . . (7.267–69)

> . . . Poseidon,
> who hampered [*katedēsas*, aor] me from my way, letting
>   loose [*ephormēsas*, aor] the winds upon me
> and stirred [*ōrinen*, aor] up an unspeakable sea . . . (271–73)

> For now the stormwind scattered [*dieskadas'*, aor] [the raft]
>   far and wide, and I now
> made my way across [*dietmagon*, aor] the great gulf by swim-
>   ming, (275–76)

> so I backed away and swam again, until I came to [*epēlthon*,
>   aor]
> a river, and this at last seemed [*eeisato*, aor] to me to be the
>   best place (280–81)

Homer's version, while significantly longer, differs little—grammatically
speaking—save for the switch from first to third person.

Seventeen days he sailed, making his way over the water,
and on the eighteenth day there showed [*ephanē*, aor] the
shadowy mountains
of the Phaiakian land (5.278–80)

[Poseidon] let loose [*orothunen*, aor] all the stormblasts
of all the winds together (292–93)

Poseidon, shaker of the earth, drove [*ōrse*, aor] on a great
wave (366)

so the raft's long timbers were scattered [*dieskadas'*, aor]
(370)

. . . but when he came [*hixe*, aor], swimming along, to the
mouth of
a sweet-running river, this at last seemed [*eeisato*, aor] to
him the best place. (441–42)

In fact, during this same performance Odysseus himself switches into the third person in order to narrate his companions' encounter with Circe (10.208–43) during his absence. In so doing he effectively assumes Homer's voice. He then quotes Eurylochos's report of this encounter, who speaks in the first person (10.251–60) — a story within a story within a story, all told in a single monologic language.

The same holds true for Ugaritic epic. Though less developed and refined than Homeric epic, it too evokes a certain unity of heroic experience. Unlike biblical narrative, therefore, it gives its characters traditional epithets: "Mighty" (*aliyn*) Baal, "Maiden" (*btlt*) Anat. As in Homer, this unity of experience is related to the patently formulaic nature of these poems and its presumed link to an oral tradition.[96] In fact, as Edward Greenstein has already observed: "In Ugaritic epic, the language of discourse is the same as the language of narration because they share the dramatic character. In the Bible, the narrative frame is past-oriented, while the embedded dialogue takes on the dramatic form of presentation."[97] For this reason the tense system of Ugaritic narrative poetry, like biblical poetry but unlike biblical prose, does not differentiate between narration and discourse. While Ugaritic epic and biblical poetry employ both a prefixal (imperfect) and a suffixal (perfect) verb form, these alternate without apparent distinction.

In light of my analyses of biblical narrative, I would like to draw particular attention to the use of repetition in the Ugaritic narrative poems.

k̠trṣmdm.ynḥt.	Kothar fashions the weapons
wypʿr.šmthm.	And he proclaims their names:
šmkat/ ygrš.	"Your name, yours, is Yagarrish:
ygrš.gršym	Yagarrish, drive Yamm,
gršym.lksih/	Drive Yamm from his throne,
[n] hrlkh̠t̠drkth.	[N]ahar from the seat of his dominion.
trtqṣ.bdbʿl.	May you leap from Baal's hand,
kmnš/ r.buṣbʿth.	Like a raptor from his fingers.
hlm.ktp.zbl.ym	Strike the torso of Prince Yamm,
bnydm/ [t̠p] t̠nhr.	Between the arms of [Jud]ge River."
yrtqṣ.ṣmd.bdbʿl.	The weapon leaps from Baal's hand,
km.nšr/ [bu] ṣbʿth.	Like a raptor from his [fin]gers.
ylm.ktp.zblym.	It strikes the torso of Prince Yamm,
bn.ydm.t̠pt̠[nh]r.	Between the arms of Judge River. (1.2.4.11-17)[98]

This rather typical example of repetition functions according to what Simon Parker aptly refers to as "transposition," that is, the repeated lines vary only as required by grammar, the switch from second to third person, and so forth.[99] Though one moves in this passage from reported speech to narrative report, the poem's language does not—indeed, cannot—admit of those stylistic nuances that separate biblical narration from discourse. On those occasions when a repeated passage actually deviates from the first passage, the deviations typically are formulae themselves.

ap.yṣb.yt̠b.bhkl/	Yassib, too, sits in the palace;
wysrnn.ggnh	And his spirit instructs him this way:
lk.labk.yṣb	"Go to your father, O Yassib,
lk/ l[a] bk.wrgm.	Go to your father and say,
t̠ny/ lk[rt.a] d[nk.]	Declare to Ki[rta, your sire]:
ištm[ʿ] / wtqǵ [.udn.]	'Hearken, alert [your ear]!'" (1.16.6.25-30)

ytbʿ.yṣb ǵlm.	Yassib the Young departs,
ʿl/ abh.yʿrb.	He enters his father's presence.
yšu.gh/ wyṣh.	He raises his voice and proclaims:
šmʿ mʿ.lkrt/t̠ʿ.	"Hear now, O Noble Kirta!
ištmʿ.wtqǵ.udn/	Hearken, alert your ear!" (1.16.6.39-42)

Thus, while the second passage "fulfills" the first using different language, one finds each line of the latter passage formulaically "transposed" in other passages.

wttb°.š°tqt/	Shataqat then departs, (1.16.6.2)
°l/ abh.y°rb[100]	He enters his father's presence. (1.16.1.11–12)
yšu.gh/ wyṣḥ	He raises his voice and proclaims:
šm°.lmtt/ ḥry/	"Listen, O Lady Huraya!" (1.16.6.15–17)
tšm°.mtt.ḥry/	Lady Huraya listens; (1.16.6.19)

The formulaic, repetitive style of the poems thus precludes any linguistic distinction between narration and discourse. The poems are entirely discourse. For this reason one finds expressive constructions not only in reported speech but in narrative as well, where one attributes their expressive force to the narrator—as with the following examples of the paronomastic infinitive absolute.[101]

almnt.škr/ tškr.	The widow, verily will/does she hire. (1.14.4.22–23)
°wr/ mzl.ymzl/	The blind, verily does he suffer. (1.14.4.25)
bt.krt.bu.tbu	The house of Kirta verily she enters. (1.16.6.2–3)

The narrator's use here of such constructions is entirely appropriate, for it is the job of the singer to emote and thereby enrapture his audience. The biblical writers, conversely, composing their history in an anonymous solitude, would fashion their literary prose precisely by denying themselves such an expressive outlet. In the world they would fashion, events would be made to seem as though they narrated themselves, and personages alone would reserve the right of self-expression.

Writing makes possible the distinction between language and speech; it makes conceivable the removal of expressivity from that style I have been calling narration. As we have seen, in Biblical Hebrew the sentence containing the narrative preterite, the consecutive, constitutes the first of Banfield's "unspeakable sentences," the sentence of "pure narration." It enabled biblical writers to fashion that impersonal style required for recounting an objective sequence of events, namely, to write history. But the knife that divides language cuts both ways. For with the emergence of an impersonal style, the language of discourse becomes marked as such. This rift within language in turn foregrounded for the biblical writers the representational problems and possibilities posed by the human subject. Discourse—no longer coterminous with language itself but restricted to the speech of characters—would enable these writers to explore and develop the interiority of these characters to a degree unthinkable for the epic singer. Hence, as has already been demonstrated by others, dialogue becomes a medium for the Bible's cunning and subtle characterizations. Epic singers, conversely, working with the unitary medium of traditional formulae, cannot use discourse—as yet coterminous with the very language of the tradition—to similar effect. Therefore its characters, as Auerbach so brilliantly demonstrated, are fully "externalized."[102]

If biblical narrative uncannily anticipates the modern novel, even more surprising is its ability to represent consciousness. For, as I will argue in the next chapter, biblical writers discovered a limited yet fully realized means for representing the perception of its characters. It is the second of Banfield's "unspeakable sentences."

•4•

REPRESENTED CONSCIOUSNESS
IN BIBLICAL NARRATIVE

[Flaubert], by the entirely new and personal use that he made
of the past definite, the past indefinite, the present participle
and certain pronouns and prepositions, renewed our vision of
things almost as much as Kant, with his Categories, renewed
our theories of Cognition and of the Reality of the external
world.
　　　　　　　　　　—Marcel Proust, "On Flaubert's Style"

The "he" is a typical novelistic convention; like the narrative
tense, it signifies and carries through the action of the novel; if
the third person is absent, the novel is powerless to come into
being, and even wills its own destruction.
　　　　　　　　　　—Roland Barthes, *Writing Degree Zero*

As we can see, then, the "he" has split in two: on the one hand,
there is something to tell, and that is the *objective* reality as it is
immediately present to the interested gaze, and on the other
hand, this reality is reduced to a constellation of individual
lives, *subjectivities*, a multiple and personalized "he," a manifest
"ego" under the veil of an apparent "he."
　　　　　　　　　　—Maurice Blanchot, "The Narrative Voice"

Opaque Minds

In a well-known story in Numbers, Moses sends twelve Israelite spies to re-
connoiter the as yet unconquered land of Canaan. Awed by what they
see, they convince the Israelites not to enter the land for fear of its mighty
inhabitants: "And there we saw the Nephilim, Anakites of the Nephilim.
And we were like grasshoppers in our eyes, and so we were in their eyes"
(Num. 13:33). The rabbis provide a shrewd reading of this passage by
imagining God's response to the spies' narrative report: "They said, 'And
we were like grasshoppers in our eyes' (Num. 13:33); the Holy One,
blessed be he, said, 'I forgive them.' But then they said, 'And so we were

in their eyes' [ibid.]; and He said, 'Do you know what I made you like in their eyes? Who can say that you were not like angels in their eyes?'" (Numbers Rabbah 16:11). In other words, the rabbis (and God) detect a note of dissimulation in this report. For as they rightly perceived, in rendering transparent the inner judgments and perceptions of the land's inhabitants—what Dorrit Cohn describes as the "singular power possessed by the novelist"[1]—these spies, like the novelist, tell lies, they narrate fiction. This epistemological tension seems to have disturbed the translators of the Jewish Publication Society's *Tanakh*, who, in an apparent attempt to soften the jarring effect of the Hebrew, added a modal— "and so we *must have* looked to them"—where, strictly speaking, none exists in the original, whose syntax, in fact, indicates a pointed symmetry between the two reported events. It would appear, then, that this narrative world distinguishes between those facts available to public scrutiny and those available solely to private introspection. Thus, by transgressing this epistemological boundary, the spies betray the disingenuousness of their "slanderous report" (*dibbat*, 13:32).[2] In fact, as I shall argue in this chapter, the biblical writers not only observed this distinction but exploited it, discovering perhaps for the first time in the history of literature a linguistic means for representing consciousness.

In the previous chapter I presented evidence for identifying a number of constructions and particles in Biblical Hebrew as "expressions," namely, formal linguistic realizations of the subjectivity of the "speaker," the "I" that stands behind every speech-act. Part of the evidence that this theory helps explain is their distribution: one finds them solely in direct discourse, never in narration. Biblical Hebrew, however, does possess one expressive element, *hinnēh* ("look"), which, unlike most of the constructions discussed in the previous chapter, regularly appears not only in discourse but in narration as well. In this context, the construction beginning with *hinnēh* constitutes a species of what, following Banfield, I will call "represented consciousness"—also known as *style indirect libre* and *erlebte Rede*—another linguistic realization of subjectivity, but this time attributed to a "he."

Several scholars writing on *hinnēh* have already provided a number of insights in this regard, but these have usually resided in the intuition of the critic and have stopped short of the theorist's formal precision. Thus, these discussions have not dealt satisfactorily either with the syntax of this construction or with the relation of its role in narration to its role in discourse. In this chapter I will provide a general theory of its overall syntax, analyzing numerous examples of this construction in both discourse and narration. This theory, in turn, will allow me to argue that its grammatical behavior provides further evidence for the disappearance of the speaker from biblical narration. For, as we will see, the expressive force of *hinnēh* can attach to the subjectivity of a third person only in the absence of the first. The evidence of Ugaritic myth will further corroborate this theory by providing a glimpse into the historical development of the use of *hinnēh* from the (oral) poetry of Ugarit to the literary prose of the Bible. It is my second "unspeakable sentence."

Before turning to *hinnēh* in the Bible, however, let me briefly review the phenomenon of represented consciousness as such. Represented speech and thought refers to that style that has traditionally been understood as a mixture of direct and indirect discourse, whence designations such as French *style indirect libre* (that is, both "free" or independent, and "indirect") and modern Hebrew *maba' meshulav* (literally, "combined discourse"). On the one hand, such sentences do not directly quote a character speaking in the first person but "represent" a speech-event, typically in the third person, thus resembling indirect discourse in certain respects. On the other hand, by taking the form of coordinate (free) rather than subordinate (bound or embedded) clauses, they are able to capture some of the immediacy of directly quoted speech. Consider the following passage from Joyce's short story "The Dead," in which I have emphasized sentences of represented consciousness.

> Gabriel, leaning on his elbow, looked for a few moments unresentfully on her tangled hair and half-open mouth, listening to her deep drawn breath. *So she had had that romance in her life: a man had died for her sake. It hardly pained him now to think how poor a part he, her husband, had played in her life.* He watched her while she slept as though he and she had never lived together as man and wife. . . .
> *Perhaps she had not told him all the story.* His eyes moved to the chair over which she had thrown some of her clothes. . . . He wondered at his riot of emotions of an hour before. *From what had it proceeded? From his aunt's supper, from his own foolish speech, from the wine and dancing, the merry-making when saying good-night in the hall, the pleasure of the walk along the river in the snow. Poor Aunt Julia! She, too, would soon be a shade with the shade of Patrick Morkan and his horse.*[3]

This passage comprises not a simple linear narration but rather a dual sequence of events. For the italicized sentences represent "mental events" that occur simultaneously with a series of physical acts: Gabriel thinks such thoughts as he leans, looks, watches, moves, and so forth. This inner "monologue," however, is not reported as indirect discourse since it takes the form of independent rather than embedded sentences. In fact, several of these sentences are non-embeddable, explaining the unacceptability of the following:

> *He said that so she had had that romance in her life.
>   ("so" in initial position non-embeddable)
> *He said that poor Aunt Julia!
>   (exclamations non-embeddable)
> *He wondered from what had it proceeded?[4]
>   (inverted questions non-embeddable)

Such syntactic features, related to the notion of "expressivity" discussed in the previous chapter, might lead one to construe these sentences as direct discourse were it not for their shifted tense and person. In direct discourse one would expect to find first-person pronouns alongside a different set of tenses (primarily the present and the present perfect), as follows (changes emphasized):

> So she *had* that romance in her life: a man *died* for her sake. It hardly *pains me* now to think how poor a part *I*, her husband, *have* played in her life. . . .
>   Perhaps she *has* not told *me* all the story. . . . From what *did* it *proceed?* From *my* aunt's supper, from *my* own foolish speech, from the wine and dancing, the merry-making when saying good-night in the hall, the pleasure of the walk along the river in the snow. Poor Aunt Julia! She, too, *will* soon be a shade with the shade of Patrick Morkan and his horse.[5]

As with indirect discourse, the representation of consciousness entails a shift in person and tense. It is this shifted tense that leads to the anomalous co-occurrence of past tense, deictics, and third person. And even when one finds represented consciousness in first-person narratives—Proust's monumental novel is the paradigmatic example—one must distinguish between the I-as-character (cotemporal with the past) and I-as-narrator (cotemporal with the present), a more subtle shift of person related to the opaque reference of indirect discourse.[6]

Banfield has provided a generative linguistic account of the syntax of represented consciousness that accounts for these grammatical peculiarities.[7] For my purpose, I am primarily concerned with the differences between quoted speech and represented speech (more generally, represented consciousness). As I have noted, both are syntactically "free," that is, non-embedded. What distinguishes represented consciousness, then, is its opaque reference, its shifted tense and person. The linguistic behavior of "expressions" and deictics brings this into particular focus. As we have seen, expressions generally cannot be embedded. Furthermore, expressions and deictics together point to a subjectivity or "self" located in a "here" and a "now." Typically, as in quoted speech, one identifies these as the "I" who speaks in the "present." In represented consciousness, however, due to the shift of person and tense, this subjectivity refers instead to a third person whose "here" and "now" is located in the narrative "past." It is an obvious yet important fact that this "self" cannot be both "I" and "he"; nor can "now" be both "present" and "past." What is more, the first-person "speaker" and the "present" take priority over the third person and the "past"; that is, whenever possible, one must refer the "self" and "now" of expressions and deictics to the "speaker" and the "present."[8] Banfield thus concludes that the sentence representing consciousness can have neither "speaker" nor "present." In other words, it too is "unspeakable."

To return to my example from Joyce, Gabriel's actions (look, watch, etc.) establish the "past," which is cotemporal with "now" ("It hardly pained him now . . . ."). And various expressive elements (e.g., the exclamation, "Poor Aunt Julia!") evoke a "self." Since there is no first-person speaker, one refers this "self" to the numerous third-person, masculine, singular pronouns. In this case context and the agreement of person, gender, and number make Gabriel the only plausible candidate.

The Presentation of Sense-Data in Discourse

The basic significance of *hinnēh* has long been recognized. S. R. Driver already observed in his classic study of the Hebrew tense system that it "introduces something specially arresting the attention"[9]—hence the traditional translations "Lo!," "Behold!," and "Look!" Its equivalent in English is "here is" and "there is"; in French *voici* and *voilà*. Its syntactic force is clearest when *hinnēh* introduces a noun phrase—possibly its "primitive" role[10]—pointing, as it were, to the referent (in the narrative world) of the noun in question.[11] In such cases one easily imagines an accompanying physical gesture on the part of the speaker.

hinnēnî (Gen. 22:1)
Here I am.
Me voici!

hinnēh hā'ēš wĕhā'ēṣîm (Gen. 22:7)
Here is the fire and the wood.
Voilà le feu et le bois.[12]

There is a patently deictic quality to these constructions, which various proposals have attempted to account for: "demonstrative,"[13] "predicator of existence,"[14] and, of course, "presentative."[15] A precise linguistic analysis of *hinnēh*, however, has eluded scholars.

I propose that *hinnēh* possesses that syntactic force I referred to in the previous chapter as "expressivity."[16] In other words, it is not merely a temporal or spatial deictic—though it does evoke the sense of a "here" and a "now." Rather, it entails reference to a "self" or subjectivity. In this regard, the traditional designation "presentative" turns out to be the most accurate. It was presumably imported from traditional French grammar, where it refers to *voici* and *voilà*,[17] but the idea of "presentation" has a long-standing place in philosophy as well.[18] Of particular interest here is Russell's understanding of the notion: "I think the relation of subject and object in presentation may be identified with the relation which I call 'acquaintance.'"[19] "Presentation," in other words, entails reference to a "self," namely, the subject of "acquaintance." In fact, he implicitly provides the philosophical notion with a grammatical form: "Concerning the immediate objects in illusions, hallucinations, and dreams, it is meaningless to ask whether they 'exist' or are 'real.' *There they are,* and that ends the matter."[20] "There they are" is a plural version of what I have identified as the presentative in English. Through this construction, language gives syntactical "expression" to the mental image or sensation of some object, whether mental (dreams) or physical (a table), as it registers on a person's consciousness.

To return to other grammatical definitions of *hinnēh*, one should note that Russell's discussion of the presentative effectively distinguishes it from the existential predicate. It is simply "meaningless" (redundant) to assert the existence of something that is already present to one's consciousness. Grammar confirms this distinction. Compare the meaning of "There is a book on the table" with "There is the book." The former, an existential construction, takes an indefinite noun; the definite noun in the latter, conversely, necessitates a presentative reading.[21] The predicator of existence does not tolerate the definite noun because definiteness in this context indicates a prior "acquaintance" with the book. The presentative, conversely, can take an indefinite noun: "Here is a book that I think you will like."[22] But in this case the restrictive clause seems to give the book in question a certain "definiteness"—not just any book but this particular one.[23]

One must similarly distinguish between the presentative and demonstrative. True, there is a certain resemblance.

hinnēh hā‘ām hayyōṣē' mimmiṣrayim waykas 'et-‘ên hā'āreṣ (Num. 22:11)

Here is this people that comes out of Egypt and covers the surface of the land.[24]

hinnēh dam-habbĕrît 'ăšer kārat yhwh ‘immākem ‘al kol-haddĕbārîm hā'ēlleh (Exod. 24:8)

Here is the blood of the covenant which the Lord has made with you concerning all these things.

In such examples, one could easily substitute the demonstrative *zeh/'ēlleh* ("this" / "these") for *hinnēh*, resulting in a sentence like:

'ēlleh 'ĕlōhêkā yiśrā'ēl 'ăšer he‘ĕlûkā mē'ereṣ miṣrāyim (Exod. 32:4)

These are your Gods, Israel, who brought you out of the land of Egypt.

They are not, however, fully equivalent (interchangeable).

mî-'ēlleh (Gen. 48:8)

Who are these?

lō' zeh hadderek wĕlō' zōh hā‘îr (2 Kings 6:19)

This is not the way, and this is not the city.

But,

*mî hinnām

*Who are here-they-are?

*lō' hinnô hadderek wĕlō' hinnĕnâ hā‘îr[25]

*Here-it-is is not the way, and here-it-is is not the city.

These latter two examples are ungrammatical because the presentative is not simply a demonstrative but an expression, and as such it cannot be embedded in another clause but only coordinated with it. In fact, one never finds an embedded *hinnēh* clause in these texts;[26] and one finds *wĕhinnēh* precisely when it has been coordinated with the preceding clause.[27]

In most cases *hinnēh* actually functions as an interjection introducing a sentence, but it carries the same expressive force as the presentative proper, which it attaches, in effect, to the succeeding sentence.[28]

> *kî lĕyāmîm ʿôd šibʿâ ʾānōkî mamṭîr ʿal-hāʾāreṣ* (Gen. 7:4)
>
> For in seven days I am causing it to rain on the earth . . .
>
> *waʾānî hinĕnî mēbîʾ ʾet-hammabbûl mayim ʿal-hāʾāreṣ* (Gen. 6:17)
>
> As for me, look, I am bringing the flood waters upon the earth . . .
>
> *ʾăḥōtî hîʾ* (Gen. 26:7; cf. 12:19 and 20:2)
>
> She is my sister.
>
> *ʾak hinnēh ʾištĕkā hîʾ wĕʾêk ʾāmartā ʾăḥōtî hîʾ* (26:9)
>
> Yet, look, she is your wife! So why did you say, "She is my sister"?
>
> *ʿeglat bāqār tiqqaḥ bĕyādekā wĕʾāmartā lizbōaḥ lyhwh bāʾtî* (1 Sam. 16:2)
>
> Take a heifer in your hand and say, "To sacrifice to YHWH have I come."
>
> *hinnēh-bāʾtî ʾēlêkā ʿattâ* (Num. 22:38)
>
> Look, I have come to you now.
>
> *kāʿēt māḥār ʾešlaḥ ʾēlêkā ʾîš mēʾereṣ binyāmin* (1 Sam. 9:16)
>
> At about this time tomorrow, I will send to you a man from the land of Benjamin.
>
> *wĕhinnēh ʾešlaḥ ʾet-hannaʿar* (1 Sam. 20:21)[29]
>
> And, look, I will send the lad . . .

I offer these pairs of contrastive examples to illustrate *hinnēh*'s role as an expressive interjection. Note that *hinnēh* functions identically no matter what type of clause follows, whether verbless (with or without participle) or verbal (perfect or imperfect). As one should by now expect, *hinnēh* never co-occurs with the consecutive.[30] Turning to the first pair of examples, I do not mean to suggest that P's version of the Flood (Gen. 6:17) is more catastrophic than J's (7:4) but rather that the presence and absence of *hinnēh* match the sense of relative urgency with which God conveys his message in each. In the second pair of examples, *hinnēh*'s absence corresponds nicely to the patriarch's poker-faced lie (Gen. 26:7), and its presence to Abimelech's indignant unmasking of that lie (26:9). Next, note how Balaam draws attention *to* his arrival (Num. 22:38), Samuel *away from* his (1 Sam. 16:2). In the latter verse God has just revoked Saul's kingship and instructed Samuel to anoint his replacement. As part of a ruse to throw off any suspicion of subversive activity, Samuel must, without a hint of guile, explain his presence in Bethlehem: to sacrifice to the Lord. The pre-posed element—"to sacrifice"—perhaps further focuses attention on the pretense and away from himself—"have I come." Balaam, conversely, stresses his arrival in order to appease his impatient customer, Balaq. The final pair of examples also functions along these lines.

Finally, one might note again the co-occurrence of *hinnēh* with other expressive elements and deictics in direct discourse.[31]

ʿattâ ("now")[32]

> *hăkî qārāʾ šĕmô yaʿăqōb . . . ʾet-bĕkōrātî lāqāḥ wĕhinnēh ʿattâ lāqaḥ birkātî* (Gen. 27:36)

Is he not indeed called Jacob? . . . He has taken my birthright, and, look, now he has taken my blessing.

wĕgam ("indeed")[33]

> *yādaʿtî kî-dabbēr yĕdabbēr hûʾ wĕgam hinnēh-hûʾ yōṣēʾ liqrāʾtekā* (Exod. 4:14)

I know that he can speak well, and indeed, look, he is coming to you.

Infinitive Absolute[34]

> *meh ʿāśîtā lî lāqōb ʾōyĕbay lĕqaḥtîkā wĕhinnēh bēraktā bārēk* (Num. 23:11; cf. 24:10)

What have you done to me? I brought you to curse my enemy, and, look, you have *actually* blessed them!

In all these examples, the "now" and "self" evoked by the temporal deictic, *hinnēh*, and other expressive elements are all co-referential with each other and with the "speaker" and the "present."

The Representation of Sense-Data in Narration

Unlike other expressive constructions, the *hinnēh* clause appears quite regularly in narration. Our initial impulse might be to anchor such clauses in a "speaker" and a "present." They would then provide evidence of a narrator. In fact, in a few instances I admit precisely this interpretation.

> *ʿal-kēn qārāʾ labbĕʾēr bĕʾēr laḥay rōʾî hinnēh bên-qādēš ûbên bāred* (Gen. 16:14)

Therefore the well is called Beer Lahai Roi. Look, it is between Kadesh and Bered.

> *ʿal-kēn qārĕʾû lammāqôm hahûʾ maḥănēh-dān ʿad hayyôm hazzeh hinnēh ʾaḥărê qiryat yĕʿārîm* (Judg. 18:12)

Therefore they have called that place Mahaneh Dan until this day. Look, it is beyond Kiriath Jearim.

> *wayyōʾmer lĕlammēd bĕnê-yĕhûdâ qāšet hinnēh kĕtûbâ ʿal-sēper hayyāšār* (2 Sam. 1:18)

And he told [them] to teach the children of Judah [the Song of] the Bow. Look, it is written in the Book of Jashar.

In these three examples—to my knowledge the only such occurrences of *hinnēh* in Genesis–Kings—one hears, at least for a moment, the "voice" of the writer. This "speaker" is located in a "here"—from which he points to that place *beyond* Kiriath Jearim[35]—and a "present"—cotemporal with "this day" (Judg. 18:12) and the (implicit) present tense of all three examples. As should be apparent, however, these three verses are instances of *authorial intrusion*. It is no coincidence that these are the only three instances of *hinnēh* without the conjunction *wĕ* ("and") outside of direct discourse. Asyndeton marks these clauses as discourse, and their insertion into narration, known for its ubiquitous "and," effects a syntactic interruption of the narrative sequence, indicating the writer's *intrusion* into the narrative from the scene of writing. The underlying force of *hinnēh*, meanwhile, has not changed.

These three exceptions aside, *hinnēh* clauses in narration always begin with the conjunction *wĕ* not because *wĕhinnēh* has a different syntactical status but because all clauses in biblical narration begin in this manner.[36] As commentators have long observed, it represents the consciousness of characters. S. R. Driver noted early on that such *hinnēh* clauses signify "*the impression* [some circumstance] *produces* upon the principal subject."[37]

> *wayhî haššemeš bāʾâ waʿălāṭâ hāyâ wĕhinnēh tannûr ʿāšān wĕlappîd ʾēš*
> *ʾăšer ʿābar bên haggĕzārîm hāʾēlleh* (Gen. 15:17)

And then the sun had gone down and it had become very dark. And here was an oven of smoke and a torch of fire which had passed between these pieces.

> *wayhî hēmmâ hōlĕkîm hālôk wĕdabbēr wĕhinnēh rekeb ʾēš wĕsûsê ʾēš* (2 Kings 2:11)

And then they were walking, talking as they went. And here were a chariot of fire and horses of fire.

In these two verses one finds *hinnēh* as the presentative proper directly taking a noun complement. As sentences of narration, however, they evoke "self" and "now" that coincide not with "speaker" and "present" but rather with a third-person character in the narrative "past." The first example represents Abraham's fearful encounter with the tokens of the divine presence—note as well the demonstrative "these" anchored in Abraham's point of view. The second represents the spectacular arrival of heavenly chariot and horses as it registers on Elisha's and/or Elijah's consciousness. Rather than the presentation of sense-data, we have their representation.

In light of the analogy I have drawn between *hinnēh* and *voici/ voilà*, it is worth noting Flaubert's use of the French presentative in passages of represented consciousness.

> *Peut-être, cependant, s'était-il trompé en quelque chose? Il cherchait, ne trouvait pas. Mais les plus fameux chirurgiens se trompaient bien.* Voilà ce qu'on ne voudrait jamais croire! *On allait rire, au contraire, clabauder!*[38]

Perhaps, however, he had made a mistake in something? He considered this, but found nothing. But even the most famous surgeons made mistakes. *Here was something no one would ever believe!* On the contrary, there would be laughter and derision!

Voilà comment se constituait la féodalité de l'argent, pire que l'autre! *Mais qu'on y prenne garde!*[39]

Here was how the feudalism of money was formed, worse than the other one! But let them beware!

Il pouvait donc lui être utile. Le voilà *qui entrait dans son existence, dans son cœur!*[40]

He could, then, be of use. *Here he was,* entering into her existence, into her heart!

Au lieu de la rupture qu'il attendait, voilà que l'autre, *au contraire, se mettait à la chérir et complètement, depuis le bout des cheveux jusqu'au fond de l'âme. La vulgarité de cet homme exaspérait Frédéric.*[41]

Instead of the break he had been expecting, *here was that man,* on the contrary, beginning to cherish his wife, and completely at that, from the ends of her hair to the depths of her soul. The vulgarity of that man was exasperating to Frederic.

In these passages, Flaubert represents the inner *speech* of various characters using the French presentative. As one would expect of represented speech and thought in French, one finds the *imparfait* in these examples, along with the occasional expressive element (*donc*) and deictic (*cet*). The punctuation itself adds to the evocation of speech, signifying the inflections of questions and exclamations. However, it lacks the specifically visual dimension of the Hebrew presentative.

Oddly enough, one finds the exact equivalent of the Hebrew presentative in Virginia Woolf's writings. Here she describes the very literary effect one finds in biblical narrative, in what seems like a novelist's gloss on Russell's philosophy: "The mind receives a myriad impressions—trivial, fantastic, evanescent, or engraved with the sharpness of steel. From all sides they come, an incessant shower of innumerable atoms; and as they fall . . . the accent falls differently from of old; the moment of importance came not *here* but *there*."[42] According to Woolf, it is the task of modern fiction to represent these impressions: "Let us record the atoms as they fall upon the mind in the order in which they fall, let us trace the pattern . . . which each sight or incident scores upon the consciousness."[43] What she means by all this becomes clear in a short story entitled "Mrs. Dalloway in Bond Street," a type of preparatory study for her famous novel, in which she provides a preliminary sketch of this "shower of atoms."[44]

Oh, right under the horses' noses, you little demon! and there she was left on the kerb stretching her hand out, while Jimmy Dawes grinned on the further side. (152)

There was St James's palace; and now—she had passed Bond Street—she was by Hatchard's book shop. The stream was end-less—endless—endless. . . . And there was that absurd book, Soapey Sponge, which Jim used to quote by the yard; and Shakespeare's Sonnets. (154–55)

. . . here was an open motor car with a girl, alone. (155)[45]

There was a roll of cloth in the window, and here just one jar on a black table, incredibly expensive; . . . (155)

There, like a Queen at a tournament, raised, regal, was Lady Bex-borough. . . . and now, there she is, thought Clarissa. (156)

There she was in her place. (157)

"There!" she exclaimed. (158)[46]

This use of the presentative is not peculiar to Woolf. One finds the same construction in Joyce put to much the same use.

And Jacky Caffrey shouted to look, there was another and she leaned back . . . and they all saw it and shouted to look, look there it was and she leaned back ever so far to see the fireworks.[47]

In all these examples, it is the presentative that "records" the impressions these visual "atoms" make on consciousness. It is a species of represented consciousness that specifically represents visual perception.

To return to biblical narrative, what one finds most often in narration is *hinnēh* as an interjection, but it retains its presentative function, intro-ducing a sentence (more precisely, an "expression") that describes some circumstance present to a perceiving subject.[48] In fact, the two *hinnēh* clauses I considered earlier (Gen. 15:17 and 2 Kings 2:11) provide the only two examples of the presentative proper (*hinnēh*—noun) in narration. Henceforth I will focus on *hinnēh* as an interjection. I begin with examples demonstrating the range of "expressions" introduced by *hinnēh*: verbless with and without participle; and verbal with the perfect tense only—the future-imperfect is not surprisingly unattested in this construction in nar-ration. These begin to demonstrate how *hinnēh* retains the syntactical force it has in discourse.

wayyiśśā᾽ ʿênāyw wayyar᾽ wĕhinnēh gĕmallîm bā᾽îm (Gen. 24:63)

And [Isaac] lifted his eyes and looked. And, look, camels were coming.

wayyāšob rĕ᾽ûbēn ᾽el-habbôr wĕhinnēh ᾽ên-yôsēp babbôr (Gen. 37:29)

And Reuben returned to the pit. And, look, Joseph was not in the pit.

wayyipnû ᾽anšê hā ʿay ᾽aḥărêhem wayyir᾽û wĕhinnēh ʿālâ ʿăšan hā ʿîr haššāmaymâ (Josh. 8:20)

And the men of Ai turned around and looked. And, look, the smoke of the city had gone up toward heaven.

In the first example Isaac has been mourning over the recent death of his mother; meanwhile Abraham has sent the trusted family servant away in search of a suitable wife for his son Isaac. In this verse, then, *hinnēh* subtly evokes Isaac's sense of anticipation as he sees what appears to be his father's servant and camels returning from their nuptial quest. Next Reuben discovers, to his utter dismay, the empty pit. Finally, the men of Ai realize too late that their city has been pillaged and burned behind their backs.

Representative *hinnēh* and Speech

In my brief discussion of represented consciousness in the novel, we saw that one of its defining characteristics is its proximity to direct discourse, the apparent blurring of the boundary between narration and discourse. As the following examples make clear, such is the case in Biblical Hebrew as well.

wayyō᾽mer . . . hinnēh ᾽ānōkî niṣṣāb ʿal ʿên hammāyim (Gen. 24:12, 13; cf. vv. 42, 43)

And he said, ". . . Look, I am standing by the spring."

wayyābō᾽ ᾽el hā᾽îš wĕhinnēh ʿōmēd ʿal haggĕmallîm ʿal hā ʿāyin (Gen. 24:30)

And he went to the man. And, look, he was standing by the camels at the spring.

wayyĕdabbēr parʿōh ʾel yôsēp bahălōmî hinĕnî ʿōmēd ʿal śĕpat hayʾōr
(Gen. 41:17)

And Pharaoh said to Joseph, "In my dream, look, I was standing
on the bank of the Nile."

wayhî miqqēṣ šĕnātayim yāmîm ûparʿōh hōlēm wĕhinnēh ʿōmēd ʿal hayʾōr
(Gen. 41:1)

And then it was two years later, and Pharaoh was dreaming. And,
look, he was standing on the Nile.

*ʾānî ṭerem ăkalleh lĕdabbēr ʾel libbî wĕhinnēh ribqâ yōṣēʾt wĕkaddāh ʿal
šikmāh* (Gen. 24:45)

I had not yet finished speaking to myself, and, look, Rebekah was
coming out, and her jar was on her shoulder.

*wayhî hûʾ ṭerem killâ lĕdabbēr wĕhinnēh ribqâ yōṣēʾt . . . wĕkaddāh ʿal
šikmāh* (Gen. 24:15)

And then he had not yet finished speaking, and, look, Rebekah
was coming out . . . and her jar was on her shoulder.

wayyōʾmer ʾel ʾeḥāyw hûšab kaspî wĕgam hinnēh bĕʾamtaḥtî (Gen.
42:28)

And he said to his brothers, "My money has been returned to me.
And indeed, look, it is in my sack!"

wayyarʾ ʾet kaspô wĕhinnēh hûʾ bĕpî ʾamtaḥtô (Gen. 42:27)

And he saw his money. And, look, it was in the mouth of his sack.

*wayyaʿan ʿākān ʾet-yĕhôšuaʿ wayyōʾmar ʾomnâ ʾānōkî ḥāṭāʾtî lyhwh
ʾĕlōhê yiśrāʾēl . . . wāʾēreʾ* [qere] *baššālāl . . . wāʾeqqāḥēm wĕhinnām
ṭĕmûnîm bāʾāreṣ bĕtôk hāʾohŏlî wĕhakkesep taḥtêhā* (Josh. 7:20, 21)

And Achan answered Joshua and said, "Truly, I have sinned
against the Lord God of Israel. . . . And I saw the spoil . . . and I
took them. And, look, they are hidden in the ground inside my
tent and the silver is beneath it."

*wayyišlaḥ yĕhôšuaʿ malʾākîm wayyāruṣû hāʾohŏlâ wĕhinnēh ṭĕmûnâ
bĕʾohŏlô wĕhakkesep taḥtêhâ* (Josh. 7:22)

And Joshua sent messengers and they ran to the tent, and, look, it
was hidden in his tent and the silver was beneath it.

wayyōʾmer yônādāb ʾel hammelek hinnēh bĕnê hammelek bāʾû (2 Sam. 13:35)

And Jonadab said to the king, "Look, the king's sons have come."

wayhî kĕkallōtô lĕdabbēr wĕhinnēh bĕnê hammelek bāʾû (2 Sam. 13:36)

And then, just as he finished speaking, look, the king's sons came.

wayyarʾ haṣṣōpeh ʾîš ʾaḥēr rāṣ wayyiqrāʾ haṣṣōpeh ʾel haššōʿēr wayyōʾmer hinnēh ʾîš rāṣ lĕbaddô (2 Sam. 18:26)

And the watchman saw another man running, and the watchman called to the gatekeeper and said, "Look, a man is running by himself."

wayyiśśāʾ ʾet ʿênāyw wayyarʾ wĕhinnēh ʾîš rāṣ lĕbaddô (2 Sam. 18:24)

And he lifted his eyes and looked, and, look, a man was running by himself.

[Note as well the contrast between *hinnēh* clause and the direct object.]

wayyōʾmer nātān ʾel bat-šebaʿ . . . hinnēh ʿôdāk mĕdabberet šām ʿim hammelek waʾănî ʾābōʾ ʾaḥărayik (1 Kings 1:11, 14)

And Nathan said to Bathsheba . . . "Look, while you are still speaking there with the King, I will come after you."

wĕhinnēh ʿôdennâ mĕdabberet ʿim hammelek wĕnātān hannābîʾ bāʾ wayyaggîdû lammelek lēʾmōr hinnēh nātān hannābîʾ (1 Kings 1:22, 23)

And, look, while she was still speaking with the King, Nathan the prophet came. And they said to the King, saying, "Here is Nathan the prophet."

ʿôdennû mĕdabbēr wĕhinnēh yônātān ben ʾebyātār hakkōhēn bāʾ (1 Kings 1:42)

And while he was still speaking, look, Jonathan the son of Abiathar the priest came.

wattōʾmer ḥay yhwh ʾĕlōhêka . . . wĕhinĕnî mĕqōšešet šĕnayim ʿēṣîm (1 Kings 17:12)

And she said, "As the Lord your God lives . . . and, look, I am gathering some wood."

wayyābōʾ ʾel petaḥ hāʿîr wĕhinnēh šām ʾiššâ ʾalmānâ mĕqōšešet ʿēṣîm (1 Kings 17:10)

And he came to the entrance of the city, and, look, a widow was gathering wood.

wayyaggîdû lāhem lēʾmōr bāʾnû ʾel maḥănēh ʾărām wĕhinnēh ʾên šām ʾîš wĕqôl ʾādām (2 Kings 7:10)

And they told them, saying, "We came to the camp of Aram, and, look, there was no one there, nor the sound of a person."

wayyābōʾû ʿad qĕṣēh maḥănēh ʾărām wĕhinnēh ʾên šām ʾîš (2 Kings 7:5)

And they came to the edge of the camp of Aram, and, look, there was no one there.

If represented consciousness in the Bible specifically takes the form of visual sensation or perception—of "the atoms," in Woolf's words, that "fall upon the mind"[49]—it seems fair to suggest, in light of the verbal proximity of these parallels, that the biblical writers represented these atoms as an inner speech that flashes across a character's consciousness.[50] Furthermore, these parallel passages help to locate the shift involved from *hinnēh* in discourse to *hinnēh* in narration. In discourse the particle's expressive force attaches to the first-person "speaker"; in narration this expressive force shifts to a third-person "self." By understanding this shift as opaque reference, one need not regard these two usages of *hinnēh* as two separate phenomena. Rather, the *hinnēh* clause is fundamentally a form of speech, an "expression." Represented consciousness in the Bible, then, consists of the transposition of expressivity from discourse into narration.

As a visualized approximation of represented speech, *hinnēh* in narration should be able to co-occur with other deictics and expressive constructions, just as it does in discourse. In fact, one does find a few examples where this is precisely the case.[51]

wayhî haššemeš bāʾâ waʿălāṭâ hāyâ wĕhinnēh tannûr ʿāšān wĕlappîd ʾēš ʾăšer ʿābar bên haggĕzārîm hāʾēlleh (Gen. 15:17)

And then the sun went down and it became very dark, and, here was an oven of smoke and a torch of fire which had passed between *these* pieces.

wayyiškab wayyîšan taḥat rōtem ʾeḥād wĕhinnēh zeh malʾāk nōgēaʿ bô wayyōʾmer lô qûm ʾĕkōl (1 Kings 19:5)

And he lay down and slept under a broom tree, and, look, *this* was an angel touching him, and he said to him, "Rise, eat."[52]

wĕkol hāʾāreṣ bôkîm qôl gādôl wĕkol hāʿām ʿōbĕrîm wĕhammelek ʿōbēr bĕnaḥal qidrôn wĕkol hāʿām ʿōbĕrîm ʿal pĕnê derek ʾet hammidbār wĕhin-nēh gam ṣādôq wĕkol halwiyyim ʾittô nōśĕʾîm ʾet ʾărôn bĕrît hāʾĕlōhîm (2 Sam. 15:23–24)

And all the land was weeping in a loud voice, and all the people were crossing over, and the king was crossing over the river Kidron, and all the people were crossing over the desert on the path. And here was, indeed, Zadok, and all the Levites with him were carrying the ark of the covenant of God.

In the first two examples, the demonstratives *zeh* and *ʾēlleh* function as deictics centered on the character's point of view: Abraham sees the divine symbol passing between *these* pieces, and Elijah senses *this* angel touching him.[53] The syntax of the third example is susceptible to more than one interpretation. One possibility, however, is to construe *gam*, co-occurring with *hinnēh*, as a speaker-oriented adverbial. If this is so, the verse registers the shock of seeing even Zadok the priest himself going into exile with the Levites and the ark of God.

This is admittedly sparse evidence. In stark contrast to *hinnēh* in direct discourse, one does not find "now" with this construction, nor (save the possible example just given) any of the expressive constructions I discussed in the previous chapter. Nonetheless, I think it an instance of taxonomic excess (typical of pragmatic, text-linguistic analyses) for Miller to imply that we need another stylistic category to describe represented consciousness in the Bible: "The functions of [*wĕhinnēh*] in Biblical Hebrew are thus simultaneously narrower and broader than free indirect discourse. . . . If free indirect discourse is to be used to describe the appearance in Hebrew narrative of [*wĕhinnēh*], it must be done with a clear understanding of the significant ways in which the ancient Hebrew and modern European literary traditions diverge."[54] What one finds in biblical narrative is a fully realized species of represented consciousness. If the biblical writers did not fully explore or exploit the possibilities of represented consciousness—which were, I suggest, latent in the medium of Biblical Hebrew prose—as novelists would almost three millennia later, this does not in any way diminish their remarkable achievement.

Representative *hinnēh* and Tense

Another defining characteristic of represented consciousness is its system of tense. On the one hand, tense is "shifted" as in indirect discourse, but these tenses are now defined deictically with respect to the "self" in the narrative "past." Thus, in the previously cited passage from Joyce's "The Dead" verbs in the present and present perfect tense were shifted into past and past perfect: "So she had had that romance in her life: a man had died for her sake. It hardly pained him now to think how poor a part he, her husband, had played in her life"; instead of "so she had," "a man died," "it hardly pains me now." On the other hand, there is often a progressive aspect to represented consciousness, which is especially clear in a language such as French, where the *imparfait* predominates in this style. For the *imparfait* is a past progressive form, rendering a secondary event that is cotemporal with a primary event recounted in the *passé simple* ("past"). Hence Proust's interest in *cet éternel imparfait* of Flaubert's style: "This everlasting imperfect then, comprised in part of the characters' own words which Flaubert is in the habit of reporting in the indirect style so that they merge with the rest . . . this imperfect then, so new in our literature, alters the aspect of things and of people entirely, as a lamp does when it is moved, or the arrival in a new house, or the old one if it is nearly empty and one is in the midst of moving."[55] Proust, in other words, perceives in "the indirect style" (his term for *style indirect libre*) a certain "aspect," as when "one is in the midst of moving," namely, the sense of a progression. Consider the function of this tense in the following examples of represented thought taken from Flaubert.

> [*Charles*] *se leva pour aller boire à son pot à l'eau et il ouvrit la fenêtre,* le ciel était couvert d'etoiles, un vent chaud passait; au loin des chiens aboyaient.[56]

> [Charles] got up to drink some water from his pitcher and opened the window. *The sky was covered with stars, a warm breeze was blowing; in the distance dogs were barking.*

> *Emma mit un châle sur ses épaules, ouvrit la fenêtre et s'accouda.* La nuit était noire. Quelques gouttes de pluie tombaient.[57]

> Emma wrapped a shawl around her shoulders, opened the window and leaned out on her elbows. *The night was dark. A few drops of rain were falling.*

In such passages the *imparfait* represents some sense-datum as it registers on a third-person "self" in a "now."[58] What is perceived is a progression — the rain falling, the dog barking — cotemporal with the primary narrative "past" — in both cases opening the window.

Biblical narrative makes the same use of tense in represented consciousness. In narration *hinnēh* as interjection introduces a circumstantial clause, which interrupts the narrative sequence. Andersen thus remarks the parallel syntax between the so-called *hinnēh* clause and circumstantial clause: "The difference between a clause like Ge 18[8b]—wĕhū ʾ ʿōmēd ʿālēhem, *and he is standing beside them*—and Ge 24[30]—wĕhinnē ʿōmēd ʿal-haggĕmallîm, *and behold he is standing beside the camels*—is that the latter is seen through Laban's eyes."[59] This clause, in turn, typically contains either the perfect or participle; less frequently it is verbless, but its implied copula functions like the participle. As I demonstrated in the previous chapter, the perfect tense in discourse deictically refers to a "past" with respect to the speaker's "present." When, conversely, the perfect tense in narration interrupts the narrative sequence as part of a circumstantial clause, it loses its deictic character but often recounts, by an analogous logic, an event *anterior to* the primary narrative event — the pluperfect.

> *wayyābōʾ bĕʾōhel rāḥēl wĕrāḥēl lāqĕḥâ ʾet-hattĕrāpîm wattĕśimēm bĕkar haggāmāl wattēšeb ʿālêhem* (Gen. 31:33–34)

And [Laban] entered Rachel's tent. And Rachel had taken the household idols, and had placed them in the camel's saddle, and had sat on them.

Laban's entry into Rachel's tent (in the consecutive) constitutes the primary narrative event, by which time Rachel *had already* stolen the idols. Note how once the pluperfect has been established, the consecutive as continuative tense can render a sequence of pluperfect events. One can easily imagine inserting *hinnēh* here to represent Laban's discovery of his idols:

> **wayyābōʾ bĕʾōhel rāḥēl wĕhinnēh lāqĕḥâ bittô ʾet-hattĕrāpîm wattĕśimēm bāʾōhel*

And Laban entered Rachel's tent. And, look, his daughter had taken the household idols, and had placed them in her tent.

This hypothetical example closely resembles Esau's bitter complaint to his father regarding his conniving brother, though in this example of quoted speech one does not shift the perfect verb into the pluperfect; it is anchored instead in Esau's "present."

wĕhinnēh ʿattâ lāqaḥ birkātî (Gen. 27:36)

And, look, he has now taken my blessing.

Conversely, one also finds analogous examples in narration.

wayyipnû ʾel-ʾōhel mô ʿēd wĕhinnēh kissāhû heʿānān wayyērāʾ kĕbôd yhwh (Num. 17:7)

And they turned toward the tent of meeting. And, look, the cloud had covered it, and the glory of the Lord had appeared.

The people turn around (*wayyipnû*) and discover that the cloud of God's presence *had covered* the tent of meeting. Here the perfect (*kissāhû*) once again signifies the pluperfect (recall, as well, Josh. 8:20, discussed earlier). But at the same time *hinnēh*'s expressive force restores the perfect's deictic quality by anchoring the secondary event's anteriority in the subjectivity ("self") of the people, whose moment of consciousness ("now") is cotemporal with the "past."

The same logic determines the use of participial clauses in this construction. The participle (technically an adjectival form), in its function as a predicate, describes a progressive action cotemporal with some other event. In discourse it signifies the present progressive, simultaneous with the act of utterance. In narration it occurs without *hinnēh* in circumstantial clauses that describe a past progressive event cotemporal with one of the events in the narrative sequence (typically recounted by a verb in the consecutive tense). With *hinnēh*, conversely, the participial clause in narration maintains this past progressive sense, but it is now anchored within a subjective point of view—"self" and "now."[60] Since such a circumstantial clause has neither "speaker" nor "present," the "self" and "now" evoked in it by the presentative are co-referential, respectively, with the third person, usually the subject of the previous sentence of narration, and the "past." (I thus give linguistic precision to the differentiation noted by Andersen and others between the circumstantial clause and the narrative *hinnēh* clause.) The participle, in other words, behaves just like the French *imparfait*.

Returning to biblical narrative, I have placed side by side in the following groups of examples circumstantial clauses with corresponding *hinnēh* clauses as a type of experiment highlighting the literary effect involved.

ʿôdennû mĕdabbēr ʿimmām wĕrāḥēl bāʾâ ʿim-haṣṣōʾn ʾăšer lĕʾābîhā (Gen. 29:9)

While he was still speaking with them, Rachel came with her father's sheep.

wĕhinnēh ʿôdennâ mĕdabberet ʿim-hammelek wĕnātān hannābîʾ bāʾ (1 Kings 1:22)

And, look, she was still speaking with the king, and Nathan the prophet came.

ʿôdennû mĕdabbēr wĕhinnēh yônātān ben-ʾebyātār hakkōhēn bāʾ (1 Kings 1:42)

He was still speaking, and, look, Jonathan the son of Abiathar the priest came.

wattēlek tāmār bêt ʾamnôn ʾāḥîha wĕhûʾ šōkēb (2 Sam. 13:8)

And Tamar went to the house of Amnon her brother, and he was lying down.

wayyābōʾû kĕḥōm hayyôm ʾel-bêt ʾîš bōšet wĕhûʾ šōkēb ʾēt miškab haṣṣohŏrāyim (2 Sam. 4:5; cf. v. 7)

And they came during the heat of the day to the house of Ish-boshet, and he was taking a midday rest.

wayyābōʾû hammalʾākîm wĕhinnēh hattĕrāpîm ʾel-hammiṭṭâ ûkĕbîr hāʿizzîm mĕraʾăšōtāyw (1 Sam. 19:16)

And the messengers came. And, look, the idol was in the bed and the goats' hair cushion was at its head.

wayyābōʾ dāwīd waʾăbîšay ʾel-hāʿām laylâ wĕhinnēh šāʾûl šōkēb yāšēn bammaʿgāl waḥănîtô mĕʿûkâ-bāʾāreṣ mĕraʾăšōtāw (1 Sam. 26:7)

And David and Abishai came to the people at night. And, look, Saul was lying, sleeping in the trench, and his spear was stuck in the earth next to his head.

wayyaʿăbōr ʾittay haggittî wĕkol-ʾănāšāyw wĕkol-haṭṭap ʾăšer ʾittô wĕkol-hāʾāreṣ bôkîm qôl gādôl wĕkol-hāʿām ʿōbĕrîm wĕhammelek ʿōbēr bĕnaḥal qidrôn wĕkol-hāʿām ʿōbĕrîm ʿal-pĕnê-derek ʾet-hammidbār (2 Sam. 15:22-23)

And Ittai the Gittite crossed over, and all his people and all the little ones who were with him, and [meanwhile] all the land was weeping in a loud voice, and all the people were crossing over, and the king was crossing over the river Kidron, and all the people were crossing over the desert on the path.

wĕhinnēh gam-ṣādôq wĕkol-halwîyim ᵓittô nōśᵉᵓîm ᵓet-ᵓărôn bĕrît hāᵓĕlōhîm (2 Sam. 15:24)

And, look, even Zadok and all the Levites with him were carrying the ark of the covenant of God.

In these examples a transition from consecutive to participle (or implied copula) takes us from a primary narrative event to a simultaneous progressive event. The presence or absence of *hinnēh*, in turn, simply determines whether or not this progressive event is represented as registering on the consciousness of some character(s).

Representative *hinnēh* and Direct and Indirect Discourse

Though perhaps an obvious point, one should, finally, note that the expression introduced by *hinnēh* in narration is neither direct nor indirect discourse. In the first place, as we have seen, these sentences require the shifted tense and person characteristic of represented consciousness (and indirect speech) rather than the present of direct discourse. Thus, if Gen. 42:27 were direct discourse, one would expect: "And he saw his money, and [he thought], look, it *is* in the mouth of *my* sack"—instead of the actual verse, "and, look, it *was* in the mouth of *his* sack." Other examples follow:[61]

wayyōᵓmer ᵓabrām hēn lî lōᵓ nātattâ zāraᶜ wĕhinnēh ben bêtî yôrēš ᵓōtî wĕhinnēh dĕbar yhwh ᵓēlāyw lēᵓmōr (Gen. 15:3-4)

And Abram said, "Look, [since] *you* have not given *me* offspring, and, look, [therefore] a servant of *my* house will be *my* heir." And, look, the word of the Lord came to *him* saying, . . .

[Note that in direct discourse one finds Abram's "I" addressed to God's "you," whereas in narration Abram's first-person deictic center shifts to the third person.]

wayyābē³ yādô bĕḥêqô wayyôṣi³āh wĕhinnēh yādô mĕṣōra°at (Exod. 4:6)

And he put his hand to his breast and took it out, and, look, his hand was leprous like snow.

wayyiśśā³ °ênāyw wayyar³ wĕhinnēh ³îš °ōmēd lĕnegdô wĕḥarbô šĕlûpâ bĕyādô (Josh. 5:13)

And he lifted his eyes and saw, and, look, a man was standing against him and a sword was drawn in his hand.

The opaque pronominal reference and the shift in tense thus differentiate the *hinnēh* clause in narration from that in direct discourse. Rather than "quote" thought, these clauses "represent" it.

If one cannot construe represented *hinnēh* clauses as directly quoted speech, neither can one regard them as indirect discourse. I claimed earlier that *hinnēh* clauses are non-embedded. I will now provide evidence for this assertion. I have noted that *hinnēh* most commonly introduces a circumstantial clause. Thus, in most of the examples given thus far, the reader will not find a verb but only a participle or implied copula, and such clauses follow subject-predicate word order (see, for instance, Exod. 4:6 and Josh. 5:13 cited earlier). The same clauses, however, invert to predicate-subject word order when following the subordinating conjunction *kî* ("that"). In the following examples, my translations attempt to replicate their reversed word order.

rā³â kî ("see that")[62]

wayyir³û bĕnê hā³ĕlōhîm ³et bĕnôt hā³ādām kî ṭōbōt hēnnâ (Gen. 6:2)

And the sons of God saw the daughters of humanity, that good were they.

wayyar³ hā°ām kî bōšēš mōšeh lāredet min hāhār . . . (Exod. 32:1)

Now when the people saw that delaying was Moses to come down from the mountain . . .

yāda° kî ("know that")[63]

raq °ēṣ ³ăšer tēda° kî lō³ °ēṣ ma³ăkāl hû³ ³ōtô tašḥît (Deut. 20:20)

Just the tree which you know that not a fruit tree is it, that shall you destroy.

ʾāz yādaᶜ mānôaḥ kî maPʾak yhwh hûʾ (Judg. 13:21)

Then Manoa realized that a messenger of YHWH was he.

hălôʾ yādaᶜtî kî bōḥērʾattâ lĕben yišay (1 Sam. 20:30)

Don't I know that choosing are you the son of Jesse?

šāmaᶜ kî ("hear that")[64]

wayyišmĕᶜû kî qĕrōbîm hēm ʾēlāyw (Josh. 9:16)

And they heard that neighbors were they to him.

šāmaᶜnû kî malkê bêt yiśrāʾēl kî malkê ḥesed hēm (1 Kings 20:31)

We have heard that the kings of the house of Israel, that loyal kings were/are they.

higgîd kî ("tell that"; indirect speech, proper)[65]

mî higgîd lĕkā kî ᶜêrōm ʾattâ (Gen. 3:11)

Who told you that naked were/are you?

wayyaggēd yaᶜăqōb lĕrāḥēl kî ʾăḥî ʾābîhā hûʾ wĕkî ben ribqâ hûʾ (Gen. 29:12)

And Jacob told Rachel that a relative of her father was he and that the son of Rebecca was he.

wĕhiggadtî lô kî šōpēṭ ʾănî ʾet bêtô ᶜad ᶜôlām (1 Sam. 3:13)

And I have told him that judge would I his house forever.

While one finds variations in word order—in the preceding notes I have listed "counterexamples," namely, subordinate clauses following anomalous subject-predicate word order—perhaps indicating some sort of emphasis or topicalization, the preponderance of examples demonstrates the rule clearly enough. And although the syntax of the perfect tense is such that its word order does not distinguish between embedded and non-embedded clauses, one can safely assume that kî and hinnēh either do or do not subordinate regardless of the tense of the subsequent verb.

The contrary syntactic force of these two conjunctions explains why one doesn't find kî hinnēh: hinnēh is non-embeddable.[66] It also contradicts exaggerations made as to their similar meaning and function. For instance, Kogut, pointing to examples where *hinnēh* occurs in similar contexts to *kî*, reasons that they must be "parallel" in function; he apparently means by this that they are entirely interchangeable, sharing both meaning and function, since his notation indicates in several examples that *hinnēh* = *kî*.[67] Their mutually exclusive distribution, however, suggests instead a contrast in their functions and/or meanings. In fact, as Berlin rightly perceives, the non-embedded form effects a sense of interiority through its proximity to direct discourse, while the embedded clause presents an exterior view.[68] One finds this contrast in literary effect in the narrative progression of Genesis 1. Six times in the course of creating the universe God stops to consider what he has made; at these points the narrative conveys the content of God's thought through an embedded clause: "And God saw *that it was good*" (*kî ṭôb*—vv. 4, 10, 12, 18, 21, 25). But at the end of the sixth day one finds: "And God saw all that he had created, *and, look, it was very good*" (*wĕhinnēh-ṭôb mĕʾōd*, v. 31). At the climax of creation the writer turns to the non-embedded form to represent God's appraisal of the world as an interior thought. One perceives a similar contrast in effect in the following examples.

> *wayyēdaʿ nōaḥ kî qallû hammayim mēʿal hāʾāreṣ* (Gen. 8:11b)

> And Noah knew that the waters had subsided from the earth.

> *wattābōʾ ʾēlāyw hayyônâ lĕʿēt ʿereb wĕhinnēh ʿālēh zayit ṭārāp bĕpîhā* (Gen. 8:11a)

> And the dove came to him at the time of evening. And, look, a plucked olive leaf was in its mouth.

> *wayyāsar nōaḥ ʾet miksēh hattēbâ wayyarʾ wĕhinnēh ḥārĕbû pĕnê hāʾădāmâ* (Gen. 8:13)

> And Noah removed the cover of the ark. And, look, the surface of the earth had dried up.

> *wayyōʾmer lāhen rōʾeh ʾānōkî ʾet pĕnê ʾăbîken kî ʾênennû ʾēlay kitmōl šilšōm* (Gen. 31:5)

> And he said to them, "I see your father's demeanor, that it is not toward me as before."

> *wayyarʾ yaʿăqōb ʾet pĕnê lābān wĕhinnēh ʾênennû ʿimmô kitmōl šilšôm* (Gen. 31:2)

And Jacob saw Laban's demeanor. And, look, it was not with him as before.

wayyuggad lišlōmōh lēʾmōr hinnēh ʾădōnîyāhû yārēʾ ʾet hammelek šēlōmōh wĕhinnēh ʾāḥaz bĕqarnôt hammizbēaḥ (1 Kings 1:51)

And it was told to Solomon, saying, "Look, Adonijah is afraid of King Solomon, and, look, he has grabbed the horns of the altar."

wayyuggad lammelek šēlōmōh kî nās yôʾāb ʾel ʾōhel yhwh wĕhinnēh ʾēṣel hammizbēaḥ (1 Kings 2:29)

And it was told to King Solomon that Joab had fled to the tent of the Lord. And there he was, next to the altar.[69]

In these passages indirect discourse gives an externalized abstraction of the content of the underlying speech or thought. In the parallel examples with *hinnēh*, however, the writer represents the interior subjective apprehension of the same information.[70]

Transparent Minds

In a telling contrast, epic, unlike biblical narrative, cannot *represent* consciousness. The oral tradition is animated by the singer's voice (the "speaker") and thus cannot give expression to a third-person "self." True, some claim to have discovered passages of represented consciousness in Homer. Irene J. F. de Jong, in particular, applying Mieke Bal's narratological system to the *Iliad*, proposes numerous examples of what she calls "implicit embedded focalization."[71] In a slightly earlier study she had similarly claimed that the famous recognition scene surrounding Odysseus's scar constitutes a "flash-back taking place in the mind of Eurykleia."[72] Turning to this latter passage, however, one finds that this digression is, in effect, an extended subordinate clause that modifies the noun "scar," whereas represented consciousness, as we have seen, takes the form of an independent clause.

> She came up close and washed her lord, and at once she recognized
> that scar, which [*tēn*] once the boar with his white tusk inflicted [*ēlase*, aor] on him
> when he went to Parnassos, to Autolykos and his children.
> (19.392–94)

As a result, this flashback simply cannot conform to the syntax of represented consciousness. It lacks expressive constructions that explicitly evoke a "self" whom we could identify as Eurykleia. Nor are there deictics pointing to a "here" and "now." Even if one makes allowance for a poetic medium, true represented consciousness would read something like: "Here was the scar that that boar had inflicted so long ago upon her lord" (note the presentative construction, the deictic "here," the demonstrative "that," and the kinship term "lord"). Crucially, there is also no change in tense, no past progressive, no pluperfect, just the expected aorist, which in Homer, as we saw in the previous chapter, defines the past with respect to the speaker, namely, the epic singer.

In fact, the scar is alluded to three more times, but in directly quoted speech. The subordinate clause that begins the full digression continues to follow the scar around in the narrative, a type of extended epithet. Consider Odysseus's own reference to the scar:

> But come now, let me show you a proof that shall be mani-
> fest,
> so that you may know me for sure and trust my identity;
> that scar, which [*tēn*] once the boar with his white tusk
> inflicted [*ēlase*] on me,
> when I went to Parnassos with the sons of Autolykos.
> (21.217–20)

Besides the switch from third to first person, there is no substantive *grammatical* difference between narrative report and direct discourse.[73] Similarly, Eurykleia later tells Penelope:

> But here is another proof that is very clear. I will tell you.
> That scar, which once the boar with his white tusk inflicted
> on him. [= 19.393]
> I recognized it while I was washing his feet, and I wanted
> to tell you about it, but he stopped my mouth with his
> hands, would not
> let me speak, for his mind sought every advantage . . .
> (23.73–77)

And, finally, Odysseus reveals himself to his father, using the same token:

> First, then, look with your eyes upon this scar and know it,

which [*tēn*] on Parnassos the boar inflicted [*elasen,* aor]
   with his white tusk
when I went there; for you and my queenly mother sent me
to Autolykos, my mother's dear father, so I could be given
those gifts, which he promised me and consented to when
   he came to us. (24.331–35)

In the previous chapter I demonstrated the monologic character of the oral tradition: the language of narration coincides with that of discourse. Here one can similarly observe, with respect to represented consciousness, that there is nothing perspectival in any of these descriptions of the scar that could be assigned to a private point of view. For the world of epic is populated with transparent minds, transparent not just to the godlike singer but to all. The monologic tradition therefore speaks in unison.[74]

By extension, the recognition of this scar does not lead to the partial revelation of an intimate inner world particular to this or that individualized character but rather to the total externalization of a character's private but stereotypical emotions through highly conventionalized gestures. Thus, when Odysseus's herdsmen saw the scar "they burst out weeping and threw their arms around wise Odysseus, / and made much of him, and kissed him on his head and his shoulders" (21.223). After hearing Eurykleia's account of the scar, Penelope similarly wonders "whether to keep away and question her dear husband, / or to go up to him and kiss his head, taking his hands" (23.86–87). Finally, Odysseus's own father "threw his arms around his dear son" (24.347). To return to Eurykleia, if the disguised Odysseus prevents her from exposing his true identity, this does not hinder the clear expression of her deepest feelings: "Pain and joy seized her at once, and both eyes / filled with tears, and the springing voice was held within her" (19.471–72). The reaction to Odysseus's homecoming is treated as a type of universal experience. Contrary to de Jong's over-reading of the digression as a flashback within Eurykleia's mind, Homer's art does not particularize experience into an intimate representation of individual consciousness.

Thus, Scott Richardson may be right when he states that the absence of represented consciousness in Homer is, in a sense, compensated for by the frequent use of "interior monologue": "[T]he soliloquies—those spoken to one's θυμός, 'spirit,' seem especially to be a record of the words passing through the character's mind."[75] But Homer's use of interior monologue is, in its turn, markedly different from the Bible's, further demonstrating how radically different are their respective narrative arts.

> Now Odysseus the spear-famed was left alone, nor did any
> of the Argives stay beside him, since fear had taken all of
>   them.
> And troubled, he spoke [*eipe*] then to his own great-
>   hearted spirit [*megalētora thumon*]:
> "Ah me, what will become of me? It will be a great evil
> if I run, fearing their multitude, yet deadlier if I am caught
> alone; and Kronos' son drove to flight the rest of the
>   Danaans.
> Yet still, why does the heart [*thumos*] within me debate on
>   these things?
> Since I know that it is the cowards who walk out of the
>   fighting." (*Il* 11.401–408)

One already senses the stereotypical nature of the hero's dilemma, a quality only further heightened by the fact that it is a "type-scene," namely, a scene consisting of a conventionalized or formulaic sequence of actions (see chapter 6). Although in the following passage Menelaos retreats, enacting heroism's failure, he still fits into the convention since any decision to stand and fight entails the possibility of flight.[76]

> Deeply troubled, [Menelaos] spoke [*eipe*] then to his own
>   great-hearted spirit [*megalētora thumon*]:
> "Ah me; if I abandon here the magnificent armour,
> and Patroklos, who has fallen here for the sake of my ho-
>   nour,
> shall not some one of the Danaans, seeing it, hold it against
>   me?
> Yet if I fight, alone as I am, the Trojans and Hektor
> for shame, shall they not close in, many against one, about
>   me?
> Hektor of the shining helm leads all of the Trojans
> here. Then why does my own heart [*thumos*] within me de-
>   bate this?
> . . . .
> Therefore, let no Danaan seeing it hold it against me
> if I give way before Hektor, who fights for God . . ." (17.90–
>   97, 100–101)

Note, for instance, that 11.403, 407 are identical in the Greek with 17.90, 97. Furthermore, there is a fundamental agreement between the inner thought (within the *thumos*) and outward action whether to fight or flee, so that even interior monologue does not reveal a private as opposed to a public face. This identity between thought and act, combined with the conventionality of the decision itself, give epic heroes a transparent quality.[77]

Interior monologue in the Bible, by contrast, plays an entirely different role. Here an angry Esau plots against his brother: "And Esau resented Jacob on account of the blessing which his father bestowed upon him, and Esau said in his heart [*lēb*], 'The days of mourning for my father are approaching, when I will kill Jacob my brother'" (Gen. 27:41).[78] Apparently he mumbles these words out loud to himself since they are reported to his mother in the following verse. But neither Esau's outward demeanor (one suspects he is not the shrewdest of men) nor the very fact that Jacob has just stolen his blessing suffices to alert the others as to his true, inner intentions. The biblical protagonist (he is rarely a hero) is opaque; the interior thoughts, desires, and motivations lurking in his heart are usually left to inference. Not coincidentally, then, the inner self becomes a moral problem in biblical religion.[79]

In the same way Ugaritic epic is unable to represent consciousness. In light of my discussion of the presentative in biblical narrative, one should note that Ugaritic possesses several expressive elements—*hn* and other particles—related functionally and sometimes etymologically to Hebrew *hinnēh*.[80] Although these carry the same expressive force, as I will now demonstrate, the singer of Ugaritic epic puts it to different use. These differences will provide empirical evidence for the stylistic shift by which I have proposed to explain the novelty of biblical narration, also adding a historical dimension to the argument of this chapter. I proceed by first pointing out where one does and does not find *hn* in Ugaritic myth and then comparing this distribution to that in biblical narrative.

Not surprisingly, one finds the Ugaritic presentative in direct discourse, where it functions like *hinnēh* in direct discourse.[81]

1.24:7–8	*hl ǵlmt*	Behold, the young woman,
	tld b[n . . .]/	Shall give birth to a child.
1.14.3.14–16	*whn . špšm / bšbᶜ*	Then [/Look], at sunrise, on the seventh,
	wl . yšn . pbl / mlk .	King Pabuli will sleep no more,
1.14.3.3–5	*mk . špšm / bšbᶜ .*	Then [/Look], at sunrise on the seventh:
	wtmǵy . ludm / rbt .	When you arrive at Udum the great . . .

In the first two examples *hl* and *hn* almost certainly carry the expressive force of *hinnēh;* given the close parallel between the third and second examples, *mk* may function in this way as well.[82] In all three examples the presentative functions as an interjection, introducing a second sentence with expressive force. As one has come to expect, I assign "self" evoked by the presentative to the "speaker."

What is interesting, however, is that one does *not* find the presentative in the context of sight, an absence all the more conspicuous for the striking—indeed, cognate—relationship between the Ugaritic and the Hebrew in this regard.

1.19.3.14–15	*bnši ʿnh.wyp<h>n/*	Raising his eyes, he sees,
	yḥd hrgb.ab.nšrm/	Notes Hargub, Father of Birds.
1.19.3.18–19	*ibqʿ.kbd[h]/waḥd.*	I'll split his belly and look.
	hm.iṯ.šmt.	If there's fat,
	hm.iṯ [ʿṣm]/	If there's [bone],
1.19.3.24–25	*ybqʿ.kbdh.wyḥd/*	He splits his belly and looks:
	in.šmt.	There's no fat!
	in.ʿṣm.	There's no bone!

Note the first example's close parallel in idiom—raising one's eyes—to Biblical Hebrew. Yet one does not find a clause introduced by *whn;* rather, in the second line one finds another verb of sight followed by a direct object. The second and third examples, direct discourse and third-person narrative, respectively, are precise parallels of each other, including the verb tenses. In these examples the act of seeing is followed by a circumstantial clause, as opposed to direct object, but they still lack an introductory *whn*. These lines do tell us what the character (Danel) sees, but only the externalized content of the perception; one would do well to recall the contrast effected in Biblical Hebrew by the presence and absence of *hinnēh* before a clause. That is, they do not yet provide any *explicit* syntactic signs of interiority, neither deictics nor expressive constructions. They do not yet realize genuine represented consciousness.

One finds a similarly instructive contrast between biblical and Ugaritic dream passages.[83]

1.14.1.31–38	*bm . bkyh. wyšn /*	As he cries, he falls asleep;
	bdmʿh . nhmmt /	As he weeps, there's slumber.
	šnt . tluan / wyškb .	Sleep overwhelms him, he lies down;
	nhmmt / wyqmṣ .	Slumber, and he crumples.

bḥlmh / il. yrd .	Now in his dream, El comes down;
bḏhrth / ab . adm [.]	The Father of Man in his vision.
wyqrb / bšal . krt .	Now El approaches, asking Kirta:
1.14.3.50–51 *krt . yḫt . wḥlm /*	Kirta awakes—it's a dream!
ʿbd . il . whdrt /	The Servant of El—a vision!

In this passage from the Kirta epic one finds a narrated dream analogous to examples found in biblical narrative. Ugaritic poetry, however, does not represent dreams as impressions registering on a character's inner eye. Rather, the dream itself consists of a sequence of narrative events, primarily dialogue. Even El's descent (*il yrd*), an inherently visual event, is not introduced by *whn*—is not represented, that is, as it registers on Kirta's consciousness. Compare this with Jacob's analogous dream vision.

wayyaḥălōm . . . wĕhinnēh malʾăkê ʾĕlōhîm ʿōlîm wĕyōrĕdîm bô (Gen. 28:12)

And he had a dream. . . . And, look, angels of God were ascending and descending on [the ladder].

Then, when Kirta awakes (1.14.3.50–51) the narrator tells us: "it's a dream! / . . . a vision!" One could perhaps regard this verse as an incipient version of represented consciousness. But one must also reckon with the role of these lines in forming an inclusion of the dream, a formal reminder *to the audience* that the more than one hundred preceding lines were, in fact, only a dream (*bḥlmh / bḏhrth*, 1.14.1.35–36). Once again Kirta's waking realization crucially does not take the form of represented consciousness; there are no deictic or expressive constructions here. The biblical writers, conversely, often choose to render the recognition of a dream precisely through the representation of consciousness.

wayyîqaṣ parʿōh wĕhinnēh ḥălôm (Gen. 41:7; see also 1 Kings 3:15)

And Pharaoh woke up. And, look, it was a dream.

In this instructive contrast, the biblical writer uses *hinnēh* to explicitly represent Pharaoh's sudden awareness that he has been dreaming as a subjective experience.

Thus, the expressive particle in Ugaritic narrative poetry is absent in precisely those third-person narrative contexts—I don't believe these narratives contain narration in Benveniste's technical sense—where one might expect to find represented consciousness. Conversely, when one does find *hn* and other expressive elements outside of quoted speech, these do not seem to represent consciousness.

1.23:39–40	*il. aṭtm. kypt.*	El charms the pair of maids.
	hm. aṭtm. tṣḥn	If the maiden pair cries out:
	ymt. mt.	"O husband! husband!" . . .
1.23:42–44	*whm/ aṭtm. tṣḥn.*	But if the maiden pair cries out:
	y. ad. ad.	"O father! father!" . . .
1.23:46–47	*whn. aṭtm. tṣḥn.*	Lo! The maiden pair cries out:
	y. mt. mt	"O husband! husband!"
1.3.2.5–7	*whln. ʿnt. tm/ tḥs. bʿmq.*	And look! Anat fights in the valley,
	tḥtṣb. bn/ qrytm	Battles between the two towns. . . .
1.3.2.17–18	*whln. ʿnt. lbth. tmgýn/*	And look! Anat goes to her house,
	tštql. ilt. lhklh	The goddess takes herself to her palace,
1.4.4.24–26	*hn[.] ym. wṭn.*	There! [/Look!] For a day and a second,
	tikl/ išt[.] bhtm	A fire burns in the house,
	nblat/ bhk[l] m.	A flame in the palace.
1.1.1.21–22	*hlm/ ilm. tphhm.*	There! [/Look!] the gods perceive them,
	tphn. mlak. ym	They perceive Yamm's messengers,
	tʿdt. ṭpṭ[. nhr]	The legation of Judge [River.]

The first example consists of three excerpts from a short narrative poem (1.23). Though the narrator eschews all use of the first person—keeping in mind, however, that small portions of the text are missing—one still finds an explicit sign that the narrative stems from an oral performance, the non-indicative mood. In other words, the singer uses conditionals to consider various narrative possibilities (*hm . . . whm*) before dramatically indicating the actual outcome—*whn*! The "self" evoked by *hn*, in other words, attaches to the "speaker," namely, the singer in performance. In the remaining examples, all of which are taken from the Baal Cycle, one finds the presentative (*hn/ hln*) in a third-person narrative context. Although the narrator—avoiding the first-person and the non-indicative moods—has begun to retreat into the background, I nonetheless believe that here, too, one should assign the presentative's expressive force to the narrator rather than a character. At the pragmatic level of interpretation, I do not think one can convincingly link the "self" and "now" in these examples to any of the characters within the story. No one looks on; rather, the narrator himself draws attention to the report of certain events in his story.

Regarding the presentative in Ugaritic narrative poetry, then, a number of features converge—the absence of the presentative in dreams and perceptions; the use of non-indicative moods in third-person narrative; pragmatic considerations—all of which indicate that, in stark contrast to the Bible, the presentative in third-person narrative contexts signifies the narrator's subjectivity as it is expressed in an oral performance. To this one might add those studies that find evidence of an oral formulaic style in Ugaritic poetry.[84] In other words, one does not find narration in Ugaritic narrative poetry but only discourse, which grammar assigns either to a character or to a narrator. Expressions in Ugaritic thus confirm the predictions of Banfield's linguistic rule, namely, the priority of the "speaker." In the Bible it is precisely narration—a style other than discourse—that allows *hinnēh* to detach from the "speaker" and to represent third-person consciousness.

Comparison with Ugaritic poetry thus brings into relief represented consciousness in the Bible as a historical innovation. I propose that it did not—indeed, could not—occur to the Canaanite singers to employ *hn* as it would later be used in biblical narrative because they could not have disassociated the presentative's expressive force from their own voice— unless, of course, the singers were quoting or imitating (in the narrow sense of *mimesis*) a character. Only with the disappearance of the voice from biblical narration do the Israelite writers seize upon this newly created opportunity to utilize *hinnēh* in third-person contexts. It is precisely writing, language without sound, that made this innovation possible.

Fraught with Interior

The discovery of what we think of as a modernist technique in these ancient stories should not in any way suggest that the biblical writers were dealing with the historically specific concerns of modernism. As the examples discussed earlier make clear, the technique did not receive complex, extended treatment at the hands of the ancient Israelite writers. They were not anticipating stream of consciousness. They did manage to break much ground, however, in the literary representation of subjective interiority, and their simplicity and, above all, concision do not indicate lack of subtlety and ingenuity. The biblical writers brilliantly exploited this new technique to represent crucial narrative moments. To conclude this chapter, I would like to consider briefly two particularly exemplary instances of represented consciousness in two of the Bible's most famous stories: the Binding of Isaac and the Flood.

If in the Bible, as Alter observes, narration plays a "highly subsidiary role . . . in comparison to direct speech by the characters,"[85] both of these stories distinguish themselves through their conspicuously spare use of dialogue. The Binding of Isaac begins with God's sudden and mysterious decision to test Abraham. In response to God's initial summons, Abraham, a paragon of obedience, says nothing save a single word of faithful service, *hinnēnî*, "Here I am!" Only then does God utter his command: "Take now your son, your only son, whom you love, Isaac, and go to the land of Moriah, and offer him there as a burnt offering on one of the mountains which I will tell you" (Gen. 22:2). In the face of this most startling demand, Abraham says not a word. This is clearly not the same Abraham who bargained with God over the fate of Sodom and Gomorrah, asking, "Shall not the judge of all the earth do justice?" (Gen. 18:25). The narrative then recounts a brief interchange between father and son, words burdened with irony: "And Isaac said to Abraham his father, saying, 'My Father.' And he said, '*hinnēnî*, my son.' And he said, '*hinnēh*, the fire and the wood, but where is the lamb for the burnt offering?' And Abraham said, 'God will see to the lamb for the burnt offering himself, my son'" (22:7, 8). Each *hinnēh*, spoken under the duress of the situation, points to the emotions suppressed beneath the surface of the narrative, what Auerbach calls "the thoughts which remain unexpressed" in biblical speech.[86] Then, at the last possible moment, God appears *ex machina* in order to circumvent the abominable human sacrifice: "And the angel of the Lord called out to him from the heavens and said, 'Abraham, Abraham!' And he said, '*hinnēnî*.' And he said, 'Do not stretch out your hand against the lad and do nothing to him, for now I know that you fear God" (vv. 11–12). Only now, at this crucial moment—is the knife in hand still stretched out to strike the son?—does Abraham lift his eyes: "*wĕhinnēh*, a ram had been caught in the thicket by its horns."[87] The writer represents or recaptures this experience, opening, if only for a moment, a window into Abraham's soul, suggesting if not expressing in words his unspeakable relief.

The Flood story begins with a similarly fateful moment: God's decision to destroy virtually all life on earth (Gen. 6:5–8). He informs Noah alone of the impending judgment, giving him detailed instructions for building an ark that will save him, his family, and a remnant of each species of animal (vv. 13–21). Noah, in response, says nothing but simply obeys. In fact, he remains speechless throughout the yearlong ordeal within his floating box, even as every living thing perishes without. And when he finally opens his mouth, it is only to curse his son Ham (8:25–27). These three verses are all that is recorded in biblical narrative of this mythic figure's words. The narrative does affirm in no uncertain terms his "righteousness" and his "blameless" character (6:9), and it twice recounts his perfect obedience (6:22; 7:5), but all is expressed through a cold, objective eye. In this way the story denies us even the slightest glimpse into Noah's inner world. Perhaps the writer realized that obedience under such duress demanded silence; consider Job, whose initial reticence gives way to a monumental curse (Job 3) that unleashes a torrent of words that only God himself will eventually stop. Then, one day, after the rains have finally passed, Noah sends forth a dove: "And the dove came to him at the time of evening, *wĕhinnēh*, a plucked olive leaf was in its beak. And Noah knew that the waters had abated from the earth" (Gen. 8:11). With a handful of words briefly representing Noah's consciousness, the writer is able to suggest all that that spare twig signifies to his hero.[88]

In this case, one can contrast Noah's reserve to the loquaciousness of his Mesopotamian avatar(s). Atrahasis-Utnapishtim, unlike his biblical counterpart, fully externalizes his inner turmoil through word and deed. In *Atrahasis* the hero does not silently endure the suffering of humankind at the hands of the gods but rather complains to his patron god, Enki: "How long (?) [will the gods make us suffer]? / Will they make us suffer illness forever?" (1.7).[89] Apparently—there are gaps in the text—these intercessions repeatedly save humanity from extinction. Even when the climactic judgment begins, against which no intervention is possible, namely, the flood, he does not retreat silently into the ark: "But he went in and out, / Could not stay still or rest on his haunches, / His heart was breaking and he was vomiting bile" (3.2). And when the rains finally pass, Utnapishtim, at least in the version of the story he tells Gilgamesh, similarly puts his emotions on full display:

> I looked at the weather; silence reigned,
> For all mankind had returned to clay.
> The flood-plain was flat as a roof.
> I opened a porthole and light fell on my cheeks.
> I bent down, then sat. I wept.
> My tears ran down my cheeks. (*Gilgamesh* 11.3)

This is the very point of the story where biblical narrative will quietly represent Noah's perception of the dove returning to him with a leafy symbol of hope—a mere hint of Noah's underlying psychological tempest. From Mesopotamian epic to the Bible, then, one witnesses what Erich Kahler has famously called the "inward turn of narrative"—made possible, I suggest, by the prose medium developed in ancient Israel.

The Ancient thus uncannily anticipates the Modern. If the former does not yet fully realize certain possibilities of language, neither can we dismiss it as in any way primitive. For alongside the objectivity of narration and the expressivity of direct discourse, the biblical writers discovered the syntactic means to represent consciousness in order to suggest the unspoken inner thoughts of their characters. And beyond the very fact of such stylistic innovation, they exploited their newly developed literary and linguistic devices with supreme subtlety and skill. If these stories are, to borrow Auerbach's phrase, "fraught with background," it is only because the Bible's psychological realism and, in particular, its ability to represent interiority allow and demand the projection of such depths. Against the backdrop of history, one now finds the variously expressed, suppressed, and enacted thoughts and desires of human subjects. In this respect, these various layers of biblical narrative work together to create this perspectival play of foreground and background, surface and depth.

In this and the previous chapters I analyzed the language and style of biblical prose narrative, all the while tracing a set of differences separating biblical narrative and the novel, on the one hand, from epic, on the other. In the following two chapters I will move from the level of grammar to that of narrative technique. Specifically, I will consider the realization of time in, and the contrastive techniques of, biblical narrative and epic. Even at this new level I will continue to map the divide between biblical narrative and epic, providing further evidence for my theory of biblical narrative and its relationship to earlier epic traditions.

Coda: Syntax or Context?

While it would contribute little to the primary analysis given earlier, I think it useful to consider certain analyses put forward by Andersen and Berlin. They ultimately subordinate the syntax of the Hebrew presentative to its context in the "text" or "discourse." Their approach, if correct, would thus contradict the syntactical account of represented consciousness I have presented here. By critically reviewing their discussions, I hope to demonstrate, to the contrary, the shortcomings of their descriptive, pragmatic approach—typical, I would add, of most studies of Biblical Hebrew.

Andersen undertakes what he calls a "discourse grammar," namely, "a taxonomy of Hebrew inter-clause constructions."[90] His analysis of the presentative amounts to a taxonomy of its occurrences in various discourse contexts: "participant perspective" (his term for represented conscious-ness), "dream reports," and "first event clauses."[91] Thus, while he points to a visual dimension common to both "dream reports" and "participant per-spective," he treats them as two separate phenomena. But represented dreams are, in fact, merely a species of represented consciousness. That is, this type of dream sequence is represented as it registers on the dreamer's inner eye. Recall the connection Russell draws between the presentative and dreams: "there they are, and that ends the matter." This emerges most clearly in a dream that Jacob *reports* to his wives:

wā'eśśā' 'ēnay wā'ēre' bahālôm wĕhinnēh hā'attudîm hā'ōlîm 'al haṣṣō'n 'ăquddîm nĕquddîm ûbĕruddîm (Gen. 31:10)

And I lifted my eyes and saw in a dream. And, look, the rams that were mounting the flock were striped, speckled, and mottled.

Though this dream is actually reported in discourse, note the first-person version of the formula we have seen so often — "he lifted his eyes and saw, and, look"—which makes explicit the underlying relation between the representation of dreams and the representation of consciousness. I therefore propose that one understand such dream sequences in the third person in like manner.

wayyahǎlōm wĕhinnēh sullām muṣṣāb 'arṣâ wĕrō'šô maggîa' haššāmāymâ wĕhinnēh mal'ăkê 'ĕlōhîm 'ōlîm wĕyōrĕdîm bô wĕhinnēh yhwh niṣṣāb 'ālāyw wayyō'mar . . . wayyîqaṣ ya'ăqōb miššĕnātô wayyō'mer . . . (Gen. 28:12–16)

And he had a dream. And, look, a ladder was standing on earth, and its top was reaching up to heaven, and, look, angels of God were ascending and descending on it, and, look, the Lord was standing upon it; and he said. . . . And Jacob awoke from his sleep, and he said . . .

The consecutive verb externally recounts the dream-event as a whole (*wayyahǎlōm*), but the dream itself (at least its beginning) is represented as a chain of images (participles) registering on Jacob's inner eye. The partici-ples then give way to a consecutive verb (*wayyō'mar*), at which point the dream moves into the mode of pure narration. In other words, we quit the representation of Jacob's inner thoughts and resume the narrative se-quence for the remainder of the dream, which, in turn, seamlessly connects with subsequent events in the external world: "And Jacob awoke" (*wayyîqaṣ*).

wayhî miqqēṣ šĕnātayim yāmîm ûparʿōh ḥōlēm wĕhinnēh ʿōmēd ʿal hayʾōr
wĕhinnēh min hayʾōr ʿōlōt šebaʿ pārôt yĕpôt marʾeh ûbĕrîʾōt bāśār . . .
wĕhinnēh šebaʿ pārôt ʾaḥērôt ʿōlôt ʾaḥărêhen min hayʾōr rāʿôt marʾeh
wĕdaqqôt bāśār wattaʿămōdnâ ʾēṣel happārôt ʿal śĕpat hayʾōr
wattôʾkalnâ happārôt raʿôt hammarʾeh wĕdaqqōt habbāśār ʾet šebaʿ
happārôt yĕpōt hammarʾeh wĕhabbĕrîʾōt wayyîqaṣ parʿōh (Gen. 41:1–4)

And then it was two years later, and Pharaoh was dreaming. And,
look, he was standing on the Nile. And, look, from the Nile seven
cows were coming up, sleek and fat. . . . And, look, seven more
cows were coming up after them from the Nile, ugly and gaunt.
And they were standing with the [first] cows on the bank of the
Nile, and the ugly, gaunt cows were eating the sleek, fat cows. And
Pharaoh awoke.

wayyîšān wayyaḥălōm šēnît wĕhinnēh šebaʿ šibbŏlîm ʿōlôt bĕqāneh ʾeḥād
bĕrîʾôt wĕṭōbôt wĕhinnēh šebaʿ šibbŏlîm daqqôt ûšĕdûpōt qādîm ṣōmĕḥôt
ʾaḥărêhen wattiblaʿnâ haššibbŏlîm haddaqqôt ʾēt šebaʿ haššibbŏlîm
habbĕrîʾôt wĕhammĕlēʾôt wayyîqaṣ parʿōh wĕhinnēh ḥălôm (Gen. 41:5–
7)

And he fell asleep and dreamt a second time; and, look, seven ears
of grain were coming up on one stalk, plump and good; and, look,
seven ears of grain, meager and scorched by the east wind, were
sprouting after them. And the seven meager ears swallowed the
seven plump and full ears. And Pharaoh awoke; and, look, it was a
dream.

Not unlike Jacob's dream, in both these examples the participles eventually give way to consecutive verbs. In the absence of direct discourse, however, the entire dream (both participles and consecutives) may, I think,
be construed as represented consciousness.

By way of contrast, one should note that the biblical writers could also
narrate dreams. Here one finds no *hinnēh*, no participle, just the unbroken chain of consecutive verbs.

wayyābōʾ ʾĕlōhîm ʾel ʾăbîmelek baḥălôm hallāylâ wayyōʾmer lô . . .
waʾăbîmelek lōʾ qārab ʾēlêhā wayyōʾmer . . . wayyōʾmer ʾēlāyw hāʾĕlōhîm
baḥălōm . . . wayyaškēm ʾăbîmelek babbōqer . . . (Gen. 20:3–8; see also
Gen. 15:1)

And God came to Abimelech in a night dream, and he said to
him. . . . But Abimelech had not approached her, and he said. . . .

And God said to him in the dream. . . . And Abimelek arose early in the morning . . .

wayyābōʾ ʾĕlōhîm ʾel-lābān hāʾărammî bahălōm hallāylâ wayyōʾmer lô . . . wayyaśśēg lābān ʾet-yaʿăqōb . . . (Gen. 31:24, 25)

And God came to Laban the Aramean in a night dream, and he said to him. . . . And Laban caught up with Jacob . . .

bĕgibʿôn nirʾâ yhwh ʾel šĕlōmōh bahălôm hallāylâ wayyōʾmer ʾĕlōhîm . . . wayyōʾmer šĕlōmōh . . . wayyîṭab haddābār bĕʿênê ʾădōnāy . . . wayyōʾmer ʾĕlōhîm ʾēlāyw . . . wayyiqaṣ šĕlōmōh wĕhinnēh hălôm (1 Kings 3:5–15)

In Gibeon the Lord appeared to Solomon in a dream of the night, and God said. . . . And Solomon said. . . . And it was pleasing in the Lord's sight. . . . And God said to him. . . . And Solomon awoke, and, look, it was a dream. (Cf. 1 Kings 9:2; 2 Chron. 1:7)

Not coincidentally, these dreams are not descriptive but dramatic; that is, they each comprise a sequence of speech events. They take the same form, one might add, as did the second half of Jacob's dream wherein God speaks to him (Gen. 28:12–16). The consecutives in these examples, as sentences of pure narration, establish the objectivity of the dream. For it is crucial to the logic of the divine oracle that God really appear to these characters, albeit within their mind. The dream sequence therefore forms a single continuous narrative sequence with the surrounding narration of external events.

After discussing these dream reports, Andersen classifies other occurrences of the presentative as "first event" clauses: "There are other uses of wĕhinne clauses in which the feature of an unexpected visual experience is not prominent or may be quite absent. . . . [It] looks like the first event clause, and not circumstantial. Examples: Ge 15[12, 17], 29[25], 38[27, 29]."[92] For the sake of discussion, I provide these passages below:

wayyēred hāʿayiṭ ʿal happĕgārîm wayyaśśēb ʾōtām ʾabrām wayhî haššemeš lābôʾ wĕtardēmâ nāpĕlâ ʿal ʾabrām wĕhinnēh ʾêmâ hăšēkâ nōpelet ʿālāyw wayyōʾmer lĕʾabrām . . . wayhî haššemeš bāʾâ waʿălāṭâ hāyâ wĕhinnēh tannûr ʿāšān wĕlappîd ʾēš ʾăšer ʿābar bên haggĕzārîm hāʾēlleh (Gen. 15:11–17)

And the birds of prey descended upon the carcasses, and Abram drove them away. And then the sun was about to set and a deep sleep fell on Abram, and, look, dark dread was falling upon him.

And [God] said to Abram. . . . And then the sun had set and it was very dark, and here was an oven of smoke and a torch of fire which had passed between these pieces.

wayhî bāʿereb wayyiqqaḥ ʾet lēʾâ bittô wayyābēʾ ʾōtāh ʾēlāyw wayyābōʾ ʾēlêhā . . . wayhî babbōqer wĕhinnēh hîʾ [qere] *lēʾâ wayyōʾmer ʾel lābān mah zōʾt ʿāśîtā lî* (Gen. 29:23, 25)

And then it was evening, and [Laban] took Leah his daughter and brought her to [Jacob], and he went into her. . . . And then it was morning, and, look, it was Leah. And he said to Laban, "What's this you've done to me?"

wayhî bĕʿēt lidtāh wĕhinnēh tĕʾômîm bĕbiṭnāh wayhî bĕlidtāh wayyitten yād wattiqqaḥ hamyalledet wattiqšōr ʿal yādô šānî lēʾmōr zeh yāṣāʾ rîʾšônâ wayhî kĕmēšîb yādô wĕhinnēh yāṣāʾ ʾāḥîw wattōʾmer mah pāraṣtā ʿālêkā pāreṣ wayyiqrāʾ šĕmô pāreṣ (Gen. 38:27–29)

And then it was the time for her to give birth, and, look, twins were in her womb. And then she was giving birth, and he put forth his hand, and the midwife tied a scarlet thread on his hand, saying, "This has come out first." And then he was withdrawing his hand, and, look, his brother came out. And she said, "What a breach you have made for yourself!" And he was named Perez.

In all these examples *hinnēh* follows *wayhî* ("And it was"), whence Andersen's notion of "first event clause." In his treatment of these examples, however, the shortcoming of an approach that merely describes and categorizes surface structure becomes evident. Just as native speakers of English, for instance, do not apply special grammatical rules to the initial sentence of a paragraph, so one should not propose a special interpretation for the *hinnēh* clause that happens to occupy "first event" position—unless one finds additional, compelling evidence.

In fact, these examples clearly constitute further examples of represented consciousness. In the passage from Genesis 15, the clauses preceding *hinnēh* in verses 11–12 clearly establish Abram as the relevant subject of consciousness. Even though one does not find one of the common introductory formulas—namely, "he came" or "he saw"—there is no reason not to assign point of view to him as dark dread falls upon him. One can easily interpret verse 17 as a representation of Abram seeing the tokens of the divine presence performing the covenant ceremony. A problem arises, however, in that verse 12 informs us that he is sleeping, while the narrative context makes no reference to a dream, suggesting that Abram saw the spectacle while awake. Indeed, the very logic of the rite requires that Abram really perceive the divine sign and not just imagine it in a dream.[93] In this instance, source critics provide the needed solution: a later hand inserted verses 12–16.[94] In this view, Abram would be awake in verse 17, and syntax would agree with source criticism. In Genesis 29 the context suggests one assign the *hinnēh* clause to Jacob's consciousness—it represents his discovery the morning after. In fact, if one brackets verse 24 as a parenthetical, one uncovers the expected sequence: verb of movement—*hinnēh*. That it is Jacob who immediately confronts his father-in-law further supports this assignment of point of view. Finally, Gen. 38:27–29 distills three moments out of Tamar's labor, each located by *wayhî*. The first (v. 27) and third (v. 29) of these moments are cotemporal with represented consciousness.[95] In verse 27 she and/or the midwife realizes that she is about to give birth to twins; however unlikely, the midwife somehow figures this out before the actual fact as she anticipates, with great professionalism, the need to identify the firstborn and thus manages to tie a thread around the first hand that ventures forth from the birth canal. Then, in verse 29, the hand is withdrawn at the last moment, and to Tamar's amazement the other is born first. I assign this perception specifically to Tamar since she is the one who immediately exclaims her surprise and names her firstborn son.

Berlin, for her part, does not practice text-linguistics or discourse analysis per se, but she similarly introduces confusion into the analysis of *hinnēh* by dissolving its syntactical force into a pool of interpretive, pragmatic concerns—specifically, the control of narrative information: "When the unexpected information is perceived by a character, and the reader or another character already knows it, we can speak of a shift in point of view."[96] According to this view, the "shift in point of view" (the representation of a third-person consciousness) has nothing to do with the syntax of the Hebrew presentative itself but rather with narrative context, what information has or has not yet been provided. Thus, she finds this "shift in point of view" in passages without *hinnēh:* "And Tamar went to the house of her brother Amnon, and he was lying down" (*wĕhû' šōkēb*, 2 Sam. 13:8). She reasons that since verse 6 already informs us that he is lying down, the writer must have indulged in this repetition in order to represent Tamar's perception.[97] Now Tamar certainly saw her brother lying there as she came in. The language itself, however, in no way renders a sense of Tamar's interiority at the moment of perception. And as we saw earlier, *hinnēh* makes all the difference in this narrative effect. Conversely, when *hinnēh* is present, she still reduces "point of view" to a question of redundant narrative information:

When the information is new to the reader as well, as in Gen. 38:27 and 29, it is more difficult to identify whose point of view is being represented. It is precisely on this issue that the usage in Ruth 2:4 becomes complicated. . . . Did Ruth know Boaz's name at this point? This, in turn, directs our attention to a gap in the story. . . . It would be more appropriate to have '*wehinneh* the owner of the field came', for this is the operative relationship between Ruth and Boaz at this moment.

Since the verse fails the criterion of repetition, that is, it gives new information to the reader, she concludes: "More likely, 2:4 is information to the reader, representing the reader's perception of Boaz's entrance into the scene, with an explanation of where he had been beforehand. . . . I would translate the phrase 'At that point, Boaz arrived from Bethlehem'" (94). Let us analyze this passage for ourselves.

> *wattēlek wattābô' wattēlaqqēṭ baśśādeh 'aḥărê haqqōṣĕrîm wayyiqer miqrehā*
> *ḥelqat haśśādeh lĕbô'az 'ăšer mimmišpaḥat 'ĕlîmelek wĕhinnēh bō'az bā'*
> *mibbêt leḥem wayyō'mer laqqôṣĕrîm yhwh 'immākem wayyō'mĕrû lô*
> *yĕbārekēkā yhwh* (Ruth 2:3, 4)

And she walked and came and gleaned in the field after the gleaners; and she chanced upon the portion of field that belonged to Boaz, who was of the family of Elimelech. And, look, Boaz had come from Bethlehem, and he said to the gleaners, "May YHWH be with you." And they said to him, "May YHWH bless you."

I would propose assigning the represented perception to the gleaners (*qōṣĕrîm*): they perceive Boaz's arrival, who in turn immediately greets them, and vice versa. These gleaners plausibly know Boaz's name and perhaps even of his trip to Bethlehem, thus solving Berlin's epistemological problem.

Berlin similarly reasons from context when she observes of another set of examples: "[T]hey mark the entrance of a new figure into a scene after the scene has been set by previous narration. They are all part of narration (not direct discourse), and all stand first in their verses and involve a verb of motion" (94). Note again how she, like Andersen, categorizes uses of *hinnēh* according to context. For the sake of discussion, I include them here.

> *wayyō'mer mōšeh 'el šōpĕṭê yiśrā'ēl hirgû 'îš 'ănāšāyw hannişmādîm*
> *lĕba'al pĕ'ôr wĕhinnēh 'îš mibbĕnê yiśrā'ēl bā' wayyaqrēb 'el 'eḥāyw 'et*

hammidyānît lĕʿênê mōšeh ûlĕʿênê kol ʿădat bĕnê yiśrāʾēl wĕhēmmâ bōkîm
petaḥ ʾōhel môʿēd wayyarʾ pînĕḥās ben ʾelʿāzār ben ʾahărōn hakkōhēn
wayyāqom mittôk hāʿēdâ wayyiqqaḥ rōmaḥ bĕyādô (Num. 25:5–7)

And Moses said to the judges of Israel, "Each of you kill his men
who have joined themselves to Baal of Peor." And, look, a man of
the children of Israel came and brought to his brothers the Midi-
anite, in the sight of Moses and in the sight of all the congregation
of the children of Israel, and they were crying at the entrance of
the tent of meeting. And Phinehas the son of Eleazar the son of
Aaron the priest saw and rose up from the midst of the congregation and took a spear in his hand . . .

wayyābōʾû hammalʾākîm gibʿat šāʾûl waydabbĕrû haddĕbarîm bĕʾoznê
hāʿām wayyiśʾû kol hāʿām ʾet qôlām wayyibkû wĕhinnēh šāʾûl bāʾ ʾaḥărê
habbāqār min haśśādeh wayyōʾmer šāʾûl mah lāʿām kî yibkû waysappĕrû
lô ʾet dibrê ʾanšê yābēš (1 Sam. 11:4, 5)

And the messengers came to Gibeah of Saul and spoke these
words in the hearing of all the people, and the people lifted their
voice and wept. And, look, Saul was coming behind the cattle
from the field. And he said, "What is wrong with the people that
they weep?" And they recounted to him the words of the men of
Jabesh.

wayyaʿaś ḥāg libnê yiśrāʾēl wayyaʿal ʿal hammizbēaḥ lĕhaqṭîr wĕhinnēh
ʾîš ʾĕlōhîm bāʾ mîhûdâ bidbar yhwh ʾel bêt ʾēl wĕyārobʿām ʿōmēd ʿal
hammizbēaḥ lĕhaqṭîr (1 Kings 12:33–13:1)

And he made a feast for the children of Israel, and he went up
next to the altar to burn incense. And, look, a man of God came
from Judah by the word of YHWH to Bethel, and Jeroboam was
standing next to the altar to burn incense.

wayyēlek wayyimṣāʾēhû ʾaryēh badderek waymîtēhû wattĕhî niblātô mušleket
badderek wĕhaḥămôr ʿōmēd ʾeṣlāh wĕhāʾaryēh ʿōmēd ʾeṣel hannĕbēlâ
wĕhinnēh ʾănāšîm ʿōbĕrîm wayyirʾû ʾet hannĕbēlâ mušleket badderek wĕʾet
hāʾaryēh ʿōmēd ʾeṣel hannĕbēlâ (1 Kings 13:24, 25)

And he went, and a lion found him on the road, and it killed him,
and his body was thrown on the road, and the donkey was standing beside it, and the lion was standing beside the body. And,

look, men were coming, and they saw the body thrown on the
road and the lion standing beside the body.

Again, one can easily account for these examples as represented consciousness. Numbers 25 actually provides a splendid example of represented consciousness. Verse 6 does appear rather abruptly, but given what
immediately follows—Phinehas sees the crime and in his zealous rage exe-
cutes the offending couple—one should assign the point of view to this
soon-to-be high priest. In this instance, then, the writer chooses to represent the perception before recounting the actual act of seeing, but the effect is still the same. The expressive force of *hinnēh* reflects his disgust as
he sees the transgression, with Moses and the people looking on, while
they affect a pious attitude by weeping at the tent of meeting.[98] In 1 Sam.
11:5 I can find no reason not to assign point of view to the people, or some
subset thereof, who have gathered to hear the messengers from Jabesh;
not unlike the gleaners in Ruth, they see someone coming, who in turn
engages them in dialogue. In 1 Kings 13.1 it seems obvious enough that
since Jeroboam has just ascended the altar—rendered through a verb of
movement not unlike other instances I have considered—the man of
God's approach registers on his consciousness. Finally, later in the same
story, this same man of God is killed by a lion. His corpse is lying on the
ground, when some men walk by. Berlin and Miller both suggest that *hinnēh*
introduces these new characters since there is no one else to see them approach. It is difficult, if not impossible, to assign point of view here to a
character within the narrative.[99] But one need not, on the basis of this passage, assign another function to *hinnēh*, which retains its primary syntactical force as an expressive particle. Nor would I identify it as another
authorial intrusion since it seamlessly continues the narrative. Rather, I
think in this one instance one must assign point of view to an authorial
presence who tells this tale. I would only add that a counterexample—and
this is the best one I have found thus far—does not suffice to disprove a
theory: what at first appears to be a counterexample may be successfully
reinterpreted within the original theory; one might revise the original
theory to account for such counterexamples; or, finally, one might eventually propose a countertheory with greater explanatory power.

My criticism of Berlin's and Andersen's analyses should not be taken
to mean that context is irrelevant. On the contrary, it supplies us, for instance, with those subjects whose points of view are represented. But context is not everything. All of the syntactic features of represented
consciousness discussed in this chapter have a reality independent of
context. Recall the passage I discussed from "The Dead." I identified cer-

tain sentences as represented speech and thought on the basis of their inherent syntactic features: various deictic and expressive constructions that were centered on a third-person "self." It had nothing to do with pragmatic, contextual criteria, such as whether it repeated information provided earlier in the story, as Berlin would have it. For the record, as this Joycean passage makes abundantly clear, represented consciousness has nothing to do with redundant information. Nor was it a matter of categorizing "inter-clause constructions," as Andersen suggests. The challenge is to discover "the real" within the autonomous realm of syntax.

•5•

BIBLICAL TIME AND EPIC TIME: FROM GRAMMAR TO NARRATIVE TECHNIQUE

[I]t is never possible for a novelist to deny time inside the fabric of his novel: he must cling however lightly to the thread of his story, he must touch the interminable tapeworm, otherwise he becomes unintelligible, which, in his case, is a blunder.

I am not trying to be philosophic about time, for it is (experts assure us) a most dangerous hobby for an outsider. . . . I am only trying to explain that as I lecture now I hear that clock ticking or do not hear it ticking, I retain or lose the time sense; whereas in a novel there is always a clock. The author may dislike his clock. Emily Brontë in *Wuthering Heights* tried to hide hers. Sterne, in *Tristram Shandy*, turned his upside down. Marcel Proust, still more ingenious, kept altering the hands, so that his hero was at the same period entertaining a mistress to supper and playing ball with his nurse in the park. All these devices are legitimate, but none of them contravene our thesis: the basis of a novel is a story, and a story is a narrative of events arranged in time sequence.

—E. M. Forster, *Aspects of the Novel*

Each time I've been to Jouy I've seen a bit of canal in one place, and then I've turned a corner and seen another, but when I saw the second I could no longer see the first. I tried to put them together in my mind's eye; it was no good. But from the top of Saint-Hilaire it's quite another matter—a regular network in which the place is enclosed. Only you can't see any water. . . . To get it all quite perfect you would have to be in both places at once; up at the top of the steeple of Saint-Hilaire and down there at Jouy-le-Vicomte.

—Marcel Proust, *Swann's Way* (*In Search of Lost Time*)

The car had gone, but it had left a slight ripple which flowed through glove shops and hat shops and tailors' shops on both sides of Bond Street. For thirty seconds all heads were inclined the same way—to the window. Choosing a pair of gloves— should they be to the elbow or above it, lemon or pale grey?— ladies stopped; when the sentence was finished something had

happened. Something so trifling in single instances that no
mathematical instrument, though capable of transmitting
shocks in China, could register the vibration; yet in its fulness
rather formidable and in its common appeal emotional; for in
all the hat shops and tailors' shops strangers looked at each
other and thought of the dead; of the flag; of Empire. In a public house in a back street a Colonial insulted the House of
Windsor which led to words, broken beer glasses, and a general
shindy, which echoed strangely across the way in the ears of
girls buying white underlinen threaded with pure white ribbon
for their weddings. For the surface agitation of the passing car
as it sunk grazed something very profound.
—Virginia Woolf, *Mrs. Dalloway*

Time and Narrative Form

In his famous study of nationalism Benedict Anderson draws attention to
the novel's striking ability (taken for granted by most of its readers) to recount simultaneous events:

> Consider first the structure of the old-fashioned novel, a structure
> typical not only of the masterpieces of Balzac but also of any con-
> temporary dollar-dreadful. It is clearly a device for the presenta-
> tion of simultaneity in "homogeneous, empty time," or a complex
> gloss upon the word "meanwhile." . . . That all these acts are per-
> formed at the same clocked, calendrical time, but by actors who
> may be largely unaware of one another, shows the novelty of this
> imagined world conjured up by the author in his readers' minds."[1]

"What then," he asks, "actually links" such characters as they live out their
lives together in mutual anonymity? In answer to this question, he invokes
the "idea of the nation": "[T]hey are embedded in 'societies,'" which, by
embodying "the idea of a sociological organism moving calendrically
through homogeneous, empty time," provide "a precise analogue of the
idea of the nation, which also is conceived as a solid community moving
steadily down (or up) history" (25, 26). By appealing to the notion of "homogeneous, empty time"[2]—time as an undifferentiated (homogeneous) flow,
bereft (empty) of any theological or transcendent meaning—Anderson
means to distinguish the novel's modern "apprehension of time" from the
theological view that held sway in medieval Europe, as expounded by
Auerbach in his account of "figural interpretation": "The horizontal, that

is the *temporal and causal,* connection of occurrences is dissolved; the *here and now* is no longer a mere link in an earthly chain of events, it is simultaneously something which has always been, and which will be fulfilled in the future; and strictly, in the eyes of God, it is something eternal, something omni-temporal, something already consummated in the realm of fragmentary earthly event."[3] In this medieval conception of time and history, both the pure ("temporal and causal") succession of what Anderson calls "clocked, calendrical time," or *histoire,* and that movement from future to present to past ("the here and now" as a "link in an earthly chain of events") experienced by the human subject, or *discours,* dissolve within an unearthly, "omnitemporal" moment.

Although Anderson correctly links the novel's striking treatment of time to a modern historical consciousness emerging out of the theological mind-set of late antiquity, he mistakenly dismisses the possibility of ancient precursors, claiming instead that the representation of simultaneity is unique to modern literature: "This polyphony decisively marks off the modern novel from so brilliant a forerunner as Petronius's *Satyricon.* Its narrative proceeds single file. If Encolpius bewails his young lover's faithlessness, we are not simultaneously shown Gito in bed with Ascyltus" (25 n. 37). Unfortunately, Anderson is not alone in his myopic celebration of the recent literary past.

In her influential study of realism and temporal perspective, Elizabeth Deeds Ermarth likewise treats simultaneity as a uniquely modern achievement.[4] What is interesting is that the role simultaneity and the modern sense of time play in her theory of realism is strikingly similar to the role they play in Anderson's interpretation of nationalism as an "imagined community." According to Ermarth, synchronization is "essential" to realism in the novel because of its implicit conceptualization of time (and space):

> [T]he narrative structure coordinates present and present, past and past, so that the various points of view all belong to a single temporal continuity that approaches clock time. . . .
>
> One of the most important of these synchronizing devices is the "meanwhile" clause, which brings the action in one plot into synchrony with the action in another. . . . The narrative order thus reassures the reader of the possibility, essential to realism, that the gaps between one point of view and another can be mediated and therefore that the problems of discontinuity that the characters face are solvable. (81)

In her account this "single temporal continuity" functions much as "homogeneous, empty time" does in Anderson's, but instead of projecting it onto an "imagined community," namely, "the idea of the nation," she bases her theory of realism on the notion of "consensus," which the realist novel's "narrative order," posited in the previously cited passage, makes possible:

> My use of the term "consensus," it should be noted, indicates a formal agreement about the conditions of perception, not an agreement about this or that thing perceived. . . . Whereas from Homer to Milton the universe presented various fixed and eternal definitions that were beyond control by mortals and that limited and shaped all mortal projects, the neutral media of modernity claim to present no such a priori obstacles to choice and development and precisely put all projects into human hands; in fact, they make possible the concept "human" as a species definition. (xix-xx)

If "the idea of the nation" provides Anderson with a communal space, Ermarth's "consensus" carves out a public realm of agreed-upon facts. For, she later explains, this "formal agreement . . . objectifies the world . . . by virtue of universal inclusion. Any and all perspectives would see the same world. . . . This construction and the power of formal agreement essential to it did not exist before the Renaissance" (xxi). As these latter two passages ("from Homer to Milton" and "before the Renaissance") make clear, the various literary phenomena linked to realism—synchronization, consensus, and so forth—are in her view strictly modern.

It goes without saying that realism and nationalism, in their historical specificity, constitute uniquely modern phenomena. Nonetheless, one must revise literary history in such a way as to free it from the nominalist tendency to treat such particulars to the exclusion of certain universals of literary form—in other words, to recognize ancient precursors to modern literary achievements without denying either its historical particularity. In fact, Auerbach himself leads the way, for he recognized how the medieval in turn marked a radical departure from classical antiquity, whose sense of history and of time is actually closer to the novel's and our own:

> This conception of history is magnificent in its homogeneity, but it was completely alien to the mentality of classical antiquity, it annihilated that mentality down to the very structure of its language, at least of its literary language, which—with all its ingenious and nicely shaded conjunctions, its wealth of devices for syntactic arrangement, its carefully elaborated system of tenses—became

wholly superfluous as soon as earthly relations of place, time and cause had ceased to matter, as soon as a vertical connection, ascending from all that happens converging in God, alone became significant.[5]

Ermarth and Anderson would surely agree that both we and the novel take for granted "earthly relations of place, time and cause." Contrary to the nominalist thesis, classical antiquity may not inhabit a totally different literary universe after all.

It should not surprise us, then, that biblical narrative already knew what modernity ostensibly discovered, that the biblical writers perceived the depth of historical time and developed a narrative realism adequate to its representation—in particular, the representation of simultaneity. What is interesting is that synchronous events are unknown in Homeric epic. For Homer observes what is known as "Zielinski's law," a phenomenon named after Thaddeus Zielinski, who demonstrated that Homer never truly realizes simultaneous events, maintaining instead a smooth temporal surface.[6] To be sure, he can switch scenes, alternating, say, between the battlefield and the walls of Troy, but his narrative "clock," as it were, never stops "ticking." (His famous digressions, such as that on Odysseus's scar, constitute a special case that, as I will demonstrate, can still be accounted for along the lines of Auerbach's essay.) Biblical narrative, conversely, freely violates this law, interrupting the forward flow of time in order to recount simultaneous narrative sequences within the relentless linearity of language.[7] To return to my strictly historical thesis, Israelite literary practice marks a departure from the narrative conventions of the ancient Near East. Ugaritic epic, as we will see, once again corresponds to the Homeric paradigm. It, too, obeys Zielinski's law.

In a sense, I merely expand upon Auerbach's insight into the radically different realizations of time and space in Homer and the Hebrew Bible. Homer, on the one hand, is all "surface," lacking both spatial and temporal perspective. Biblical narrative, on the other, is "fraught with background," that is, depth in time and space. For my purposes I would only add that simultaneity is closely related to perspective. The point of such a contrast is not, as is sometimes thought, to demonstrate the "superiority" of biblical narrative. Why, after all, should a perspectival aesthetic be inherently superior to an aesthetic of surface? Rather, it is to bring to light different possibilities of narrative art. Toward this end I will further argue that a formal distinction exists between two narrative modes defined with reference to their temporal structure, namely, memory and history. Memory embodies a subjective notion of time, organized around the central perspective of the epic singer. History—the correlative of Benveniste's *histoire* (narration)—lacks a central organizing perspective, so that events take their place in an objectively conceived temporal succession. In other words, if Homer recalls a past that he in some sense witnesses through the Muse, biblical narrative recounts a past "alienated" from experience.

The Problem of Simultaneity

For my purposes Zielinski himself provides an ample discussion of the problem of simultaneity. He begins by positing three principles of human perception. (1) In an unchanging, stable scene, one can perceive multiple objects at once. Looking down a city street, for example, you could simultaneously see, at least peripherally, both the parked car in the background and the fire hydrant in the foreground. (2) A gradual uniform process seizes one's attention at its beginning and end, but is like a stable scene in the middle. Thus, you might turn your gaze on that car if a person entered it and began driving it down the street, but once it was in motion, you could resume taking in the street as a whole. (3) Ongoing action requires continual focus. If that same car recklessly weaves through pedestrian traffic on its way down the street, it will likely attract your full attention the whole while.

The determining factor of these three principles is change, the perception of which demands one's dedicated focus. One can perceive foreground and background in a stable scene because it does not change. A uniform process requires one's attention only at its beginning and end because change takes place at these junctures. Genuine action monopolizes one's field of vision because it constitutes change by its very nature. From these principles Zielinski deduces what he calls "the law of psychological incompatibility": "[M]ultiple simultaneous actions are incompatible within our visual perception."[8] In accordance with this law, Zielinski proposes three methods for achieving the effect of simultaneity in narrative, three ways of creating the awareness and/or actual perception of simultaneous events. The simplest way of describing these is to imagine three different types of movies.

In standard film practice the "narrative clock," so to speak, never stops moving forward. That is, in the overwhelming majority of movies the action will variously slow down, speed up, and even skip ahead, but it will generally not step back in time; as with Homer, flashbacks are an apparent exception to this rule. The effect of simultaneity, then, results from switching between scenes in (as Zielinski puts it) "desultory" fashion. But simultaneity is in this case an illusion since no event actually overlaps temporally with another. Just as the film itself provides the illusion of continuity through a quick succession of discrete, frozen images, so the splicing together of two or more parallel sequences provides the illusion of simultaneity through the seamless interlacing of nonsimultaneous events. In fact, we perform this trick every day in real life whenever we divide our attention between two or more objects of interest, focusing first on one and then on the other but never truly on both *at the same time.* Let us call this effect "pseudosimultaneity."

In a smaller set of films one finds "retrospective simultaneity." This is achieved not through camera work and scene splicing but rather through the retrospective correlation of synchronous events that are reported by characters within the narrative world—"to put them together in [the] mind's eye," as Proust describes it in one of the epigraphs to this chapter. Akira Kurosawa's *Rashomon* comes immediately to mind. Here a court summons and interrogates various witnesses as part of a murder investigation. Each witness provides, in succession, a partially overlapping account of the same stretch of narrative time. The goal, of course, is to solve the crime by combining these simultaneous but partial versions of the day in question to create an overall account of the murder. The fact that in this particular film they cannot be combined into a single coherent account does not change the underlying temporal structure of the film. At the diegetic level (the court proceedings), narrative time continues to move forward in accordance with standard film technique. But at the intradiegetic level (the events narrated by the witnesses), the clock turns back each time a new witness steps forward.

These first two methods are both "naturalistic" inasmuch as they are available to us in everyday life. But the third method, "true simultaneity"—what Zielinski calls "the complete solution" to the problem of simultaneity[9]—is impossible in real time, at least until someone invents a time machine, for it entails control over time and space. Here one reverses time itself, so that one can witness two simultaneous chains of events in succession. To turn again to Proust, it's a matter of being "in both places at once." Even in motion pictures, where turning back the clock is as easy as splicing film, one will only occasionally encounter this type of temporal artifice, where events themselves (not their reportage by characters within the narrative world) are displaced, presented out of their actual temporal sequence. One recent example is the German film *Run, Lola, Run,* in which we witness the same stretch of time—indeed, the same narrative sequence —over and over again, with only slight variations, in what amounts to a realization on the silver screen of the idea of "multiple universes." If this film, strictly speaking, doesn't so much present simultaneity as alternate realities, the point is nonetheless clear enough. Its artistic effect resides in the technique of turning back time, enabling the audience to follow the same day over and over again.

Time in Homer: Zielinski's Law

Let me return to Zielinski's law in light of his analysis of simultaneity. More precisely, it states that Homer realizes only pseudosimultaneity— *never* retrospective or true simultaneity. By narrating events in an uninterrupted linear succession, he maintains an unbroken temporal surface, what Zielinski refers to as Homer's *Einplanigkeit* (one-dimensionality). In fact, the singer maintains this technique at the expense of what a modern (literary) audience would consider narrative realism, so that from case to case one can detect varying degrees of resultant strain on the narrative. In order to clarify what all this means, I will rehearse Zielinski's discussion of a few of the examples he adduces from the *Iliad*.

In Book 3 of the *Iliad* Homer alternates between four scenes: the Argive ships, the battlefield, the Trojan wall, and Paris's home.[10] We begin in the field of battle, where two great armies approach each other (1ff.). Before any fighting begins, however, Paris proposes a duel—winner take all—between himself and Menelaus (67-75). Hector wins approval for the proposal in negotiation (76-110), the armies disarm (111-15), and messengers are sent to Troy to summon King Priam to put his seal on the agreement (116-17). The armies maintain a holding pattern as they await the duel, and the messengers, having once set off, are likewise in a "uniform process" en route to the city. Our attention is free, in other words, to take up other narrative threads. Thus, we turn to Helen, weaving in her Trojan lord's hall. Iris approaches her (121-44), and at her bidding Helen walks forth to the wall (145). While we may suspect that we have backtracked in time, Homer makes clear the uninterrupted flow of time through what Zielinski refers to as "synchronisms," as in Iris's summons to Helen: "[N]ow they are all seated in silence, the fighting has ended; / they lean on their shields, the tall spears stuck in the ground beside them" (134-35). Similarly, at the wall the narrative reminds us periodically of the armies sitting on the field (166-70, 192, 225, 230), who in their stasis resemble and function like an observed painting, as Priam, in conversation with Helen, gazes upon and asks, in turn, about Agamemnon (166-70), Odysseus (191-98), and Ajax (225-27). Helen finally points out Idomeneus among the warriors (230-31), when the messengers, dispatched over one hundred lines before, finally arrive with news from the battlefield. In this way the narrative makes us minimally conscious of the battlefield as we stand upon the wall, but it actually maintains an unbroken temporal surface inasmuch as nothing takes place "out there."[11]

This narratological principle stands out more clearly as we approach more difficult representational challenges, as on those occasions when certain events are sacrificed to the law of nonsimultaneity. Book 4, for instance, takes place in three locales: the Greek and Trojan sides of the battlefield and Olympus.[12] We begin in Olympus, where the gods devise a catalyst for the stalled battle (1-74). Lines 75-126 find us in the Trojan camp, as Pandarus, tricked by Athena, makes an illicit attempt on Menelaus's life during the agreed-upon cease-fire. We next jump over to the Greek side, where Agamemnon and company are tending to his wounded brother (127-219). Suddenly the narrative informs us of the Trojans' approach: "While they were working over Menelaos of the great war cry / all this time came on the ranks of the armoured Trojans" (220-21). In fact, we have heard nothing of them since Pandarus's treacherous shot. Apparently Hector, learning that one of his own fired the first shot, resigned himself to war and mustered the troops. As Zielinski suggests, perhaps Pandarus himself boasted of his deed (see 4.93-103, 5.102-105, 206-208). At any rate, Homer refuses—or simply never thinks—to narrate these developments in the Trojan camp since such a procedure would violate the principles underlying his representation of time. He therefore simply passes over them in silence in favor of Menelaus's medical treatment.

In some instances the very course of events is distorted so as to accommodate this temporal law.[13] Toward the end of Book 8, as the sun sets on yet another day of battle (8.485), each side gathers to discuss the day's events. Hector immediately calls the Trojans together (489), and Book 8 draws to a close with their adjourning for the night and setting up campfires (542-65). As Book 9 opens, however, the Achaeans are only just calling their meeting to order. One would naturally assume that they congregated right after battle, as did the Trojans. What else would they do in the meantime? And yet, as the Achaeans finally assemble, Nestor alludes specifically to the Trojan campfires already glowing ominously in their vicinity: "[C]lose to our ships the enemy / burn their numerous fires" (76-77). Unrealistic though it seems to us, the Greeks have apparently stood by patiently while the Trojans held counsel, allowing Homer to present first one and then the other assembly. What in principle are two simultaneous events have been resolved into a linear succession.

Such temporal distortion reaches its extreme limit when dealing with days and not hours.[14] After his argument with Agamemnon, Achilles complains to his mother of his slighted honor and proposes his fateful request of Zeus (1.357–427). Logically she should leave immediately and relay her son's request to Olympus. As she informs him, however, Zeus is indisposed:

> For Zeus went to the blameless Aithiopians at the Ocean
> yesterday to feast, and the rest of the gods went with him.
> On the twelfth day he will be coming back to Olympos,
> and then I will go for your sake to the house of Zeus,
>   bronze-founded,
> and take him by the knees and I think I can persuade him.
>   (423–27)

Thetis must therefore await Zeus's return—as must the war. Why this seemingly arbitrary delay? It gives Odysseus time, while all else is suspended, to return Chryseis to her father, Chryses, priest of Apollo (430–87). Without this delay the narrative would have to backtrack from Odysseus's mission to Thetis's visit with Zeus (493–532). If, conversely, one reconstructs the events logically as they "really happened," namely, by understanding Achilles' and Thetis's conversation as coinciding with Odysseus's voyage, then the night following the latter's sacrifices to Apollo—"Afterwards when the sun went down and darkness came onward" (475)—corresponds neatly to the night that falls upon Olympus after Thetis's transaction with Zeus—"Afterwards when the light of the flaming sun went under" (605). Thus, as Zielinski shrewdly observes, when Athena approaches Odysseus (2.167–83) to boost Achaean morale, she finds him on the beach near his ship, suggesting that within the story's underlying logic he had "really" just returned from his mission. What Homer reports instead, however, is that he had returned the day before— before, that is, Thetis's journey to Olympus (1.484–87).

Time in Biblical Narrative: Zielinski's Law Transgressed

Turning to the Bible, one finds a completely different state of affairs. Thus, in his frequently cited study of simultaneity in biblical narrative Shemaryahu Talmon can adduce numerous examples of genuinely synchronous events.[15] Although he refers to Zielinski's work in his conclusion, his own analysis unfortunately lacks the latter's precision. Talmon fails to distinguish between the three types of simultaneity, discussed earlier, offering all his examples under the rubric of a vague notion of synchronicity.

Indeed, he seems unaware of the fact that Zielinski in effect argued against the presence of actual simultaneity in Homer. What is more, Talmon mistakenly contends that the biblical writers make events simultaneous simply by employing the technique known as "resumptive repetition," or *Wiederaufnahme*: "When an editor desired to incorporate something, he frequently inserted it, and then resumed the original narrative, repeating the last sentence before the break with more or less accuracy" (117).[16] If one obvious use for such a device, as scholars have long recognized, is the editorial insertion of secondary material into an existing text, Talmon does take the next logical step, reasoning that a writer as well as a subsequent editor could use this device to insert a secondary sequence of events into a primary narrative thread. As Zielinski recognized, however, what is crucial to simultaneity isn't a mere rhetorical device but temporal structure itself.

In fact, biblical narrative realizes all three versions of simultaneity—not only pseudosimultaneity, but retrospective, and true simultaneity as well. And in the latter two cases, it does so by manipulating time itself. The biblical writers may use resumptive repetition as a literary convenience, as a means of reinforcing narrative continuity, but this has nothing to do with temporal form, as such. In this section, then, we will revisit the examples Talmon proffers and carefully discern the different methods that biblical narrative employs in order to achieve simultaneity. Due to the place Talmon's article occupies in the field, I will at the same time engage in a sustained critique of his study, in order to clarify further the issues involved.

Pseudosimultaneity

I begin with a brief example from the beginning of David's military and political career: 1 Sam. 18:20–28. This passage begins and ends with mention of Michal's love for David, which Talmon mistakes for a resumptive repetition:

> And Michal, Saul's daughter, loved David [*watteʾĕhab mîkal bat-šāʾûl ʾet dāwīd*], and they told Saul, and the thing was right in his eyes. And Saul said, "Let me give her to him, so that she might be a snare for him and that the hand of the Philistines might be against him." (18:20–21)

> And Saul saw and knew that the Lord was with David, and (that) Michal, Saul's daughter, loved him [*ûmîkal bat-šāʾûl ʾăhēbathû*]. And Saul continued to fear David more . . . (18:28–29)

He therefore suggests that this passage "is composed of two parallel-running episodes: Michal's love for David, and Saul's planning to utilize his daughter's attachment to bring about David's death at the hand of the Philistines. The splicing of the narratives is achieved by splitting the Michal component and inserting the report on Saul's evil intentions between the resulting brackets" (124). Even if, for the sake of argument, one accepts Talmon's questionable construal of verse 28b as an independent rather than subordinate clause ("And Saul saw and knew . . . and Michal loved David") and overlooks, moreover, the Septuagint's variant reading for the same, this half-verse hardly constitutes a second "parallel-running episode" simultaneous with Saul's machinations.[17] It is thus an exaggeration to speak of "splitting the Michal component" into "brackets." In fact, we should not analyze verse 28b as a resumptive repetition at all since it in no way resumes a previously interrupted narrative thread. The two half-verses, 20a and 28b, do not refer to a single event but constitute two independent reports of Michal's ongoing love for David. By connecting the dots, as it were, one understands them as referring to Michal's single continuous state, what Zielinski would call a "uniform process." This example—again, only if one accepts Talmon's construal of verse 28—would then follow the Homeric pattern for *avoiding* genuine simultaneity.[18] What little "simultaneity" one does find here results not from a resumptive repetition but purely from the syntax of 18:28. For, as we saw in chapter 3, the switch from consecutive in verse 28a—"And Saul saw and knew" (*wayyar³ šāʾûl wayyēdaᶜ*)—to perfect in verse 28b—"while/but Michal . . . loved him" (*ûmîkal . . . ʾāhēbathû*)—here signals a symmetry between these two events.[19] But since the latter half-verse points to Michal's continuing state—"love" in Hebrew is a "stative" verb—it in no way violates Zielinski's "law of psychological incompatibility."

One finds a dramatically effective use of space in Gen. 45:2-16, a scene that divides its attention between Joseph's and Pharaoh's houses. Talmon again falsely discovers a resumptive repetition, this time in verses 2 and 16a (125-26):

> And Joseph could not restrain himself in front of all those standing before him, and he called out, "Take out everyone from before me." So not a man stood with him when Joseph made himself known to his brothers. And he gave forth his voice [*qōlô*] in weeping, and Egypt heard, and Pharaoh's house heard [*wayyišmaᶜ bêt parᶜōh*]. . . . And Joseph said to his brothers . . . (45:1, 2, 4)[20]

> And he kissed all of his brothers and wept over them, and after that his brothers spoke with him. And the voice was heard in Pharaoh's house [*wĕhaqqōl nišmaᶜ bêt parᶜōh*], saying, "Joseph's brothers have come." And it was good in Pharaoh's eyes and in his servant's eyes. And Pharaoh said to Joseph . . . (45:15-17)

In verse 2, however, Pharaoh merely hears the "sound/voice" of Joseph's weeping (*qōlô bibkî*), surely an inchoate outpouring of emotion, whereas in verse 16a, "the voice" is an anonymous rumor cogently reporting in direct discourse Joseph's subsequent revelations.[21] Thus, the repetition notwithstanding, verse 16 takes place after verse 2; in any event, it makes no sense to claim, as Talmon does, that Joseph simultaneously speaks with his brothers in verses 3-15 and with Pharaoh in verses 17-20. One should compare Pharaoh's hearing the commotion in Joseph's house in verse 2 to Helen and Priam's looking out on the battlefield from the walls of Troy in Book 3 of the *Iliad*. Similarly, the disembodied "voice" in verse 16 effects a transition from Joseph to Pharaoh, much like the messenger who makes his way from the battlefield to Priam in the same scene of the *Iliad*. Such "synchronisms" may join together two narrative threads, but this "desultory" alternation between scenes merely gives the effect of simultaneity. The narrative recounts no event in Pharaoh's house that is genuinely simultaneous with some part of Joseph's recognition scene with his brothers. One has yet to violate that law that Homer followed so scrupulously.

1 Samuel 14 provides an instructive (because typical) use of resumptive repetition not to manipulate time but to insert secondary material.

> And it was a certain day, and Jonathan, Saul's son, said [*wayyōʾmer yônātān*] to the lad bearing his arms, "Come, let us cross over to the Philistine garrison, which is across over there." But he did not tell his father. And Saul was sitting [*yōšēb*] in the outskirts of Gibeah. . . . And the people with him were about 600 men. And Ahijah . . . was carrying [*nōśēʾ*] an ephod, but the people did not know that Jonathan had gone. And in the pass that Jonathan tried to cross over to the Philistine garrison was a rocky cliff on this side and a rocky cliff on that side. . . . And Jonathan said [*wayyōʾmer yēhônātān*] to the lad bearing his arms, "Come, let us cross over to the garrison of these uncircumcised . . ." (14:1-6)

Here we finally encounter a genuine resumptive repetition in verses 1 and 6, for in spite of the stylistic variation ("Philistine" versus "uncircumcised"), they both recount the same event. As Talmon correctly observes, the author uses this rhetorical device to insert verses 2-3 as a "vignette of Saul's camp" (127). Note, however, that these inserted verses do not narrate any action but rather describe like a picture the state (here, not even what Zielinski would call a "uniform process") of the Israelite camp—hence the participles *yōšēb* and *nōśēʾ*, which I render as past progressives. The passage then goes on to describe the pass which Jonathan is about to cross. In other words, in verses 2–5 no event transpires, no time passes. One has yet to find simultaneous action. The background described, verse 6 resumes Jonathan's tale with the consecutive (*wayyōʾmer*) —not the pluperfect, since there is no need to turn back the clock, the intervening description having taken no time within the narrative world. Next, Jonathan crosses over to the Philistine camp and succeeds in instigating a contagion of panic among the Philistines:

> And Jonathan went up on his hands and feet, and his arms bearer was following after him. And the Philistines fell before Jonathan, and his arms bearer was killing them off after him. And the first strike, which Jonathan and his arms bearer struck, was of about twenty men. . . . And there was a panic in the camp, in the field, and in all the people. . . . And Saul's lookouts in Gibeah of Benjamin saw, and look, the multitude was melting away this way and that.[22] And Saul said to the people who were with him . . . (14:13–17)

Once Jonathan has reduced the Philistines to a chaotic mob, the enemy camp reaches that state of gradual motion or change Zielinski would call a "uniform process." As in Homer, this allows the biblical writer to cross back over to the Israelite side, which he does, again, with a "synchronism": this time Saul's lookouts spy the Philistines' disarray (v. 16). This indication of temporal correspondence, however, indicates that we still do not have simultaneous events but rather an uninterrupted, linear temporal progression, even as we cross from Israelite to Philistine back to Israelite camp. Though Jonathan surfaces again in verse 27, when he unwittingly breaks his father's oath, he merely inserts himself into the narrative sequence without disrupting its flow. Through deft maneuvering, then, the writer maintains in "desultory" fashion two parallel narrative lines *without* actually disturbing the narrative's smooth temporal surface.

One finds an impressively developed example of pseudosimultaneity in 1 Samuel 2: a prolonged alternation between two narrative sequences, contrasting Samuel's ascension as prophet with the decline of Eli's priestly house, all the while maintaining time's forward flow.

> And Elkanah went [*wayyēlek*] home to Ramah, while the lad was serving [*hāyâ mĕšārēt*] the Lord in the presence of Eli the priest. (2:11)

> Now the sons of Eli were scoundrels; they did not know the Lord. And the custom of the priests with the people was whenever any man was making [*zōbēaḥ*] a sacrifice, the priest's lad would come

[*ûbā'*]. . . . And so the sin of the lads was [*wattĕhî*] very great in the presence of the Lord, for they treated with contempt the offering of the Lord. (2:12–17)

But Samuel was serving [*mĕšārēt*] in the presence of the Lord, a lad dressed in a linen ephod. And his mother would make [*ta'ǎśeh*] him a small coat, and she would bring [*wĕha'altâ*] it up to him. . . . And Eli would bless [*ûbērak*] Elkanah and his wife and would say [*wĕ'āmar*]. . . . And they would go [*wĕhālēkû*] back to his place. And the Lord took notice [*wayyipqōd*][23] of Hannah and she conceived [*wattahar*] and bore [*wattēled*] three sons and two daughters. And the lad, Samuel, grew [*wayyigdal*] with the Lord. (2:18–21)

Now Eli was very old [*zāqēn*] and he would hear [*wĕšāma'*] all that his sons did to all Israel. . . . And he began to say [*wayyō'mer*] to them. . . . But they would not listen [*wĕlō' yišmĕ'û*] to the voice of their father, for the Lord desired to kill them. (2:22–25)

But the lad, Samuel, was continually growing and gaining favor [*hōlēk wĕgādēl wātôb*] both with the Lord and with people. (2:26)

And a man of God came [*wayyābō'*] to Eli and said [*wayyō'mer*], "Thus says the Lord. . . ." (2:27–36)

Now the lad, Samuel, was serving [*mĕšārēt*] the Lord in the presence of Eli. And the word of the Lord was rare in those days; vision was not widespread. And it was [*wayhî*] in that day. . . . And the Lord called [*wayyiqrā'*] to Samuel . . . (3:1–4)

I provide a rather extended sampling of this chapter, which I have broken into paragraphs at the junctures between narrative threads, since the verb forms highlight those "uniform processes" that allow the "desultory" alternation between narrative threads. The passage consists almost entirely of the past progressive and the habitual past. As Elkanah leaves (v. 11)—a singular event recounted in the consecutive *wayyēlek*—Samuel immediately begins that "uniform process" which is the life of a cultic figure, grammatically captured in a past progressive—*hāyâ mĕšārēt*, a rare compound verbal construction. This allows the writer to move seamlessly to Eli's sons (vv. 12–17). Here the writer, using the habitual past—note the sequence of tense from participle (*zōbēah*) to converted perfect (*ûbā'*)— portrays their lives as a repetition of priestly malpractice. The consecutive that concludes this paragraph (*wattĕhî*) merely sums up their life of sin. The writer next returns to Samuel, again without interrupting the temporal flow (vv. 18–21). The scene begins with Samuel still serving before the

Lord—*mĕšārēt*, past progressive—though presumably some time after his father's departure, and switches quickly to a narrative sequence in the habitual past; note again the sequence of tense, this time from imperfect (*taʿăśeh*) to converted perfect (*wĕhaʿaltâ . . . ûbērak*). Although this paragraph concludes with a sequence of consecutives—*wayyipqōd . . . wattahar wattēled*—these merely signify a new development in what is still an iterated (if not genuinely habitual) past. For this single narrative sequence recounts five births, most likely over the course of at least as many years. Similarly, while the consecutive at the end of verse 21—*wayyigdal*, "and Samuel grew"—treats his growth as a single whole, one still interprets it as a gradual process spread over some length of time due to the semantics of the verb—humans don't generally grow in violent spurts. Moving this uniform process into the background, one switches back to Eli (vv. 22-25), which I understand also to recount a habitual past.[24] Analogous to 2:12-17, one begins with a stative perfect or adjective (*zāqēn*) and switches to the converted perfect (*wĕšāmaʿ*). Although one next finds a consecutive (*wayyōʾmer*), it seems to continue the habitual past, but with an incipient force, marking a transition or new development within the narrative; that is, after repeatedly hearing of his sons' transgressions, Eli finally (too late) *begins* to warn them of the consequences of their actions. Note that this tense sequence is identical to that in 2:18-21, where, following Hannah and Elkanah's frequent visits to Eli (primarily in the converted perfect), God finally *begins* to bless them through the repeated birth of children (in the consecutive). My reading of this passage also accounts for the otherwise puzzling imperfect, *yišmĕʿû*, in 2:25, which one can now interpret as Eli's sons' repeated refusal to heed their father's admonitions. Then, for a single sentence (v. 26), one returns to Samuel, this time with an emphatically progressive construction, *hōlēk wĕ*, "continually . . ." (lit. "walking and"). Again, I would point out, contra Talmon, that these repeated references to Samuel's service and to his physical and spiritual growth are not resumptive repetitions but rather a continuing refrain tracing Samuel's maturation. They do not resume an earlier point in the narrative by stepping back in time but instead refer to the same durative process at progressively later points in time. Only in the last two paragraphs does one return to the simple past (consecutive), with the first sequence of events leading in a linear chronology to the second. First a prophet comes to Eli, predicting the end of his lineage (vv. 27-36); then the word of the Lord comes to Samuel for the first time, predicting much the same thing (3:1ff.). The parting of their destinies is now complete. Samuel has attained the status of prophet, Eli's house is as good as dead, and all within a single unbroken temporal plane.

Pseudosimultaneity in biblical narrative superficially resembles the Homeric procedure examined earlier inasmuch as it does not interrupt the passage of time, that is, it does not create actual simultaneity. It achieves a certain type of perspective, however, for as these examples demonstrate, biblical narrative often uses pseudosimultaneity to set up certain contrasts: Michal's feelings for David over against Saul's; the Philistine versus Israelite camp; Eli's fall and Samuel's rise. The quick alternation between these contrastive narrative threads creates a simultaneous awareness of both, establishing a sense of tension between foreground and background.[25] Perspective becomes more explicit in the following example of retrospective simultaneity, with its complex interplay of various players and events.

Retrospective Simultaneity

In 1 Samuel 30 we find ourselves moving toward the climactic confrontation in which Saul and his sons will fall before the Philistines.

> And it was when David and his men came to Ziklag on the third day. (30:1a)

> And the Amalekites had raided [*waʿămālēqî pāšĕṭû*] the Negeb and Ziklag, and they had struck Ziklag and burned it with fire. And they had taken [*wayyišbû*] the women captive which were in it, from small to big; they killed no one. And they drove [*wayyinhăgû*] them on and went [*wayyēlēkû*] on their way. (30:1b, 2)

> And David came [*wayyābōʾ*], and his men, to the town, and look, it was burnt with fire and their women and sons and daughters were taken captive. . . . And David went [*wayyēlek*], he and 600 men who were with him. . . . And they found an Egyptian man in the field, and they took him to David and gave him food and he ate, and they gave him water to drink. . . . And his spirit returned to him, for he had not eaten food or drunk water for three days and three nights. And David said to him, "Who do you belong to, and where are you from?" And he said, "I am an Egyptian lad. I am the slave of an Amalekite man, and my lord left me for I became sick three days ago." (30:3–13)

As the reader will recall, 29:1 places David (an apparent double agent) with the Philistines in Aphek and Saul and his armies in Jezreel. Since the Philistine commanders rightly suspect David of potential treachery, they part company in verse 11. David now heads south for Ziklag, while the

Philistines head farther north toward Jezreel in order to engage the Israelite forces. On the third day David finds his home sacked and burned by
the Amalekites. He goes in search of his attackers and eventually comes
upon an Egyptian in the countryside, who informs him (in direct discourse) that the Amalekite attack took place a bit more than three days
earlier. Although the narrative leaves the chronology somewhat vague,
the repeated three-day motif suggests that David's expulsion from the
Philistine camp in 1 Samuel 29 coincides with the Amalekites' pillaging
of Ziklag. (To anticipate my discussion of true simultaneity, note as well
the pluperfect sequence in vv. 1b, 2.) Through its use of an eyewitness account, the narrative obliges the reader to retrospectively correlate the
Egyptian's report with David's recently recounted actions.

This example of retrospective simultaneity does not so much set up a
contrast between narrative threads as give an account of a key moment in
history in all its complexity, namely, the *simultaneous* relations among its
constituent parts. Where was David when his enemy Saul conveniently
fell victim to the hated Philistines? Far to the south avenging himself
upon another Israelite enemy, the Amalekites. This is made possible by
the use of direct speech, which allows a type of temporal shift, albeit one
that breaks no laws of physics. The manipulation of time is something it
shares with true simultaneity, though to a different degree. Through its
correlations of simultaneous events, true simultaneity functions like retrospective simultaneity, setting up significant historical situations. Not
coincidentally, one finds it in the story I have just been considering.

True Simultaneity

1 Samuel 30 continues with David, through the Egyptian's help, hunting
down the Amalekites and wreaking vengeance on them "from twilight till
evening of the next day" (30:17). After he has recovered his wives and
property, the narrative finally returns to Saul and the Philistines: "And
meanwhile the Philistines had been fighting [*ûpĕlištîm nilḥāmîm*] against
Israel, and the men of Israel fled from the Philistines and they fell slain on
Mount Gilboa" (31:1). In referring to this verse as a "repetitive resumption" (130) of 29:11b—"and (meanwhile) the Philistines had gone up
[*ûpĕlištîm ʿālû*] to Jezreel"—Talmon has clearly generalized the concept
far beyond its original definition. For one finds only a weak verbal correspondence between the two verses, and they clearly do not refer to the
same event—an unintentional admission on his part that this device is not
the operative one. In fact, in this case one finally comes upon the "complete solution" of the problem of simultaneity, but it arises not through a
rhetorical device but through a syntactical manipulation of time which

makes possible the resumption of an earlier point in the narrative. As Alter observes in his recent translation (which I have loosely followed here), the syntax of 31:1 suggests that Saul's defeat takes place at the same time as the immediately preceding events, namely, David's victory: "The Hebrew does not explicitly say 'meanwhile,' but it is implied by the unusual use of the participial form of the verb (literally, 'are battling') to begin the narrative unit."[26] Recall that this is the same "meanwhile" that both Anderson and Ermarth consider the key to simultaneity in the modern novel. I would only add that while one does not have here a true pluperfect, which would require the use of the perfect tense, one should still analyze it as an "anterior construction" based on the word order it shares with the pluperfect (subject followed by predicate)[27]—hence my translation "had been fighting," what I would call a "plu-past progressive." It temporarily reverses the flow of time, opening up a spatial and temporal depth within the narrative. One can further confirm this reading through another instance of retrospective simultaneity. In 2 Sam. 1:1–2 a messenger comes to David in Ziklag—again three days after the latter has recovered his stolen property and wives—and informs him of Saul's and Jonathan's demise. Since it took David and his men three days to return from Aphek to Ziklag, one can retroactively surmise that the messenger is three days in coming and that Saul and Jonathan thus fell roughly three days earlier, the very time of David's retaliatory strike against the Amalekites.[28] The plane of epic opens into the space of history.

At a similarly crucial moment—the scene immediately subsequent to Amnon's murder at the hands of his half brother Absalom—the biblical writer uses true simultaneity to establish the fugitive Absalom's whereabouts:

> And Absalom commanded his lads, saying. . . . And the lads of Absalom did to Amnon as Absalom commanded. And all the sons of the king arose and rode, each on his mule, and fled. (2 Sam. 13:28–29)

> And it was when they were on the way, and the rumor came to David, saying, "Absalom has struck down all the sons of the king, and not one of them remains." And the king arose and tore his clothes and lay on the earth. . . . And Jonadab son of Shimeah brother of David replied and said, "Let not my lord say, 'All the lads, the king's sons, they have killed,' for Amnon alone is dead. . . ." (30–33)

> [And Absalom fled (*wayyibraḥ ʾabšālôm*).][29] (34a)

And the lad on lookout lifted his eyes and saw, and look, a multitude were coming. . . . And Jonadab said, "Look, the sons of the king have come. According to the word of your servant, so it happened." And it was as he finished speaking, and look, the sons of the king came and lifted their voice and wept. . . . (34b–36)

And Absalom had fled [*wěʾabšālôm bāraḥ*] and gone to Talmai son of Amihur king of Geshur. (37a)

On the basis of the ostensible resumptive repetition between verses 34a and 37a, Talmon incorrectly observes of this scene: "The author is at pains to present the concurrent events in Amnon's house where the murder took place and in the king's palace where David is informed of Absalom's deed and his ensuing flight" (125). Clearly the anxious speculation at David's palace can only take place after Amnon's death. Furthermore, verse 34a looks extremely suspect as it stands; one should most likely excise it as a textual error. What is instructive in this case is that its deletion in no way affects the simultaneity of the events in question. Although verse 37a no longer repeats an earlier verse in the narrative, it still returns us to Absalom and picks up his story where it left off, as he seeks refuge from the king's wrath at the very time that his half brothers flee to the king's palace. Simultaneity does not depend on any repetition per se but rather on the resumption of a previously interrupted narrative sequence, on the temporal relation established by the pluperfect as it turns back the clock. Homer, in the same circumstance, would create the conceit that Absalom had been waiting patiently while other characters took the stage, fleeing only after the surviving sons of David made it home; think of the Trojan assembly at the close of *Iliad* 8, followed by the Greeks' in the opening of Book 9.

One finds the same technique, albeit more pronounced, in Genesis 38, the story of Judah and Tamar, which has been conspicuously inserted into the Joseph story. The reader will recall that Genesis 37 closes with Jacob mourning inconsolably over the apparent death of his son Joseph. Next, 38:1 suddenly announces: "And it was in that time, and Judah went down from his brothers." The events of this chapter span many years—enough for Judah to marry, raise three sons to adulthood, and eventually have a grandson through his daughter-in-law, Tamar. Equally suddenly 39:1 reaches back across these many years to resume Joseph's story where it had left off: "And Joseph had been brought down [*wěyôsēp hûrad*] to Egypt. And Potiphar bought him [*wayyiqnēhû*] . . . from the Ishmaelites who had brought him down there." In order to maintain his theory basing synchronicity on the use of resumptive repetition, Talmon (124) tries valiantly to recuperate 37:36 for J, to which the bulk of these chapters belongs—"But the Midianites had sold [*wĕhammĕdānîm mākĕrû*] him . . . to Potiphar. . . ." Unfortunately, the traditional attribution of this verse to E seems more plausible. But this does not actually matter for the point at hand. Even without the repetition, the pluperfect in 39:1 still suffices to create simultaneity,[30] for the years Joseph spends in Egypt clearly coincide with those Judah spends away from his father's house.

As Ibn Ezra shrewdly points out, the events of Genesis 38 cannot reasonably fit within the span of time Joseph spends in Egypt before being reunited with his brothers.[31] Instructively, this resembles an equally insightful observation Zielinski makes regarding the tendency of Homer's narrative technique to, as it were, lose track of a secondary process while narrating a primary action, straining credulity, albeit with impunity, for the sake of maintaining a smooth temporal surface.[32] For example, when Achilles sees Nestor returning from the battlefield with a wounded warrior in *Il* 11.595–97, he sends Patroclus to Nestor's tent in order to confirm the identity of the injured soldier (Machaon). Achilles' faithful companion departs in 11.615–16, allowing us to move seamlessly to Nestor's tent, where an extended scene plays itself out: at a leisurely pace Nestor and Machaon disembark from the chariot, wash themselves off, enter the tent, after which Hecamede, Nestor's female slave, seats them at a table and prepares them a drink, which they proceed to imbibe (11.617–42). Only then does Patroclus finally appear. As Zielinski notes, Patroclus should have arrived much sooner, but Homer wanted to give free rein to the tranquil scene gradually unfolding within Nestor's tent, so he artificially lengthens the time Patroclus takes to get there. But since, as Auerbach would say, Homer is all surface, the audience easily forgets about Patroclus as he slowly approaches in the background, and thus does not notice, much less object to, this strain on realism. In Genesis, conversely, one sees the inverse effect: J forces Genesis 38 into an unrealistically short period of time precisely in order to make two narrative sequences coincide.

I conclude this section with one final example, 1 Samuel 28–29, which strikingly demonstrates the extent to which time can be manipulated in biblical narrative.

And it was in those days, and the Philistines gathered [*wayyiqbĕṣû*] their armies for war to fight against Israel. And Achish said [*wayyō'mer*] to David, "You surely know that you will go out with me in the army, you and your men." And David said [*wayyō'mer*] to Achish . . . (1 Sam. 28:1-2)

And Samuel had died [*ûšĕmû⁾ēl m t*] and all Israel had mourned [*wayyispĕdû*] him and buried [*wayyiqbĕrūhû*] him in Ramah, in his town. And Saul had removed [*wĕšāʾûl hēsîr*] all the mediums and the diviners from the land. (28:3)

And the Philistines were gathered [*wayyiqqābĕṣû*], and they came [*wayyābōʾû*] and camped [*wayyaḥănû*] in Shunem. (28:4)

And Saul gathered [*wayyiqbōṣ*] all Israel and camped [*wayyaḥănû*] in Gilboa. And Saul saw the camp of the Philistines and he was afraid and his heart trembled greatly. . . . And Saul said to his servants, "Seek out for me a woman medium . . ." (28:5-7)

And the Philistines gathered [*wayyiqbĕṣû*] all their armies at Aphek, while Israel was camping [*wĕyiśrāʾēl ḥōnîm*] at the well which is in Jezreel. And the Philistine lords were crossing over [ʿōbĕrîm] by hundreds and by thousands, and David and his men were crossing over [ʿōbĕrîm] at the rear with Achish. And the Philistine lords said [*wayyōʾmĕrû*], "Who are these Hebrews?" . . . And David rose early [*wayyaškēm*], he and his men, to go in the morning and to return to Philistine land, while the Philistines went [*ûpĕlištîm ʿālû*] up to Jezreel. (29:1-11)

This chapter alternates between the Philistines (and David) and Saul. In his discussion (127-30) Talmon again misapplies the notion of a resumptive repetition, this time to 28:1 and 29:1, mistakenly claiming that "the self-contained Witch of Endor episode [28:5-25] . . . occurred at the very time of Achish's altercation with the other Philistine leaders over David's admissibility into their camp [29:1-11]" (129). He apparently failed to notice that 28:1, 28:4, and 29:1 place the Philistines in three different locales, rendering his reading untenable. Although 28:1 gives no location, one can confidently place it somewhere far in the south, in Philistine territory, since it recounts the initial mobilization of their troops—recall specifically that Achish and David, the two characters in verse 1b, are based, respectively, in Gath (27:2) and even farther south in Ziklag (v. 6).[33] In 28:4 we next find the Philistines in Shunem, far to the north, near Jezreel and Mount Gilboa, where the battle eventually takes place (31:1-13). Finally, in 29:1 we find the Philistines back in Aphek, a considerable distance south of Shunem. In other words, not only are 28:1, 28:4, and 29:1 not simultaneous, they are out of geographical and therefore chronological order. Noting this inconsistency, Driver correctly concludes that 28:3-25 (the "Witch of Endor" episode) is "out of its proper place," belonging instead after chapters 29-30.[34] At the same time, however, I think

Driver's comment misses the point, inasmuch as the writer apparently intentionally displaced 28:3–25 precisely in order to create an alternation between David's rise and Saul's fall, in particular juxtaposing David's calculated dealings with Achish (28:1–2; 29:1–11) and Saul's desperate consultation with the medium of Endor (28:5–25). This sort of chronological manipulation is inconceivable for Homer, with his smooth temporal surfaces and well-behaved flashbacks. Indeed, I noted earlier that Homer sacrifices narrative realism for the sake of temporal continuity. Biblical narrative inversely sacrifices realism for the sake of temporal manipulation. If Driver is correct, it results from a secondary textual maneuver, an editorial displacement of a narrative block already fixed in written form.

Memory and History

I have now analyzed the strikingly different approaches to simultaneity in Homer and the Bible. Homeric time, even when approximating synchronicity, flows smoothly forward, constituting an uninterrupted surface. Biblical narrative, conversely, recounts genuinely simultaneous events, causing ruptures or breaks in time but achieving thereby historical depth or perspective. In order to account for this fundamental dichotomy, I propose that a formal distinction exists between two narrative modes: history—which, following Benveniste, one might call *histoire*—and memory—what one might correspondingly designate *mémoire*. As these names suggest, this narrative dichotomy is analogous with but not identical to the strictly grammatical distinction, discussed at length in chapter 3, between narration and discourse.

Narrative memory, by which I refer primarily to oral epic, gives narrative form to what I will call "subjective time."[35] This is a deictic conception of time, centered on the present, the moment of speech. Like the grammatical notion of tense—past, present, and future—the "epic past" is defined with respect to the "now" of the singer, who recalls this past in the "present" of performance. Epic singers conventionally register this fact by invoking the muse, the personification of memory. Narrative history—under which I include biblical narrative and the novel, in addition to what is thought of as history proper—gives narrative form to what I will call "objective time."[36] This non-deictic notion of time does not define moments as past, present, or future, instead establishing relations between moments: earlier than, simultaneous with, later than. Its corresponding system of verb forms makes no reference to a speaker or subject, no appeal to a privileged moment called the "present" or "now." Rather, it recounts a linear temporal succession of event following event, employing various objective temporal markers, especially dates.[37] In effect, memory and history account for the temporal relation a narrative may or may not have with the present.[38] While I would not posit any straightforward correspondence between these two narrative modes and established genres—in the terms offered here, an autobiographical memoir, for example, may very well assume the narrative form of a history, albeit in the first person[39]— they do correspond to two of Northrup Frye's "radicals of presentation": "Words may be acted in front of a spectator [drama]; they may be spoken in front of a listener [epic]; they may be sung or chanted [lyric]; or they may be written for a reader [novel]."[40]

Barthes seems to have a similar distinction in mind when he observes that "the Photograph [is] never, in essence, a memory [*souvenir*] (whose grammatical expression would be the perfect tense, whereas the tense of the Photograph is the aorist)."[41] For the aorist characterizes the photograph precisely because the latter, at least according to Barthes, belongs to history:[42] "With regard to many of these photographs, it was History [*l'Histoire*] which separated me from them. Is History not simply that time when we were not born?"[43] In Barthes's view, in other words, such photographs cannot speak to us in the perfect tense of memory because they record "that time when we were not born." They recount, instead, a history in "the absolute past of the pose (aorist)," where "absolute" specifies that past having no connection to the present.[44] Thus, in *Writing Degree Zero* Barthes famously observes of the *passé simple* (aorist) in the novel that it no longer functions as a "tense"—in other words, it is no longer deictic. Meanwhile, the perfect—what Benveniste calls the tense of the "witness"[45]—is the "grammatical expression" of memory because it maintains a connection between past and present. It is therefore incompatible with history, with that time preceding our birth, which we could not possibly have witnessed. "[I]mpossible for me to believe in 'witnesses.' . . . Michelet was able to write virtually nothing about his own time," Barthes parenthetically observes apropos of history.[46]

What is interesting is that simultaneity is conceivable only in objective time, in history. Since by definition the subjective time of memory relates an event-object to a speaker-subject, it cannot, as such, relate one event to another, which would fall under the domain of objective time. Rather, each event is either past, present, or future *to the subject*. Thus, in his analysis of time Russell explicitly relegates both simultaneity and succession to what he calls "physical time" because both describe a "relation between objects."[47] In fact, history not only makes simultaneous action conceivable but, as Talmon notes, necessary: "Recording such episodes one after the other would result in the impression that they came about in a chronological sequence and not simultaneously. Such an arrangement would thus distort the 'historical truth.'"[48] Barthes similarly observes of the rhetoric of history: "[T]his type of discourse—though linear in its material form—when it is face to face with historical time, undertakes (so it would appear) the role of amplifying the depth of that time. We become aware of what we might call a zig-zag or saw-toothed history."[49] This temporal zigzag—two parallel lines (simultaneous narrative sequences) joined by a diagonal (turning the clock back)—is the precise image Zielinski uses to represent true simultaneity: a figure resembling a backwards "N."[50]

By the same logic, simultaneity is inconceivable within human memory as well. For I can relate two remembered events to each other only by secondary reflection, linking each to external temporal markers (dates are especially useful here) and comparing these in order to determine their temporal relation: earlier than, later than, simultaneous with. As Russell observes, "[O]ur power of thus immediately perceiving temporal distances is very limited; beyond the immediate past, events remembered are simply past, and their greater or less distance from the present is a matter of inference."[51] This secondary reflection (Russell's "inference") is nothing less than the transformation or objectification of memory into history. Banfield makes similar remarks in her study of Proustian memory, in which she contrasts remembering to recounting:

> It is true that we assume it is possible to remember when or how many times something happened, but our analysis suggests that what is being invoked is not strictly speaking memory but a second order act starting out from memory. . . . To remember when and how many times, to count, is to perform *another operation* upon the data of memory, comparing them with other data; it requires an *inference*, a *deduction*. One knows one has done something more than once, habitually, time and time again, or even rarely, but in order to determine how many times and when, one must put one's memories, by nature without a date and without an exact number, *in relation to* other facts established by other means than by memory—by consulting datebooks, calendars, newspapers, diaries, and subjecting this data to calculations. . . . In other words, what is remembered is then recounted, the two linguistic operations contributing to constitute narrative.[52]

In Banfield's account, memory in a sense provides us with "raw" data, events from the subject's remembered past. In order to construct history, one must, through "inference" and "deduction," bring event "in relation to" event. In this way history recounts events that are simultaneous with some and that succeed and precede others.

Permit me to reexamine biblical narrative in this light. As we saw, biblical narrative achieves both retrospective and true simultaneity. Common to both techniques is what I would call "narrative geometry," that is, the setting up of spatial and temporal relationships within the narrative world that carve out a sense of perspective or depth. In retrospective simultaneity a character recalls events that coincide temporally with other events, whether recalled by other characters, as in *Rashomon*, or recounted in the narration itself, as in 1 Samuel 30–2 Samuel 1. True simultaneity establishes the same logical-temporal structure, but this time both events are recounted in narration. In either case, by correlating event to event the narrative establishes the logical relation of simultaneity between two or more events.[53]

In both types of simultaneity the use of verbs plays a crucial role. For tense in effect sets up logical relations: past, present, future for deictic verbs; earlier than, simultaneous with, later than for non-deictic verbs. In the case of retrospective simultaneity, a character within the narrative world recalls an event, usually in direct discourse using the perfect tense.[54] While the perfect tense locates this event deictically with respect to the character's subjective present, it also leads to the retrospective construction of secondary logical relations: earlier than the objectively defined moment the character occupies within the narrative, and, more to the point, simultaneous with some other independent event—that is, an event lying outside of that character's experience. This retrospective process objectifies the character's subjective experience and incorporates it into a larger history. In the case of true simultaneity, the pluperfect plays a role analogous to that of the perfect quoted in direct speech, except that here all the relevant events are recounted in narration. It relates an objectively defined moment in the narrative past to an event in the more distant past. At the same time it thereby makes this antecedent event simultaneous with some independent event. Not coincidentally, in Biblical Hebrew the pluperfect takes the form of a circumstantial clause, *wĕ*-X-perfect ("and X had —ed"). The perfect in this construction retains its logical structure as a retrospective preterite (earlier than), but it places this antecedent event not in relation to the speaker's present (which would make it deictic) but rather in relation to another objectively defined moment within the narrative.[55] Like the *passé simple*, the pluperfect is a non-deictic tense, for it does not relate event to speaker but event to antecedent event. Thus, in both cases of simultaneity the verb constructs geometrical relationships that transcend the pure surface of linear narrative succession by relating events that do not lie within a single plane but rather occupy points that, taken together, map out, as it were, a three-dimensional volume.[56]

Auerbach anticipates my argument in his insights into the Bible's realization of character:

> Abraham's actions are explained not only by what is happening to him at *the moment,* nor yet only by his character (as Achilles' actions by his courage and his pride, and Odysseus' by his versatility and foresightedness), but by his *previous history;* he remembers, he is constantly conscious of, what God has promised him and what God has already accomplished for him.[57]

Note the switch in Auerbach's commentary from present ("remembers . . . is") to present perfect ("has promised . . . has . . . accomplished"), replicating what in the narrative would be a switch from the past to past perfect tense. This sense of anteriority transforms surface into depth. Thus, he continues:

> How fraught with background, in comparison, are characters like Saul and David! How entangled and stratified are such human relations as those between David and Absalom, between David and Joab! Any such "background" quality of the psychological situation as that which the story of Absalom's death and its sequel (II Samuel 18 and 19, by the so-called Jahvist) rather suggests than expresses, is unthinkable in Homer. Here we are confronted not merely with the psychological processes of characters whose depth of background is veritably abysmal, but with a purely *geographical background* too. For David is absent from the battlefield; but the influence of his will and his feelings continues to operate, they affect even Joab in his rebellion and disregard for the consequences of his actions. . . . With this, compare, for example, how Achilles, who sends Patroclus first to scout and then into battle, loses almost all "presentness" so long as he is not physically present. But the most important thing is the "multilayeredness" of the individual character; this is hardly to be met with in Homer, or at most in the form of a conscious hesitation between two possible courses of action; otherwise, in Homer, the complexity of the psychological life is shown *only in the succession* and alternation of emotions; whereas the Jewish writers are able to express the *simultaneous* existence of various layers of consciousness and the conflict between them.[58]

In light of the preceding discussion, I would gloss Auerbach's reference to the Bible's depiction of "geographical background" as none other than the awareness of simultaneous events taking place "out there" while the narrative recounts events "over here." Simultaneity is an aspect of narrative perspective.

What is interesting is that even when discussing a different dimension of narrative representation, Auerbach, like Zielinski, specifically draws attention to Homer's smooth narrative surface. Although time itself does not constitute an explicit part of his argument, it seems no coincidence that Auerbach contrasts the "succession . . . of emotions" in Homeric characters to the "simultaneous existence" of the same in biblical characters. However, while Zielinski linked the smooth surface of Homeric narrative to the lack of simultaneity, Auerbach links it to the hero's lack of a past, of biographical succession. In fact, these insights complement each other, for together they disclose the fact that Homer does not relate event to event within his narrative. Homeric epic, in contrast to biblical narrative, lacks an internal narrative geometry.

On the one hand, Homer disallows retrospective correlations of events by restricting what characters can report. True, characters will occasionally speak of their past, and yet they speak of a past that belongs solely to them, that cannot be correlated to other events. Consider Odysseus's visit with the Phaiakians, which interlude provides us with large portions of Odysseus's exploits. First he informs his hosts of his immediate past, how he came to their shores from Calypso's Island (7.240–97). Next, their own Demodokos sings of Odysseus's involvement in the end of the Trojan War (8.72–82, 499–520). Finally, Odysseus regales his hosts with the lengthy tale of his adventures between these two endpoints, from his departure from Troy to his arrival at Calypso's home (9.1–12.453). While his story has thus been analyzed into parts and then, in effect, re-synthesized, there is no geometry here, for together they merely form a seamless whole, a continuous narrative sequence. Moreover, Homer recalls no other events that transpire during this period and that could, as a result, be correlated with Odysseus's struggles.[59] For these take place before the narrative time of the *Odyssey*, which begins in medias res on Calypso's Island. In this sense, the true purpose of Odysseus's stories is precisely to flesh out his experiences for the benefit of Homer's audience. They have no current significance within the narrative world for Odysseus and his audience. Indeed, Homer is loathe to sing of the same event twice, so that Odysseus speaks not only for himself but for the entire oral tradition when he declares: "Why tell the rest of / this story again, since yesterday in your house I told it / to you and your majestic wife? It is hateful to me / to tell a story over again, when it has been well told" (12.450–53).[60] In spite of the complicated narratorial structure of the *Odyssey*, all the pieces fall into place within a single narrative plane.

On the other hand, Homer never achieves true simultaneity because he never employs a genuine pluperfect, whether in a particular verb form or syntactical construction.[61] As Pierre Chantraine observes: "The pluperfect is none other than the preterite of the perfect and presents, in the preterite, the same value as the perfect. . . . The pluperfect, which *does not properly express anteriority*, sometimes serves to indicate in express fashion that the verbal process is already realized."[62] He notes that the aorist does occasionally denote "an action anterior to that which is noted by the adjoining proposition, but this signification results from context and is not a proper value of the aorist."[63] Let us consider a few examples.[64]

> But when [*epei*] they (had) arrived [*hikonto*, aorist] at the
>   wide camp of the Achaeans,
> they dragged [*erussan*, aorist] the black ship onto dry land.
>   (*Il* 1.484–85)

Here one might arguably translate with the pluperfect, inasmuch as Homer uses the aorist—"arrived"—to narrate an event at a moment that just precedes the rest of story, but, as Chantraine notes, only the logic of the context and not an actual verb form or syntactical construction suggests the anterior past.[65]

> There came [*Ēlthe*] a town beggar . . . (*Od* 18.1)
> Arnaios was his name, for his lady mother (had given)/
>   gave [*theto*, aor] it to him
> from birth [*ek genetēs*], but all the young men used to call
>   him Iros
> because he would go and bear messages when anyone
>   asked.
> So he came [*elthōn*] to chase Odysseus out of his own
>   home. (18.5–8)

> Drawing near, she washed her lord, and immediately she
>   recognized [*egnō*]
> that scar [*oulēn*], where once [*pote*] the boar [*sus*] with his
>   white tusk [*leukǭ odonti*] had struck [*ēlase*, aor] him
> when he went to Parnassus [*Parnēsond' elthonta*], to Auto-
>   lycus and his children. . . . (*Od* 19.392–94)
> . . . [His parents] asked about everything,

about the wound [*oulēn*] that he suffered. He told his story
   well
how while hunting, a boar [*sus*] struck [*elasen*] him with his
   white tusk [*leukō odonti*]
when he went to Parnassus [*Parnēsond' elthonta*] with the
   sons of Autolycus.
Holding him in the palms of her hands, the old woman
recognized [*gnō*] (19.463-68)

Both of these passages contain an example of those famous Homeric flashbacks or digressions. Of particular interest here is the use of the resumptive repetition in each. A minimal verbal correspondence (between 18.1 and 18.8) suffices to signal a resumption after the brief flashback in *Odyssey* 18. A rather more complex set of clues (see lines 19.392-94 and 19.463-68) seems necessary to resume the main narrative after the lengthy digression on Odysseus's scar. Unlike the previous example in *Il* 1.484, they narrate genuinely anterior events, but Homer accomplishes this merely by establishing a new point in the past—"from birth" (18.6), "once" (18.393)—jumping to this new point in time and then using the aorist, as opposed to any sort of anterior construction, to report these earlier events—"gave" (*Od* 18.5), "struck" (19.393). These digressions do not carry a true pluperfect sense because they do not refer to an earlier point in time from the perspective of another privileged moment within the narrative. And since these digressions—just like the stories Odysseus tells—reach back far beyond the temporal limits of the narrative proper, they do not entail any chronological overlap. In fact, Homer uses these digressions, like Odysseus's turns as bard, solely to provide information to his audience, so that they have no current significance for the events unfolding in the primary narrative. The resumptive repetition thus functions as an inclusion, hermetically sealing the anterior sequence in a verbal parenthesis. As a result, the epic lacks that internal narrative geometry needed to create a sense of spatial and temporal depth.

Again one finds an analogous comment in Auerbach:

And this procession of phenomena takes place in the foreground —that is, in a local and temporal present which is absolute. One might think that the many interpolations, the frequent moving back and forth, would create a sort of perspective in time and place; but the Homeric style never gives any such impression. The way in which any impression of perspective is avoided can be clearly observed in the procedure for introducing episodes, a syntactical

> construction with which every reader of Homer is familiar. . . . To
> the word scar (v. 393) there is first attached a relative clause . . .
> which enlarges into a voluminous syntactical *parenthesis* . . . until,
> with verse 467 ("The old woman now touched it . . ."), the scene
> which had been broken off is *resumed.*[66]

I would only add that what is equally decisive in this Homeric procedure, in addition to the relative clause, is the absence of a proper pluperfect construction. For without such a construction, there can be no
relations internal to the past. The story of Odysseus's scar is retold not as
a past event impinging on the hero's present but as an unconnected sequence of events—"absolute," to use Auerbach's term. In other words,
all events lie in the foreground while being told because each defines its
temporal position not in relation to another event within the narrative
but with respect to the same privileged moment, the present of the
singer and his audience.[67] The Homeric privileging of foreground derives from the organizing premise of narrative memory: the perspective
of the singer who recalls the past from the present. If Homer's epic is
"one-dimensional" (*einplanig*) —as Zielinski, like Auerbach, observes—
this is because each event is related only to this central perspective and
not to each other.

    In Ugaritic epic one finds a temporal surface smoother still than
Homer's. Parker correctly observes: "Fast or slowly, the plot progresses directly forward. There are no asides, no anticipatory confidences to the lis-
tener/reader, no summaries or generalizations, no moralizing lessons
drawn, no explanations of older customs, no references to the present
day."[68] I would only add that one finds neither Homer's flashbacks nor the
Bible's zigzags through time. As regards this issue, although there is no direct point of comparison within the Ugaritic tradition with respect to the
formal realization and manipulation of time, there is an instructive example of a resumptive repetition in Ugaritic.

> Sleep overwhelms him, he lies down;
> Slumber, and he crumples.
> Now in his dream [*bḥlmh*], El comes down [*il . yrd*];
> The Father of Man [*ab . adm*], in his vision [*bdhrth*].
> Now El approaches, asking Kirta: (1.14.1.33–38)
> "Whom El [*il*] has given in my dream [*dbḥlmy*],
> The Father of Man [*ab. adm*] in my vision [*bdrty*];
> Who will bear a child for Kirta,
> A lad for the Servant of El."

Kirta awakes—it's a dream [*wḥlm*]!
The servant of El—a vision [*whdrt*]! (1.14.3.46-51)

This resumptive repetition does not join together independent simultaneous narrative threads one might find in biblical narrative, nor does it effect a flashback, as in Homer. Throughout this passage, time continues to flow forward, neither backtracking nor digressing—the dream is a temporal event, not a nontemporal description. On some level one could say that this device resumes Kirta's waking existence. More to the point, it really serves to remind the audience that Kirta has been dreaming, a fact which has gradually faded during the course of the dream's two columns of text. The Ugaritic narrative poems would also seem to follow Zielinski's law and thus to embody the subjective time of narrative memory.

In this way epic memory assumes the point of view of the singer who recalls the past from his present. Zielinski himself imputes such a subjective perspective to Homer's epics by framing his discussion of simultaneity as a problem of perception and asking, in effect: How might a human observer perceive two simultaneous events?[69] By observing the law of psychological incompatibility, Homer chooses (if one can speak of it as a choice) to tell his story as though he had witnessed the events. As Blanchot observes: "The distant epic narrator recounts exploits that happened and that he seems to be reproducing, whether or not he witnessed them. But the narrator is not a historian. His song is the domain where the event that takes place there comes to speech, in the presence of a memory [*souvenir*]; memory [*la mémoire*]—muse and mother of muses—contains within it truth, that is, the reality of what takes place."[70] The epic singer not only practices an art of memory in his formulaic style but, by invoking the Muse, explicitly summons divine aid in order to recall the past.[71] Furthermore, as Richard Martin has cogently argued, Homer's epics themselves embody in their overall form a "feat of memory," which he identifies as one of the "heroic genres of speaking" that the characters within the epic employ—epic as the very genre of memory.[72] While it is harder to fit Ugaritic epic into this scheme, it is worth pondering under what circumstances these poems were performed and preserved. It is instructive that *Aqhat* (1.17.6, left edge), *Kirta* (1.16.6, left edge), and *Baal* (1.4.8, left edge; and 1.6.6.54-58) are all signed by the scribe (*spr*) Ilimilku.[73] I do not mean to suggest that he was their singular author but only that his appended name helps indicate the subjective origin of this form of narrative.[74] One wonders, in fact, whether in this culture a text's authority may have derived from its scribe/author. Consider *Baal*'s extended genealogy:

> The scribe is Ilimalku the Shubanite,
> Student of Attenu the diviner,[75]
> Chief of the priests
> Chief of the shepherds,
> The Thaite of Niqmaddu,
> King of Ugar[it]
> Lord of YRGB,
> Master of THRMN (1.6.6.54–58)

Progressing from scribe to teacher to ruler, these lines constitute a transparent gesture of textual legitimation.[76] The link between the Ugaritic texts and the originating subject has yet to be severed.

Biblical narrative, conversely, is infamously anonymous—hence a book such as Friedman's *Who Wrote the Bible?*, which has some of the suspense of a detective novel. As I indicated in my introductory chapter, even if Ezra the scribe edited the Pentateuch, as Friedman has plausibly conjectured,[77] he receives no credit for this, and as he recites from the Book of the Law of Moses, authority seems to inhere within the text itself (Nehemiah 8).[78] Inasmuch as biblical narrative denies or effaces its subjective origins, it betrays the impulse of history, that "objective" form of narrative. Thus, one sees signs of this objectivity in various formal literary features of biblical narrative. As I argued at length in chapters 3 and 4, the very language of biblical narration lacks the grammatical signs of subjectivity and thus constitutes *histoire*. Now one sees that its temporal logic, too, derives from the objectivity of narrative history.

In light of this dichotomy between memory and history, I would like to consider one final example from the Bible: Judges 4 and 5. As the reader will recall from chapter 2, Halpern has convincingly argued that the prose account in Judges 4 is a historical reconstruction of a crucial battle based on the Song of Deborah in Judges 5. Furthermore, as I argued in that chapter, the Song of Deborah may well originate in an oral tradition analogous to Homer's. It is telling, then, that in writing this history the author of Judges 4 found it necessary to treat certain events as having taken place simultaneously, and thus turned to the pluperfect.

> And the Lord discomfited Sisera and all the chariots and all the army by the mouth of the sword before Barak. And Sisera dismounted from his chariot, and he fled on foot [*wayyānos běraglāyw*]. But Barak pursued the chariots and the army as far as Haroshet-hagoyim. And all the army of Sisera fell by the mouth of the sword; no one was left. Now Sisera had fled on foot [*wěsîsěrāʾ nās běraglāyw*] to the tent of Yael. (Judg. 4:15–17)

The narrative splits into two threads as Sisera abandons (15b), and Barak pursues (16a), the Canaanite forces. We follow first Barak as he pursues and kills Sisera's men (16). Although the length of time that elapses in this verse is unspecified, dispatching the enemy no doubt took time as well as effort.[79] This affords Sisera a significant head start, and so the writer turns back the clock with a pluperfect in order to recount the general's fate in turn: "Now Sisera had fled on foot" (17a), a resumptive repetition of 15b ("and he fled on foot"), though a mere single verse intervenes. While Barak and company slay the Canaanite rank and file, Yael is given the honor of vanquishing the hated Canaanite general. These events are also recalled in the Song of Deborah, but there, as one might now expect, they take place in a strictly linear temporal succession: the battle (5:19-21), flight (5:22), and Sisera's death (5:24-27).[80] In a telling contrast, the prose writer, in order to fashion a coherent, adequate historical account—that is, to explain Sisera's liaison with Yael and Barak's absence during the same—found it necessary to depart from the linear sequence. We see before our very eyes the transformation of "epic memory" into "history."

Defamiliarizing Temporal Form

Given my overarching thesis, I would, finally, like to return to the question of writing. Memory, almost by definition—except for that rare "photographic" variety, whose metaphorical name, not coincidentally, takes as its vehicle a fixed, "textual" medium—is unordered and unfixed in textual form. Thus, as we saw in Banfield's reading of Proust, it is writing, in the form of datebooks, calendars, and so forth, that enables the ordering of the data and that, as a medium, next fixes the data in a stable form, thereby transforming memory into history. This is the same process, observed from a different angle, whereby, in Barthes' words, the author seeks "to reduce reality to a point of time, and to abstract, from the depth of a multiplicity of experiences, a pure verbal act, freed from the existential roots of knowledge, and directed towards a logical link with other acts, other processes, a general movement of the world."[81]

One can easily imagine how Zielinski's law, as a principle of narration, functioned in the oral tradition, like the formulaic style, as an aid to memory and to improvisational performance.[82] By presenting each scenario one after the other, the performer need not keep track of two or more independent narrative lines. Even the frequent digressions in Homer do not make inordinate demands on the singer's attention; by discretely containing them within verbal parentheses, the performer avoids leaving loose narrative threads. Though Zielinski himself does not make this connection—he was, after all, working in the days before the Parry-Lord hypothesis—certain of his observations are relevant here. Drawing an explicit analogy between the representation of time in narrative and that of space in the nonplastic visual arts, he notes that in the history of art the depiction of the one-dimensional, the surface, is the "original" (*ursprüngliche*) form, "the natural and unmediated" (*Natürliche und Unmittelbare*), preceding any sense of perspective, which is "the derivative and artificial" (*das Abgeleitete und Künstliche*).[83] In other words, certain forms are presumed to be "original," "natural," and "unmediated." Art, by imposing varying degrees of "artifice" upon its medium (cf. *Kunst* and *künstlich*), creates "derivative" and "artificial" forms. By implication, then, it was an artistic impulse subsequent—and hence unknown—to Homer that eventually led to a new literary realization of time.

Ben Perry takes this line of reasoning a step further by raising the issue of writing with respect to what he perceives in early Greek literature as the "capacity for viewing things separately."[84] Since in the linear flow of narrative viewing things separately means none other than viewing phenomena successively rather than simultaneously, his notion provides a nice counterpart to Zielinski's law. Not coincidentally, Perry, like Zielinski, places Homer at the beginnings of a literary history. He sees Homer's narrative mode as evincing a preclassical Greek mentality: "[Homer's] mind is here functioning in a purely natural and unrestrained fashion" (404). Aware now of the problem of orality, he contrasts Homer's style specifically to that of later writers: "Since epic poety [*sic*] is oral in origin and early, its syntax and style of composition are consequently more spontaneous and less logical in many respects than the syntax and style of later authors" (410). In Perry's account, reminiscent of Zielinski's, later writers distance themselves from Homer's "spontaneous," "natural," and "unrestrained" language—which I would gloss as the singer's relative proximity to the spoken language—by imposing upon their syntax and style a more austere "logical" form.

To oppose, as Perry and Zielinski do, Homer's "natural" and "spontaneous" style to subsequent literary developments is not to deny or in any way denigrate the artistry of Homer's *Kunstsprache* but merely to place it in a certain position with respect to speech and writing. For, as Perry implies, writing creates a divide between Homer and post-epic literature. While Homer's arsenal of finely honed oral formulae in dactylic hexameter already bears witness to an artistic reshaping of language, writing brings linguistic operations of another order. Hugh Kenner, for instance, remarks of that quintessential writer, the author of the modernist novel:

> These are not the maneuvers of a man speaking, but of a man writ-
> ing: a man setting down twelve or fourteen selected words and de-
> termining in what order to arrange them. A man speaking
> arranges larger structural units than words. Frank Budgen recalls
> their discussion of what had been for Joyce a solid day's work: two
> sentences. "You have been seeking the *mot juste?*" "No," said Joyce,
> "I have the words already. What I am seeking is the perfect order
> of words in the sentence. There is an order in every way appropri-
> ate. I think I have it."[85]

The singer, performing under the temporal constraints of improvisation, works at the level of the phrase; he thus relies on a matrix of formulae created and perfected to precisely this end by his oral tradition. The writer, composing under temporal constraints of an entirely different order of magnitude, labors at the level of words; thus, he must not only find his *mots justes* but string these together into an order "in every way appropriate." As Joyce's art amply demonstrates, this "perfect order" need be only distantly related to those sentences generated in natural, spontaneous speech.

Beyond the level of style, writing also brings with it new aesthetic possibilities through a fundamental shift in verbal technique. Specifically, the medium of the written word makes possible at the level of verbal form that artistic technique known as "defamiliarization," namely, inducing aesthetic perception by making the objects of perception strange and unfamiliar. In this sense Zielinski's law gives way to the law of the letter. Indeed, Shklovsky himself, who first proposed defamiliarization as a (or the) defining characteristic of literature, notes in his reading of *Tristram Shandy* how the "ordinary novel" defamiliarized the epic treatment of time: "In an ordinary novel [such as *Don Quixote*] digressions are cut off by a return to the main story. If there are two, or only a few, story lines in the novel, their fragments alternate with one another. . . . Zielinksi notes something entirely different in Homer. Homer never shows two simultaneous actions. If by force of circumstances they ever had to be simultaneous, they were reported as happening in sequence."[86] Sterne would go further still. He "allowed actions to occur simultaneously, and he even parodied the development of the story line and the intrusions of the new material into it."[87] In this way he "lays bare the technique of combining separate story lines to make up the novel. . . . By violating the form, he forces us to attend to it; and, for him, this awareness of the form through its violation constitutes the content of the novel."[88]

Biblical narrative similarly violates, makes strange, the temporal form inherited from the traditions of the ancient Near East, in effect making myth and epic the object of renewed aesthetic perception. At the same time, in achieving simultaneity and employing the technique of defamiliarization, it anticipates important formal features of the modern novel. By recognizing these analogies between the Bible and the novel, the way is cleared for a renewed perception of the literary history of the West. For inasmuch as the history of *literature*, of written verbal art, traces a process of defamiliarization, it begins not with the novel, nor with Homer, but with the Bible. In fact, defamiliarization affects not only the temporal structure of biblical narrative but the operation of a whole array of narrative devices. In the following chapter I will consider the notion of defamiliarization in more detail and trace its workings in one representative formal device common to both biblical narrative and epic, namely, the type-scene.

•6•

THE ART OF BIBLICAL NARRATIVE AS TECHNIQUE: MAKING STRANGE THE TRADITION

> The indication of tone of voice and varying speeds of utterance.
> In that, Homer is never excelled by Flaubert or James or any of
> 'em. But it needs the technique of one or more life times.
> —Ezra Pound, *Letters: 1907–1941*

> It is doubtful whether in the course of the centuries, though we
> have learnt much about making machines, we have learnt much
> about making literature. We do not come to write better; all that
> we can be said to do is to keep moving, now a little in this direc-
> tion, now in that, but with a circular tendency should the whole
> course of the track be viewed from a sufficiently lofty pinnacle.
> —Virginia Woolf, "Modern Fiction"

The Bible as Literature

In the preceding chapters I have provided a series of arguments for viewing biblical narrative as the product of a written verbal art that should be
counterposed to the oral verbal art of Homer and the Ugaritic narrative
poems. At the same time, however, biblical narrative shares certain formal
compositional devices with oral-traditional poetry, and a number of scholars have taken these as evidence of the Bible's orality. I noted in chapter 1,
for instance, how Umberto Cassuto—though not concerned with oral traditions per se—called biblical literature a "continuation of the old in its
forms"[1] based on the "linguistic tradition" of "fixed idioms and expressions" apparently joining Ugaritic poetry to the Bible,[2] thus inaugurating
that scholarly school of thought emphasizing the formal continuities that
exist between the Bible and its predecessors.

This project finds perhaps its fullest expression in the work of Susan
Niditch, who has linked biblical literature to the purportedly oral culture
of ancient Israel.[3] In her summation of this area of research, she observes:

161

Biblical authors of various periods and persuasions composing in a variety of genres share a set of traditional ways to express particular ideas or to create particular images. We cannot link these seeming formulas with systematic metrical and prosodic patterns, nor with strictly poetic texts at all, but the language of the Bible is much more stylized and conventionalized, than, for example, the writing in a modern novel or poem and involves variations on certain formulaic patterns of language.

She therefore hypothesizes:

While biblical works cannot be proven in any instance to have been orally composed, the written works of the Hebrew Bible evidence traits typically associated with ascertainably orally composed works. They belong somewhere in an "oral register." This phrase refers not to modes of composition but to the style of compositions whether the works were created orally or in writing, whether they are performed or read to oneself.[4]

If Niditch shrewdly avoids the strong thesis of an oral composition, her notion of an "oral register," comprising both oral and written works, whether performed or read to oneself, is nonetheless too broad. In fact, even the most "conventionalized" or "stylized" literature is not necessarily "oral" in any meaningful way. As Robert Alter aptly observes, all literature follows certain conventions, albeit to varying degrees:

A coherent reading of any art work, whatever the medium, requires some detailed awareness of the grid of conventions upon which, and against which, the individual work operates. It is only in exceptional moments of cultural history that these conventions are explicitly codified, as in French neoclassicism or in Arabic and Hebrew poetry of the Andalusian Golden Age, but an elaborate set of tacit agreements between artist and audience about the ordering of the art work is at all times the enabling context in which the complex communication of art occurs.[5]

In the present context Virgil is even more to the point. As an "epic" consciously imitating Homer's style, Niditch would undoubtedly place the *Aeneid* somewhere in an "oral register," but to posit any connection between this written work and orality as such would be a grave error. To imitate an oral tradition is not to be a part of that tradition. For the same reason, "oral register" is equally misleading as a description of biblical narrative. I appeal once again to David Bynum's incisive remark: "One obvious historical fact is that the four Samson stories are not epic, ballad, or folktale. They are patently annalistic. . . . Whatever traces of oral traditional diction might subsist in them have therefore surely entered the Hebrew text through the agency of a literary retailer rather than by dictation from an oral traditional *raconteur*."[6] In other words, traces of oral diction may "subsist" in a literary work without it for that reason being "oral," for the activity of the "literary retailer" crucially divides between the "annalistic" and the "oral traditional." It only remains to justify the differentiation between oral and written verbal art at the level of formal composition.

I believe one finds such an argument in the examination of technique. While biblical narrative shares with oral-traditional epics certain formal features, and while they likely point to an actual historical relationship between the two, careful analysis reveals that these two modes of narrative operate according to fundamentally different aesthetic principles that bestow upon their respective traditions different narrative possibilities. Specifically, one must distinguish between the conventions of literature and the rules of tradition. In order to account for this distinction, I will invoke two theories of verbal art: Walter Benjamin's description of the storyteller's craft and Victor Shklovsky's definition of art as "defamiliarization." The evidence for my thesis comes from one formal compositional device common to both biblical narrative and oral epic, namely, the type-scene.[7] I will not attempt to discover previously undetected examples of this narrative device, nor give it a radically new interpretation. Rather, I have the more modest aim of using the type-scene as a point of comparison for bringing the distinctive features of our two narrative traditions into proper relief.

The Familiar and the Strange

Victor Shklovsky begins his programmatic essay "Art as Technique" by confronting the very problem of defining art, especially literature.[8] He rejects those definitions based on a particular device or rhetorical figure—imagery, for example—in favor of one based on technique itself, that is, the manner in which any given device is employed, thus crucially generalizing the criterion of art. He specifically proffers a technique he calls "defamiliarization": "The purpose of art is to impart the sensation of things as they are perceived and not as they are known. The technique of art is to make objects 'unfamiliar,' to make forms difficult, to increase the difficulty and length of perception because the process of perception is an aesthetic end in itself and must be prolonged."[9] In fact, art not only defamiliarizes concrete objects of perception but artistic form itself: "By violating the form, he forces us to attend to it; and, for him, this awareness of the form through its violation constitutes the content of the novel."[10] He thus defines literature self-referentially as the manipulation of literary form, so that form itself becomes the object of renewed aesthetic perception.

One might well wonder whether this definition of art encompasses all of its varieties, or whether it encodes, however brilliantly, merely one of several aesthetic possibilities. In fact, over against Shklovsky's theory of art stands Benjamin's account of the storyteller's craft. It is based not on innovation but on the conservation of tradition. The greatness of a story lies not in its originality but in its seamless derivation "from the speech of the many nameless storytellers," from "that slow piling one on top of the other of thin, transparent layers which constitutes the most appropriate picture of the way in which the perfect narrative is revealed through the layers of a variety of retellings."[11] It is this traditional mode of art, unoriginal in a sense but perfect, that Benjamin means to capture through the designation "craft."

Not coincidentally, Benjamin's storyteller bears a strong resemblance to the epic singer described by Milman Parry, who, as I have already noted, laid the foundation for a revolution in our understanding of Homer precisely by freeing that epic tradition from the aesthetic standards of our modern, literate culture. Already in his master's thesis, in which he reconsiders the implications of Homer's "artificial" *Kunstsprache*, Parry argues that an artistic principle unknown to modern readers underlies the Homeric poems, using ancient Greek sculpture as an analogue:

> By following this traditional design and expression Phidias has filled his work with the spirit of a whole race. . . . Nor, by accepting these broader lines, has he hampered the strength or subtlety of his own personality. He has used them for the further perfection and purification of the popular ideal.
>
> Such is the role of convention in Greek sculpture, and we can now see that its role in epic poetry is much the same. We realize that the traditional, the formulaic quality of the diction was not a device for mere convenience, but the highest possible development of the hexameter medium to tell a race's heroic tales.[12]

His claim that such a style has not "hampered" the poet's "own personality" already anticipates certain objections: What of Homer's presumed "originality"? It is a complicated problem, which I shall not presume to enter into here, raising as it does vexing questions regarding the origins of the Homeric epics. Nonetheless, if the question of Homer's "originality," which, I suggest, is the question of the relationship of his epics to writing—that is, to what degree they are transcriptions of an oral performance or literary compositions merely based on an oral tradition—has yet to be answered definitively, Parry's fundamental thesis concerning the traditional nature of Homer's art still seems unassailable: "For the character of this language reveals that it is a work beyond the powers of a single man, or even of a single generation of poets; consequently we know that we are in the presence of a stylistic element which is the product of a tradition and which every bard of Homer's time must have used."[13] While some critics argue that a certain "individual genius" shines through Homer, suggesting, at least to some extent, the influence of that writerly art more akin to modern sensibilities, the poems still work largely within the inherited tradition.

In this light, let me return to Shklovsky in order to see what he excludes from his theory of literature as not literary. He specifically rejects Potebnya's theory of poetry as "thinking in images" because imagery accounts neither for the history of poetry nor for the poet's individual achievement: "[I]mages change little; from century to century, from nation to nation, from poet to poet, they flow on without changing. . . . The more you understand an age, the more convinced you become that the images a given poet used and which you thought his own were taken almost unchanged from another poet."[14] He highlights instead the question of technique: "The works of poets are classified or grouped according to the new techniques that poets discover and share, and according to their arrangement and development of the resources of language; poets are much more concerned with arranging images than with creating them. Images are *given* to poets; the ability to *remember* them is far more important than the ability to create them."[15] While I do not mean to salvage a theory of art based on imagery, I would like to draw attention to what precedes technique in Shklovsky's theory, namely, those unchanging images which are "given to poets" and which they, in turn, must "remember"—in a word, tradition. One finds, in other words, a temporal distribution of the familiar (traditional) and the defamiliarized, each with its corresponding principles. I propose that Shklovsky's and Benjamin's theories of art do not exclude but rather complement each other. If Benjamin's storyteller, like Parry's Homer, practices a "craft" that Shklovsky's theory does not account for, Shklovsky's notion of defamiliarization, I suggest, gives critical precision to that vague aesthetic criterion referred to often in Homeric studies of all persuasions, namely, the artist's "originality" or "individuality."[16]

The complementarity of oral tradition and literature finds further corroboration in Shklovsky's understanding of perception and its relationship to art. Over against the defamiliarizing "poetic" use of imagery Shklovsky opposes the "practical": "[T]here are two aspects of imagery: imagery as a practical means of thinking, as a means of placing objects within categories; and imagery as poetic, as a means of reinforcing an impression."[17] Practical language observes what he calls "the law of the economy of creative effort," namely, "economizing the reader's or the hearer's attention. To so present ideas that they may be apprehended with the least possible mental effort."[18] Again, what Shklovsky ends up excluding from his theory—those "practical images" that poets must defamiliarize—is precisely tradition.[19] The familiarity of tradition not only facilitates the singer's improvised performance but his audience's live reception as well. Conversely, defamiliarization—that attempt to "reinforce an impression," "to make forms difficult, to increase the difficulty and length of perception" for aesthetic ends—constitutes by definition the very antithesis of any economy of effort.[20]

The precise opposition between Benjamin's and Shklovsky's theories is no mere coincidence, for these two modes of art correspond to two radically different conceptions of experience. For Benjamin authentic experience is "communicable" (i.e., traditional):

> One reason for [the loss of the ability to exchange experiences] is obvious: experience has fallen in value. . . . With the World War a process began to become apparent which has not halted since then. Was it not noticeable at the end of the war that men returned from the battlefield grown silent—not richer, but poorer in communicable experience? . . . For never has experience been contradicted more thoroughly than strategic experience by tactical warfare, economic experience by inflation, bodily experience by mechanical warfare, moral experience by those in power. A generation that had gone to school on a horse-drawn streetcar now stood under the open sky in a countryside in which nothing remained unchanged but the clouds, and beneath these clouds, in a field of force of destructive torrents and explosions, was the tiny, fragile human body.[21]

"Communicable experience," in turn, provides the storyteller with his material, which his craft conserves and disseminates. In stark contrast, Shklovsky defines experience precisely in opposition to routine, to boredom: "If we start to examine the general laws of perception, we see that as perception becomes habitual, it becomes automatic."[22] He invokes Tolstoy to get at this peculiarly modern problem of everyday life:

> I was cleaning a room and, meandering about, approached the divan and couldn't remember whether or not I had dusted it. Since these movements are habitual and unconscious, I could not remember and felt that it was impossible to remember. . . . If some conscious person had been watching, then the fact could be established. If, however, no one was looking, or looking on unconsciously, if the whole complex of lives of many people go on unconsciously, then such lives are as if they had never been.[23]

The purpose of art therefore, at least as Shklovsky understands it, is to redeem experience from the corrosive effect of habit: "Habitualization devours works, clothes, furniture, one's wife, and the fear of war. . . . And art exists that one may recover the sensation of life; it exists to make one feel things, to make the stone *stony.*"[24]

For Benjamin modern warfare destroyed the past's stable, habitual experience of life; for Shklovsky even the fear of war must be rescued from habitualization. What ultimately separates the two is their attitude toward modernity. Shklovsky's understanding of genuine experience is premised on a certain peculiarly modern ideal, namely, a life full of the promise of endless novelty. In his view habit—and, one might add, tradition—is nonexperience, analogous to oblivion ("such lives are as if they had never been"). Benjamin, on the other hand, sees tradition as the very *habitus* of authentic experience. He therefore mourns the passing of the world of his fathers and the subsequent loss of those shared and therefore "communicable" experiences that depended for their existence on the stability of a traditional, unchanging, and consequently habitual world. For this reason the world of the novel is inimical to that of the storyteller. As he regretfully observes, echoing Paul Valéry, modernity has no place for habit:

> The intellectual picture of the atmosphere of craftsmanship from which the storyteller comes has perhaps never been sketched in such a significant way as by Paul Valéry. "He speaks of the perfect things in nature, flawless pearls, full-bodied, matured wines, truly developed creatures, and calls them 'the precious product of a long chain of causes similar to one another.'" The accumulation of such causes has its temporal limit only at perfection. "This patient process of Nature," Valéry continues, "was once imitated by men. Miniatures, ivory carvings, elaborated to the point of greatest

perfection, stones that are perfect in polish and engraving, lacquer work or paintings in which a series of thin, transparent layers are placed one on top of the other—all these products of sustained, sacrificing effort are vanishing, and the time is past in which time did not matter. Modern man no longer works at what cannot be abbreviated."[25]

Valéry's craftsman, imitating the patience of Nature, provides Benjamin with a paradigmatic figure of the storyteller's art: "We have witnessed the evolution of the 'short story,' which has removed itself from oral tradition and no longer permits that slow piling one on top of the other of thin, transparent layers which constitutes the most appropriate picture of the way in which the perfect narrative is revealed through the layers of a variety of retellings."[26] Modernity's impatience and its insatiable desire for change preclude the *durée* of the storyteller's traditional craft.

While Shklovsky and Benjamin both deal with the threshold of modernity, I believe one can detach their arguments from such historical particulars and focus instead on the transition from oral tradition to literature. For if Shklovsky implicitly addresses the question of a written verbal art, Benjamin's attention falls explicitly on "what can be handed on orally, the wealth of the epic," which he opposes to "what constitutes the stock in trade of the novel."[27] Returning to the terms I used in my reading of Judges 4 and 5, let me suggest instead that the relevant threshold is that between the traditional and the post-traditional. While any number of historical factors—which one cannot entirely predict in advance—might contribute to the twilight of tradition, it is surely no coincidence that writing figures in all the evidence invoked thus far.[28] As Plato's Socrates recognized in *Phaedrus* (274–75), its power to *preserve* what once was *conserved* through memory leads to the atrophy of the latter. As a result, the *preservation* (and concomitant petrification) of a once living tradition causes, in turn, the *conservative* art of oral tradition to give way to the *innovative* art of literature.

Specifically, I propose that the oral tradition, comprising *la longue durée*, has that temporal aspect grammarians call "habitual" or "iterative." It is in its "variety of retellings," its countless repetitions in oral performance, that the tradition has its being. Existing as it does in this habitual mode, traditional art is an *art of the familiar*.[29] Literature, coming *after* the tradition, operates according to that other aesthetic principle, namely, *defamiliarization*. As in some sense an "abbreviated" art form (which I will return to in the conclusion to this chapter), it manifests itself not in the iterative series of oral performance but in that singular but fixed event known as the text. As I shall now argue, Homer and biblical narrative correspond, respectively, to traditional and post-traditional modes of art.

Homeric Type-Scenes

In 1933 Walter Arend published a groundbreaking study entitled *Die typischen Scenen bei Homer,* in which he analyzed Homer's tendency to recount certain repeated actions using much the same language, details, and form, or, in his own words, to "repeatedly represent the customary course of an action."[30] In his review of the same, Milman Parry quickly recognized the relevance of these recurring narrative patterns for his own developing theory of Homer's traditional compositional style.[31] To his mind, Arend's "fine and thorough" analysis had contributed to a "real advance of Homeric studies" by "mak[ing] plain how Homer builds his tale by joining and interworking the traditional schemes of composition" and by "mak[ing] clear with exactness wherein [Homer] differs in form from more modern poetries" (405). Parry criticizes him, however, for his explanation of the phenomenon: "Yet for all that he so clearly sees the schematization of Homer's composition, Arend fails almost altogether to understand the reasons for it. . . . Having nothing better, Arend outlines a philosophic and almost mystic theory" (405). The "mystic theory" Parry disapprovingly refers to is Arend's appeal to a vague notion of the supposed Greek insight into *das Wesentliche,* the essential: "To sum up, the Greek sees right through to the essential, and brings it out in the presentation: the structure, the form, the [*eidos*]. But the essential of an incident is that which is constant in all the repetitions. And therefore this type of *journey by land* can and must recur whenever a like happening comes up."[32] Parry offers as an alternative his own theory for Homer's type-scenes, one based on his developing theory of Homer's dependence on an oral tradition:

> The singer of tales, unlike the writer of poetry, is never free of his tradition. He has not learned his art from a varied reading, but only from listening to older singers. He has no pen and ink to let him slowly work out a novel way of recounting novel actions, but must make up his tale without pausing, in the speed of his singing. This he can do only by telling each action as it comes up in more or less the usual way, and in more or less the usual verses which go with that way. . . . The fixed action-patterns and the fixed formulas, of course, depend on one another: an action which each time took a new form would call for new words, and in the same way the

formulas are useful only inasmuch as the singer uses the schemes
of composition in which they are meant to serve. (406)

Drawing an explicit analogy between "fixed action-patterns" and "fixed
formulas," Parry in effect hypothesizes that at both the level of the line
and the scene the singer generates narrative by following the rules of the
tradition.

Parry goes too far, however, in dismissing as "meaningless" Homer's
"play of norm and variation" (407). Objecting to Arend's professed interpretation of type-scenes as "the play between fixed form and varying em-
bellishment . . . between the necessary and the chance, between the typical
and the individual, between repetition and variation,"[33] Parry observes
with relief: "Happily the theory of 'type' and 'variation' is so tenuous a
thing that it has had almost no effect at all upon Arend's analysis itself,
which thus remains good. . . . The healthy result . . . shows itself in his not
finding falsely subtle meanings in the repetitions, as meant to recall an earlier scene where the same words are used" (407). In other words, Parry suggests that it would be a modern interpretive gesture to look for the telling
deviation from the norm in Homeric type-scenes. Despite of the danger of
"falsely subtle" interpretations, an adequate theory—even one that strives
to reconstruct a *traditional* aesthetic—should account for rather than sum-
marily dismiss as irrelevant the variation as well as the type. In his book-
length treatment of the battle scenes in the *Iliad,* Bernard Fenik in effect
addresses this weakness in Parry's theory while remaining true to its underlying premise:

> The passage is, therefore, a *unique* combination of *familiar* details.
> The technique shows that when the poet, who constructed all his
> battle scenes out of typical details, wished to narrate an especially
> long, difficult, or important fight, he did so not by inventing a new
> action or new details, but by the larger than average accumulation
> of familiar details. An especially significant combat is given the
> weight and length that it deserves by the simple process of addi-
> tion and lengthening.[34]

In other words, even the variation of a type-scene derives from the tradition itself, is "typical" on some larger scale. Homer's use of the type-scene,
like the formula, must be understood as part of a still living tradition
which can generate type-scenes, variations and all. It is not a question of
defamiliarizing convention but of more or less fully realizing it.

In order to characterize more precisely Homer's technique for playing with convention, I would like to draw a loose analogy with transformational grammar. If one thinks of the fixed basic pattern as the type-scene's primary narrative "syntax," its "deep structure," then Homer varies the arming scenes by inserting optional "modifiers," yet he never "transforms" the pattern's fundamental structure. Think of a simple sentence such as: "The cat sat on the rug." It is perfectly well formed on its own. One could add adjectives, even certain subordinate clauses, without transforming or altering the sentence's basic syntax, its underlying structure: "The black cat sat on the Persian rug." Or, "The black cat sat on the Persian rug that was in the middle of the room." Such is not the case with a sentence such as, "On the rug there sat a cat." In this case one finds the wholesale "transformation" of the original sentence into a secondary form. The analogy with generative grammar is admittedly imprecise from a linguistic standpoint, but it does help to define the technique shaping Homer's type-scenes: variation without transformation. For, as I will now demonstrate, however Byzantine Homer's additions to the type-scene's basic form, they remain discrete insertions within his narrative syntax. In this sense the variations observable within the Homeric type-scene are "well behaved," that is, they operate within precisely defined boundaries.

One sees this in Homer's use of the "arming" type-scene, which occurs four times in the *Iliad:* the arming of Paris (3.328–38), Agamemnon (11.16–46), Patroclus (16.130–44), and Achilles (19.364–91) (see table).[35] All four scenes perfectly conform to a fixed underlying pattern: six obligatory elements, always in the same order (italicized in the table). Thus, each begins with an introduction signaling to the audience the type-scene's onset: each hero "puts on" or "helms" himself with "armor" or "shining bronze." Next, he puts on "greaves" and "corselet" in the course of three lines, which appear verbatim in all four scenes, highlighting the formulaic nature of Homeric technique: "First he placed along his legs the fair greaves linked with / silver fastenings to hold the greaves at the ankles. / Afterwards he girt on about his chest the corselet" (3.330–32 = 11.17–19 = 16.32–34 = 19.69–71). Then, in the remaining four sections, the hero takes up precisely the same four implements in precisely the same order: sword, shield, helmet, and spear. This fixed sequence of elements constitutes what one might think of as the type-scene's primary "syntax" or "deep structure."

Each required element can and does receive an optional "modifier" in at least one of the arming scenes (roman typeface). By calling such passages "modifiers," I mean to suggest that they function like adjectives and adverbs within the scene's "syntax." They particularize each scene with respect to its hero by elaborating or expanding upon the basic elements of

The "Arming" Type-Scene in the *Iliad*

Paris (3.328–38)	Agamemnon (11.16–46)
while he put [eduseto] *about his shoulders his splendid armour* (teuchea), brilliant Alexandros, the lord of lovely-haired Helen.	*. . . while he himself put* [eduseto] *the shining bronze* [nōropa chalkon] *upon him.*
First he placed along his legs the fair greaves linked with silver fastenings to hold the greaves at the ankles. Afterwards he girt on about his chest the corselet of Lykaon his brother since this fitted him also.	*First he placed along his legs the fair greaves linked with silver fastenings to hold the greaves at the ankles. Afterwards he girt on about his chest the corselet* that Kinyras had given him once, to be a guest present. For the great fame and rumour of war had carried to Kypros how the Achaians were to sail against Troy in their vessels. Therefore he gave the king as a gift of grace this corselet. Now there were ten circles of deep cobalt upon it, and twelve of gold and twenty of tin. And toward the opening at the throat there were rearing up three serpents of cobalt on either side, like rainbows, which the son of Kronos has marked upon the clouds, to be a portent to mortals.
Across his shoulders he slung the sword with the nails of silver, a bronze sword,	*Across his shoulders he slung the sword, and the nails upon it were golden and glittered,* and closing about it the scabbard was silver, and gold was upon the swordstraps that held it.
and above it the great shield, huge and heavy.	*And he took up the man-enclosing elaborate stark shield, a thing of splendour.* There were ten circles of bronze upon it, and set about it were twenty knobs of tin, pale-shining, and in the very centre another knob of dark cobalt. And circled in the midst of all was the blank-eyed face of the Gorgon with her stare of horror, and Fear was inscribed upon it, and Terror. The strap of the shield had silver upon it, and there also on it was coiled a cobalt snake, and there were three heads upon him twisted to look backward and grown from a single neck, all three.
Over his powerful head he set the well-fashioned helmet with the horse-hair crest, and the plumes nodded terribly above it.	*Upon his head he set the helmet, two-horned, four-sheeted, with the horse-hair crest, and the plumes nodded terribly above it.*
He took up a strong-shafted spear that fitted his hand's grip.	*Then he caught up two strong spears edged with sharp bronze* and the brazen heads flashed far from him deep into heaven. And Hera and Athene caused a crash of thunder about him, doing honour to the lord of deep-golden Mykenai.

Patroclus (16.130–44)	Achilles (19.364–91)
. . . *and Patroklos was helming* [korusseto] *himself in bronze that glittered* [nōropi chalkǭ].	. . . *within whose midst brilliant Achilleus helmed* [korusseto] *him.* A clash went from the grinding of his teeth, and his eyes glowed as if they were the stare of a fire, and the heart inside him was entered with sorrow beyond endurance. Raging at the Trojans he put on [*duseto*] the gifts of the god, that Hephaistos wrought [*teuchōn*] him with much toil.
First he placed along his legs the fair greaves linked with *silver fastenings to hold the greaves at the ankles.* *Afterwards he girt on about his chest the corselet* *starry and elaborate of swift-footed Aiakides.*	*First he placed along his legs the fair greaves linked with silver fastenings to hold the greaves at the ankles.* *Afterwards he girt on about his chest the corselet.*
Across his shoulders he slung the sword with the nails of silver, *a bronze sword,*	*Across his shoulders he slung the sword with the nails of silver,* *a bronze sword,*
and caught up the great shield, huge and heavy.	*and caught up the great shield, huge and heavy* and from it the light glimmered far, as from the moon. And as when from across water a light shines to mariners from a blazing fire, when the fire is burning high in the mountains in a desolate steading, as the mariners are carried unwilling by storm winds over the fish-swarming sea, far away from their loved ones; so the light from the fair elaborate shield of Achilleus shot into the high air.
Over his powerful head he set the well-fashioned helmet *with the horse-hair crest, and the plumes nodded terribly above it.*	*And lifting the helm he set it* *massive upon his head, and the helmet crested with horse-hair* shone like a star, the golden fringes were shaken about it which Hephaistos had driven close along the horn of the helmet. And brilliant Achilleus tried himself in his armour, to see if it fitted close, and how his glorious limbs ran within it, and the armour became as wings and upheld the shepherd of the people.
He took up two powerful spears that fitted his hand's grip, only he did not take the spear of blameless Aiakides, huge, heavy, thick, which no one else of all the Achaians could handle, but Achilleus alone knew how to wield it, the Pelian ash spear which Cheiron had brought to his father from high on Pelion to be death for fighters.	*Next he pulled out from its standing place the spear of his father,* huge, heavy, thick, which no one else of all the Achaians could handle, but Achilleus alone knew how to wield it, the Pelian ash spear which Cheiron had brought to his father from high on Pelion to be death for fighters.

the narrative form. Perhaps the most famous example is that devoted to Achilles' shield (19.74–80), a type of coda to the celebrated description of the same shield found in 18.478–616. It gives suitable heft to that greatest of heroes, arming him with the handiwork of Hephaestus himself. Homer describes Achilles' spear at similar length: "[H]uge, heavy, thick, which no one else of all the Achaians / could handle, but Achilles alone knew how to wield it; / the Pelian ash spear which Cheiron had brought to his father / from high on Pelion to be death for fighters" (19.388–91). Interestingly, these lines appear verbatim in Patroclus's scene (16.141–44) with one telling difference: "only he did not take the spear of blameless Aiakides" (16.140). Great though he is, Patroclus is no Achilles. As a final example, one might note that, as befits the leader of the Achaean host, an august portent accompanies Agamemnon's arming scene as a whole: "And Hera and Athena caused a crash of thunder about him, / doing honor to the lord of deep-golden Mykenai" (11.45–46).

In this way Homer's conventional technique does not violently force individual heroes into an inflexible mold; rather, it allows for the supple adaptation of a fixed pattern. At the same time, however, the underlying pattern retains its integrity as a generic form, for one could delete any or all of the lines in any of the modifiers from any of these scenes without altering its structure or diminishing its internal coherence. Thus, in spite of the considerable amplitude of variation tolerated by the arming type-scene, the nature of Homer's technique is such that all four instances equally embody the convention's form. For this reason Fenik spoke of the "unique combination," the "larger than average accumulation," of "familiar details."[36] One does not find deviations from the expected but rather realizations, with varying degrees of elaboration, of the scene's underlying syntax. From line to scene, all is meant to facilitate rather than impede the perception of narrative form. It is as an "art of the familiar."

Relatedly, the purpose of the variations from one arming scene to another is precisely to facilitate interpretation, namely, by guiding the audience in its evaluation of each hero. Indeed, Homer follows an almost algebraic logic. He adds a mere two lines of modifier to Paris's arming (3.329, 333), six to Patroclus's (16.134, 140–44); Achilles, meanwhile, receives 19.5 additional lines (19.65–68, 74–80a, 82–86, 88–91), Agamemnon an impressive 22 (11.20–28, 30–31, 33–40, 44–46). Paris pales in comparison to Agamemnon; Patroclus may wear Achilles' armor, but he cannot wield his spear. True, Agamemnon and Achilles seem to be virtually equal, at least in terms of their arming scenes. While Achilles dons the gifts of Hephaestus, Hera and Athena punctuate Agamemnon's arming with a clap of thunder. But the conflict between these two heroes, both of whom claim to be the "best of the Achaeans," lies at the very heart of the *Iliad.*

Krischer makes much the same point, on a larger scale, in his impressive analysis of Homer's "aristeiai" (literally "excellences"), large-scale compositional units in the *Iliad* that include as one of its elements an arming type-scene. Each "aristeia" focuses on and tailors itself to the heroes involved, for it is the primary means of establishing their individual worth, that is to say, their relative "excellence": "Without differences between *aristeiai*, all heroes would be equal. Nevertheless the variation is not arbitrary, but it follows clearly defined principles."[37] Such principles, in other words, constrain variation. As with the type-scene, the aristeia's "sequence of elements is never changed, though the number and weight of the individual elements are. The aristeia is thus varied through omission of expected elements and through shift in emphasis" (15).[38] In fact, Homer operates according to a principle that Krischer refers to as an "economy of differences," that is, he achieves as much variation as possible through minimal differences (15). Differences must be economized because the epic performer cannot afford to defamiliarize the tradition and thereby shock his audience, which would only result in confusion. On the contrary, the "analysis of the system" of the aristeiai allows us to discover "the rules of the game which one must know in order to be able to understand the poet's game in his movement" (77–78). In other words, Homer's compositional rules do not serve as the point of departure for ingeniously unexpected deviations, but by guiding the audience at every step they establish the very ground for comprehension. To return to Shklovsky, Homer's technique is not "poetic," in the sense of "increas[ing] the difficulty and length of perception,"[39] but "practical" in the sense of "economizing the reader's or the hearer's attention. To so present ideas that they may be apprehended with the least possible mental effort."[40] It presumes and exploits the audience's *familiarity* with the tradition. This is not to deny the palpable artistry of the *Iliad* and the *Odyssey* but rather to suggest that Homer's storytelling is not "literary." One can better appreciate Homer's traditional craft by considering the radically different art of biblical narrative.

Biblical Type-Scenes

It was Robert Alter who first introduced type-scene analysis to biblical studies.[41] In fact, he did so precisely by reinterpreting Robert Culley's study of biblical narrative as "oral prose."[42] Here is how he recalls his process of discovery: "As I stared at Culley's schematic tables, it gradually dawned on me that he had made a discovery without realizing it. For what his tables of parallels and variants actually reveal are the lineaments of a purposefully deployed literary convention. The variations in the parallel episodes are not at all *random*, as a scrambling by oral transmission would imply."[43] He then goes on to define this "literary convention":

> In order to define this basic convention of biblical narrative, I am going to borrow a concept from Homer scholarship, though a couple of major modifications of the concept will have to be made.[44] Students of Homer have generally agreed that there are certain prominent elements of repetition, one of which has been designated "type-scene." The notion was first worked out by Walter Arend in 1933 (*Die typischen Szenen bei Homer*) before the oral-formulaic nature of the Homeric poems was understood. Since then, the type-scene has been plausibly connected with the special needs of oral composition, and a good deal of recent scholarship has been devoted to showing the *sophisticated* variations on the set patterns of the various type-scenes in the Homeric epics. (50; emphasis added)

Inasmuch as Alter takes Homer's use of the type-scene as a close analogy for the Bible's, he implicitly treats the former as a *literary* artist. This, however, entails an unjustified aesthetic prejudice: the literary is distinguished by its "purposefulness" and "sophistication" from the "random" and presumably unsophisticated character of the oral.[45] Part of the problem is that Culley speaks of "oral transmission" and not oral composition as such. Within a pre-literate culture, a given oral tradition may comprise various lines of transmission, whose variations may appear to be more or less random. (Whether such variation is indeed random or interpretable at some broader cultural level is a separate question which need not concern us here.) However, within a single transmission of an oral tradition—the *Iliad*, for instance—various instantiations of a type-scene may coexist, and their synchronic variation will likely exhibit "the lineaments of a purposefully deployed" (50) verbal art. As we have just seen, however, this art is not "literary."

This is not to dismiss the comparison Alter makes between the Bible's narrative patterns and Homer's type-scenes, but merely to suggest that he glosses over important differences in the deployment of this device in our two traditions. Significantly, Alter himself invokes the Russian formalists in his analysis of the biblical type-scene: "The process of literary creation, as criticism has clearly recognized from the Russian Formalists onward, is an unceasing dialectic between the necessity to use established forms in order to be able to communicate coherently and the necessity to break and remake those forms because they are arbitrary restrictions and because what is merely repeated automatically no longer conveys a message" (62). In light of my analysis of Homer, his oblique reference to Shklovsky's notion of "defamiliarization" already suggests that a fundamentally different principle is at work in biblical narrative. All that remains is to demonstrate the operation of this technique in the Bible's type-scenes. If in the process it becomes apparent that Alter has overestimated the similarity between Homeric and biblical type-scenes, this will not contradict his findings so much as give them their proper significance.

In biblical narrative key births often play themselves out in the form of an "annunciation" type-scene, the importance of the hero being partly indicated by the very employment of this established narrative convention.[46] The Midrash on Genesis already demonstrates an awareness of this convention in a typically astute if elliptical comment: "Wherever 'she had not' [a child] is found, it means that eventually she did have."[47] This type-scene, not unlike Homer's, presupposes an underlying narrative syntax, a set of primary "generative rules," so to speak: the initial fact of barrenness; the annunciation of the apparently impossible and hence portentous birth; and, finally, the conception and birth of the son. At this point, however, the similarity between Homer and the Bible ends. We have already seen that any of the arming scenes in Homer could serve equally well as the model or paradigm of the convention. It is striking, then, that none of the annunciations actually found in biblical narrative conforms precisely to this putative underlying form. This is because the variations exhibited in biblical type-scenes do not consist of mere modifiers. Rather, the very structure of the type-scene changes from example to example. One should not, therefore, conclude that there is no convention; it makes good interpretive sense to posit or reconstruct this implicit norm. But it indicates already the biblical writers' restless impulse to innovate, to transform and reinterpret convention. To continue the analogy I have drawn with generative grammar, if the type-scene's basic underlying form, the convention's norm, constitutes its "deep structure," the biblical writers depart from convention, and play with literary form, by "transforming" this primary narrative syntax.[48] In the next section I will examine how the annunciation type-scene plays itself out in the lives of three successive generations of matriarchs in Genesis. Specifically, I will point out four "transformations" that the biblical writers use to defamiliarize the narrative convention: "substitution," "parenthesis," "movement," and "deletion."[49] Because I view the use of type-scenes as a compositional rather than an editorial technique, I will refer to the underlying Pentateuchal sources, not the redacted (final) version of the text.[50]

"Substitution": Gen. 18:9-15

In Gen. 18:9-15 the so-called Jahwist (J) recounts the annunciation of Isaac's birth. The shock or unfamiliarity of this scene consists partly in its "substitution" of Abraham for Sarah, since the annunciation typically centers on the would-be mother. Sarah's barrenness, established in J as far back as 11:30, has just been emphasized in her abortive attempt to gain a son through her servant, Hagar (16:1-13) — in J the episode immediately preceding this one. Thus, when God's messenger asks Abraham where his wife is, convention would seem to dictate that he now summon her and make his announcement. But the messenger proceeds instead to inform Abraham of Sarah's impending pregnancy, emphasizing his unique significance as the first "patriarch." Sarah, meanwhile, assumes a conspicuously marginal role, played out within the scene as well in her liminal position at the tent door, from which vantage point she merely overhears the annunciation that should be hers. Although J gives no indication of Abraham's personal response to this startling message, Sarah's laughter (18:12) nonetheless stands in marked contrast to the faith her husband demonstrated less than forty verses earlier (according to J): "And he believed in the Lord, and he reckoned it to him as righteousness" (15:6).

A genuine violation of the type-scene ("most peculiar[]," in Alter's words [120]), this transformation is unlike any of the variations in Homer. For an analogy, one might turn to Athena's arming scene in *Il* 5.733-47, inasmuch as here an immortal, as opposed to mortal hero, arms for battle. But, of course, it is no surprise to see the gray-eyed daughter of Zeus preparing for war, as it would be in the case of, say, Helen or Aphrodite. This type-scene admittedly does not follow the tradition's rules (so far as one can discover them) with the same degree of fidelity as the four arming scenes I have already discussed, most likely in recognition of Athena's divine stature.[51] It nonetheless preserves the same general outline and fulfills the same basic function, celebrating the hero in all her splendor and signaling to the audience her impending mission "to smite Ares with painful strokes and drive him out of the fighting" (*Il* 5.763) for the sake of the Achaeans. In syntactical terms, one might think of Athena as representing a particular class of noun—female and divine rather than male and mortal— which necessitates certain syntactical adjustments, while still preserving the overall structure of the scene. Thus, Athena does not simply put on armor over her civilian clothes, as do her male counterparts. Rather, she changes her entire demeanor as a woman, so that the "introduction" (733-

35) to this scene describes her slipping off (*katecheuon*) her "dress which she herself had wrought with her hands' patience" (*peplon . . . hon rh' autē poiēsato kai kame chersin*). She does not put on "greaves" and "corselet," as would a mere mortal, but instead dresses herself in the very "war tunic of Zeus who gathers / the clouds" (*chitōn' . . . Dios nephelēgeretao* [736]).[52] For the same reason, she can do without a sword, taking up instead the aegis (the divine equivalent of a shield) along with a helm and spear—notably in the expected order and with several echoes of other arming sequences (738-47).[53] Finally, the fact that Athena's second arming scene at 8.384-96—I include here for the sake of argument the preparation of the chariot, which may or may not be part of the arming scene proper—repeats verbatim 5.733-37 and 745-752 from her first arming scene[54] demonstrates the formulaic nature of these two scenes, quite apart from their minor divergences from mortal arming scenes.

"Parenthesis": Gen. 18:9-15

Abraham's scene also surprises the knowing reader through the addition of a narrative "parenthesis" that inserts itself between the annunciation of Isaac's birth in 18:9-15 and J's account of the birth itself in 21:1a and 2a[55]—namely, the destruction of Sodom and Gomorrah in Gen. 18:16-19:38.[56] This fateful interlude further emphasizes Abraham's central role in God's designs. God's emissaries decide to inform Abraham of their plans for Sodom and Gomorrah precisely in recognition of his future role, namely, to teach his descendants to "observe the way of the Lord, to do righteousness [*ṣĕdāqâ*] and justice [*mišpāṭ*]" (18:19). I have just noted how J juxtaposes Sarah's incredulous laughter to Abraham's "righteous" faith (*ṣĕdāqâ*, 15:6). J further develops the motif of Abraham's righteousness— while giving us a first glimpse into his emerging role in history—by having him accompany his mysterious visitors toward Sodom and Gomorrah— Sarah has been completely left behind at this point—and bargain with God over the fate of the cities of the plain (18:20-33). In fact, the key term "righteous" (*ṣaddîq / ṣaddîqîm*) functions as a *Leitwort* in this conversation, in the course of which Abraham presumes to ask God: "Shall not the judge of all the earth do justice [*mišpāṭ*]?" (18:25).

Looking beyond the parenthesis to the type-scene's conclusion, one finds that Abraham's divinely sanctioned lineage stands in stark contrast to Lot's incestuously conceived offspring. The contrast is all the more naked in J's narrative, for without Genesis 20, which scholars attribute to the Elohist (E), Isaac's birth immediately follows the birth of Lot's sons. Within the narrative world, in fact, they take place simultaneously. One has it on good authority that Isaac will be born about a year after the announcement

made in Genesis 18—"I will surely return to you at this season next year"
(18:10). Allowing for the usual gestation period, one can likewise surmise
that the events of Genesis 19—from the destruction of Sodom and Gomorrah to the birth of Lot's sons—span approximately one year. A pluperfect,
often lost in translation, makes this temporal coincidence explicit: "And
the Lord *had taken* notice [*wayhwh pāqad*] of Sarah as he had said. And
Sarah conceived and bore to Abraham a son in his old age" (21:1a, 2a). In
other words, after following Lot's story as it unfolds in the hazy aftermath
of divine judgment, J turns back about nine months in order to recount
the parallel fulfillment of divine promise. Lot and Abraham's parting of
ways, begun in Genesis 13 (also in J), comes to term here in the synchro-
nized if antithetical births of the fathers of Israel and of its enemies Moab
and Ammon.

Inasmuch as Alter invokes the Russian formalist notion of "free motif"
(optional elements within a narrative) as one possible means of variation
among instances of a type-scene (118), one might be tempted to analyze
this parenthetical episode as just such a motif.[57] What one finds here, however, is the intrusion of an entirely independent motif. It does not add an
element integrally related to the type-scene proper but altogether interrupts it with foreign narrative material—though, to be sure, the insertion
still has interpretive significance. Meanwhile Homer, as we saw, inserts a
great many optional "modifiers" which—since they can be omitted without disrupting the logical continuity of the scene, but once added fit seamlessly into the scene's progress—constitute genuine "free motifs." To
return briefly to Achilles' arming scene, its expansion results purely from
the addition of a number of "modifiers": 19.365–67, 374–79, 384–86, 388–
91. These free motifs may take the form of additional narrative events:

> A clash went from the grinding of his teeth, and his eyes
>   glowed
> as if they were the stare of a fire, and the heart inside him
> was entered with sorrow beyond endurance (365–67)

or of an adjectival phrase:

> huge, heavy, thick, which no one else of all the Achaians
> could handle, but Achilleus alone knew how to wield it,
> the Pelian ash spear which Cheiron had brought to his
>   father
> from high on Pelion, to be death for fighters in battle.
>   (388–91)

This second example even swerves briefly into a narrative flashback ("spear which Cheiron had brought"), but it in no way constitutes an interruption of the type-scene, since it is syntactically and logically dependent on the crucial noun, namely, the spear.[58] In both cases they provide additional detail to some component of the scene and are thus entirely interpretable within the convention itself, but they are nonetheless entirely expendable.

"Movement": Gen. 25:21–26a

Sarah's promised son, Isaac, eventually marries Rebekah, who receives her annunciation, in turn, in Gen. 25:21–26a (J). Here an element is "moved" out of position, the annunciation taking place *after* conception. Rather than predict the conception and birth, it therefore turns to describing the fate of her sons. In this way a mere change in order alters the content of the annunciation and the very function of the scene. It is worth noting here, in light of my discussion of "free motifs," that the type-scene's basic constituents are "bound motifs" in that changing their order affects the logical sequence of the narrative. This scene also makes of Rebekah a striking counterpart to the marginalized Sarah. In stark contrast to her mother-in-law, Rebekah does not passively receive her oracle but rather goes in search of it. It continues the Rebekah of the betrothal type-scene in Genesis 24 (J), who single-handedly waters the camels under Abraham's servant's care. It anticipates the Rebekah of Genesis 27 (also J), who will help her favorite, Jacob, deceive both her husband and her firstborn son.

As such, the technique of biblical narrative marks a radical departure from the Homeric. As we have seen, Homer's type-scenes consist of an unchanging outline of events. In all four instances we find the same six components in precisely the same order. Even Athena's arming scene (5.733–47), allowing for the slight adjustments analyzed earlier, follows more or less the expected order: introduction, aegis, helm, and spear.

"Deletion": Gen. 30:1–3 and 22–23a[59]

Finally, Rebekah's chosen son, Jacob, marries Rachel, who as the next matriarch in line after Sarah and Rebekah, seems destined to receive her annunciation in turn. But in Gen. 30:1–3 E brings us instead to the limits of formal deformation, raising the possibility of a type-scene only to deflect or "delete" it. The narrative immediately establishes Rebekah's barrenness, which under normal circumstances would signal the onset of the type-scene. Instead, a frustrated Rachel tries, in effect, to dispense with formalities, demanding of Jacob rather than God that he provide her with sons. In his heated response, Jacob (with a touch of literary self-referentiality) seems to object to her plea on the grounds that her impossible demand not only usurps God's role but violates the convention's protocol. E further teases the reader with the elided type-scene in his account of Rachel's eventual pregnancy, which reads like the fulfillment of a typical annunciation: "And God remembered [*wayyizkōr*] Rachel, and God heard her and opened her womb. And she conceived and bore a son [*wattahar wattēled bēn*]" (30:22–23a). Compare this with the conclusion of Hannah's annunciation scene: "And Elkanah knew Hannah his wife, and the Lord remembered her [*wayyizkĕrehā*]. And it was at the period of days, and Hannah conceived and bore a son [*wattahar . . . wattēled bēn*]" (1 Sam. 1:19b–20a). The fulfillment of Rachel's longing for a son, suggesting as it does that she did eventually direct her request to God, only foregrounds the excluded middle of the annunciation itself. In fact, the specter of this deleted type-scene will haunt the would-be matriarch. While she eventually bears two sons, she will die while giving birth to the second. In the ensuing family drama that sets her firstborn, Joseph, against his brothers, the eponymous ancestors of the tribes of Israel, Joseph will be displaced as a future tribe by his own sons, Ephraim and Manasseh. And neither of these half-tribes will produce the royal line of the future kingdom of Israel. That honor will fall to a son of Rachel's rival and sister, Leah.

Again, the biblical technique departs from the Homeric. One does find two partially realized arming scenes in the *Iliad*, but these are not deflected or deleted in the same way. Here is Teucer's:

> [Aias] spoke, and Teukros put away the bow in his shelter
> and threw across his shoulders the shield of the fourfold
>   ox-hide.
> Over his mighty head he set the well-fashioned helmet
> with the horse-hair crest, and the plumes nodded terribly
>   above it.
> Then he caught up a powerful spear, edged with sharp
>   bronze,
> and went on his way, running fast, and stood beside Aias.
>   (*Il* 15.478–83)

This scene skips over the introduction, greaves-corselet, and sword.[60] Even in this shortened form, however, Teucer picks up shield, helmet, and spear in proper order. One must also consider that Teucer's bow has just been rendered useless by Zeus, leading Ajax, his brother, to cry out: "Dear brother, then let your bow and your showering arrows / lie. . . . / But take a long spear in your hands, a shield on your shoulder" (15.472–74). Not only does this directive help explain why Teucer opts not to take up his sword, but it effectively signals his arming scene, rendering otiose the more conventional "introduction," for as soon as he puts down his bow the audience knows that he is following his brother's advice. Furthermore, since Teucer is already in the midst of battle, the greaves-corselet sequence—appearing verbatim in the four examples examined earlier—also becomes unnecessary. Teucer's arming is partial because his need for preparation is partial. What one does find falls entirely within the bounds of tradition. Similarly, Athena's second arming scene (8.384–91), alluded to briefly earlier, presents a shortened version of the convention, eliminating mention of aegis and helmet. Otherwise, however, it repeats verbatim her first arming. It seems likely, then, that this second scene is neither "deflected" nor "distorted" but rather curtailed through a type of narratorial "shorthand" meant to limit verbatim repetition. The ellipsis takes place at the level of reportage—not at the level of the underlying form—of the events themselves. Such shorthand may be further motivated by the fact that, not unlike Teucer's "inconsequential" arming, Athena does not complete this second mission with Hera but aborts under threat of punishment at the hands of her all-powerful father (8.425–37). In neither scene, then, does Homer depart from convention.

Ugaritic Type-Scenes

The Ugaritic narratives again conform to the mode of epic. Although the evidence is scant, it will prove instructive to consider the two examples of the annunciation type-scene found in Ugaritic epic. The *Aqhat Epic* begins with the childless Danel trying to invoke divine assistance for begetting an heir. Simon Parker rightly identifies it as a type-scene, though he does not focus on the annunciation as such: "The course of this section of the poem is a familiar one in ancient Near Eastern literature. Its main structural elements are as follows: (1) the introduction of the hero as childless; (2) the appeal to the god; (3) the god's favorable response; (4) conception and birth"[61]—the very convention we have seen in biblical narrative. Modifying Parker's outline slightly, I would like to focus on the scene of annunciation itself:[62]

1.17.1.15–16	Arrival (Baal to Danel/El)
1.16–33	Appeal for blessing (Baal to El)
1.34–48	Blessing (El to Baal)
2.1–8	Annunciation (El to Baal or messenger to Danel)

2.8–23	Danel's reaction
2.24–40	Danel's fertility rite with the Katharat
2.41–46	Conception and birth

Although Parker interprets El's annunciation to Kirta in the *Kirta Epic* as a "marriage blessing" (162), it too foretells the birth of sons and daughters, presenting a strikingly similar scene:

1.15.2.11	Arrival (gods to Kirta)
2.12–16	Appeal for blessing (Baal to El)
2.16–3.16	Blessing and annunciation (El to Kirta)
3.17–19	Departure of gods
3.20–25	Conception and birth

As expected, we find more or less the same events in the same order.[63] Although the annunciation to Danel occurs in two stages—El first speaking to Baal, who then relays the message to the mortal hero (possibly through a messenger, though one cannot know for certain due to damage to the text)—this has little impact on the logical progression of the type-scene.[64] It is striking, furthermore, that in both narratives Baal serves as an intermediary between the hero and El:

Aqhat: "Bless him [*ltbrknn*], Bull, El my father,
      Prosper him [*tmrnn l*], Creator of Creatures" (1.17.1.23–24)
Kirta: "Won't you bless [*ltbrk*] the Noble Kirta?
      Prosper [*ltmr*] the Pleasant, [Lad] of El?" (1.15.2.14–16)

The actual blessings, corresponding to the initial requests, are equally typical:

Aqhat: "El takes [a cup] in his hand [(*ks*) *yiḥd.il.!bdh*].
      He blesses [*ybrk*] [Dan]el, man of Rapiu,
      Prospers [*ymr*] the hero, [man of the] Harnemite": (1.17.1.34–36)
Kirta: "[El] holds a cup in his hand [*ks. yiḥd / (il. b)yd.*]
      A chalice he holds in his right.
      He blesses, yes, blesses [*brkm. ybrk*] [his servant];
      El blesses [*ybrk*] Kirta [the Noble,
      Prosp]ers [(*ymr*) *m*] the Pleasant, Lad of El": (1.15.2.16–20)

Danel's reaction to the annunciation as well as his performance of a fertility rite (ritual meal) with the Katharat, neither of which has a counterpart in Kirta's scene, seem to be "optional modifiers." Since they are both relevant to the type-scene, however, they do not constitute a parenthesis like the one between the annunciation and actual account of Isaac's birth. In fact, one might compare Danel's fertility rite with the Katharat, unanticipated, as far as one can tell, by any instruction in El's blessing or Baal's annunciation, with Kirta's unsolicited vow to Asherah (1.14.4.34–43) —also a fertility rite inasmuch as he seeks to secure a wife as a necessary precondition for begetting children—perhaps a clue that this, too, is a traditional plot motif.

Parker is thus right to contrast biblical to Ugaritic narrative:

> In Ugaritic literature, the plot progresses through largely stereotyped descriptions of actions which may be extended and slowed down by epic repetition or repetition with a numerical framework. . . . Speeches too may be quite conventional and may be repeated to fill out a scene. . . . Biblical narrative . . . may be characterized generally by contrast with these features. . . . The more flexible use of language—a function of prose composition, as against traditional verse composition—allows more sensitive portrayal of character and more subtle recounting of and commenting on action. (228)

More precisely, biblical narrative—especially at the level of narrative form—defamiliarizes the tradition. The reader may have observed, for instance, that in Aqhat and Kirta the human recipient of the annunciation is male, which, Parker observes, is generally the case in ancient Near Eastern traditions: "It is again characteristic of many of the biblical stories that the central character is the childless *woman*—whereas all the ancient Near Eastern treatments of the subject focus on the man" (105). In other words, in biblical narrative the very convention of the annunciation already depends on a revision, a reappropriation of the tradition from the perspective of the mother manquée. Ironically, by defamiliarizing the convention yet again, the annunciation featuring Abraham as the center of attention returns it like a double negative to the original form.[65]

Transformational Art

Through such juxtapositions, the respective techniques of Homer and the Bible come into proper perspective. On the one hand, Homer follows certain primary rules of composition in order to generate his type-scenes, variations and all. In this way he never leaves the familiar terrain of tradition. Biblical narrative, on the other hand, performs secondary operations, or "transformations," upon the convention's underlying syntax or "deep structure." Its defamiliarizing art treats the type-scene's norm as a mere point of departure. Inasmuch as one thinks of narrative, first and foremost, as a sequence of events, the "movement transformation" perhaps brings most clearly into focus the issue at hand. Homer, for whom it would be unthinkable to distort the formal conventions of his art, works entirely within the constraints of the tradition, composing type-scenes that all follow the same basic order of events. Meanwhile, the biblical writers systematically displace, distort, and even delete the type-scene's expected constituents, forcing their readers to perceive literary form anew.

As a consequence, the function and meaning of biblical type-scenes differ radically from one example to the next. It sheds light in unpredictable ways on the mother or father of the soon-to-be-born child, while providing information of the child's birth or even destiny. It is instructive that one finds an occasional hint of self-referential play, as in Rachel's attempt to circumvent the annunciation type-scene. In fact, as Alter has observed, the biblical writers could distort the convention to the point of satire and parody, as in Eli's unwitting annunciation to Hannah in 1 Samuel 1 or Elisha's coldly perfunctory transaction with the Shunamite woman in 2 Kings 4:8–17.[66] One should, finally, mention the annunciation Samson's parents receive in Judg. 13:2–25. In this example the divine proclamation in a sense takes place three times: the "real" annunciation to the mother; her report of it to her husband; and the "command performance" for Manoah himself. At each step the point of this parodic repetition is Manoah's obtuseness: like father, like son. Such ironic effects would be unthinkable for Homer, who still fully inhabits his tradition. Here the variations particularize or individualize each occurrence of the type-scene, yet always in the interest of characterizing the hero, especially with respect to his place within the heroic hierarchy: Agamemnon before Paris, Achilles before Patroclus.

Once again writing marks the crucial boundary, this time between the aesthetic principles of familiarity and defamiliarization. The exigencies of oral performance necessitated Homer's economy of style, the formal purity of his type-scenes. To defamiliarize the tradition as the biblical writers did, conversely, is a more costly procedure. The pen, like a scalpel, can dissect and reassemble literary form, but only through the lengthy procedure of writing and rewriting.

It is no coincidence, then, that when we turn to a written epic, even one that consciously imitates Homer's art, we find it making strange the conventions inherited from its great predecessor. This, at least, is what Krischer convincingly demonstrates concerning "scene-patterns" in Virgil: "Vergil has taken over Homeric content but not Homeric form, and so used Homeric motifs to produce an unhomeric effect."[67] In Virgil's writerly practice, as in the Bible's, one can genuinely speak of disappointed expectations: "Each single motif brings with it from Homer an expectation about where it will stand in a scene, what kind of scene it will stand in, how the motif will be connected with other motifs and what function and significance it will have. By not fulfilling these expectations Vergil systematically achieves original and meaningful effects" (143). He thus demonstrates how Virgil displaces motifs, alters their function, changes their context, or deletes an expected motif, much like the "transformations" in biblical narrative. Virgil, as an epic *writer* following in the wake of the tradition, practices an art of defamiliarization.

While the use of formulae is often taken as the hallmark of oral composition, some scholars believe the type-scene may prove to be more crucial for identifying oral-traditional narratives. For instance, Mark Edwards, in a bibliographic survey and summary of type-scenes research, observes: "Use of type-scenes is probably a better test for orality, at least in Greek poetry, than use of formulae."[68] He echoes earlier observations by Parry ("The arguments by the characterization of oral style [of which the most important is probably the theme (type-scene)] will prove only the oral nature of the Homeric poems")[69] and Michael Nagler ("By his use of this type of structure and technique [and not, I fear, by formula count] the spontaneous-traditional poet really differentiates himself from the writer").[70] Presumably these scholars reason that a writer can more easily affect a traditional style at the level of the formula than at the level of the scene. In light of my comparative analysis, however, we must contend with the possibility of type-scenes—and other ostensibly oral-traditional *devices* —that are yet un-Homeric or post-traditional. Following Shklovsky's lead, I therefore propose that one make *technique* itself the crucial touchstone of tradition and of literature. The oral improviser, fully inhabiting his still living tradition, composes entirely according to its rules. The writer, at least to the extent that he has grown apart from the tradition—I will not, in other words, dismiss the possibility of a hybridization of writing and oral tradition—unavoidably (not unlike the non-native speaker of a language) departs from the tradition, instinctively making its forms strange in order to convey his or her post-traditional vision.

Now, from our modern literary perspective it will seem to some that I have exalted the art of biblical narrative at Homer's expense, that I have made the latter into a "primitive" who practices a simplistic art regrettably constrained by tradition. While it is true that I consider Homer's to be a more "natural" art—that is, relatively free of literary "artifice"—I nonetheless maintain that such an accusation would be false. As a parting thought, then, permit me to suggest what in Homer's art is no longer within our reach.

Virginia Woolf, in her brief but remarkable essay "Modern Fiction," makes certain comments on literary history not unrelated to defamiliarization:

> In making any survey . . . of modern fiction it is difficult not to take it for granted that the modern practice of the art is somehow an improvement upon the old. With their simple tools and primitive materials, it might be said, Fielding did well and Jane Austen even better, but compare their opportunities with ours! Their masterpieces certainly have a strange air of simplicity. And yet the analogy between literature and the process, to choose an example, of making motor cars scarcely holds good beyond the first glance. It is doubtful whether in the course of the centuries, though we have learnt much about making machines, we have learnt much about making literature. We do not come to write better; all that we can be said to do is to keep moving, now a little in this direction, now in that, but with a circular tendency should the whole course of the track be viewed from a sufficiently lofty pinnacle.[71]

What she resignedly concedes here is that our modern, post-traditional impulse to innovate, to defamiliarize, comes only at a price: with no overarching principle or goal spanning the generations, writing can only press forward in fits and starts, always from a new starting point, so that in the end its history merely traces an endlessly recapitulating circle.

Not so with the oral tradition. As Benjamin saw so clearly, if the storyteller's craft is conservative, evolving only gradually over time, it is, by that same cumulative logic, capable of attaining to a perfection beyond the reach of the solitary writer. For the storyteller, like the craftsman Paul Valéry describes, imitates that "patient process of Nature," that "long chain of causes similar to one another . . . [that] has its temporal limit only at perfection."[72] Parry came to a very similar conclusion when he recognized in the monumental perfection of Homer's *Kunstsprache* "a work beyond the powers of a single man, or even of a single generation of poets"[73]—just as earlier he argued that Phidias contributed to the "further perfection and purification of the popular ideal."[74] In fact, as Benjamin again recognized, repetition and perfection are but two aspects of the same patient process: "We have witnessed the evolution of the 'short story,' which has removed itself from oral tradition and no longer permits that slow piling one on top of the other of thin, transparent layers which constitutes the most appropriate picture of the way in which the perfect narrative is revealed through the layers of a variety of retellings."[75] *La longue durée* of oral tradition, in other words, is not only "iterative" or "habitual" but also, as the grammarians would say, "progressive." For these retellings accumulate through the generations like thin layers, approaching, however asymptotically, that "perfection" which is its "temporal limit," namely, the realization and refinement of the inherent possibilities of the tradition's underlying medium. Thus, as tradition recedes into the past, so too does the ideal of a truly perfected art.

I don't mean to suggest that the writer cannot work to refine his or her craft. In an important sense, however, the art of writing—whether of the novel, the short story, or biblical narrative—is "abbreviated," living and dying with the individual writer. The writer comes after the tradition and therefore stands outside it. While he assumes his place in what one might call the "literary tradition," this does not so much inspire him as constrain him. As Barthes observes in his discussion of the writer's freedom: "True, I can today select such and such mode of writing, and in so doing assert my freedom, aspire to the freshness of novelty or to a tradition; but it is impossible to develop it within duration without gradually becoming a prisoner of someone else's words and even of my own."[76] The fate of writing is the necessity of this freedom. And so writing keeps moving, now in this direction, now in that, but never with a *telos* in sight. Thus, if Ezra Pound's comparison of Homer with Flaubert, James, and company is right, it is not, as he himself implies, entirely fair: "The indication of tone of voice and varying speeds of utterance. In that, Homer is never excelled by Flaubert or James or any of 'em. But it needs the technique of one or more life times."[77]

•7•

CONCLUSION: TOWARD AN ARCHAEOLOGY OF ANCIENT ISRAELITE KNOWLEDGE

> [T]he mental life of primitives (and consequently their institu-
> tions) depend upon this essential primary fact that in their rep-
> resentations the world of sense and the other make but one.
> —Lucien Lévy-Bruhl, *Primitive Mentality*

> For it is quite obvious that Realism is necessarily dualist, and
> that an ontological dualism is always "realist."
> —Alexandre Kojève, *Introduction to the Reading of Hegel*

> [A]lthough different novelists have given different degrees of
> importance to the internal and the external objects of con-
> sciousness, they have never completely rejected either; on the
> contrary, the basic terms of their inquiry have been dictated by
> the narrative equivalent of dualism—the problematic nature of
> the relation between the individual and his environment.
> —Ian Watt, *The Rise of the Novel*

> The concept of God held by the Jews is less a cause than a symp-
> tom of their manner of comprehending and representing things.
> —Erich Auerbach, *Mimesis*

The Novelty of Biblical Religion

There is a tradition of scholarship attempting to account for biblical narrative's peculiar artistic merits with reference to the distinctiveness of Israelite religion. Von Rad, for instance, in his study of Israel's historical
writing, found one of its enabling factors in the "unique religious conceptions of this people":

From the earliest times Israel had been accustomed to see in every
unusual event the direct intervention of God. Old Testament man

190

attributed to Yahweh even those occurrences of public or private life which every other religion would have traced to the activity of demons, or other anonymous intermediate beings. . . . Israel owes to its unique religious faith a capacity to see and understand as history what is really no more than a succession of isolated occurrences.[1]

Even Cassuto, who, as we saw, exaggerated the formal continuity between Canaanite and biblical literature, claimed that the Bible was "new" in its "content and spirit."[2] What he means by "new" becomes clear in his reconstruction of "The Epic of the Revolt of the Sea," in which he carefully excavates certain mythic motifs scattered throughout various books of the Bible: "Needless to say, there is a vast difference between the myths of the heathen peoples and those of Israel. The Israelites gave to the traditional material current in the East the distinctive stamp of their ethos, and transformed it in consonance with its own character. . . . The quarrels and fighting between the gods, could not possibly find a place in the poetry of the Israelites, who believed in only One God."[3] Talmon, recognizing, as Cassuto did not, the significance of biblical narrative's *prose*, observes:

> The outstanding predominance in the Bible of straightforward prose narration fulfills the functions for which other literatures revert to the epic genre: heroic tales, historiography, even myth and cosmogony. The phenomenon is too striking to be coincidental. It appears that the ancient Hebrew writers purposefully nurtured and developed prose narration to take the place of the epic genre which by its content was intimately bound up with the world of paganism and appears to have had a special standing in the polytheistic cults. The recitation of epics was tantamount to a reenactment of cosmic events in the manner of sympathetic magic. In the process of total rejection of the polytheistic religions and their ritual expressions in the cult, epic songs and also the epic genre were purged from the literary repertoire of the Hebrew authors.[4]

Citing this very passage, Alter drew attention specifically to the literary consequences of this newly developed prose art: "What is crucial for the literary understanding of the Bible is that this reflex away from the polytheistic genre had powerfully constructive consequences in the new [prose] medium which the ancient Hebrew writers fashioned for their monotheistic purposes."[5]

Some have questioned this school of thought. Edward Greenstein, on the one hand, has argued against those who think that "the development of prose narrative in ancient Israel reflects an ideological innovation," proposing instead that the Bible's preference for prose narration is "purely literary, the result of a difference in genre and not in thought."[6] This "purely literary" choice, in turn, rests on the generic contrast between the "dramatic" character of Ugaritic epic and the "past-oriented" nature of biblical narrative. While Ugaritic epic used the dramatic language of discourse in both its narratives and dialogues in order to maintain its dramatic presentation, biblical narrative emphasized the pastness of the events recounted, reserving the language of discourse for the quoted speech of its characters. Greenstein's argument, however, does not actually solve the problem of the relation between genre and thought but merely defers it. Why did the biblical writers prefer past-oriented narrative—and, indeed, exert much effort in developing it as an art form—while virtually all their neighbors, past and present, and with strikingly few exceptions, preferred the drama of epic? In fact, it is an extreme formalism indeed that would maintain the total isolation of a genre from its historical context. Thus, while I may make a similar distinction between epic and biblical narrative, I draw entirely different conclusions from it. Like scholars of the novel, who link its origins to certain material and intellectual conditions in modernity, such as the printing press[7] and Cartesian philosophy,[8] I will situate the rise of biblical narrative within analogous developments in ancient Israel.

On the other hand, the very claim that Israelite religion was somehow distinctive within the ancient Near East has met with increasing skepticism, partly in reaction to the presumably apologetic impulse informing such arguments, partly on methodological grounds.[9] Peter Machinist, for instance, characterizes the history of scholarship on the supposed "distinctiveness" of biblical Israel as a "cautionary tale."[10] In light of the steady flow of archaeological discoveries from the ancient Near East, he questions whether the search for "trait lists" has unearthed anything genuinely distinctive within Israelite culture:

> On the one hand, there has been a determined search for clear concepts and behaviors which would neatly separate Israel from the cultures being compared with it, which in our present instance means the rest of the ancient Near East. The goal here has been a kind of "trait list." . . . But establishing such traits is an elusive business, to say the least. . . . Indeed, as the increasing volume of archaeological discoveries makes clear, some correspondence always seems to be waiting to be found somewhere in the ancient Near East, not to mention in other regions of the world, for what is proposed as a distinctive concept or behavior in ancient Israel.[11]

As a corrective to this apparently misguided line of research, he continues:

> [A] second approach to distinctiveness has been tried. Here the possibility is allowed that Israel and her Near Eastern neighbors may have shared much the same pool of ideas and behaviors. What, then, is distinctive about each community are the ways in which the ideas were patterned and emphasized. Not individual, pure traits, in short, but configurations of traits become the focus of the modern historian, if he wants to understand the distinctiveness of ancient Israel—or of any culture. . . . There is much in this search for distinctive configurations which makes sense. . . . Plainly, however, there are problems here as well. For how can we be sure that the configurations we have discerned in the data are actually there? And even if they are there, how representative of the given culture are the data we are using?[12]

Machinist raises two different objections. In the latter passage he confronts the considerable problems arising from the limited extent of our data and their ability to support our theories. This is a problem of corroboration, however, and does not impugn the legitimacy of the search itself. A true statement about the past remains so regardless of our ability to excavate compelling evidence in support of it. In fact, this problem casts its shadow on every aspect of research into the Bible and its world—and clearly scholarship has come to live with this unfortunate state of affairs. What is more, inasmuch as the focus throughout this study has been on *biblical* narrative, that is, the canonized sources of ancient Israel, the "official" religion constitutes an entirely appropriate backdrop for my study. Since I will consciously *not* concern myself here with the so-called popular religion of ancient Israel,[13] I can legitimately bracket the otherwise pressing question raised by Machinist as to "how representative" the biblical data is of ancient Israel as a whole. In the former passage, however, he raises the question of distinctiveness as such. What, he asks in effect, should the search for distinctiveness aim to discover?

In the history of thought—or, perhaps better, of knowledge—one finds a number of breaks between what Foucault, the culminating figure in a tradition of French philosophy,[14] famously refers to as "epistemes."[15] In his preface to *The Order of Things*, for instance, he observes of his study:

> Quite obviously, such an analysis does not belong to the history of ideas or of science: it is rather an inquiry whose aim is to rediscover on what basis knowledge and theory became possible; within what

space of order knowledge was constituted; on the basis of what historical *a priori*, and in the element of what positivity, ideas could appear, sciences be established, experience be reflected in philosophies, rationalities be formed. . . . [W]hat I am attempting to bring to light is the epistemological field, the *episteme* in which knowledge, envisaged apart from all criteria having reference to its rational value or to its objective forms, grounds its positivity and thereby manifests a history which is not that of its growing perfection, but rather that of its conditions of possibility; in this account, what should appear are those configurations within the *space* of knowledge which have given rise to the diverse forms of empirical science. Such an enterprise is not so much a history, in the traditional meaning of that word, as an "archaeology."[16]

By opposing his "archaeology" to "history, in the traditional meaning of that word," Foucault indicates that he will dig beneath those surface phenomena treated in traditional intellectual history ("ideas," "science") in order to bring to light the "space" and "configurations"—in a word, the epistemes—that constitute the ground, the "historical *a priori*," of knowledge itself. Furthermore, while this archaeology traces a historical development, the history it maps does not consist of a continuous evolution but rather a series of revolutions, of epistemic ruptures or breaks:

Now, this archaeological inquiry has revealed two great discontinuities in the *episteme* of Western culture: the first inaugurates the Classical age (roughly half-way through the seventeenth century) and the second, at the beginning of the nineteenth century, marks the beginning of the modern age. The order on the basis of which we think today does not have the same mode of being as that of the Classical thinkers. Despite the impression we may have of an almost uninterrupted development of the European *ratio* from the Renaissance to our own day . . . all this quasi-continuity on the level of ideas and themes is doubtless only a surface appearance; on the archaeological level, we see that the system of positivities was transformed in a wholesale fashion at the end of the eighteenth and beginning of the nineteenth century. . . . [A]rchaeology, addressing itself to the general space of knowledge, to its configurations, and to the mode of being of things that appear in it, defines systems of simultaneity, as well as the series of mutations necessary and sufficient to circumscribe the threshold of a new positivity. (xxii–xxiii)

It is these "discontinuities" and "mutations" that archaeology seeks to discover. At such moments knowledge suddenly reconfigures itself, and with it the possibilities of thought. Archaeology, in other words, is no mere notational variant of history. As such, I believe it provides an approach to the problem of the so-called distinctiveness of Israelite religion that responds to those objections recently encountered.

Despite the temptation to draw an analogy between Foucault's notion of "configurations within the space of knowledge" and what Machinist refers to as the search for "configurations of traits," one should note that the former exist at a much deeper level than the latter. For the shifts Foucault discovers mark profound and radical breaks within "the space of knowledge," not within some repertoire of surface "traits," of "concepts and behaviors." (Whether these are conceptually organized as a "list" or a "configuration" makes little difference at this level of analysis.) In Milner's reading of Foucault, in fact, the surface effects of these epistemic breaks constitute what he refers to as "Foucault's thesis": "There are cuts in thought such that there is absolutely no synonymy between the two sides of the cut."[17] In this light one would do well to reconsider Machinist's caution that ostensibly distinctive features of Israelite religion inevitably seem to find "some correspondence . . . somewhere in the ancient Near East," for such correspondences may be only apparent, that is, lacking genuine synonymy.

Since this archaeology seeks to discover the crucial "discontinuities" in the history of knowledge, the expanse of this history will not be of uniform interest. From this point of view, Machinist, laboring under the understandable but unrealistic desire to level (in essence, to "democratize") the field of history, ultimately trivializes the notion of "distinctiveness" by implying that every culture is equally distinctive as a unique combination of an otherwise common store of traits: "What, then, is distinctive about *each community* are the ways in which the ideas were patterned and emphasized. Not individual, pure traits, in short, but configurations of traits become the focus of the modern historian, if he wants to understand the distinctiveness of ancient Israel—or of *any culture.*"[18] Perhaps some such claim could serve as an axiom for the anthropologist, constituting each and every human culture equally as the object of study. For the archaeologist of knowledge, however, not all cultures and historical moments are of equal interest and import. Rather, the archaeologist's attention focuses on particular points in history, such as the rise of science in early modern Europe.

Inasmuch as this archaeology purports to *discover* some real if abstract event in the history of knowledge rather than to *invent* or *construct* some idealized entity—Biblical Israel, Classical Greece, Western Modernity—it does not suffice to dismiss it as a mere instance of cultural chauvinism. Does "Galilean science" constitute its own episteme *distinct* from earlier versions of "science"?[19] The demonstrable successes of modern science — and of physics in particular — suggest that it does. Similarly, I propose that earlier scholars, while perhaps lacking certain analytical tools — as they would eventually be developed by Foucault, for instance — rightly perceived in the rise of biblical religion an intellectual event that marked Israel off from its neighbors.[20] It is no doubt the case that an apologetic impulse often led (and still leads) certain scholars to exaggerate such arguments — for instance, by attributing an "absolute" distinctiveness to Israel, which presumably would provide evidence for some sort of divine revelation within human history. Although in such instances appeal to the divine necessarily remains extraneous to any strictly empirical study, having once bracketed such an appeal, the empirical remains. Thus, Patrick D. Miller can observe of G. Ernest Wright's study *The Old Testament Against Its Environment:* "It is an attempt to argue for the revelatory uniqueness of Israel's faith by laying her religion alongside that of her Near Eastern neighbors to demonstrate both its singular character and its superiority as a religious expression."[21] And yet he is quick to add: "Some of his analyses of the differences, however, may hold up better than is presently recognized."[22]

Such apologetic transgressions do help bring into focus one final contrast between the archaeology of knowledge and previous searches for the distinctive. While the latter takes as its object a given culture — sometimes, as we have seen, even privileging it as some sort of irruption of the absolute into history — Foucault's archaeology takes as its object the history of knowledge as such. Israel, as I will argue, may be a locus of an event in this history and hence privy to a novel mode of thought, but this is neither to limit this event to Israel nor to attribute distinctiveness to Israel in and of itself. One therefore need not deny the possibility that certain neighboring cultures also participated in this epistemic shift, not only the Egypt of Akhenaton but also the immediately adjacent and contemporary cultures of Ammon, Moab, and Edom. Halpern, citing the example of these very cultures, remarks:

> This distribution of evidence reflects Israel's place among the "Hebrew" successor-states to the Egyptian empire in Asia, all of which crystallized at the close of the Bronze Age along the major trade routes from Mesopotamia to Egypt. These states appear uniformly to have devoted themselves to the worship of the national god. . . . On the Mediterranean littoral, adherence to the cult of a

single high god seems to have been taken early as the natural way of things.[23]

Admittedly, maintaining that these neighboring cultures were indeed monolatrous or even monotheistic is not necessarily to place them with Israel to one side of an epistemic break, for an apparent correspondence does not necessarily entail a synonymy of terms. Nonetheless, it seems plausible—even probable—that whatever epistemic break took place in biblical Israel affected such immediately neighboring cultures as well. One would not speak of "Galilean science," for instance, as a specifically Italian intellectual event; mention must also be made of such figures as the Polish astronomer Copernicus and the German physicist Kepler. Furthermore, one should also (as Machinist does) raise the possibility of independent, parallel developments: "[S]ome correspondence always seems to be waiting to be found somewhere in the ancient Near East, not to mention in *other regions of the world.*"[24] While I have already objected to his notion of "correspondence," it seems conceivable that an archaeology of knowledge could discover historically isolated though structurally analogous epistemic breaks. The so-called Axial Age, for instance, may well point to the existence of some set of comparable though unconnected events in the history of knowledge.[25]

I cannot hope to undertake here a full-dress archaeology of ancient Israelite knowledge, let alone of the ancient Near East as a whole or of antiquity at large. In the brief remarks that follow I will simply account for the frequently noted distinctiveness of Israelite religion in terms of an underlying epistemic break, which I will simultaneously attempt to describe. Whether Egypt anticipated this break or Ammon, Moab, and Edom shared in it I leave as open questions whose answers in no way affect my thesis. As an "archaeologist" I will not recount the history of the idea of monotheism in Israel, which is no monolith of religious thought, nor will I focus on the surface concept of monotheism as such. Instead, I will look "within the space of knowledge" for the epistemic break that made it possible for monotheism to be thought at all. As monotheism's "historical *a priori*," it does not coincide with some fully developed version of monotheism—it does not even belong to a history of that idea—but altogether precedes it both temporally and logically. Although I believe this break took place early in Israel's history—one could perhaps find traces of it already in archaic poetry—I will simply present some evidence for it in certain pre-exilic prose sources, a mere "preliminary excavation" to a proper archaeology of ancient Israelite knowledge.

Monotheism and Dualism

In what way does Israelite monotheism constitute or provide an index of an event within the history of knowledge? I take as my starting point the distinction Yehezkel Kaufmann draws between Israelite and pagan religion: "[T]he Bible is utterly unaware of the nature and meaning of pagan religion."[26] Note how the notion of an epistemic break and the lack of synonymy across that break would account for this striking fact. "The mark of monotheism," he continues, "is not the concept of a god who is creator, eternal, benign, or even all-powerful; these notions are found everywhere in the pagan world. It is, rather, the idea of a god who is the source of all being, not subject to a cosmic order, and not emergent from a pre-existent realm; a god free of the limitations of magic and mythology. The high gods of primitive tribes do not embody this idea."[27] Later he similarly observes: "The basic idea of Israelite religion is that God is supreme over all. There is no realm above or beside him to limit his absolute sovereignty. He is utterly distinct from, and other than, the world; he is subject to no laws, no compulsions, or powers that transcend him. He is, in short, non-mythological. This is the essence of Israelite religion, and that which sets it apart from all forms of paganism."[28] It is worth noting that in spite of the intervening years, Baruch Halpern has recently endorsed Kaufman's identification of Israel's "mark of monotheism" in his insightful study of the history of monotheism in Israelite religion: "Although this description may be controversial in its individual components, it does have the virtue of representing fairly some of the characteristic properties of Western monotheisms."[29]

Rather than focus on monotheism as such, however, I would like to draw attention to the configuration of thought implicit in Kaufman's description of Israelite theology, namely, the dualism of mind and matter.[30] Apparently for the first time in the history of knowledge, a metaphysical distinction, however implicit, is made between mental and physical entities. For in conceiving of God as "not subject to a cosmic order" and "utterly distinct from, and other than, the world," the biblical writers/ thinkers abstracted or projected divinity outside of the physical universe, simultaneously constituting the realms of spirit and of matter as such.[31] The God of Israel is primarily and essentially a Will, the ground of subjectivity. By reducing the material world to a mere object henceforth submitted to his Will, Yahweh becomes (as has frequently been noted) the God of history. I would suggest that it is this gesture of thought, whose first appearance is typically attributed to the pre-Socratic philosophers in ancient Greece,[32] that lies at the heart of what has generally been referred to as the distinctiveness of biblical religion.

One finds a similar argument with Henri and H. A. Frankfort, who distinguish between ancient and modern thought precisely according to the epistemological relationship each takes with respect to the external world: "The fundamental difference between the attitudes of modern and ancient man as regards the surrounding world is this: for modern, scientific man the phenomenal world is primarily an 'It'; for ancient— and also for primitive—man it is a 'Thou.' "[33] Unable to make an "It" of the world, "primitive man cannot withdraw from the presence of the phenomena because they reveal themselves to him in the manner we have described. Hence the distinction between subjective and objective knowledge is meaningless to him."[34] For ancient and primitive thought, in other words, the world is a monism. This is the implication of John A. Wilson's study of Egyptian thought as well. He poses the question: "Did the ancient Egyptian see an essential difference in substance between man, society, the gods, plants, animals, and the physical universe?"[35] He answers in the negative: "[T]o the ancient Egyptian the elements of the universe were consubstantial."[36] This metaphysical system he aptly describes as "monophysite," that is, "many men and many gods, but all ultimately of one nature."[37] Similarly, according to the Frankforts, in Mesopotamian thought "the divine was immanent in nature."[38] Conversely, the Frankforts, like Kaufman, assert: "The dominant tenet of Hebrew thought is the absolute transcendence of God. Yahweh is not in nature. Neither earth nor sun nor heaven is divine; even the most potent natural phenomena are but reflections of God's greatness."[39] Although they never quite say so explicitly, they seem to perceive a dualism within Israelite thought: "This conception of God represents so high a degree of abstraction that, in reaching it, the Hebrews seem to have left the realm of mythopoeic thought."[40] In other words, as they conclude elsewhere, "It would seem that the Hebrews, no less than the Greeks, broke with the mode of speculation which had prevailed up to their time."[41] Nature bereft of the divine becomes an "It."

Machinist, as one might expect, takes exception to these claims. While he concedes to Kaufmann that Israel "knew of transcendent divinity," he counters that "it was not the only ancient Near Eastern culture that did. One does not have to search too far among the 'great gods' or 'sky gods' of, say, Mesopotamia to find a deity like Enki/Ea, who, as the extant texts make clear, is no mere 'genius' of the 'sweet waters,' but has a cosmic range as god of wisdom and creation."[42] And yet, if one examines the narrative "Enki and the World Order," which he adduces in support of this claim, one finds that Enki has a bull for his biological father (lines 2 and 62), a brother (64), and perhaps a place of birth (Sumer) figured as the divine maternal womb: "Your fecund matrix, the place where the gods are born." His "cosmic range," in other words, does not prevent him from having a meaningfully material existence that is, in fact, explicitly connected to the mundane, physical world:

> After father Enki lifted his eyes over the Euphrates,
> He stood up like a rampant bull lusting for battle
> Lifts (his) penis, pours out his semen
> Filled the Euphrates(!) with continually flowing water,
> It (the Euphrates) is a cow mooing in the pastures for its
>   young, the scorpion infested stall,
> The Tigris [stands(?)] at his side like a rampant bull,
> He lifted (his) penis, he brought a bridal gift,
> The Tigris rejoiced (in) its heart like a great wild bull,
>   when it was fashioned. . . . (251-58)[43]

The land between the two rivers, in other words, derives its fertility directly from the reproductive potency of Enki's body. As becomes clear, one must specify the meaning of "transcendent." For Machinist it seems to indicate a divinity that has "transcended" its original role as a personification of nature ("no mere genius of the sweet waters"). Conversely, Kaufman, who, as we saw, readily admits that "all-powerful" gods "are found everywhere in the pagan world,"[44] has in mind the more technical meaning of altogether leaving behind the physical world, which is another matter entirely from that of extent of power and/or range.[45]

Monotheistic Mythology

In order to demonstrate the operation of this new episteme, I would like to examine various stories from the so-called Primeval History (Genesis 1-11). While these function as myth inasmuch as they explain how the present world came to be the way it is— indeed, they share a number of motifs with other ancient Near Eastern myths—they present an understanding of the world entirely at odds with "pagan" myth, which is based upon a monistic cosmos. Like the traces of oral tradition still visible in the decidedly literary narratives of the Bible, these mythological motifs demonstrate a legacy of ancient Near Eastern mythology which was nonetheless transformed by Israel's dualist, post-mythic mode of thought.

The Priestly account in Genesis 1—which, following what one might refer to as an Israeli scholarly tradition, I place in the pre-exilic period[46]—

begins by describing the very dualism I have proposed: "When God began to create heaven and earth, the earth was welter and waste, and darkness was upon the face of the deep and the wind of God was hovering upon the face of the waters" (vv. 1–2). While God is described here metaphorically as a wind, he does not, as do the gods in *Enuma Elish,* actually derive from the physical world.[47] Kaufmann thus observes how the motif of "pre-existent stuff" takes on a new significance in biblical cosmology: "In pagan myth . . . the primordial realm is the necessary presupposition for theogony. Divine beings and powers must have a derivation. . . . Lacking a theogony, the Bible has no need of a pre-existent realm."[48] What is equally significant is that the physical world does not derive from God, which fact, in the absence of a precise metaphysical vocabulary, might also have imputed physical substance to the divine. Again, to quote Kaufmann: "Creation is not depicted as a sexual process, nor does it proceed from the seed of the god, his blood, spittle, tears, or the like. The idea of a material emanation from the creator is foreign to the Bible."[49] Instead, the primordial stuff of the universe, like God, has no origin. The originary opposition of wind and water functions in the narrative as a hypostasis of the dualism between spirit and matter. As different as J's account is from P's, he too begins with this dualism of God and material world: "In the day the Lord God made earth and heaven, and no shrub of the field was yet on the earth, and no plant of the field had yet sprouted . . . a flood[50] would rise up from the earth and would water the whole face of the land" (Gen. 2:4b–6). It is upon a blank slate of wet soil that God "made earth and heaven." Although one does not find here P's primordial symmetry between God and deep, this beginning similarly comprises two irreducible realities, neither of which can be said to derive from the other.[51] In both J and P, there is no interest in, no conception of, what precedes a certain point in time. Kaufmann is therefore wrong to argue for a creation *ex nihilo* in Genesis.[52] While the material realm does not precede God, it does not follow that God must therefore precede the world of matter. As we have seen, both versions of creation hold to a third option, an originary dualism. I would add, however, that creation *ex nihilo* is not crucial to Kaufmann's central thesis; one need only revise his characterization of Israel's God as follows: he is not "the source of all being,"[53] nor is there "no realm above or *beside* him to limit his absolute sovereignty."[54] According to both J and P, God did not create everything from nothing. He did not exercise the philosopher's absolute freedom but rather confronted a preexisting material order, a certain necessity. Perhaps the Bible, strictly speaking, "has no need of a pre-existent realm," as Kaufmann suggests, but it remained for Deutero-Isaiah, systematically working out the implications of monotheism in the exilic period, to insist, contra P (Gen. 1:2–3), that God created darkness as well as light (Isa. 45:7).[55]

The creation of humankind in J and P proves similarly instructive. While they share with Mesopotamian tradition the idea that humans are somehow like god(s), somehow different in kind from the beasts, they conceive of this relationship to the immortal realm in a fundamentally different way. In *Enuma Elish,* just as the gods derive from the physical world (and vice versa), so humans derive from the gods. Specifically, they are created out of the blood of a god who is put to death—gods are not quite immortal here—for his part in an unsuccessful attempt to maintain the primal order of the chthonic gods (Tiamat et al.). As a result, there is a mutual, substantive interchange between mortals and immortals, which are thus metaphysically joined. It is humanity's consubstantiality with the divine, a type of numinous genetic legacy, that makes humans like the gods.[56] In stark contrast, Gen. 2:7 recounts how God forms the first man out of "dust from the ground," thus maintaining the metaphysical divide between mortals and the immortal. God may animate this man with the "breath of life" (*nišmat ḥayyîm*), but it merely represents the principle of life as it derives from God. It does not indicate a divine–human material continuity. Thus, at this initial stage they are not yet "like God," having only the ontological status of a "living being" (*nepeš ḥayyâ*), which they share with the rest of the animal kingdom (2:19). To be "like God," as both the serpent promises (3:5) and God later concedes (3:22), is to have knowledge. Humans, according to J, don't passively acquire it by partaking of the divine substance but rather by seizing it for themselves in the form of a magical fruit—a supernatural substance, to be sure, but one having no connection to the immortal body.[57] In Genesis 1 one finds a similar situation in P's notion of the "image" (*ṣelem*) and "likeness" (*dĕmût*) of God. While these terms might be taken to suggest a physical resemblance, such an interpretation seems unlikely within the context of P's patently abstract theology, which scrupulously avoids anthropomorphizing God.[58] Rather, if one compares the blessings bestowed upon humans in 1:28 with those bestowed upon sea creatures in 1:22, the additional obligations enjoined upon humans imply that what separates humans from animals is their cognitive ability, above and beyond the instinctual drive and the biological capacity to propagate, to assume a role, namely, to "conquer" (*kābaš*) and "rule" (*rādâ*). Friedman is right to suspect that the image of God is none other than "consciousness."[59] P's notion of god-likeness is the very opposite of a physical contiguity, namely, an immaterial, abstract resemblance.

In both creation stories, as Kaufmann notes, it is instructive that there is a complete absence of theogony and theomachy.[60] But the absence of these, I suggest, is not in and of itself the decisive factor. Halpern, for instance, correctly points out that the Ugaritic tradition may share this feature with the Bible:

> Kaufmann identified the absence of theogony in Israel and the battle-free cosmogony of Genesis 2–3 as hallmarks of an early monotheism. . . . But it is worth noting the Caaanite evidence . . . in the tablets from Ugarit. . . . [T]here is not the faintest hint that the [Baal-Yamm] cycle involves creation at Ugarit; indeed, El is repeatedly called "the creator/progenitor of all creatures/progeny," and "father of man," and the gods, as in Israel, are called "sons of El." Too, references to villages in the Haddu-Yamm cycle suggest that the conflict is situated after the creation of the world. This is what one would expect, given that El is so much in control of the cosmos that he alone dispenses permits for palace construction while his "sons," Haddu, Yamm, and Mot, administer the regions of land/sky, sea, and underworld under his supervision. Thus, theogony and cosmogonic theomacy [*sic*] may already be absent at Ugarit. . . . [Ugaritic myth] may represent a sort of middle between the extremes of the Babylonian theogony-cosmogony and the Israelite Genesis.[61]

Although such an argument ultimately rests on silence—one cannot rule out the possibility of a lost Ugaritic theogony—as the evidence stands there is a surface similarity between Ugarit and Israel, forcing me, once again, to formulate Kaufmann's case more precisely: the absence of theogony and cosmogony is merely a surface manifestation of a deeper configuration in Israelite thought—namely, dualism—and this epistemic feature is categorically unknown in Ugaritic thought.

In other words, one must address the question of synonymy and homonymy, namely, whether a surface resemblance between two notions in fact has the same meaning or merely the same "lexical form."[62] This is particularly important in the case of the Ugaritic tradition because of its general linguistic and cultural proximity to biblical literature. On the surface El seems to be a theological—indeed, a linguistic—cognate of Israel's God; his unchallenged supremacy, not unlike Yahweh's, seems to preclude theogony and theomachy. Such surface resemblances, however, merely mask the underlying break separating Israelite from Ugaritic and Babylonian thought. Like Ea, his Babylonian counterpart, and in stark contrast to Yahweh, El exists, along with the rest of the Ugaritic pantheon, within the material realm and is subject to biological processes: El is understood to have fathered offspring; one of his "sons" acquires real estate and dies; he mourns as a father; and so forth. From the perspective of an epistemic analysis, therefore, the mythopoeic continuum Halpern would construct from Israel to Ugarit to Mesopotamia is beside the point.

The question of synonymy again comes to the fore in that supremely "mythological" moment in Genesis, namely, J's story of the nephilim (6:1–4). Its presence in the Bible has long been a stumbling block for scholars precisely because they assume that a cognate word, phrase, or motif must have the same meaning in entirely different historical and cultural contexts. Hendel, in his recent study of this myth, rightly objects to earlier assumptions that this story somehow slipped past an Israelite censor whose mission was to suppress foreign myths: "I find this . . . hard to conceive: what could be more mythological than the sexual mingling of gods and mortals and the birth of semidivine offspring? Surely if the Yahwist were averse to myth as such he would simply have omitted Gen. 6:1–4. That the Yahwist included it in the Primeval Cycle of Genesis 2–11 indicates that he did not find it objectionable and that it is indeed an authentic Israelite myth."[63] One must qualify the term "mythological," however, by specifying, as Kaufmann does, what in this story makes it an "authentic" Israelite myth: "It was not felt to be foreign . . . because its protagonists on both sides are creatures of God, not God himself. That any conscious censorship has been at work here to purge these stories of pagan features is improbable in view of the folk naïveté that permeates the legends of Genesis 2–11. It was rather that the religion of YHWH instinctively excluded such motifs and was unable to assimilate them."[64] I would only add that it is not a question of instinct or even choice but of logical necessity; that which can no longer be thought cannot be assimilated.

Although Gen. 6:1–4 refers to "the sons of the god" (*běnê hā'ělōhîm*), this episode in no way specifies their actual relationship to Yahweh. No stories are recounted dealing with genuine interactions between these gods and God, who seems more concerned with the earthly rather than the heavenly realm. Furthermore, according to J, before God's personal name is somehow discovered by humans in 4:26, characters refer to him as "God" (*'ělōhîm*) —without a definite article—which seems to function provisionally as his proper name (3:1 and 3).[65] The locution "the sons of the god" (*běnê hā'ělōhîm*), with its definite article, is thus tantalizingly vague as to any putative biological paternity these "sons" may claim. In both its occurrences in this story, it is directly opposed as a category to "the daughters of the human" (*běnôt hā'ādām*), with a corresponding definite article, which one might compare with the locution "sons of the human" (*běnê hā'ādām*) in Gen. 11:5. In other words, divine boys meet human girls. As with such designations as "Israelites" (*běnê yiśrā'ēl*) and "Benjaminites" (*běnê yāmîn*), this locution should not be taken strictly literally but rather as an "ethnic" classification based on a kinship metaphor. Meanwhile, in the cognate Ugaritic phrase "sons of El" (*bn il*), "El" (*il*) is a proper name, so that the locution designates not merely a class of beings but a biological clan. The Hebrew phrase has an entirely different meaning, for the Ugaritic phrase conceives of biological relationships among divine beings, whereas the Hebrew, strictly speaking, does not even seem to entertain such a possibility.

Admittedly, this story imputes a biological reality to the divine realm— or, at least to certain divine men, for God himself takes absolutely no part in these fleshly events—but the very possibility of such intercosmic coupling is represented precisely as an ancient and unrepeatable aberration. Within J it constitutes part of a process through which the immortal and mortal realms, once contiguous (though always distinct), gradually and irrevocably separate.[66] Early on, for instance, J presents a highly anthropomorphized version of God, but one should not take this as a straightforward depiction of Yahweh but as a literary conceit. As Friedman has pointed out, within J itself God shows signs of receding from the world, suggesting an affected naïveté in the portrayal of the divine in his Primeval History.[67] Similarly, the first humans live in God's garden (Gen. 2:8-14), perhaps implicitly understood as his backyard (cf. Ezek. 28:11-13). Even after they leave the garden (3:22-24), gods and humans, at least in the antediluvian past, both continue to walk the earth. Thus, these immortal men seem to encounter mortal women simply by chance as the latter "increase upon the face of the ground" (6:1). In fact, there is no hint of vertical movement from heaven to earth in these stories until we reach the story of the Tower of Babel, where precisely the growing distance between these two realms is at issue:[68] "And they said, 'Come, let us build ourselves a city and a tower, with its head in the heavens. And let us make ourselves a name, lest we be scattered upon the face of the whole earth.' And the Lord came down [*wayyēred*] to see the city and the tower that the sons of the human had built" (11:4-5). To return to the story of the nephilim, God's response to this supreme instance of miscegenation is telling, for he decrees, in effect, the separation of "spirit" and "flesh": "My spirit [*rûḥî*] will not be strong in the human forever, in that, indeed, he is but flesh [*bāśār*]" (6:3).[69] As the divide between heaven and earth grows, the former essentially turns into spirit, the latter into flesh. Humans, suspended between the kingdom of God and the animal kingdom, retain something of the divine, but only within the temporal limits of a human life span.

I would, finally, add here that this dualism also finds expression in the aniconism of Israelite religion: How can one visually represent that which exists outside of the physical universe? As with monotheism, the notion of aniconism develops over time, leading Tryggve N. D. Mettinger to distinguish between the "programmatic" aniconism of the Deuteronomistic tradition and the "de facto" aniconism that preceded it.[70] If the latter term suggests a practice devoid of broader significance, Hendel rightly adds that "any religious phenomenon, however conventional, has an implicit theology (or put more simply, implicit meanings) that requires interpretation."[71] Specifically, the aniconism of Israelite religion, even in its de facto stage, implies the nonmateriality of God, putting into perspective whatever anthropomorphisms of God we do find in the Bible.[72] If biblical narrative often imputes a bodily form to God, we find its mitigating factor, as Hendel shrewdly points out, in the motif of the danger of seeing God.[73] Furthermore, the biblical writers themselves, much like the characters within their stories, observe the unspoken rule of what Howard Eilberg-Schwartz calls "the averted gaze":

> [O]n a number of occasions various Israelites are said to have seen God. And in these "God sightings," or "theophanies" . . . various Israelite leaders see the deity in what appears to be a human form. But it is a human form in which the sex of God is carefully obscured. The question of God's genitals was an extremely delicate one for ancient Jews, a question to which any answer would have been troubling and disconcerting. And it is in part an attempt to sidestep this question that explains why the divine body is so carefully veiled.[74]

Hendel correctly revises Eilberg-Schwartz's explanation of this literary phenomenon: "I would suggest that in Israel the dominant issue is more the relation between God and humans than God's sexuality as such. The non-depiction of God's sexual qualities is in this light a sign of his difference from humans."[75] This difference has to do specifically with the metaphysical division between spirit and flesh. The aversion to gazing upon God's body, both by writers and their characters, shares with the aniconism of Israelite religion the problematization of God's body as such.

These arguments are not meant to suggest that the idea of God-as-spirit does not undergo continuous refinement. But it is surely no coincidence that various lines of evidence converge on the nonmateriality of God: the absence of stories dealing with God's biological existence; the so-called disappearance of God; aniconism; the averted gaze. Preceding all of these, I would suggest, is an epistemic revolution leading to a sudden and profound shift in the very concept of God.

The Creation of the Internal and External Worlds

This dualism in turn had productive consequences for Israelite thought. One must admit that in one sense it entailed the loss of mythic wholeness, the "alienation" from the numinous-natural world. As Henri Frankfort interestingly observes of the nonmythic character of Israelite religion:

> The keeping of Yahweh's covenant meant relinquishing a great deal. It meant, in a word, sacrificing the greatest good ancient Near Eastern religion could bestow—the harmonious integration of man's life with the life of nature. . . . In Hebrew religion—and in Hebrew religion alone—the ancient bond between man and nature was destroyed. Those who served Yahweh must forego the richness, the fulfilment, and the consolation of a life which moves in tune with the great rhythms of earth and sky.[76]

But one must also recognize what was gained. It is not merely a matter, as Frankfort suggests, of "freedom," of "the emancipation of thought from myth," but of regaining that which was lost.[77] Specifically, I think one can profitably relate this dialectic of loss and compensation to Althusser's understanding of alienation:

> In short, the final historical totality, which marks the end of alienation, is nothing but the reconquered unity of the labourer and his product. This end is simply the restoration of the origin, the reconquest of the original harmony after a tragic adventure. . . .
>
> Yet it is only in a formal sense that the final unity is the restoration of the original unity. The worker who reappropriates what he himself produces is no longer the primitive worker, and the product he reappropriates is no longer the primitive product. Men do not return to the solitude of the domestic economy, and what they produce does not revert to being what it once was, the simple object of their needs. This *natural* unity is destroyed; the unity that replaces it is *human*.[78]

In other words, alienation, though a "tragic adventure," has productive consequences. Through it the proletariat comes to possess the product of its labor in a "human" rather than merely "natural" way. Conversely, that which is inalienable cannot be truly possessed.[79] In the case of the ancient Near East, I would like to suggest that the "natural unity" of mortals, gods, and nature within the world of myth is transformed, through alienation, into a "human unity" within history. Barthes makes a similar point with respect to history and the novel: "The teleology common to the Novel and to narrated History is the *alienation* of the facts: the preterite is the very act by which society affirms its *possession* of its past and its possibility."[80] The progression from "alienation" to "possession" suggests an Althusserian argument, according to which the "facts" of history and the novel undergo a twofold alienation. First, facts are alienated from the subjective, allowing a society to possess "its past" as a set of empirical rather than solipsistic events. Second, facts are alienated from necessity, so that a society may possess "its possibility," that is, recognize its own contingency—the merely possible cannot be necessary. If the first derives history from memory (a process I discussed in chapter 5), the second derives it from myth. Myth is the narrative mode of the necessary and essential, whereas history is the narrative mode of the contingent and accidental.[81] It is the second that will concern me here as it works itself out in the relationships joining God, humankind, and nature.

I note first that Yahweh, by transcending nature—that is, being alienated from it—comes to reign over it in a proper sense, and this notion of a divine force working upon nature from without gives new significance to earthly events. In the monistic world of "pagan" religions, the human and divine realms are metaphysically one; events on the human plane are thus inherently connected—often through recurring mythic patterns and sympathetic magical rituals—to divine counterparts. The Mesopotamian New Year festival, for instance, culminated in the recital of *Enuma Elish,* which was thought to reestablish Marduk's reign. As such, mythic time emphasizes the cycles of nature conceived of as recurring expressions of the eternal and necessary order of the gods.[82] In the dualism of Israelite religion, conversely, events are imagined as the manifestation of Yahweh's will,[83] so that they lose their link to necessity and eternity, instead becoming contingent upon something more or less arbitrary.[84] As a result, biblical time emphasizes that which changes through time, the linear movement of history as one generally thinks of it. Correspondingly, one sees the tendency in Israel to historicize festivals, to make them commemorations of divinely appointed events in history.

Furthermore, in Israel there are no longer autochthonous relationships joining land, god, and people. On the one hand, neither Israel nor its God enjoy native ties to the land of Canaan. According to various archaic biblical traditions, Yahweh comes from the south or southeast, from outside of the promised land;[85] meanwhile Abraham is said to come from "Ur of the Chaldeans" (Gen. 11:31). Similarly the Israelites, after joining God outside of Canaan at Mount Sinai/Horeb in that liminal time and place known as the "Wilderness Period," belatedly come to receive the "promised land" through a "historical" if largely fabricated event, namely, the conquest.[86] In this way the Israelites come to possess a land, not theirs of necessity, through a contingent event in the past. In an instructive contrast, *Enuma Elish* concludes with the exaltation of Marduk and the founding of Babylon, linking a people to a place and a god in a mythic past. Similarly, as we saw in "Enki and the World Order," Enki's potency expresses itself in the fertility of Mesopotamia. Baal, too, reigns over Ugarit from atop his throne on Mount Zaphon, which visibly looms over the local landscape, as some sort of native divinity. In other words, such myths conceive of Mesopotamia and Ugarit as the inalienable territory of a certain god and people, and inasmuch as one can speak of a past event—the founding of Babylon, for instance—one cannot connect it to the present through a linear, horizontal sequence but only vertically to an eternal and necessary order.[87] Conversely, the very relationship joining God to the Israelites is in some sense an accident of history. Yahweh becomes the God of Israel, and Israel the "chosen" people, within a history that could have—and nearly did—turn out otherwise.[88] Meanwhile, in the myths I have been discussing, Marduk and Baal, as native gods, do not encounter their subjects by chance in historical time; rather, their respective reigns over the inhabitants of Babylon and Ugarit are part of the eternal order. In ancient Israel this historical relationship between God and man specifically takes on the form of a covenant.[89] It is no coincidence that the biblical idea of covenant, as Nahum Sarna attests, constitutes a "revolutionary expansion of the original treaty concept in that God and an entire people become parties to the covenant."[90] This "revolutionary" appropriation of the treaty concept was needed precisely to compensate for the loss of any mythic bond that would otherwise have united Yahweh, Israel, and the Promised Land.

This reinterpretation of the covenant in turn led to an unprecedented concern with subjectivity. The notion of a transcendent god who yet confronts man led to what the Frankforts call "the myth of the Will of God": "Although the great 'Thou' which confronted the Hebrews transcended nature, it stood in a specific relationship to the people. . . . Thus God's will was felt to be focused on one particular and concrete group of human beings."[91] The will of God, in turn, helps lead to a corresponding emphasis on human obligation. For instance, Walther Eichrodt, claiming that "the unconditional obligation of the will of God [was] the basis of the Old Testament view of man,"[92] concludes: "[I]t may be affirmed without exaggeration that in no other people of the ancient East is the sense of the responsibility of each member of the people so living, and the personal attitude so dominant. The explanation lies in the religious basis of the Law of Israel."[93] Citing Eichrodt, G. E. Wright specifically emphasizes the connection between the developing concern with the individual as moral agent and that legal form known as "apodictic law": "The Lord's 'Thou shalt' in the law broke through the collectivisim of primitive man and imposed in the covenant an unconditional obedience, not only on the group, but on the individual as well."[94] What is interesting is the unusual emphasis placed on this type of law in the Bible. As Sarna observes regarding the Ten Commandments: "We find only 'You shall' or 'You shall not'—unqualified, absolute declarations without definitions, limitations, or threat of punishment. While this apodictic style . . . is not original to the Torah, its use in Near Eastern treaties is very rare, and the conditional formulation is customary" (142). This surprising shift in emphasis finds its explanation in the fact that apodictic law provides the appropriate mode of address for an absolute will as it singles out the individual subject. Finally, since humankind confronts this will in history—it is not mythically created into servitude as in *Enuma Elish*[95]—it cannot merely play its fated (necessary) part in the cosmos but must willingly choose—just as it was chosen—to fulfill its obligations. The human subject so conceived therefore becomes an object of increasing religious and moral concern.[96]

Ecriture Biblique

In their suggestive survey entitled "The Consequences of Literacy,"[97] Jack Goody and Ian Watt touch upon a number of interesting developments they believe derived from widespread literacy—particularly with respect to "alphabetic culture and Greek thought" (42–55)—such as the distinction between myth and history (44–49), increased emphasis on the individual (61–63),[98] and a general skepticism toward tradition (46, 48, and 67–68)—developments, in other words, equally characteristic of biblical thought. Can similar arguments be made regarding the role literacy played in Israel's remarkable intellectual and literary achievements? The alphabet is, after all, an invention of the Near East, and ancient Israel was among the first to make use of it. Perhaps, as I. J. Gelb argues, the lack of vowels in this so-called alphabet makes it in principle a syllabary, for unlike the Greek alphabet it does not yet constitute "a system of signs expressing single sounds of speech."[99] Nonetheless, it reduced the number of needed signs to the dimensions of our current alphabet by treating vowels, in effect, as a variable contained within each sign, and it simplified each individual sign as well.[100] As such, in Israel it led to a fuller exploration of the possibilities of writing and possibly to the spread of literacy as well.[101]

In fact, as a symptom of this new technology, the world of biblical narrative exhibits a thoroughgoing and—Niditch's assertions to the contrary notwithstanding[102]—mundane familiarity with writing without parallel, moreover, in Homeric, Ugaritic, and Mesopotamian narrative traditions. In Judg. 8:14, for instance, we read: "And [Gideon] captured a young man of the people of Succoth and questioned him. And he wrote [*wayyiktōb*] for him [the names of] the leaders and elders of Succoth, seventy-seven men."[103] While there is no reason to posit an actual event behind this verse, it nonetheless betrays a casual attitude toward writing on the part of the writer: this anonymous young man could simply produce this text for his captors, who, in turn, could read it. In Homer, conversely, one finds only one clear reference to writing:

> [Proitos] shrank from killing him, since his heart was awed
>   by such action,
> but sent him away to Lykia, and handed him murderous
>   symbols [*sēmata*],
> which he inscribed [*grapsas*] in a folding tablet [*pinaki*],
>   enough to destroy life,
> and told him to show it to his wife's father, that he might
>   perish. (6.167–70)

Even here scholars are split regarding the actual nature and significance of these *sēmata*.[104] Are they letters, ideograms, or symbols? Did the Homeric tradition comprehend the mechanics of this writing? Unfortunately, while this contrast is instructive, the witness of the Bible does not ultimately suffice to establish any sort of general literacy in Israel.[105] If Goody and Watt are justified in attributing a critical mass of functional literacy to Athens on the basis of certain democratic institutions that presume the existence of a literate citizenry,[106] one does not find corresponding institutions in Israel.

An emphasis on literacy, however, may be misplaced as far as the consequences of writing are concerned. Writing is certainly, as Goody observes, a "technology of the intellect,"[107] but if the "development of an easy system of writing," as he and Watt jointly argue, was thus crucial to "the Greek achievement" (67) —and to the Israelite achievement as well—this technological development did not necessarily make its primary contribution toward any such achievement through a consequent increase in literacy. For the nature and being of writing is independent of its possible reception. That is, one can imagine a literate intelligentsia exploring the implications of writing and being helped, furthermore, by advances in its technology without consideration for the existence or size of their reading public. This is not to reject literacy as a legitimate topic of research, especially for anthropology and sociology, but as regards an epistemic analysis of ancient Israel, it is writing itself and not the spread of literacy that provides the crucial factor.

The French critical tradition, in fact, supplies its own term for this factor: *écriture*. As Banfield observes, the entry of this loanword into English indicates that it signifies something other or more than mere "writing," something especially visible in the grammar of French.[108] For the opposition between *écriture* and *parole* (speech)[109] coincides with a grammatical dualism within the French language.[110] The features of *l'écriture*, according to various French theorists, are most fully realized in the language of the novel, specifically in what Barthes refers to as certain "formal signs of Literature," in particular the "preterite" and the "indirect style," namely, *style indirect libre* or represented consciousness (67). These are precisely those constructions in the language of fiction that Banfield identifies as "unspeakable," that is, they occur only in the written language. The significance of this mode of language becomes clear in certain of Barthes's previously cited comments regarding *l'écriture du Roman:* "The teleology common to the Novel and to narrated History is the alienation of the facts: the preterite [*passé simple*] is the very act by which society affirms its possession of its past and its possibility" (32–33). The "part [the preterite] plays is . . . to abstract, from the depth of a multiplicity of experiences, a pure verbal act, freed from the existential roots of knowledge" (30). *L'Ecriture*, in other words, designates the alienation of language from the speaking subject; it has to do with an impersonality of language, "the death of the author."

Beyond this core meaning, what Banfield calls *écriture*'s "empirical content," lies a further institutional significance. For Barthes it has to do with the modern concept of Literature: "Obsolete in spoken French, the preterite, which is the cornerstone of Narration, always signifies the presence of Art; it is part of a ritual of Letters [*Belles-Lettres*]" (30). He links Literature's origins specifically to "a tragic awareness (around 1850)": "This was precisely the time when Literature (the word having come into being shortly before) was finally established as an object" (3). This tragic awareness, he explains later, derives from the loss of a universal bourgeois ideology:

> Until [the revolution of June 1848], it was bourgeois ideology itself which gave the measure of the universal by fulfilling it unchallenged. The bourgeois writer, sole judge of other people's woes

and without anyone else to gaze on him, was not torn between his social condition and his intellectual vocation. Henceforth, this very ideology appears merely as one among many possible others; the universal escapes it, since transcending itself would mean condemning itself; the writer falls a prey to ambiguity, since his consciousness no longer accounts for the whole of his condition. Thus is born a tragic predicament peculiar to Literature. (60)

Foucault, not unlike Barthes, conceives of *écriture* in relation to Literature, but he locates Literature's origins not in the class struggle but in the ascendance of modern philology and its "demotion of language":

> [T]he last of the compensations for the demotion of language, the most important, and also the most unexpected, is the appearance of literature, of literature as such—for there has of course existed in the Western world, since Dante, since Homer, a form of language that we now call "literature." But the word is of recent date, as is also, in our culture, the isolation of a particular language whose peculiar mode of being is "literary." This is because at the beginning of the nineteenth century, at the time when language was burying itself within its own density as an object and allowing itself to be traversed, through and through, by knowledge, it was also reconstituting itself elsewhere, in an independent form, difficult of access, folded back upon the enigma of its own origin and existing wholly in reference to the pure act of writing. Literature is the contestation of philology (of which it is nevertheless the twin figure): it leads language back from grammar to the naked power of speech, and there it encounters the untamed, imperious being of words.[111]

In both accounts Literature thus arises in response to a loss. It provides a solace to the painful knowledge of modernity.[112]

As we have seen in the preceding chapters, the signs of *l'écriture* are discernible in Biblical Hebrew prose as well. Like the writing of the novel, *écriture biblique* is impersonal, alienated from the speaking subject, signifying the death of the rhapsode. Furthermore, it too describes not only the "real" in the grammar of Biblical Hebrew but also an institution of letters in ancient Israel. If it cannot be part of that modern ritual of Letters called *Belles Lettres*, it is yet a ritual of letters, and as such it substitutes for other, spoken, rituals. As I noted in my introduction, von Rad observes of the Succession Narrative: "Admittedly the conception of Yahweh's activity through the ancient sacral institutions has become obsolete, but the belief that he is active in history most certainly had not."[113] He similarly argues that the traditions J uses in the Hexateuch have been "historicised": "[T]heir inner content has actually been removed bodily from its narrow sacral context into the freer atmosphere of common history."[114] Similarly Cross, in effect revisiting von Rad's study of the Hexateuch through the lens of the Parry-Lord hypothesis, claims that J likely worked "at a time when Israel's cultic institutions, notably the covenant festivals of the league, in which the epic events were recited and enacted, had fallen into desuetude, and epic tradition thus loosened from its primary setting and function."[115] While such attempts at reconstructing a historical context for the Bible's narrative sources are necessarily speculative, the intuitions they try to account for are themselves well founded and bear eloquent witness to biblical narrative's mode of being as *écriture.*

Not unlike *Belles Lettres, écriture biblique* compensates for a loss—the loss of the consolations of myth, ritual, and their institutions. We have already seen how biblical narrative communicates a new knowledge appropriate to the episteme of ancient Israel: knowledge of a transcendent God, of history, of the human subject. This knowledge finds expression in certain biblical themes: the succession of covenants between God and humankind; history as the neutral ground of these encounters; and the problematic dialectic of divine demand and human response. Confronted by such knowledge, speech falls silent, unable to bear its burden. Thus, as von Rad, Cross, and others attest, within these narratives the rhapsode's voice has fallen silent, and with it the power of ritual has vanished. Yet biblical narrative also provides solace, the hope of redemption.[116]

But what actual, historical ritual of letters does *écriture biblique* take part in? In other words, if it is, for obvious reasons, an anachronism to invoke here the idea of *Belles Lettres,* of Literature in the modern sense, how shall one name this biblical counterpart? Perhaps Ezra the scribe provides the needed clue. The scribe (*sōpēr*) is merely the keeper, the servant, of a Scroll (*sēper*), whose words he neither animates nor authorizes. He is no author, and if he were, he could not be acknowledged as such. For this Scroll derives its authority solely from "the whiteness of a piece of paper . . . possess[ing] neither sound nor interlocutor . . . ha[ving] nothing to say but itself, nothing to do but shine in the brightness of its being."[117] In ancient Israel *écriture,* the death of the rhapsode, announces the birth of the scribe, the advent of Scripture.

NOTES

1. Introduction

1. Throughout this discussion I use Allan Bloom's translation, which appears in *The Roots of Political Philosophy: Ten Forgotten Socratic Dialogues*, ed. Thomas L. Pangle (Ithaca, N.Y.: Cornell University Press, 1987), 356-70. Unless otherwise noted, all other translations are my own.

2. It is worth noting that at first, as in this passage, Socrates refers to Ion unambiguously as *hermēneus*, meaning simply "interpreter." Later, however, he uses the more ambiguous term *hypokritēs* (536a), meaning not only "interpreter" but "actor," which seems more to the point and of questionable merit for Plato. For the problem of "acting" (*hypokrisis*) seems related to the problem of "representation" (*mimēsis*) in Book 3 of *The Republic*. Just as Socrates here distrusts the actor who, borrowing Homer's voice, would speak of many arts without knowing any of them, so in *The Republic* he doubts the rectitude of any man who would "represent many things" (*polla . . . mimeisthai*, 394e), that is, play the parts of other men. One should also note the remark of Antisthenes in Xenophon's Banquet: "Do you know any tribe more stupid [or simple] than the rhapsodes?" (quoted in Allan Bloom, "An Interpretation of Plato's *Ion*," in *Roots of Political Philosophy*, ed. Pangle, 371). For a more positive assessment of the rhapsodes' place in the evolution of Homeric epic, see Gregory Nagy, *Homeric Questions* (Austin: University of Texas Press, 1996).

3. For a brief discussion of these issues, see Richard Elliott Friedman, *Who Wrote the Bible?* (New York: Summit Books, 1987), 150-60, 217-33.

4. This oral recitation in no way changes the written character of the text. Albert Lord himself has observed: "Oral epics are performed orally, it is true, but so can any other poem be performed orally. What is important is not the oral performance but rather the composition *during* oral performance" (*The Singer of Tales* [Cambridge, Mass.: Harvard University Press, 1960], 5). Even more to the point in the case of the Bible is the remark he makes in the related footnote: "It should be clear from this . . . that sacred texts which must be preserved word for word, if there be such, could not be *oral* in any except the most literal sense" (280 n. 9).

5. See Gerhard von Rad, *Studies in Deuteronomy* (London: SCM Press, 1953), 13-14; Jacob M. Myers, *Ezra-Nehemiah*, AB 14 (Garden City, N.Y.: Doubleday, 1965), 151-53; Joseph Blenkinsopp, *Ezra-Nehemiah* (Philadelphia, Pa.: Westminster Press, 1988), 283-88. This passage poses several problems, such as deciding what, precisely, the Levites did, the meaning of *mĕpōrāš*, and the likelihood of secondary additions. But these do not obscure my main point, namely, that "interpretation" here is aimed not at the audience's affects but at their intellects (*śekel, bînâ*).

6. In this study "biblical narrative" refers to the prose narratives found in Genesis through Kings. Broadly speaking, these texts originate from the same period of Israelite history (during the monarchy and before the fall of Jerusalem in

587 B.C.E.) and are written in what is often referred to as Classical Biblical Hebrew. Later texts such as Esther, while affecting a "classical" style, betray the influence of Late Biblical Hebrew. My literary and linguistic analyses will therefore focus on this body of texts, and my claims will not necessarily hold outside of it.

7. Wolfram von Soden, for instance, simply states that "outside of Israel . . . there was no historical writing in the ancient Orient in the strict sense of the term" (*The Ancient Orient: An Introduction to the Study of the Ancient Near East* [Grand Rapids, Mich.: Eerdmans, 1994], 46).

8. Gerhard von Rad, "The Beginnings of Historical Writing in Ancient Israel," in *The Problem of the Hexateuch and Other Essays* (Edinburgh: Oliver & Boyd, 1966), 167; subsequent references are given parenthetically.

9. Gerhard von Rad, "The Form-Critical Problem of the Hexateuch," in *Problem of the Hexateuch*, 1–78; subsequent references are given parenthetically.

10. I borrow the term from Hans Frei, *The Eclipse of Biblical Narrative* (New Haven, Conn.: Yale University Press, 1974).

11. Umberto Cassuto, "Biblical and Canaanite Literature," in *Biblical and Oriental Studies*, vol. 2, *Bible and Ancient Oriental Texts* (1942–43; reprint, Jerusalem: Magnes Press, 1975), 16; subsequent references are given parenthetically.

12. Von Rad, "Form-Critical Problem of the Hexateuch," 68.

13. Ibid., 64.

14. Cassuto, "Biblical and Canaanite Literature," 18. Regarding this "new content," see especially Cassuto, "The Israelite Epic," in *Biblical and Oriental Studies*, 2:69–109.

15. Frank Moore Cross, "The Epic Traditions of Early Israel: Epic Narrative and the Reconstruction of Early Israelite Institutions," in *The Poet and the Historian: Essays in Literary and Historical Biblical Criticism*, ed. Richard Elliott Friedman (Chico, Calif.: Scholars Press, 1983), 13–39; subsequent references are given parenthetically.

16. One might mention here Shemaryahu Talmon's similar observation that "the ancient Hebrew writers purposefully nurtured prose narration to take the place of the epic genre" ("Did There Exist a Biblical National Epic?," in *Literary Studies in the Hebrew Bible: Form and Content* [Jerusalem: Magnes Press, 1993], 105), which position Robert Alter would later adopt (*The Art of Biblical Narrative* [New York: Basic Books, 1981], 24–26). Although he and Talmon take issue with Cross's use of the term "epic" (and vice versa), their respective positions, as I try to suggest, do not differ as radically as one might imagine.

17. Erich Auerbach, *Mimesis: The Representation of Reality in Western Literature* (Princeton, N.J.: Princeton University Press, 1953), 3–23; subsequent references are given parenthetically.

18. Alter, *Biblical Narrative*, 24 and 29. In the latter point he advances a modified version of the claims made by Herbert N. Schneidau in *Sacred Discontent: The Bible and Western Tradition* (Baton Rouge, La.: Louisiana State University Press, 1976).

19. Alter, *Biblical Narrative*, 31.

20. In his preface Alter informs us that he originally considered devoting a chapter to style but later decided against it since it would have required knowledge of Hebrew on the reader's part (x).

21. David Damrosch, *The Narrative Covenant: Transformations of Genre in the Growth of Biblical Literature* (San Francisco: Harper & Row, 1987), 60. Regarding

ancient Near Eastern historiography, he mentions the following studies: Bertil Albrektson, *History and the Gods: An Essay on the Idea of Historical Events as Divine Manifestations in the Ancient Near East and Israel* (Lund, Sweden: Gleerup, 1967); and John Van Seters, *In Search of History: Historiography in the Ancient World and the Origins of Biblical History* (New Haven, Conn.: Yale University Press, 1983). I should note here that Cross, in his somewhat controversial notion of the Pentateuch's "epic sources" (namely J and E), partly meant for the term "epic" to serve as a mediating term between myth and history: "If we eschew the designations 'mythic narrative' and 'historical narrative' as inappropriate or misleading in describing the constitutive genre of early Israelite oral narrative preserved in the Tetrateuch, we do find a third literary genre which fits snugly, namely *epea*, traditional epic" ("Epic Traditions of Early Israel," 14).

22. Gerald K. Gresseth, "The Gilgamesh Epic and Homer," *Classical Journal* 70 (1975): 1–18.

23. Damrosch, *Narrative Covenant*, 36–50. Simon B. Parker's study *Stories in Scripture and Inscriptions: Comparative Studies on Narratives in Northwest Semitic Inscriptions and the Hebrew Bible* (Oxford: Oxford University Press, 1997) takes an analogous approach, though on a smaller scale, organizing his comparative analyses around story genres, such as "petitionary narratives" and "military campaigns."

24. Damrosch, *Narrative Covenant*, 1.

25. Edward Greenstein, "On the Genesis of Biblical Prose Narrative," *Prooftexts* 8 (1988): 349.

26. Ibid.

27. The terminology of "verbal art" as modified by the adjectives "oral" and "written" was suggested to me by Ann Banfield. It is meant to avoid the often unnoticed oxymoron of "oral literature," on the one hand, and the normative, evaluative connotations of the current usage of such terms as "literature" and "literary," on the other. I will nonetheless not refrain from using these latter terms.

28. Walter Benjamin, "The Storyteller: Reflections on the Works of Nikolai Leskov," in his *Illuminations* (New York: Schocken Books, 1968), 87.

29. Marcel Proust, "To Be Added to Flaubert," in *Against Sainte Beuve and Other Essays* (New York: Penguin, 1988), 89.

30. Proust, "On Flaubert's Style," in *Against Sainte Beuve*, 261.

31. Roland Barthes, *Writing Degree Zero* (New York: Noonday Press, 1968). This study was originally published in French in 1953.

32. Barthes's 1968 pronouncement (reprinted as "The Death of the Author" in *The Rustle of Language* [Berkeley: University of California Press, 1989], 49–55) has generally been misunderstood as a profession of literary atheism vis-à-vis the author. As Jacques Lacan recognized, however, "God is dead" is not the "true formula of atheism" but rather "God is unconscious" (*The Four Fundamental Concepts of Psycho-Analysis* [New York: Norton, 1978], 59). In fact, like Nietzsche's death of God, one should understand the death of the author as a particular event in the history of literature—Alain Robbe-Grillet's *nouveau roman*, according to Christine Brooke-Rose ("Narrating Without a Narrator," *TLS*, December 31, 1999, 12).

33. Barthes, *Writing Degree Zero*, 17.

34. See Ann Banfield, "*Écriture*, Narration and the Grammar of French," in *Narrative: From Malory to Motion Pictures*, ed. Jeremy Hawthorn (London: Edward Arnold, 1985), 1–22.

35. Emile Benveniste, "The Correlations of Tense in the French Verb," in his

Problems in General Linguistics, trans. Mary Elizabeth Meek (Coral Gables, Fla.: University of Miami, 1971), 205–15. This study was originally published in French in 1959.

36. Ibid, 206.

37. Käte Hamburger, *The Logic of Literature,* 2d. ed. (Bloomington: Indiana University Press, 1993). This study was originally published in German in 1957.

38. It should be pointed out, however, that Hamburger overextends her notion of the "epic preterite" to cover too much data. Her mistake begins, I believe, with the phenomenological distinction she posits between the reading of fiction and the reading of history (59–63). For the fact that we cannot always be sure which category a given narrative belongs to—biblical narrative is a signal example —suggests, to the contrary, that the phenomenology of the primary reading experience is identical for both, and that we should instead assign the reception of the divergent truth claims made by each to a secondary cognitive experience. Working under this false premise, however, Hamburger claims that the preterite of a "statement" (*die Aussage*) is experienced as referring to the past, while the so-called epic preterite of "fictional narration" (*das fiktionale Erzählen*) "loses its grammatical function of designating what is past" (66). I would not object to this claim if it were limited to *erlebte Rede,* which, as we will see, represents a past as *present* to a subject of consciousness. However, Hamburger clearly means for her "epic preterite" to account for all occurrences of the preterite in fictional narration. Thus, according to her the sentence "Mr. X was on a trip," if found in a novel, signifies "not that Mr. X *was* on a trip, but that he *is* on a trip" (70). This reading follows upon her interpretation of the fact, alluded to earlier, that fiction does not make the historian's claim to truth. Fiction does not refer to reality, ergo it cannot refer to a past, ergo its preterite loses its normal grammatical function. As I shall argue in chapter 3, however, the preterite in narration, whether fictional or historical, refers to a past, but without respect to a present. It is a non-deictic preterite.

39. For her discussions of *die Aussage* and *das fiktionale Erzählen,* see Hamburger, *The Logic of Literature,* 23–54 and 59–194, resp.

40. One current orthodoxy related to the axiomatic status of the narrator is the ascendancy of "discourse." Alter, for instance, laments the overuse of this term: "As a binary opposite to narration (*récit*), 'discourse' has a definite utility, but nowadays one finds it used instead of style, rhetoric, speech, diction, narrative technique, narrative structure, fictional representation, language as a formal system, and a good deal else" (*The Pleasures of Reading in an Ideological Age* [New York: Simon and Schuster, 1989], 18). An insatiable "discourse" has swallowed up its binary opposite by turning "narration" into the "discourse" of a narrator.

41. I draw from two of his essays, "Where Epistemology, Style, and Grammar Meet: A Case Study from Japanese," and "Reflections on the Foundations of Narrative Theory—from a Linguistic Point of View," both reprinted in *The 'Whole of the Doughnut: Syntax and Its Boundaries* (Ghent: E. Story-Scientia, 1979), 185–203 and 205–31, resp.; see also Ann Banfield's summary of Kuroda's work in *Unspeakable Sentences: Narration and Representation in the Language of Fiction* (Boston: Routledge and Kegan Paul, 1982), 11–12.

42. Kuroda, in fact, refers to Bertrand Russell's distinction between "indicating facts" and "expressing the state of the speaker" ("Epistemology, Style, and Grammar," 185); see Bertrand Russell, *An Inquiry into Meaning and Truth* (London: George Allen & Unwin, 1980), 204–25.

43. "Poetic" here alludes to the distinction in Aristotle's *Poetics* between those genres based on "creating" (*poiein*) and those based on "speaking" (*legein*), the very distinction Hamburger refers to as well.

44. Banfield, *Unspeakable Sentences;* subsequent references are given parenthetically.

45. The terms "narration" and "discourse" have become so entrenched in Anglo-American literary theory that I have chosen to retain "discourse" in favor of Banfield's admittedly more precise "communication."

46. Benveniste writes: "Discourse excludes the aorist, but historical narration, which employs it constantly, retains it only in the forms of the third person" ("Correlations of Tense," 210–11). While Hamburger refers to the novel written in the first person as a "special form," she assigns it, along with lyric, to "the statement system" (*Logic of Literature*, 311–41).

47. As Banfield points out (*Unspeakable Sentences*, 144), the first and second person are not linguistically symmetrical. While every instance of "you" necessarily presupposes an "I," not every instance of "I" addresses a "you."

48. Recall Northrop Frye's remark: "Criticism, we note resignedly in passing, has no word for the individual member of an author's audience, and the word "audience" itself does not really cover all genres, as it is slightly illogical to describe the readers of a book as an audience" (*Anatomy of Criticism: Four Essays* [Princeton, N.J.: Princeton University Press, 1957], 246–47).

49. See Milman Parry, *The Making of Homeric Verse: The Collected Papers of Milman Parry*, ed. Adam Parry (Oxford: Oxford University Press, 1987); and Albert Lord, *The Singer of Tales*.

50. Milman Parry, "Studies in the Epic Technique of Oral Verse-Making. I. Homer and Homeric Style," in *Making of Homeric Verse*, 272. This essay was originally published in 1930.

51. Ibid., 276.

52. For a fine account and appraisal of Milman Parry's thought and work, see the introduction written by his son, Adam Parry, to *The Making of Homeric Verse* (ix–lxii).

53. In an earlier note I alluded to Plato's objections to *mimēsis* ("representation" or "imitation") in *The Republic*. I would like to point out here that these objections are premised on the inseparability of epic narrative from the poet's voice. In narrative proper (*diēgēsis*) "the poet speaks as himself" (*legei te autos ho poiētēs*, 393a), but in mimetic narrative (*mimēsis*), that is, narrative employing direct discourse, "he assimilates his own speech" (*homoioun . . . tēn hautou lexin*, 393c) to that of his characters. Plato cannot imagine a narrative that is not actualized by an oral performance (as opposed to an impersonal recitation) because such did not exist in the Greek tradition—whence a figure such as Ion.

54. See, e.g., Cross, "Epic Traditions of Early Israel"; Robert C. Culley, *Oral Formulaic Language in the Biblical Psalms* (Toronto: University of Toronto Press, 1967); Stephen Geller, *Parallelism in Early Biblical Poetry* (Missoula, Mont.: Scholars Press, 1979).

55. Cross, "Epic Traditions of Early Israel," 21.

56. See, e.g., the objections of Charles Conroy, "Hebrew Epic: Historical Notes and Critical Reflections," *Biblica* 61 (1980): 1–30; and Shemaryahu Talmon, "The Comparative Method in Biblical Interpretation: Principles and Problems," in *Literary Studies in the Hebrew Bible*, 11–49.

57. I intentionally mean to echo here Chomsky's observations regarding the "creative aspect of language use," namely, the capacity of language to generate an infinite number of grammatical sentences on the basis of a severely restricted set of syntactical rules. See Noam Chomsky, *Cartesian Linguistics: A Chapter in the History of Rationalist Thought* (Lanham, Md.: University Press of America, 1966), 3–31; idem, *Language and Mind* (New York: Harcourt, Brace & World, 1968), 1–20. I also mean to suggest that the formal possibilities underlying narrative are analogous to what Chomsky calls "universal grammar." Indeed, inasmuch as some of these features of narrative consist precisely of certain rules in the grammar of the language of narrative fiction, they form a subset of universal grammar.

2. From Song to Story

1. *Semeia* 5 (1976) is devoted to "Oral Tradition and Old Testament Studies." Robert C. Culley's introduction (1–33) surveys relevant studies. For more recent developments, see Robert C. Culley, *Themes and Variations: A Study of Action in Biblical Narrative* (Atlanta, Ga.: Scholars Press, 1992); John Miles Foley, *The Theory of Oral Composition: History and Methodology* (Bloomington: Indiana University Press, 1988), 84–86; and Susan Niditch, *Oral World and Written Word: Ancient Israelite Literature* (Louisville, Ky.: Westminster John Knox Press, 1996).

2. Alter, *Biblical Narrative;* Adele Berlin, *Poetics and Interpretation of Biblical Narrative* (Sheffield, Eng.: Almond Press, 1983); Meir Sternberg, *The Poetics of Biblical Narrative: Ideological Literature and the Drama of Reading* (Bloomington: Indiana University Press, 1987).

3. See Robert C. Culley, *Oral Formulaic Language in the Biblical Psalms.* Here I must raise the related issue of Ugaritic narrative poetry. Frank Moore Cross early on linked the Ugaritic myth cycles to an oral-formulaic tradition; see his *Canaanite Myth and Hebrew Epic: Essays in the History of the Religion of Israel* (Cambridge, Mass.: Harvard University Press, 1973), 112; idem, "Prose and Poetry in the Mythic and Epic Texts from Ugarit," *HTR* 67 (1974): 1–15. See, more recently, Kenneth T. Aitken, "Oral Formulaic Composition and Theme in the Aqhat Narrative," *UF* 21 (1989): 1–16; idem, "Word Pairs and Tradition in an Ugaritic Tale," *UF* 21 (1989): 17–38.

4. Cross, *Canaanite Myth and Hebrew Epic*, 124 n. 38. See also Umberto Cassuto's series of essays touching on this question: "Biblical and Canaanite Literature," "Parallel Words in Hebrew and Ugaritic," and "The Israelite Epic," in *Biblical and Oriental Studies*, 2:16–59, 60–68, 69–109, resp.

5. See Shemaryahu Talmon, "The Comparative Method in Biblical Interpretation: Principles and Problems," in *Literary Studies in the Hebrew Bible*, 11–49; idem, "Did There Exist a Biblical National Epic?" in *Literary Studies in the Hebrew Bible*, 91–111. Alter endorses Talmon's critique in *Biblical Narrative*, 25–26. See also Conroy, "Hebrew Epic." Note, however, that Talmon addresses Cross's work only in passing, criticizing more directly and at greater length Sigmund Mowinckel, "Hat es ein israelitisches Nationalepos gegeben?" *ZAW* 53 (1935): 130–53; and Cassuto, "Israelite Epic."

6. One would do well to recall that Lord gave "oral epic" (also referred to as "oral narrative poetry") the purely formal definition "story poetry," in which the use of "formulas" and "formulaic expressions" indicates not merely "oral performance" but "composition *during* oral performance" (paraphrasing *Singer of Tales*, 4–5). He rejected thematic definitions of epic since these, at least for the purposes of his formal analysis, would exclude relevant data (6).

7. See Cross's defense of the term "epic," in response to the objections mentioned earlier, in "Epic Traditions of Early Israel," 17–19.

8. Ibid, 20.

9. For convenience' sake I will generally refer to Judges 4 and 5 as "story" and "song," respectively, and to their composers as "writer" and "poet."

10. For the dating of the Song of Deborah on the basis of linguistic evidence, see Frank Moore Cross and David Noel Freedman, *Studies in Ancient Yahwistic Poetry* (Missoula, Mont.: Scholars Press, 1975), 3–42; and D. A. Robertson, *Linguistic Evidence in Dating Early Hebrew Poetry* (Missoula, Mont.: Scholars Press, 1972). As with most issues in biblical studies, arguments have been made for the opposing view; see, more recently, Michael Waltisberg, "Zum Alter der Sprache des Deboraliedes Ri 5," *ZAH* 12 (1999): 218–32.

11. Baruch Halpern, "The Resourceful Israelite Historian: The Song of Deborah and Israelite Historiography," *HTR* 76 (1983): 380. See also Halpern's two related studies: "Doctrine by Misadventure: Between the Israelite Source and the Biblical Historian," in *Poet and Historian*, 41–73; and "Sisera and Old Lace: The Case of Deborah and Yael," in *The First Historians: The Hebrew Bible and History* (University Park: Pennsylvania State University Press, 1996), 76–103; subsequent references to Halpern's studies are given parenthetically. Although Heinz-Dieter Neef ("Deboraerzählung und Deboralied: Beobachtungen zum Verhältnis von Jdc. IV und V," *VT* 44 [1994]: 47–59) also argues that the story is a later clarification of the song, I will deal primarily with Halpern's work, which brings more clearly into focus the methodological issues at stake.

12. See Hayden White, *Metahistory: The Historical Imagination in Nineteenth-Century Europe* (Baltimore, Md.: Johns Hopkins University Press, 1973); idem, *Tropics of Discourse: Essays in Cultural Criticism* (Baltimore, Md.: Johns Hopkins University Press, 1978); idem, *The Content of the Form: Narrative Discourse and Historical Representation* (Baltimore, Md.: Johns Hopkins University Press, 1987). See also Arnaldo Momigliano's sober appraisal of White's project in "Biblical Studies and Classical Studies: Simple Reflections upon Historical Method," in his *Essays on Ancient and Modern Judaism* (Chicago: University of Chicago Press, 1994), 3–9.

13. Cf. the thesis put forward by Cross: "In both instances [Exodus 15 and Judges 5] we possess side by side prose narrative accounts (Exodus 14 and Judges 4), and in both instances the poetry is earlier, the prose secondary and derivative. We see the process of prosaizing poetic composition before our eyes" ("Epic Traditions of Early Israel," 21). As Jeffrey Kittay and Wlad Godzich observe, the transformation of oral poetry into literary prose has broad implications as an almost universal literary-historical process: "In the linguistic traditions of Hebrew, Greek, Latin, Arabic, Old Icelandic, English, Spanish, German, Wolof, and Pulaar, and on and on and on, prose comes after verse" (*The Emergence of Prose: An Essay in Prosaics* [Minneapolis: University of Minnesota Press, 1987], xi). Kristin Hanson and Paul Kiparsky describe this process in more formal linguistic terms, identifying verse (counterintuitively) as the "unmarked" form of verbal art, prose as the "marked" form ("The Nature of Verse and Its Consequences for the Mixed Form," in *Prosimetrum: Crosscultural Perspectives on Narrative in Prose and Verse*, ed. Joseph Harris and Karl Reichl [Rochester, N.Y.: D. S. Brewer, 1997], 17–44).

14. The Greek tradition provides an interesting parallel. J. B. Hainsworth points out that in the seventh century B.C.E. a post-Homeric tradition of narrative choral lyric poetry develops, which generally preserves Homeric language and

diction while jettisoning the long narrative form: "[T]heir narrative leaps from point to point and is balanced by prayers and reflections and a confident use of the first-person pronoun" (*The Idea of Epic* [Berkeley: University of California Press, 1991], 43).

15. David E. Bynum, "Samson as a Biblical φὴρ ὀρεσκῷος," in *Text and Tradition: The Hebrew Bible and Folklore*, ed. Susan Niditch (Atlanta, Ga.: Scholars Press, 1990), 59. He wrote this essay in response to Alter's arguments ("Samson Without Folklore," in *Text and Tradition*, 47–56), on different grounds, against a folkloric (oral-traditional) understanding of the Samson stories.

16. Regarding formulaic diction, consider the use of traditional word-pairs, e.g., *šimʿû* ("hear") and *haʾăzînû* ("give ear") in 5:3, *ḥālāb* ("milk") and *ḥemʾâ* ("curds") in 5:25. As for opacity, one assumes that the tribal roster (5:14–18) was more transparent for those steeped in the tradition.

17. Talmon ("Bridegroom of Blood" [in Hebrew], *Eretz Israel* 3 [1954]: 93–95) takes a vaguely folkloric approach in interpreting the mysterious episode in Exodus 4. Rather than illuminate the story through textual emendations or even on the basis of its present narrative context, he posits a wider literary or folkloric context. Thus, he interprets this "legend" (*aggadah*) against the posited background of a certain legend "type" (*sug*), which tells of various violent encounters between a traveler and a supernatural being: he mentions Jacob's struggle in Genesis 32, Balaam's encounters with the angel in Num. 22:22–34, and the "second circumcision" in Josh. 5:2–8 (there is no actual divine encounter, but perhaps the underlying rite resembles that found in Exodus 4). He does not specifically discuss the issue of oral tradition, and his approach almost amounts to a literary type-scene analysis, but the point remains that these legends point to a largely pre-literary tradition, here a class of folktales, that would clarify their obscurities. Perhaps the seemingly archaic account of Abraham in Genesis 14, which includes a sudden encounter with a mysterious priest, similarly points to an earlier stratum of the patriarchal narratives. See Yochanan Muffs, "Abraham the Noble Warrior: Patriarchal Politics and Laws of War in Ancient Israel," in his *Love and Joy: Law, Language and Religion in Ancient Israel* (New York: Jewish Theological Seminary, 1992), 67–95; a suggestive study that, in effect, sheds light on what may be the remains of a heroic tradition embedded in the patriarchal narratives.

18. Roland Barthes, "The Struggle with the Angel," in his *Image Music Text* (New York: Hill and Wang, 1977), 125–41.

19. Note that both implements are grammatically definite nouns, as though referring to the already known data of tradition.

20. Robert G. Boling also observes: "Here it appears that the prose account has taken literally the poetic parallelism of 5:26" (*Judges*, AB 6A [Garden City, N.Y.: Doubleday, 1975], 98). Oddly enough, however, his translation of 5:26 does not agree with his proposal: "With her left hand she reached for a tent peg / With her right hand for the workman's mallet" (104).

21. Besides Judg. 5:27, the verb appears seven times in the Bible and has the general sense of "hit" or "strike," not necessarily or primarily "hammer." Thus, in Prov. 23:35 it appears in parallel to *hikkâ*, apparently with the sense of a strike of the hand, which seems to be its sense in Ps. 141:5 as well. Perhaps being "overcome by wine" (*ḥălûmê yāyin*), as in Isa. 28:1, literally means being in a daze, as if one had been punched in the head. Judg. 5:22 refers to horses' hoofbeats; similarly vines are trampled underfoot in Isa. 16:8. Finally, the two attestations closest

to this case are Isa. 41:7, an overall problematic and relatively late verse, and Ps. 74:6, where once again the precise implements are obscure, both *kaššîl* and *kêlappōt* perhaps being a hatchet or an axe rather than a hammer.

22. The referent of *maqqebet* (and the relevant sense of *nqb*) is somewhat clearer; cf. 1 Kings 6:7, Isa. 44:12, and Jer. 10:4.

23. Let me emphasize that there are alternative hypotheses regarding the relationship between Judges 4 and 5, namely, that Judges 5 depends on Judges 4, or that they are independent. These are alternatives that Halpern considers and, to my mind, convincingly argues against, and so I will not discuss them further here. Instead, inasmuch as I build on his arguments, my study should be read in conjunction with his. I would also add that if my literary reading of Judges 4 and 5, based on Halpern's theory, accounts for the data in a convincing way, this does not so much confirm my initial assumptions in a circular fashion as provide additional corroboration of Halpern's thesis.

24. He makes similar statements elsewhere. "He did not invent; he merely reified the text, treated it as though it were some legal deposit intended to be read as it was written" ("Doctrine," 49). "The historian indulges his imagination insofar as is necessary to answer questions arising from a close reading of SDeb; he gives no rein at all to idle fancy" ("Sisera," 94). "The art functions steadily *within* the confines of the reconstruction, serving the historian's intention, rather than shaping it" ("Sisera," 94). "Judges 4 does not exhibit a striking internal elaboration, a living growth of its own. It sticks close to the poetic evidence" ("Israelite Historian," 395).

25. Hayden White's work is of particular relevance here (see n. 12). On the place of imagination specifically in biblical history, see Robert Alter, "Imagining History in the Bible," in *History and . . . : History within the Human Sciences*, ed. Ralph Cohen and Michael Roth (Charlottesville: University of Virginia Press, 1995), 53–72.

26. Frank Kermode, "Necessities of Upspringing," in *The Genesis of Secrecy: On the Interpretation of Narrative* (Cambridge: Harvard University Press, 1979), 75–99.

27. Ibid, 98. For instance, Henry James, in his preface to *What Maisie Knew*, describes how a "great oak" grows from a "little acorn": "The accidental mention had been made to me of the manner in which the situation of some luckless child of a divorced couple was affected, under my informant's eyes, by the re-marriage of one of its parents. . . . Whereas each of these persons had at first vindictively desired to keep it from the other, so at present the re-married relative sought now rather to be rid of it. . . . This figure could but touch the fancy to the quick and strike one as the beginning of a story—a story commanding a great choice of developments" (*The Art of the Novel: Critical Prefaces* [Boston: Northeastern University Press, 1984], 140).

28. For helpful discussions of biblical theophanies, see Cross, *Canaanite Myth and Hebrew Epic*, 91–144 and 156–77; and S. E. Loewenstamm, "The Quaking of Nature at the Appearance of God" (in Hebrew), in *Oz LeDavid: D. Ben-Gurion Jubilee Volume* (Jerusalem: Kiryat Sefer, 1964), 508–20. For parallels from antiquity, see Moshe Weinfeld, "Divine Intervention in War in Ancient Israel and in the Ancient Near East," in *History, Historiography and Interpretation: Studies in Biblical and Cuneiform Literatures*, ed. H. Tadmor and M. Weinfeld (Jerusalem: Magnes Press, 1983), 121–47.

29. Perhaps this *sûfâ* flutters in the background of the name *yam-sûf*.

30. It is Deborah's leadership, not Barak's, that is memorialized in 5:7. In fact, Barak, unlike Deborah, has no independent existence in the poem. His name appears only twice (vv. 12, 15), both times in Deborah's wake, like the second term

of a parallelistic word-pair. Linguistically this makes "Deborah" the unmarked and thus primary term. Furthermore, the writer quite likely mistook *qamtî* (v. 7), the archaic second-person feminine singular form of the verb, for the first-person singular (on which see C. F. Burney, *The Book of Judges with Introduction and Notes* [1930; reprint, New York: Ktav, 1970], 116), yet another indication to the writer that Deborah outranks Barak. All this led the writer to place Deborah before Barak in 5:1, granting her the superior position (as in Exod. 15:1, Moses is named before the people) and making the song *hers*.

31. In the ancient Near East the names of animals were sometimes used as proper names. See Martin Noth, *Die israelitischen Personennamen im Rahmen der gemeinsemitischen Namengebung* (Stuttgart: Kohlhammer, 1928), 229–30; Herbert Bardwell Huffmon, *Amorite Personal Names in the Mari Texts: A Structural and Lexical Study* (Baltimore, Md.: Johns Hopkins University Press, 1965), 151–52; Johann Jakob Stamm, *Beiträge zur hebräischen und altorientalischen Namenkunde* (Göttingen, Ger.: Vandenhoeck & Ruprecht, 1980), 329–30; and Richard S. Hess, *Amarna Personal Names* (Winona Lake, Ind.: Eisenbrauns, 1993), 193. The question naturally arises whether a given occurrence of such a name is "realistic" or "symbolic." Unfortunately, there is no prior method by which one can answer this question; one can only engage, case by case, in that inferential process known as interpretation. That three names in a single poem have, as I will argue, thematically relevant meaning strengthens but does not ultimately prove my reading. Conversely, that "Sisera" apparently does not—it is simply his name—in no way disproves it.

In fact, if one stands back, the evidence of Judges 4 and 5 falls into place as part of a larger picture. One can find several other instances in Judges of humans named after animals and other natural phenomena—Eglon ("calf"), Oreb ("raven"), Zeeb ("wolf"), and Samson (cognate with "sun")—perhaps further traces of underlying oral traditions. Two of these still seem to have thematic significance in the narrative. Eglon's ponderous flesh endows him with the inertia of a cultic statue. And note how Ehud is sent to bring Eglon an offering (*lĕhaqrîb ʾet-hamminḥâ*, 3:18), combining the political and religious meanings of *ʿābad*. Similarly, Samson's name resonates with his hot temper as well as with the use of fire in his exploits. Halpern perceives an analogous process elsewhere in biblical narrative: "Routinely in Israelite prosopography, geographic and political kinship metaphor is reified by interpreters. It should be noted that the same applies to names and epithets in transmission: Gual ben-Ebed ('the despised son of a slave,' vocalized with Josephus) and Zabul ('prince, commissioner') in Judges 9, Shemebed ('his name is lost'), along with others in Genesis 14:2, and the corrupt liturgy in 1 Chr. 25:4 (from *hᵃnānî* forward), which has produced at least five and perhaps as many as nine sons of Heman, are some examples" ("Doctrine," 53–54). In effect, in each instance a "function" begins to evolve into a character. Finally, Ian Watt, in his famous study of the origins of the novel, observes that it, too, broke with tradition through its use of names: "Characters in previous forms of literature, of course, were usually given proper names; but the kind of names actually used showed that the author was not trying to establish his characters as completely individualised entities. . . . The early novelists, however, made an extremely significant break with tradition, and named their characters in such a way as to suggest that they were to be regarded as particular individuals in the contemporary social environment" (*The Rise of the Novel: Studies in Defoe, Richardson and Fielding* [Berkeley: University of California Press, 1965], 18–19).

Of course, in our case the names do not change; rather, their original symbolic significance is lost.

32. L. Alonso-Schökel ("Erzählkunst im Buche der Richter," *Biblica* 42 [1961]: 160–61) recognizes the irony of Barak's name within the story but goes no further.

33. The various passages that I will refer to in this discussion were most likely composed after Judges 5. Nonetheless, one can easily imagine that their underlying traditions, which I posit or reconstruct through a type of triangulation, go back at least to the time of the song's composition.

34. Psalm 18 and 2 Samuel 22 exhibit several minor discrepancies, and yet they are manifestly the same psalm; one would be hard-pressed to give these differences a convincing literary interpretation. This provides an instructive contrast to the mode of articulation of biblical prose, as argued by Alter ("Samson Without Folklore"), where discriminations on the same scale often have significant interpretive consequences.

35. See Burney, *Judges*, 85, for references. Boling (*Judges*, 95) continues this line of thought.

36. As Cassuto points out ("Biblical and Canaanite Literature," 41), Ugaritic *mḫṣ* appears in various accounts of Baal vanquishing his enemies. Hebrew *māḥaṣ*, then, is part of a venerable tradition of heroes smiting their foes.

37. Yair Zakovitch, "Sisseras Tod," *ZAW* 93 (1981): 364–74.

38. Halpern similarly remarks: "In [this] case, the source is literary, a poem long canonized, with antique linguistic elements posing knotty problems to the interpreter" ("Sisera," 96).

39. Halpern provides an analogous glimpse into "the construction of a Biblical historical account" ("Sisera," 82), but he focuses on the historian's attempt to reconstruct the events.

40. See von Rad, "Historical Writing in Ancient Israel," 201–202; and I. L. Seeligman, "Menschliches Heldentum und göttliche Hilfe: Die doppelte Kausalität im alttestamentlichen Geschichtsdenken," *Theologische Zeitschrift* 19 (1963): 385–411.

41. I previously listed these: Exod. 14:24 and 23:27; Deut. 7:23; 2 Sam. 22:15 = Ps. 18:15; Ps. 144:6. Consider as well the following occurrences of *mĕhûmâ:* Deut. 7:23 and 28:20; 1 Sam. 5:9, 11 and 14:20; Isa. 22:5; Ezek. 7:7; Zech. 14:13.

42. The source text of the allusion is apparently J, while vv. 26 and 27a belong to P—following S. R. Driver, *Introduction to the Literature of the Old Testament*, rev. ed. (New York: Scribner, 1910), 29–30.

43. Here I follow Neef ("Deboraerzählung und Deboralied," 54), who shrewdly points out how the story was designed to answer precisely those questions raised by the song's gaps.

44. Halpern insightfully observes that "*ʾšt ḥbr ḥqyny* [means] either 'the wife of Heber the Qenite' or 'the woman of the Qenite community/band.' In Judg. 5:24 either rendition could apply. In Judges 4 (17a, 21), vss. 11 and 17b leave no doubt. Jael is 'the wife of Heber the Qenite,' a fact that has programmed all subsequent views about her. The author of Judges 4 has *fleshed out* and perhaps even *created a character* etiolate in or absent from SongDeb. It is probable that the prose author has *elaborated because of interpretation,* not tradition: 'Heber's' treaty with Hazor (4:17) is a detail supplied to answer the question 'why did Sisera flee to Jael's . . . tent?'" ("Israelite Historian," 393; emphasis added). This is the first step in yet another "upspringing."

45. Even Halpern concedes, with respect to Judg. 4:20, that "the historian seizes the opportunity to insinuate that the Canaanite was a coward" ("Israelite Historian," 401).

46. Neef, "Deboraerzählung und Deboralied," 56.

47. Boling, *Judges*, 97–98. Halpern, conversely, remarks: "Commentators have long speculated that Jael employed milk as a soporific. There is no evidence that the Israelites cherished it for this quality. Quite the reverse, Sisera slumbers because the drug of exhaustion has overcome the adrenalin of fear (wy^cp, 4:21g). But the *commentators' urge to find a function* for the drink expresses a sense, first, that the narrative is otherwise tightly drawn, and, second, that *this element is now otiose*. The historian has taken the element from SDeb (5:25) in order to include all the relevant action relayed by his source" ("Sisera," 83, emphasis added; cf. "Doctrine," 47). As with other details in the story, he wrongly assumes that his historiographical explanation of a narrative datum excludes the possibility of a literary interpretation of the same datum. His distinction between symbolic and nonsymbolic details finds an interesting analogue in Roland Barthes's "reality effect": "Flaubert's barometer, Michelet's little door, say, in the last analysis, only this: *we are real*" ("The Reality Effect," in *French Literary Theory Today: A Reader*, ed. Tzvetan Todorov [Cambridge: Cambridge University Press, 1982], 16). It is notoriously difficult, however, to foreclose symbolic readings of even such seemingly arbitrary details.

48. I am tempted to see such a convention of a recognition scene as a convention of these stories. After Ehud has slain Eglon and made his escape, the writer chooses to linger beside the corpse until his servants finally make the gruesome discovery (3:24, 25). One thinks as well of Gideon's triumphal and vindictive parade through Succoth and Penuel after capturing Zebah and Zalmunna (8:13–17). Perhaps Samson's secret victory over the lion plays with this convention (14:6).

49. Neef, "Deboraerzählung und Deboralied," 55.

50. Kermode, *Genesis of Secrecy*, 75.

51. Ibid., 77. In Aristotle's words: "[T]he subject represented . . . is an action; and the action involves agents, who must necessarily have their distinctive qualities both of character and thought, since it is from these that we ascribe certain qualities to their actions. . . . In a play accordingly they do not act in order to portray the Characters; they include the Characters for the sake of the action." ("Aristotle's *Poetics*," in *The Rhetoric and The Poetics of Aristotle*, trans. Ingram Bywater [New York: Random House, 1954], 1449b–1450a).

52. Kermode, *Genesis of Secrecy*, 77.

53. One should note here Ben Edwin Perry's apt remarks regarding the analogous lack of "character" in Greek myth: "Now the analogy of similar stories about Zeus may have helped at the birth of [the myth of Io], but most mythologists would agree, I think, that the *character* of Zeus and Hera was not the starting point from which this myth was 'deduced' . . . rather the myth was told in order to explain something in the history of the cult of Hera, while 'character' is something that results only for the modern or later mind. The myth-maker is oblivious to character" ("The Early Greek Capacity for Viewing Things Separately," *Transactions of the American Philological Association* 68 [1937]: 408 n. 3).

54. See Vladimir Propp, *Morphology of the Folktale*, 2d ed. (Austin: University of Texas Press, 1968). A.-J. Greimas (*Structural Semantics: An Attempt at a Method* [Lincoln: University of Nebraska Press, 1983], 197–256) continues and revises Propp's model. Unlike Aristotle and Propp, however, Greimas seeks not to account for a

particular practice, a specific body of work, but rather to provide a general structural-semantic method. See Kermode's discussion of both figures in *Genesis of Secrecy*, 79–81.

55. Kermode, *Genesis of Secrecy*, 76.

56. E. M. Forster, *Aspects of the Novel* (San Diego, Calif.: Harcourt, Brace & World, 1927), 78.

57. Kermode, *Genesis of Secrecy*, 78.

58. Ibid, 79.

59. Ibid, 81. He halfheartedly brackets the historical reconstructions of New Testament scholars: "So biblical critics solace themselves with an Aramaic Matthew or a proto-Luke or an ur-Mark, or a Passion narrative. It is at least convenient to think of the methodologically describable *fabula* as having historical existence" (79). Nonetheless, the very real historical dimension of his argument is clear.

60. In fact, the synoptic tradition quite possibly began as early Christian oral traditions. See, e.g., Werner H. Kelber, *The Oral and the Written Gospel: The Hermeneutics of Speaking and Writing in the Synoptic Tradition, Mark, Paul, and Q* (Philadelphia, Pa.: Fortress Press, 1983).

61. Kermode, *Genesis of Secrecy*, 78.

62. Recall, for instance, the progression Kermode describes "from fable to *written* story, from story to character, from character to more story" (*Genesis of Secrecy*, 98; emphasis added). To return to Perry's discussion of myth, it seems no mere coincidence that he links the "modern" penchant for thinking in terms of character to print culture: "Moreover, the number of instances in which Zeus was supposed to have made love to a mortal woman was not so present to the mind of the myth-maker as it is to us, *who peruse classical dictionaries*" ("The Early Greek Capacity for Viewing Things Separately," 408 n. 3; emphasis added).

63. In fact, as Jaakko Hintikka has observed with regard to Aristotle's view of time, "Greek culture" in general is "largely based on the spoken and not on the written word" (*Time and Necessity: Studies in Aristotle's Theory of Modality* [Oxford: Clarendon Press, 1973], 88). See also Eric Havelock, *Preface to Plato* (Cambridge, Mass.: Harvard University Press, 1963).

3. Narration and Discourse

1. It matters not that *šibbōlet* has two separate meanings since the test involves sound, not sense. I have therefore included both in my word count. What this incident actually reveals about the pronunciation of Hebrew in antiquity remains unclear. For a recent treatment that includes a survey of the problems involved and their variously proposed solutions, see Ronald S. Hendel, "Sibilants and *šibbōlet* (Judges 12:6)," *BASOR* 301 (1996): 69–75.

2. Ibid., 71–72.

3. Shklovsky specifically mentions *skaz* as an example of defamiliarization ("Art as Technique," in *Russian Formalist Criticism: Four Essays*, ed. and trans. Lee T. Lemon and Marion J. Reis [Lincoln: University of Nebraska Press, 1965], 23).

4. The notion of "monism" is meant to invoke Bertrand Russell's distinction between his own "dualist" philosophy and monistic philosophies (such as William James's pragmatism) that deny or undo the Cartesian division between "mind" and "matter." See, for instance, his *Theory of Knowledge: The 1913 Manuscript* (London: George Allen & Unwin, 1984), 5–14.

5. Emile Benveniste, "The Correlations of Tense in the French Verb," in his

Problems in General Linguistics, 205–16; subsequent references are given parenthetically.

6. Hans Reichenbach, *Elements of Symbolic Logic* (New York: Macmillan, 1947), 287–98. This theory defines tense as a complex of three "time points": S (point of speech), E (point of the event), R (point of reference). For the present tense, S = R = E; for the pluperfect, E < R < S. In order to account for non-deictic tenses with this formalism, one would have to define a second set of tenses defined solely in terms of E and R. For a standard recent account based on Reichenbach's analysis, see Bernard Comrie, *Tense* (Cambridge: Cambridge University Press, 1985).

7. Russell, *Theory of Knowledge,* 106–107.

8. Bertrand Russell, "On the Experience of Time," *The Monist* 25 (1915): 212, 220. See also J. M. E. McTaggart, "The Unreality of Time" (1908), in *The Philosophy of Time,* ed. Robin Le Poidevin and Murray MacBeath (Oxford: Oxford University Press, 1993), 23–34.

9. In this study I assume that the Biblical Hebrew verbal system is based at least partly on tense. The important problem of aspect is beyond the scope of the present work. In any case, the temporal markers I will discuss here demonstrate that temporal relations are involved. For one largely convincing account of tense and aspect in Biblical Hebrew, see Ronald Hendel, "In the Margins of the Hebrew Verbal System: Situation, Tense, Aspect, Mood," *ZAH* 9 (1996): 152–81; see also Tal Goldfajn, *Word Order and Time in Biblical Hebrew Narrative* (Oxford: Oxford University Press, 1998). Both these studies are largely compatible with the analysis given here, but since they are based on Reichenbach's system, they cannot fully accommodate my hypothesis that the consecutive is an unspoken (non-deictic) preterite.

10. Goldfajn analogously observes that "in narrative, tenses are used to locate situations which are not anchored to any specific S time [present of speech], but rather to a context-specified anchor point" (*Word Order and Time,* 59), but she still defines the "temporal perspective" of narrative with respect to Tn (Narrator's Time), which in effect merely substitutes for Ts, the present of speech (141).

11. Hans Jacob Polotsky, "A Note on the Sequential Verb-Form in Ramesside Egyptian and in Biblical Hebrew," in *Pharaonic Egypt: The Bible and Christianity,* ed. Sarah Israelit Groll (Jerusalem: Magnes Press, 1985), 159.

12. Ibid., 157. He refers to Weinrich, *Tempus: Besprochene und erzählte Welt,* 3d ed. (Stuttgart: W. Kohlhammer, 1977).

13. See Wolfgang Schneider, *Grammatik des biblischen Hebräisch,* 5th ed. (Munich: Claudius, 1982); Eep Talstra, "Text Grammar and Hebrew Bible. I: Elements of a Theory," *BibOr* 35 (1978): 169–74; idem, "Text Grammar and Hebrew Bible. II: Syntax and Semantics," *BibOr* 39 (1982): 26–38; Alviero Niccacci, *The Syntax of the Verb in Classical Hebrew Prose* (Sheffield, Eng.: Sheffield Academic Press, 1990); Robert E. Longacre, "Discourse Perspective on the Hebrew Verb: Affirmation and Restatement," in *Linguistics and Biblical Hebrew,* ed. Walter R. Bodine (Winona Lake, Ind.: Eisenbrauns, 1992), 177–89.

14. See as well their critical exchange subsequent to the publication of the first edition of *Tempus* in 1964: Käte Hamburger, "Noch einmal: Vom Erzählen. Versuch einer Antwort und Klärung," *Euphorion* 59 (1965): 46–71; and Harald Weinrich, "Tempusprobleme eines Leitartikels," *Euphorion* 60 (1966): 263–72. Recall that Banfield argues for the complementarity of Hamburger's and Benveniste's work on, respectively, the epic preterite and narration.

15. Weinrich, *Tempus,* 27.

16. Ibid., 33.

17. It makes no difference that Weinrich also speaks of writer and reader since they are mere notational variants for the *Sender* and *Empfänger* of a presumed act of *Kommunikation* (*Tempus*, 29). As we just saw, however, Benveniste claimed that the events of narration seemed to "narrate themselves" ("Correlations of Tense," 208).

18. It is still typical of scholars, especially those following Weinrich under the banner of "text linguistics" or "discourse analysis," to take Benveniste's insight as the "aware[ness] of linguistic realities beyond the level of the sentence," namely, the text or discourse. See, e.g., Jan Joosten, "The Indicative System of the Biblical Hebrew Verb and Its Literary Exploitation," in *Narrative Syntax and the Hebrew Bible*, ed. Ellen van Wolde (Leiden, Holland: Brill, 1997), 53; cf. Goldfajn, *Word Order and Time*, 78.

19. The letter *waw* (*w*) in Hebrew often functions as a prefixal conjunction meaning "and." The designation *waw*-consecutive refers (synchronically speaking) to those derivative verb forms in which the conjunction has been joined to a primary verb form. There are, in fact, two *waw*-consecutives: *waw* + imperfect (wayyiqtol), which serves as the sequential preterite, and *waw* + perfect (weqatal), which functions as the inverse, a sequential future. Given the concerns of this chapter, I will, for the sake of convenience, use the term *waw*-consecutive (or, simply, consecutive) to refer strictly to the former.

20. This is the standard historical account of the *waw*-consecutive formulated by G. Bergsträsser through comparative analysis of various Northwest Semitic languages. For a helpful survey of opinion on this tense, see Mark S. Smith, *The Origins and Development of the* Waw-Consecutive: *Northwest Semitic Evidence from Ugarit to Qumran* (Atlanta, Ga.: Scholars Press, 1991), 1–15. For an updated historical account of this tense, see Anson F. Rainey, "The Ancient Hebrew Prefix Conjugation in the Light of Amarnah Canaanite," *Hebrew Studies* 27 (1986): 4–19; see also the response articles in *Hebrew Studies* 29 (1988).

21. See Goldfajn, *Word Order and Time*, 107.

22. Smith, Waw-*Consecutive*, 22.

23. Niccacci, *Syntax*, 41–43; see also Polotsky, "Sequential Verb-Form," 159.

24. Some versions read *hammĕlûkâ* for *hammāyim*. It is difficult to account for the corruption of *hammĕlûkâ* into *hammāyim;* I take the former as an attempt at harmonization and retain the latter. There is an interesting possible parallel in the Aqhat Epic where one finds reference to *qr mym* (CTA 1.19:III:45–46), a place not far from where Aqhat is killed. The designation (perhaps a proper name) is of uncertain meaning and is typically left untranslated, though H. L. Ginsberg suggests in a note "water sources" (*ANET*, 154). Perhaps one should read here "City of Water," emending *qr* to *qrt*. In fact, a nearby parallel passage (1.19:IV:3–4) refers to the "City of ABLM" (with the expected *qrt*), another locale in the vicinity of the place of Aqhat's death.

25. Niccacci analogously if vaguely refers to "narrative" (our "narration") as the "detached" account of the "historian" (*Syntax*, 33, 102; see also Niccacci, "The Stele of Mesha and the Bible: Verbal System and Narrativity," *Orientalia* 63 [1994]: 241). He means by this that "narrative concerns persons or events which are not present or current in the relationship involving writer-reader and so the third person is used. In discourse, on the other hand, the speaker addresses the listener directly (dialogue, sermon, prayer)" (*Syntax*, 29). He seems to define narrative and comment, respectively, as being in the third and first persons. Thus, he does not

allow for the possibility of first-person narration (though, one should admit, neither did Benveniste or Weinrich), which in a meaningful sense would still be an "objective" recounting of events. Conversely, I have been arguing that speakers, even when reporting past events in the third person, often provide "subjective" accounts. Regarding first-person narration and Benveniste's failure to account for it, see Banfield, *Unspeakable Sentences*, 141–80.

26. Niccacci aptly notes such differences by contrasting non-initial QATAL in narration with initial QATAL in discourse, which he calls "QATAL for reporting." Due to his emphasis on categorization, however, he fails to give adequate or convincing explanation of these data (*Syntax*, 48–62).

27. Regarding the restriction of ʿattâ to discourse, see Niccacci, *Syntax*, 101. In fact, there are several (apparent) counterexamples. In Gen. 32:5, for instance, Jacob sends a message to Esau that "I have sojourned with Laban, and I delayed [wāʾēḥar] until now [ʿad ʿattâ]." Since this is direct speech, of concern is not the presence of the deictic as such but its co-occurrence with the consecutive. This is mitigated, however, by the preposition ʿad ("until"); the tense still locates the onset of the verb at a certain moment of time independent of "now," which then continues until the present. (The semantics of the verb allows this temporal effect since "delay" necessarily begins at a definite point in time, but can continue on indefinitely.) One finds similar examples outside of quoted speech:

And Joseph established [wayyāśem] it as a law until this day. (Gen. 47:26)

And he (Joshua?) called [wayyiqrāʾ] the name of that place Gilgal until this day. (Josh. 5:9)

These, however, are clearly examples of what is aptly referred to as "authorial intrusion"—the writer and his present briefly intrude into the text—so these deictics do not, strictly speaking, actually appear in narration. But one must still consider the co-occurrence of "now" and the consecutive. As with the first example, the preposition ʿad serves as a buffer of sorts between the moment of the event and the author's present. Furthermore, note the difficulty of giving these sentences a literal interpretation since the grammatical subject cannot be understood as continuing the action until "this day." Relatedly, one senses a blurred, indistinct transition from narration to authorial comment, in that the phrase "until this day" has been unceremoniously appended to a sentence of narration; if one were to remove this offending phrase, one would still have a perfectly grammatical sentence. Thus, I believe that such sentences have undergone deletion or (what amounts to roughly the same thing) that they have entered standard usage as a type of shorthand. For one finds fuller and logically more coherent versions of these same sentences in which, furthermore, the deictic does not co-occur with the consecutive.

And he called [wayyiqrāʾ] it Shibah—therefore [ʿal kēn] the name of the city is Beer-sheba until this day. (Gen. 26:33)

And he called [wayyiqrāʾ] its name Luz—that is its name until this day. (Judg. 1:26)

In addition to these verbless (present-tense) clauses, other analogous examples use the imperfect (Gen. 32:33 and Judg. 10:4) and the perfect (Josh. 7:26 and 23:8) —

never the consecutive—in order to narrate actions that continue from the past to the present.

28. For the full linguistic account, see Banfield, *Unspeakable Sentences*, 37–41.

29. Banfield, *Unspeakable Sentences*, 54–56; Jean-Claude Milner, *De la syntaxe à l'interprétation: quantités, insultes, exclamations* (Paris: Éditions du Seuil, 1978), esp. 198–223.

30. James Joyce, *Dubliners* (Harmondsworth, Eng.: Penguin Books, 1968), 222.

31. Takamitsu Muraoka, *Emphatic Words and Structures in Biblical Hebrew* (Jerusalem: Magnes Press, 1985), xi; subsequent references are given parenthetically.

32. Emphasis, more strictly conceived, may provide a second subcategory. The early Russell, for instance, referred to deictics as "emphatic particulars": "In a world where there were no specifically mental facts, is it not plain that there would be a complete impartiality, an evenly diffused light, not the central illumination fading away into outer darkness, which is characteristic of objects in relation to a mind? . . . [T]o me it seems obvious that such 'emphatic particulars' as 'this' and 'I' and 'now' would be impossible without the selectiveness of mind" (*Theory of Knowledge*, 40–41; see also Ann Banfield's discussion of "emphatic particulars" in *The Phantom Table: Woolf, Fry, Russell and the Epistemology of Modernism* [Cambridge: Cambridge University Press, 2000], 265–66, 328–29). Russell's emphasis has to do with a type of geometry of sight, "the central illumination fading away into outer darkness." While Russell here seems to link emphasis specifically to subjectivity, what he calls "selectiveness of mind," one might, on the basis of his own logic, give it an alternate definition in purely geometrical terms, namely, the relations of objects to a perspective that may or may not be occupied by a subject. A photograph, for instance, can be said to contain a "focal" point, deriving from the geometrical relations holding between the camera lens and the objects captured in the photograph, not from the "selectiveness" of any mind. Following this analogy, those types of emphasis related to word order and other syntactic phenomena, where certain words or phrases become the "focus" of a sentence, might be analyzed as the effects of a "geometry" of syntax. See, e.g., C. H. J. van der Merwe's discussion of "emphasis and focus" (which I take to be a hendiadys) in *The Old Hebrew Particle "gam": A Syntactic-semantic Description of "gam" in Gn–2Kg* (St. Ottilien, Ger.: EOS, 1990), 37–47.

33. Muraoka's distinction between narrative and conversation does not necessarily entail the stronger, because more specific, distinction between narration and discourse. The almost universal insistence of narrative theory that all narrative originates in a narrator telling a story to a narratee assumes that language is discourse, that narrative is a type of conversation. For a rebuttal of this view see Ann Banfield, "Narrative Style and the Grammar of Direct and Indirect Speech," *Foundations of Language* 10 (1973): 1–39.

34. Van der Merwe's study (*Old Hebrew Particle "gam"*) interprets the emphatic use of this particle solely in terms of "focus," and so his analysis is largely tangential to my own; see also C. H. J. van der Merwe, Jackie A. Naudé, and Jan H. Kroeze, *A Biblical Hebrew Reference Grammar* (Sheffield, Eng.: Sheffield Academic Press, 1999), §1.4.

35. See the similar syntax and sense in 1 Kings 1:46–48. Robert Alter has suggested to me in conversation that this verse actually alludes to 1 Sam. 4:17.

36. I take the notion of speaker-oriented adverbial from Ray Jackendoff, *Semantic Interpretation in Generative Grammar* (Cambridge: MIT Press, 1972), 47–107; Banfield adopts his notion in *Unspeakable Sentences*, 34, 116–18. He analyzes

adverbials according to the node (of the sentential tree structure) they attach to, which in turn determines their possible sentence positions. Sometimes an adverb in a given sentence position can attach to more than one node; its semantic interpretation will then vary according to which node it is attached to.

John also went to the store.

Depending on intonation, one might mean that John, in addition to Mary, went to the store, or that John went to the store as well as to the bank. These alternatives would be represented formally by attaching "also" to different nodes. In the former case it attaches to the sentence and "modifies" the subject; in the latter it attaches to the verb phrase, where it "modifies" the prepositional phrase. Consider its effect in initial position.

?Also, John went to the store.
Furthermore, John went to the store.
What is more, John went to the store.
In fact, John went to the store.
Indeed, John went to the store.
Actually, John went to the store.

In this position "also" conveys nothing about John or his action; it is oriented instead toward the speaker and her assertion. As a result, the two paraphrases given above (for "John also went to the store") do not capture the meaning of this sentence. This use of the adverbial, I suggest, approximates the effect of initial-position *gam* in Biblical Hebrew. Since "also" in initial position is not entirely idiomatic in English, I have listed other speaker-oriented adverbials which provide reasonable translations for *gam* as a speaker-oriented adverbial. Wolfgang Richter's "modal words" (under which he includes *ʾak* and *gam*) are more or less equivalent to speaker-oriented adverbials (*Grundlagen einer althebräischen Grammatik*, 3 vols. [St. Ottilien, Ger.: EOS, 1978–80], 1:188–92). See also C. J. Labuschagne, "The Emphasizing Particle *gam* and Its Connotations," in *Studia Biblica et Semitica* (Wageningen, Neth.: H. Veenman en Zonen, 1966), 193–203.

37. Richter, too, classifies occurrences of *gam* and *ʾak* (see the next section of the present chapter) as either a "conjunction" (2:38, 3:195) or a "modal" (3:176–78); in the latter case, the adverbial stands in sentence-initial position.

38. Muraoka singles out this example of *gam* as having "simple additive force" (144).

39. I have found two examples where a sentence-initial *gam* may be construed as embedded: Eccl. 7:22 and 8:16. In neither, however, does it function as a speaker-oriented adverbial.

40. BDB (s.v. "אַךְ") already gives much the same analysis of its syntactic functions. Van der Merwe, Naudé, and Kroeze similarly assign two functions to *ʾak* (but not *gam*): "focus particle" (§41.4) and "modal word" (§41.3); see also C. H. J. van der Merwe, "The Old Hebrew 'Particles' אַךְ and רק (in Genesis to 2 Kings)," in *Text, Methode und Grammatik: Wolfgang Richter zum 65. Geburtstag*, ed. W. Gross, H. Irsigler, and T. Siedl (St. Ottilien, Ger.: EOS, 1991), 297–311.

41. All poetry in the Bible is presented as direct discourse, whether explicitly as reported speech (e.g., the Song of the Sea) or implicitly as the exclamations of

a lyric persona (e.g., the psalms). (Edward Greenstein has informed me that Tur-Sinai was the first to make this observation of biblical poetry, though I have not succeeded in finding the relevant reference.) I do not mean to suggest, however, that biblical poetry follows the grammar of direct discourse in biblical narrative, but merely that it shares with direct discourse certain grammatical features: first- and second-person pronouns, expressive constructions, various spatial and temporal deictics, etc.

42. I render the somewhat surprising imperfect verb (*yāšubû*) with the past continuous. Driver (*Notes on the Hebrew Text and the Topography of the Books of Samuel*, 2d ed. [Oxford: Clarendon Press, 1913], 365) suggests it is "more picturesque" than the perfect. I have also supplied a direct object ("corpses") for the sake of idiomatic English.

43. These are the only two instances of this interesting collocation of *ʾak* and the infinitive absolute; BDB, s.v. "אַךְ."

44. In addition to the following two examples, see 2 Sam. 2:10; 1 Kings 9:24; 2 Kings 12:14; 23:9, 26, 35.

45. Reading with LXX.

46. See Martin Noth, *The Deuteronomistic History* (Sheffield, Eng.: JSOT Press, 1981), 57, 72, and 135 n. 48; Cross (*Canaanite Myth*, 287n) attributes 2 Kings 23:26–25:30 to a second edition of the Deuteronomistic history (Dtr²).

47. I should point out that Muraoka distinguishes between narrative and direct discourse in his analyses, but it is by no means clear that he maintains Benveniste's stronger definition of narration.

48. I am not suggesting the infinitive absolute is always an adverbial. It is, however, in the presence of a finite form of the same verb since the latter takes precedence as the verb.

49. One might refer to this as emphasis of the verbal action, but it is not expressive in my precise use of the term. "She looked very closely" describes an intense mode of looking. In such instances the most literal English approximation to the Hebrew would be, "She looked lookingly"—analogous, in effect, to another paronomastic construction, the X of Xs, as in "the Song of Songs." This mode of intensification, dealing entirely with *what* is described, is quite different from forcefully insisting, "She did indeed look," where it is a question of *how* the speaker asserts the proposition itself. Here a literal English translation might be, "Looking, she did look."

50. Friedman, in his recent translation of his extended J source (*The Hidden Book in the Bible* [San Francisco: HarperCollins, 1998]), shrewdly renders this construction not with a particular word or phrase but with italic typeface. Not coincidentally, one alternatively refers to italicization as "emphasis," as when an academic writer specifies whether or not emphasis has been added to a quotation. This is because italics typographically represent the *contrastive stress* of a voice in an imagined or anticipated recitation. I thus find Friedman's solution attractive. Unfortunately, he uses this convention to translate *all* occurrences of the construction—partly due, it should be noted, to his stated aim of achieving an internally consistent translation—where, in fact, an important distinction should have been made.

51. Gen. 19:9; *20:18; 26:28; 27:30;* 30:16; 31:15; 31:30 (two times); 37:33; 40:15; 43:3, 7, 20; 44:28; Exod. 2:19; 3:7, 16; 5:23; *13:19;* 15:1, 21; Lev. 5:19; *10:16; 19:20;* Num. *11:32;* 12:14; 22:30, 37; 23:11; 24:10; Josh. 3:10; 7:7; 9:24; *17:13;*

24:10; Judg. *1:28; 7:19;* 9:8; 11:25 (three times), 11:35; 15:2 (two times); 17:3; 20:39; 1 Sam. *1:10;* 2:27, 30; 10:16; 14:28, 30, 43; 20:3, 6, 28; 23:10; 27:12; 2 Sam. 1:6; 3:24; 12:14; 19:43 (two times); 1 Kings 8:13; 19:10, 14; 2 Kings 3:23; 14:10; 18:33. Italic typeface indicates narration. Though these lie outside my primary set of texts, see also Ezek. 1:3 and Ruth 2:11.

52. This verse presents difficulties regardless of which solution one chooses. Given the apparently intended repetition of this construction, I follow those who regard *niśśēʾt* as the infinitive absolute, followed by the perfect. The precise meaning of the sentence, however, is still difficult to ascertain. For a survey of the problem and some possible solutions, see Driver, *Notes on . . . the Books of Samuel*, 339.

53. See also 2 Sam. 1:6, Ezek. 1:3; and Muraoka, *Emphasis*, 88.

54. Banfield observes that in the sentence "John said that, frankly, she was lying" the adverbial "frankly" should be attributed to the quoting speaker (the implicit "I") rather than the quoted speaker, John (*Unspeakable Sentences*, 34). The distinction between quoting and quoted speaker is more difficult to perceive here since in my example Moses is both the quoted and quoting speaker. That is, it is a performative declaration, and so Moses, speaking in the first person, refers to his own act of speaking: "I hereby declare . . ."

55. See also Gen. 20:18; Lev. 10:16; Num. 11:32; Josh. 17:13; Judg. 1:28; 1 Sam. 1:10.

56. See also Gen. 27:30.

57. The infinitive absolute construction occasionally allows for the expressive use of the consecutive, which few examples constitute the only counterevidence I have found thus far to my thesis regarding the incompatibility of the consecutive and expressivity: Gen. 19:9; 31:15; Josh. 24:10; 2 Sam. 3:24. Unlike the deictic *ʿattâ* and the expressive elements *gam* and *hinnēh*, the infinitive absolute can appear after the conjugated verb, thus circumventing the switch in tense. In Gen. 31:15 the infinitive absolute might not actually be expressive, but here *gam*, which does seem to carry expressive force, for once co-occurs with the consecutive: "Are we not thought of by him as foreigners? For he has sold [*mĕkārānû*] us and indeed, has entirely consumed [*wayyōʾkal gam ʾākōl*] our money." Again, it is precisely the infinitive that allows for this syntactic anomaly, for in its absence one would find *wĕgam ʾākal*, the expressive element now co-occuring with the perfect, as one would expect. Had one found instead *wayyōʾkal gam ʾet kaspēnû*, the adverbial *gam*, in the absence of the infinitive absolute, would lose its expressive force and the phrase would mean: "And he ate our money as well."

58. Muraoka, review of *Sintassi del verbo ebraico nella prosa biblica classica*, by Alviero Niccacci, *Abr-Nahrain* 27 (1989): 188. See Goldfajn's similar criticisms in *Word Order and Time*, 74–76. In light of my criticism of Weinrich's *Textlinguistik*, it is worth noting Muraoka's similar skepticism toward Niccacci's method: "All this seems to suggest that, notwithstanding the insistence of the text linguistics that one needs to look at a unit larger than even a sentence, it is still possible to proceed on the assumption that a given tense has a certain value on its own" (189).

59. Joüon-Muraoka §118c; see also GKC §111a. Muraoka echoes this traditional view in criticizing Niccacci's view of the perfect: "Quoting Joüon (*Grammaire*, §118c), who writes that normally a narrative begins with QATAL, N[iccacci] categorically denies that such is the case, although the former adduces, in the paragraph referred to by N[iccacci] some valid examples such as Gn 4.1 / whāʾādām yādaʿ ʾet hawwā wattahar wattēled . . . /, which is hardly a case of "ante-

fatto" (so N[iccacci] in §19), unlike in Gn 3.1 /whannāḥāš hāyā ʿārum . . . /" (Muraoka, "Review," 189; ellipses in original).

60. See Ziony Zevit, *The Anterior Construction in Classical Hebrew* (Atlanta, Ga.: Scholars Press, 1998).

61. Joüon-Muraoka §118c; GKC §111a.

62. For the sake of argument I hold to a traditional reading of this verse, largely abandoned by modern translators. Of course, my argument does not depend on either reading.

63. The asyndetic beginning of this verse makes it look like the onset of a new narrative thread syntactically independent of the preceding events. Note the correspondingly broad time frame of the introductory phrase: "In those days . . .".

64. See Goldfajn, *Word Order and Time*, 90–104.

65. Cf. Banfield's observations regarding the function of dates in historical narrative ("Grammar and Memory," in *Interdisciplinary Approaches to Language: Essays in Honor of S.-Y. Kuroda*, ed. Carol Georgopoulos and Roberta Ishihara [Dordrecht: Kluwer, 1991], 39–50). In 1–2 Kings consider as well the recurring references to the year X of the rule of King Y.

66. Even when a date lies yet in the future, one can still use the simple past of narration, for a non-deictic preterite need not refer to an event in one's actual past. Consider Orwell's use of the preterite in *1984*. Hamburger thus comments with respect to the preterite in this novel: "And the fact that even [*1984*], like all other utopian visions of the future, is narrated in the past—and not in the future—tense, once again drastically discloses the a-temporal meaning of the epic preterite" (*Logic of Literature*, 112). As I indicated in my introduction, Hamburger means for the adjective "epic" to modify all occurrences of the preterite in fictive narrative.

67. Muraoka, review of *Sintassi*, by Niccacci, 189–90; ellipses in original. Niccacci, well aware of this problem in verb distribution, posits a "fundamental difference between the *WAYYIQTOL of narrative*—which is either initial or the continuation of another initial WAYYIQTOL—and the *WAYYIQTOL of discourse* which is never initial but always the continuation of a non-narrative initial construction, different, that is, from WAYYIQTOL" (*Syntax of the Verb in Classical Hebrew Prose*, trans. W. G. E. Watson [Sheffield, Eng.: JSOT Press, 1990], 107; emphasis added). As a matter of fact, as he himself recognizes, this so-called initial WAYYIQTOL in narration is never initial but is always preceded by some adverbial phrase or a construction involving the perfect (WAW-x-QATAL) typically recounting some antecedent sequence of events (the pluperfect). These he tautologically excludes from narration by relegating them to "recovered information" (48–62)—one of Weinrich's dubious linguistic notions—allowing him to maintain WAYYIQTOL's "initial" position in narration. In this ad hoc fashion the true consecutive continues to characterize narration, while the offending evidence is ostensibly brought into line. Muraoka quite justly objects to such maneuvers: "As a consequence of N.'s general thesis he has to distinguish between true and proper narrative and improper narrative" (review, 190).

68. Roland Barthes, *Camera Lucida* (New York: Hill and Wang, 1981), 64.

69. As Alter has pointed out, in biblical narrative's rendering of speech "the 'bias of stylization' affects the words assigned to the speakers" (*Biblical Narrative*, 70); as one now sees, it also affects its syntax. It is worth noting, furthermore, that even the French aorist makes occasional appearances in speech. For instance, Banfield reports: "There are archaic and conventionalized uses of the aorist with

the second person, such as formal addresses of the type delivered at the Académie Française. For instance, in the response of Claude Lévi-Strauss to the reception of Alain Peyrefitte by the Académie" (*Unspeakable Sentences*, 301 n. 6). She has further indicated to me (in a personal communication) that a museum guide may use the *passé simple* in the recited prescripted text that accompanies a tour, as may a radio sports announcer, sans interlocutor, in the isolation and anonymity of a broadcast. In these latter examples, all grammatical signs of the speaker's subjectivity, like Jephthah's, are systematically removed from language.

70. Robert Alter, *Genesis: Translation and Commentary* (New York: Norton, 1996), xxiii. In this discussion I draw upon Alter's introduction, wherein he discusses matters of translation, style, and so forth.

71. See Abba Ben-David, *Biblical Hebrew and Rabbinic Hebrew*, 2 vols. (Tel Aviv: Dvir, 1967–71).

72. Frye, *Anatomy of Criticism*, 246–47.

73. Noth, *Deuteronomistic History*, 5–6.

74. Of course, at a sufficient remove later biblical writers, such as the author of Esther and the Chronicler, would dare to return to narration.

75. Banfield, *Unspeakable Sentences*, 171–72.

76. See Maurice Blanchot, "The Narrative Voice," in *The Gaze of Orpheus and Other Literary Essays*, ed. P. Adams Sitney (Barrytown, N.Y.: Station Hill Press, 1981), 133–43.

77. I include here the *waw* of the consecutive, although it has been absorbed into this verb's morphology. See Gabriel Josipovici, "The Rhythm Established: *Bereshit bara*," in *The Book of God: A Response to the Bible* (New Haven, Conn.: Yale University Press, 1988), 53–74; see esp. 60.

78. Gen. 1:1 and 2:4b are two notable exceptions. And here one deals specifically with absolute beginnings, both source-critically and mythologically speaking. See also 2 Kings 20:1.

79. I think this effect is achieved in: Exod. 4:1; Num. 12:14; 20:3; Josh. 22:28; 1 Sam. 10:12; 21:9; 22:14; 2 Sam 18:11; 2 Kings 4:14, 41; 5:6; 7:13, 19. In 2 Kings 5:6 one actually has the text of a letter, which genre often begins with *wĕʿattâ*, indicating, I would suggest, how the letter responds to some previous correspondence or known situation. In legal texts the conspicuous *waw* seems to have another effect, as in, e.g., Exod. 30:18, 23; 31:13; Lev. 20:2; Num. 9:2; 18:25. See Cynthia L. Miller, "The Pragmatics of *waw* as a Discourse Marker in Biblical Hebrew Dialogue," *ZAH* 12 (1999): 165–91.

80. Smith, Waw-*Consecutive*, 25.

81. Joüon-Muraoka, §111a3.

82. Waltke-O'Connor, §32.3. See further references in their discussion of: Num. 23:19; Deut. 2:30; 1 Sam. 10:2; 1 Kings 3:11; 8:47. Although they do provide examples from narration (2 Kings 14:7; 21:3–4; 23:4), given the overwhelming stylistic evidence, they are deviations from classical style. Coming as they do late in the Book of Kings, perhaps they point to an evolutionary trend toward Late Biblical Hebrew. As they point out with reference to Eccles. 2:5, 9, a late text: "This use tends to replace the common *wayyqtl* in the later books, in part as the language comes more and more under the influence of Aramaic, which lacks the *wayyqtl* form" (§32.3d).

83. I offer this attested form, derived from a secondary root (see 1 Kings 18:27), in favor of the unattested primary form.

84. Alter entertains this possibility as well (*Genesis*, xxii).

85. For an overview of this problem and its solutions, see Smith, *Waw-Consecutive*, 24–27. The idea of the consecutive as a purely literary tense is obviously very attractive, given the analogy I have drawn between it and the French *passé simple*. While I have presented evidence for why this is plausibly so, such arguments are hardly conclusive. Over against the Arad Inscription just mentioned, one should note, for instance, the so-called Yavneh Yam Inscription (KAI 200:4–8), a transcription of a worker's complaint against his supervisor, in which the consecutive is used four times. One suspects the mediation of a scribe, who in formalizing the language may have introduced literary forms such as the consecutive. I must admit, however, that the worker's distraught emotional state still manages to come through in the language, and this inscription is surely one of the closest things we have to a live recording of spoken pre-exilic Hebrew. The question, then, is hardly settled. Therefore I must emphasize that the argument of this chapter does *not* rest on the consecutive's being a strictly literary tense. More important is the fact that it does not posit any relationship between the speaker and the narrated event. Similarly, while the simple past in English and the German *Imperfekt* appear regularly in the spoken language, they no doubt take on a specialized function in many novels as the tense of narration.

86. See E. A. Speiser, *Genesis* (Garden City, N.Y.: Doubleday, 1964), 195; and Alter, *Genesis*, 129.

87. See Ben-David, *Biblical Hebrew and Rabbinic Hebrew*, 1:14–15.

88. M. M. Bakhtin, *The Dialogic Imagination: Four Essays*, ed. Michael Holquist and trans. Caryl Emerson and Michael Holquist (Austin: University of Texas Press, 1981), 259–422; subsequent references are given parenthetically.

89. M. Parry, *Making of Homeric Verse*, 273.

90. A. Parry, *The Language of Achilles and Other Papers* (Oxford: Oxford University Press, 1989), 3.

91. Translations of Homer throughout this book closely follow Lattimore, with only occasional adjustments to highlight repetitions and other important effects. Richmond Lattimore, *The Iliad of Homer* (Chicago: University of Chicago Press, 1951); idem, *The Odyssey of Homer* (New York: Harper & Row, 1967).

92. Note that Russell refers to William James's pragmatist philosophy as a "neutral monism" because of the latter's refusal to distinguish between physical and mental entities, which, in turn, is based on his psychological theory equating behavior with belief—not unlike A. Parry's description of the Homeric world. See Russell, *Theory of Knowledge*, 15–32.

93. A. Parry, *Language of Achilles*, 6. Egbert J. Bakker similarly observes: "The step from Achilles' and Patroklos' discourse to that of the Homeric narrator and the voice of the Greek epic tradition presupposes a certain compatibility between the heroic discourse of Homeric characters and the poetic discourse that encapsulates this direct speech" ("Storytelling in the Future: Truth, Time, and Tense in Homeric Epic," in *Written Voices, Spoken Signs: Tradition, Performance, and the Epic Text*, ed. Egbert Bakker and Ahuvia Kahane [Cambridge, Mass.: Harvard University Press, 1997], 23–24); idem, "The Study of Homeric Discourse," in *A New Companion to Homer*, ed. Ian Morris and Barry Powell (Leiden, Holland: Brill, 1997), 284–304.

94. As Pierre Chantraine points out, the verbal system of Homeric Greek is primarily aspectual but still indicates temporal relations (*Grammaire Homérique: Tome II, Syntaxe* [Paris: Librairie C. Klincksieck, 1958], §§270–91). The aorist gives the

event, "pure and simple"; the imperfect indicates a duration. Thus, Louis Basset, on the basis of the unequal distribution of the augmented verb forms in Homer, mistakenly distinguishes between discourse and narration ("L'Augment et la Distinction Discours/Récit dans *L'Iliade* et *L'Odyssée*," in *Études Homériques* [Lyon: Maison de l'Orient Méditerranéen, 1989], 9–16). While it is true that augmented forms are significantly more frequent in direct discourse, this does not provide adequate grounds for such a grammatical distinction. The present tense similarly occurs more frequently in direct discourse than in Homer's third-person narratives, but this is because Homer primarily tells stories (in the past tense), whereas his characters occasionally tell stories but mostly talk about their present situations. If Bakker is correct in his conclusion that augmented verbs are "used in contrast with [non-augmented] forms, not to mark an event as 'past' in our sense, but as 'near,' in the sense that a given idea derives not from the collective consciousness of the tradition but from the consciousness of the individual speaker here and now" ("Storytelling in the Future," 29), then one might explain their distribution along a similar line of reasoning. Thus, as Bakker notes, the augmented forms are not only frequent in characters' speech but "de rigueur in similes"—an eternal present?

95. One might similarly compare the various references to Odysseus's scar: Homer's own digression on the scar in the famous recognition scene between Odysseus and Eurykleia (19.392–490); Odysseus's self-revelation to his herdsmen (21.218–21); Eurykleia's explanation to Penelope (23.73–77); and, finally, Odysseus's self-revelation to his father (24.331–35).

96. See Aitken, "Oral Formulaic Composition and Theme in the Aqhat Narrative"; idem, "Word Pairs and Tradition in an Ugaritic Tale."

97. Edward Greenstein, "Between Ugaritic Epic and Biblical Narrative: The Role of Direct Discourse" (paper presented at the annual meeting of the Society of Biblical Literature, Washington, D.C., November 1993).

98. Throughout this book I use the Ugaritic texts and translations found in Simon B. Parker, ed., *Ugaritic Narrative Poetry* (Atlanta, Ga.: Scholars Press, 1997); I give CTA references in lieu of page number.

99. See Simon B. Parker, *The Pre-Biblical Narrative Tradition* (Atlanta, Ga.: Scholars Press, 1989), 28–37.

100. As Greenstein points out in his translation, however, this last consonant requires an emendation: "Written *ṣ;* the scribe forgot his horizontals" (Parker, *Ugaritic Narrative Poetry*, 46 n. 112).

101. I more or less follow the translations suggested by Daniel Sivan, *Grammar of the Ugaritic Language* (Leiden, Holland: Brill, 1997), 123. As I indicate later, he renders one line with the future tense, which only strengthens the presence of an oral storyteller.

102. Auerbach, *Mimesis*, 3.

4. Represented Consciousness in Biblical Narrative

1. Dorrit Cohn, *Transparent Minds: Narrative Modes for Presenting Consciousness in Fiction* (Princeton, N.J.: Princeton University Press, 1978), 4.

2. For this understanding of *dibbâ*, see Prov. 10:18.

3. Joyce, *Dubliners*, 222.

4. The grammatical form of the *indirect* question would be: "He wondered from what it had proceeded." Note that there is neither subject-verb inversion nor a question mark.

5. It is worth noting that the passages I have transposed here into direct speech appear more or less in this form in John Huston's film adaptation of "The Dead," rendered (as are others) as a voice-over interior monologue.

6. Hamburger originally made the third person a necessary component of the "epic preterite," related to though not coterminous with represented consciousness. However, W. J. M. Bronzwaer (*Tense in the Novel: An Investigation of Some Potentialities of Linguistic Criticism* [Groningen, Neth.: Wolters-Noordhoff, 1970]) and Banfield (*Unspeakable Sentences*, 154–65) disprove her theory inasmuch as they discover examples of first-person represented consciousness. Note that with respect to the "opacity" of the represented "I" Banfield speaks of *dédoublement du moi* (159).

7. See Banfield, *Unspeakable Sentences*, 64–108; subsequent references are given parenthetically. The scholarly literature on represented consciousness is vast and rife with controversy. In general, there is a marked preference for "pragmatic" over "formal" accounts. In spite of the a priori objections of rival "theories," the explanatory power of Banfield's grammatical theory demonstrates that represented consciousness does indeed follow generative syntactical rules, susceptible to analysis and not just interpretation. Regarding rival accounts, see Brian McHale, "Free Indirect Discourse: A Survey of Recent Accounts," *PTL* 3 (1978): 249–87; idem, "Unspeakable Sentences, Unnatural Acts. Linguistics and Poetics Revisited," *Poetics Today* 4, no. 1 (1983): 17–45. Monika Fludernik has claimed to refine and extend Banfield's theory in *The Fictions of Language and the Languages of Fiction: The Linguistic Representation of Speech and Consciousness* (London: Routledge, 1993).

8. Consider the two sentences Banfield proffers as evidence (*Unspeakable Sentences*, 94).

Oh how extraordinarily nice I was! (*she thought).
Where were my paints? (*she wondered).

Without the parentheticals, one naturally attributes the subjectivity evoked in both sentences to the "I" who speaks. But adding these parentheticals, which specify a third-person subjectivity, makes them grammatically anomalous (when not read as direct discourse). This is because the third-person parentheticals contradict the fact that the expressivity of these constructions wants to be interpreted with respect to the first-person speaker. She provides similar evidence regarding "now" and the present tense (99).

How my heart was beating now, (I realized then/*I realize now).

The phrase without parenthetical is an example of represented thought, in which the "now" is cotemporal with past ("was"). Adding the first parenthetical, with past tense, is thus acceptable, but adding the second, with its present tense, results in a grammatical contradiction.

9. S. R. Driver, *A Treatise on the Use of the Tenses in Hebrew and Some Other Syntactical Questions,* 3d ed. (Oxford: Clarendon Press, 1892), §135.3 Obs.

10. Simcha Kogut offers an account of *hinnēh*'s "semantic evolution" according to which it first "came to be attached to the beginning of one-member sentences," such as nouns ("On the Meaning and Syntactical Status of הנה in Biblical Hebrew," *Scripta Hierosolymitana* 31 [1986]: 142).

11. Following Kogut, Tamar Zewi ("The Particles הנה and והנה in Biblical

Hebrew," *Hebrew Studies* 37 [1996]: 35–37) classifies these examples under a category she calls *hinnēh* introducing "one-member clause." Most of her "one-member clauses," however, are predicates in surface structure (Gen. 42:28; 2 Kings 6:20; 2 Sam. 1:18; 2 Sam. 16:3; Josh. 7:22; 1 Kings 3:21). I suspect that in deep structure these also contained subjects which were subsequently deleted, so that one should not consider these true "one-member clauses." Conversely, predicate deletion is unlikely, so one-member clauses comprising a noun phrase were probably generated as such in deep structure.

12. I quote from the *Bible de Jérusalem*, the translation directed by the École Biblique de Jérusalem (Paris: Éditions du Cerf, 1955).

13. GKC §147b; BDB, s.v. "הנה." See also Zewi, "The Particles הנה and והנה," 21–22.

14. Lambdin, §135; Kogut, "הנה in Biblical Hebrew," 142.

15. As far as I can tell, Joshua Blau introduced this term into the study of Biblical Hebrew (*A Grammar of Biblical Hebrew* [Wiesbaden, Ger.: Otto Harrassowitz, 1976], §103).

16. A more precise linguistic analysis of the *hinnēh* clause would be E: E → Quasiverb—NP (see Banfield, *Unspeakable Sentences*, 38). (The linguistic formalism means something like: "Expression can take the form of a Quasiverb followed by a Noun Phrase.") The concept of Quasiverb was proposed by Quang Phuc Dong (a.k.a. James McCawley) in order to account for certain subjectless sentences, which he called "epithets" ("Phrases Anglaises sans Sujet Grammatical Apparent," *Langages* 14 [1969]: 44–51). They contain what looks like an imperative verb, and like the imperative they have no apparent subject. On various syntactical grounds, however, he argues that this "quasi-verb" (as he calls it) does not actually constitute a verbal form. The various presentatives, I propose, fall under the category of Quasiverb: in Hebrew *hinnēh*, *hēn* (a synonym of *hinnēh*), and some uses of *rĕʾēh* (the imperative form of "to see"); *voici* and *voilà* in French; and the English and German constructions "here/there is" and "hier/da ist."

It is worth noting that *hinnēh* occasionally appears in syntactic parallelism with *rĕʾēh*, the imperative of "to see." Thus, Francis I. Andersen astutely assigns to *hinnēh* a "quasi-imperative" function—though he is wrong to identify NP as the subject of *hinnēh* (*The Sentence in Biblical Hebrew* [The Hague, Neth.: Mouton, 1974], 94; see also Zewi, "The Particles הנה and והנה," 36). In fact, NP constitutes the complement of the presentative. French makes this grammatical relationship explicit through the oblique case, as in *"me voici!"* BDB already analyzes the pronominal suffix to *hinnēh* as an accusative (BDB, s.v. "הנה") —though strictly speaking Hebrew, of course, lacks case.

17. See Ferdinand Brunot, *La Pensée et la Langue*, 3d ed. (Paris: Masson, 1936), 8; George Le Bidois and Robert Le Bidois, *Syntaxe du Français Moderne* (Paris: Picard, 1936), 122. The analysis of the French presentative has also proven difficult; linguists problematically tend to link it to the verb. See, e.g., Yves-Charles Morin, "On the Two French Subjectless Verbs *Voici* and *Voilà*," *Language* 61 (1985): 777–820.

18. The OED traces attestations of both "presentative" and "presentation" with "metaphysical" or "psychological" meaning back to 1842.

19. Russell, *The Theory of Knowledge*, 41.

20. Bertrand Russell, *Mysticism and Logic* (Garden City, N.Y.: Doubleday, Anchor Books, n.d.), 170; emphasis added. Cf. Russell's assertion elsewhere: "Of an

actually given *this*, an object of acquaintance, it is meaningless to say that it 'exists' " (*Theory of Knowledge*, 138).

21. See Roderick A. Jacobs and Peter S. Rosenbaum, *English Transformational Grammar* (Waltham, Mass.: Blaisdell, 1968), 85.

22. Zewi, in her analysis of *hinnēh* in "the role of a predicate" (i.e., *hinnēh*—Noun), understandably but mistakenly makes definiteness necessary to this construction ("The Particles הנה and והנה," 36).

23. "Here is a book" is grammatical on its own, but it seems to presuppose the prior knowledge of a desire or need that the book can fill: "I'm bored"; "Here's a book."

24. I construe this clause as *hinnēh*—NP since both noun and participle are definite. Conversely, when the noun is definite but the participle indefinite, the participle clearly functions as the predicate of the clause (e.g., Gen. 19:20 and 2 Kings 6:33). If both are indefinite, the syntax is ambiguous (e.g., Gen. 24:63 and 41:29), though it will not affect my arguments here. At any rate, I will tend to view such cases as full clauses since biblical Hebrew can avoid such an ambiguity by using *ʾăšer* ("that/which"):

> *wĕhinnēh tannûr ʿāšān wĕlappîd ʾēš ʾăšer ʿābar bên haggĕzārîm hāʾēlleh* (Gen. 15:17)

And here was an oven of smoke and a torch of fire which had passed between these pieces.

Furthermore, *hinnēh* followed by NP, by virtue of its demonstrative force, tends to "point" to nouns that are close at hand and thus often definite. In fact, Gen. 15:17 and 2 Kings 2:11 (both in narration) are the only clear examples I have found of *hinnēh*—indefinite NP. Contra Zewi, "The Particles הנה and והנה," 36.

25. I offer the hypothetical form *hinnĕnâ* as the particle inflected with the third feminine singular pronoun, a form unattested in the Bible.

26. One finds a number of apparent counterexamples in different poetic texts: *kî hinnēh*. In these cases, however, *kî* does not function as the subordinating conjunction "that" but rather as a logical connective: "For, look, . . ." Interestingly enough, the otherwise non-embeddable *voici* does occur in a fixed expression after the subordinating conjunction: *que voici*.

27. On occasion one finds *wĕhinnēh* at the beginning of a quotation, so that it is not coordinated to a preceding clause. As I discussed in the previous chapter, such "misplaced" conjunctions constitute an additional expressive element.

> *wayyōʾmer lō hinnēh nāʾ ʾîš ʾĕlōhîm bāʿîr hazzōʾt wĕhāʾîš nikbād kol ʾăšer yĕdabbēr bōʾ yābōʾ ʿattâ nēlākâ šām ʾûlay yaggîd lānû ʾet darkēnû ʾăšer hālaknû ʿālêhā wayyōʾmer šāʾûl lĕnaʿărō wĕhinnēh nēlēk ûmah nābîʾ lāʾîš* (1 Sam. 9:6, 7)

And [Saul's servant] said to him, "Look, please, there is a man of God in this city, and the man is honored. All that he says certainly comes to pass. Now, let us go there; perhaps he will tell us about our way, by which we have gone." And Saul said, "And, look, we will come, but what will we bring to the man?"

The servant's statement begins, as is more common, without "and." Saul's reply, however, begins with "and," which indicates his impatience as he apparently interrupts or appropriates what his servant just said. See also: Exod. 4:1; 2 Sam. 18:11; 2 Kings 7:19.

28. GKC §105b identifies *hinnēh* as an interjection; Stanislav Segert refers to the cognate Ugaritic particle *hn* as a "deictic interjection" (*A Basic Grammar of the Ugaritic Language with Selected Texts and Glossary* [Berkeley: University of California Press, 1984], §68). It is worth noting that in modern Hebrew one can say simply, *hinneh!*, "Here!"—cf. *Voilà!* This construction is unattested in the Hebrew Bible, where the presentative always precedes a noun or a sentence. It is thus unclear whether the lone presentative is grammatical in Biblical Hebrew. The occurrence of the presentative as an interjection does not contradict my earlier analysis of the presentative proper as a Quasiverb. Quang Phuc Dong notes that most Quasiverbs can occur alone as an exclamation, observing: "[C]es phrases indiquent l'attitude en question, mais ne spécifient pas vers quel objet l'attitude du locuteur est dirigée" ("Phrases," 49). His examples are: Fuck! Damn! Shit! Hooray!

29. See also Exod. 32:34; Josh. 24:27; Judg. 21:21; 1 Sam. 9:7; 20:2, 21; 21:15; 1 Kings 8:27.

30. One does find instances, however, where the consecutive arguably continues the initial verb of the *hinnēh* clause.

31. Because of this evidence, I do not accept Kogut's contention that *hinnēh* introduces a "content clause" ("הנה in Biblical Hebrew," 147). "Content" suggests the abstracted information of a subordinate clause (S̄), whereas one now sees that *hinnēh* specifically introduces Expressions (E).

32. See also Gen. 12:19; 1 Sam. 24:21; 2 Kings 5:6.

33. See also Gen. 38:24; 42:22, 28; Exod. 3:9; Judg. 17:2.

34. See also Lev. 13:6–7, 10–12, 21–22, 26–27, 34–35; 14:48.

35. Translations often interpret *ʾaḥărê*, literally "beyond," as "west," thus suppressing the deictic element. Even if this translation accurately captures an idiomatic sense of "beyond," however, it still has a certain "built-in" spatial deixis since "beyond" location X is west of X only with respect to the locus of points east of X. Analogous terms such as *mizrāḥ* ("east," deriving from "sunrise") and *maʿărāb* ("west," deriving from "sunset"), conversely, are non-deictic since they do not depend on the location of the speaker. Regardless of the location in which I speak, the sun rises to the east of X and sets west of it.

36. Scholars often treat *hinnēh* and *wĕhinnēh* separately, as though they were two lexical items—a result of text linguistics' misplaced emphasis on surface structure and taxonomic analysis. Consider the title, e.g., of Zewi's study: "The Particles הנה and והנה in Biblical Hebrew."

37. Driver, *Tenses*, §160, Obs. Meir Weiss analyzes it as *erlebte Rede* ("Einiges über die Bauformen des Erzählens in der Bibel," *VT* 13 [1961]: 464). If Meir Sternberg correctly links the presentative to "free indirect discourse" (see index in his *Poetics of Biblical Narrative*), he wrongheadedly refers to *wĕhinnēh* as "codified as a marker of biblical free indirect thought" (ibid., 53), as though represented consciousness weren't a syntactic phenomenon but merely something to be marked by the addition of a type of preposition. See also L. Alonso-Schökel, "Nota estilística sobre la partícula הנה," *Bib* 37 (1956): 74–80; J. P. Fokkelman, *Narrative Art in Genesis: Specimens of Stylistic and Structural Analysis* (Assen, Neth.: Van Gorcum, 1975), 50–53; Andersen, *Sentence*, 94–96; Dennis J. McCarthy, "The Uses of *wᵉhinnêh* in Biblical Hebrew," *Bib* 61 (1980): 332–33; Berlin, *Poetics and Interpreta-*

tion of Biblical Narrative, 62–63, 91–95; Hiroya Katsumura, "Zur Funktion von *hinneh* und *wᵉhinnēh* in der biblischen Erzählung," *Annual of the Japanese Biblical Institute* 13 (1987): 3–21.

38. Flaubert, *Madame Bovary* (Paris: Garnier Frères, 1971), 189.

39. Flaubert, *L'Éducation Sentimentale* (Paris: Garnier Frères, 1964), 138.

40. Ibid., 143.

41. Ibid., 185.

42. Virginia Woolf, "Modern Fiction" (1919), in *The Common Reader* (New York: Harcourt, Brace, 1925), 154; emphasis added. The "shower" of "atoms" is an apparent allusion to Russell's *Philosophy of Logical Atomism* (1918).

43. Ibid., 155.

44. Virginia Woolf, "Mrs. Dalloway in Bond Street" (1923), in *The Complete Shorter Fiction of Virginia Woolf*, ed. Susan Dick, 2d ed. (New York: Harcourt Brace Jovanovich, 1989), 152–59; subsequent references are given parenthetically. A reference to Bond Street in the 1919 essay firmly establishes the connection between the "shower" of visual "atoms" Woolf refers to and her use of the presentative in the short story.

45. I noted earlier that the presentative with an indefinite noun ("Here is a book") seems slightly odd unless one supplies a certain context. One can now see that the presentative takes an indefinite noun more naturally in represented consciousness. It simply represents the perception of an unidentified, nonparticularized object—a car, a girl, etc.

46. Other examples in Woolf are numerous and widespread.

> The feet of those people busy about their activities . . . minds eternally occupied not with trivial chatterings . . . but with thoughts of ships, of business, of law, of administration, and with it all so stately (she was in the Temple), gay (there was the river), pious (there was the Church), made her quite determined, whatever her mother might say, to become either a farmer or a doctor. (*Mrs. Dalloway* [San Diego: Harcourt Brace Jovanovich, 1953], 207; recall that the definite article precludes interpreting "there was" in the existential sense.)

> Her ladyship was coming. Here she was. (*The Years* [New York: Harcourt Brace Jovanovich, 1965], 266)

> Here was a market. Here a funeral. Here a procession with banners upon which was written in great letters. (*Orlando* [San Diego: Harcourt, Brace, 1956], 306–307)

47. James Joyce, *Ulysses* (New York: Random House, 1961), 366.

48. The linguistic formalism is: E_1, E_2. The first E is the interjection, *hinnēh;* the second the perception itself.

49. Woolf, "Modern Fiction," 155.

50. As a type of exclamation, *hinnēh* necessarily represents *reflective* consciousness. See Banfield, *Unspeakable Sentences,* 182–223, esp. 203.

51. Contra Cynthia Miller, *The Representation of Speech in Biblical Hebrew Narrative: A Linguistic Analysis* (Atlanta, Ga.: Scholars Press, 1996), 85–89.

52. BDB (261b) translates the demonstrative "this" as "here," but as another deictic it still supports my point.

53. Various translations, apparently uncomfortable with the unexpected, mute both these deictics.

54. Miller, *Representation of Speech*, 89.

55. Proust, "On Flaubert's Style," 264–65.

56. Flaubert, *Madame Bovary*, 24.

57. Ibid., 55.

58. See Banfield, "Grammar and Memory," 39–41.

59. Andersen, *Sentence*, 94.

60. Fokkelman refers to this past progressive aspect in *Narrative Art in Genesis*, 51. By specifically calling it a "durative present," he seems to perceive that in the represented *hinnēh* clause "now" is cotemporal with "past."

61. See also Gen. 15:12; 18:2; 25:24; 31:2; 38:27; 42:35; Exod. 14:10; Judg. 3:25; 11:34; 14:5; 19:27; 1 Sam. 9:14; 10:10; 25:20; 30:3; 2 Sam. 13:34; 15:32; 16:1; 19:42; 1 Kings 18:7; 19:5, 6, 9, 13; 2 Kings 6:33.

62. See also Gen. 3:6; 12:14; 28:8; 29:31; Exod. 2:2; 32:25; 33:13; Judg. 9:22; 18:26; 1 Kings 11:28; 22:33; 2 Kings 5:7. For possible counterexamples, see 1 Sam. 12:17; 2 Sam. 12:19; 1 Kings 3:28; 20:7.

63. See also Gen. 3:7; 12:11; 22:12; 38:16; 42:23, 33, 34; Exod. 18:11; 32:22; Josh. 22:31; Judg. 13:16; 14:4; 15:11; 20:34; 1 Sam. 22:17; 28:14; 29:9; 2 Sam. 17:8, 10; 1 Kings 17:24; 2 Kings 4:9; 5:7; 7:12. For possible counterexamples, see Gen. 33:13; Num. 11:16; 22:34; Josh. 3:10; 1 Sam. 12:17; 2 Sam. 14:1; 1 Kings 14:2; 20:7.

64. See also 1 Sam. 23:10; 25:4. For a possible counterexample, see 1 Sam. 25:7.

65. See also Gen. 12:18; 31:20.

66. I mentioned earlier that one does occasionally find *kî hinnēh*, but that *kî* in these instances does not function as the subordinating conjunction "that." Nor does one find *hinnēh kî*.

67. Kogut, "הנה in Biblical Hebrew," 148–51. C. J. Labuschagne is similarly guilty of exaggeration regarding the ostensible parallels between *hinnēh* and *kî* ("The Particles הן and הנה," *OS* 18 [1973]: 1–15).

68. Berlin, *Poetics and Interpretation of Biblical Narrative*, 62.

69. The conjunctive *waw* and the preceding arguments for viewing *hinnēh* as non-embeddable indicate a switch from indirect speech to represented consciousness. I am tempted to view this *hinnēh* clause as one of the only biblical examples of actual represented speech: "And it was reported to King Solomon that Joab had fled to the tent of the Lord. There, next to the altar."

70. Banfield makes a similar argument by demonstrating that indirect and direct discourse are not related to each other via a transformation; both must be generated in the phrase structure rules ("Narrative Style and the Grammar of Direct and Indirect Speech").

71. Irene J. F De Jong, *Narrators and Focalizers: The Presentation of the Story in the Iliad* (Amsterdam: Grüner, 1987), 38–39, 118–22.

72. De Jong, "Eurykleia and Odysseus' Scar: *Odyssey* 19.393–466," *Classical Quarterly* 35 (1985): 517–18

73. Compare 19.393–94: *oulēn tēn pote min sūs ēlase leukō odonti / Parnēsond' elthonta met' Autolukon te kai huias;* and 21.219–20f.: *oulēn tēn pote me sūs ēlase leukō odonti / Parnēsond' elthonta sun huiasin Autolukoio.*

74. Similar remarks could be made with respect to *Il* 7.216–18 and 18.237–38, which de Jong regards as approaching "stream of consciousness" (*Narrators and Focalizers*, 121).

75. Scott Richardson, *The Homeric Narrator* (Nashville, Tenn.: Vanderbilt University Press, 1990), 71.

76. As Auerbach observes, the "multilayeredness" of character "is hardly to be met with in Homer, or at most in the form of a conscious hesitation between two possible courses of action" (*Mimesis*, 12–13; emphasis added).

77. In fact, in Homer the hero's *thumos* and its close correlate *menos* compel him to act, just as the *thumos* of the lion compels it to fight. See Gregory Nagy, *The Best of the Achaeans* (Baltimore, Md.: Johns Hopkins University Press, 1979), 136–37.

78. Interior monologue need not take place in the *lēb* in the Bible, nor in the *thumos* in Homer, though the contrast between these two concepts is still important.

79. According to Moshe Greenberg, it is the sincerity of one's heart (*lēb*), not properly performed ritual, that brings about effective prayer (*Biblical Prose Prayer as a Window to the Popular Religion of Ancient Israel* [Berkeley: University of California Press, 1983], 47–51).

80. See Segert, *Grammar of Ugaritic*, §§58, 68; Sivan, *Grammar of Ugaritic*, 185–86.

81. I again follow Parker, ed., *Ugaritic Narrative Poetry;* for the sake of argument, I occasionally give alternate translations of key words in brackets.

82. Sivan, *Grammar of Ugaritic*, 186.

83. See also 1.6.3.10–14, a dream in the Baal Cycle.

84. See Cross, "Prose and Poetry in the Mythic and Epic Texts from Ugarit"; Aitken, "Oral Formulaic Composition and Theme in the Aqhat Narrative"; idem, "Word Pairs and Tradition in an Ugaritic Tale."

85. Alter, *Biblical Narrative*, 65.

86. Auerbach, *Mimesis*, 11.

87. Friedman points out that Gen. 22:11–14 is likely a secondary addition; in the original Elohistic story Isaac *was* actually sacrificed (*Who Wrote the Bible?*, 256–57). Even if this is true, however, it does not affect my interpretation. The redactor responsible for inserting these verses most likely composed them as well—there are no signs of a "doublet" here, which would have required two versions of the same story to be combined without harmonization of such detail—so that he was able to write these verses in such a way as to exploit fully the received narrative situation.

88. I comment here on the redacted text, but the same could be said for J and P separately, for over against J's representation of Noah's consciousness (8:11) stands P's (8:13).

89. For translations of the Mesopotamian texts I use Stephanie Dalley, trans., *Myths from Mesopotamia: Creation, the Flood, Gilgamesh and Others* (Oxford: Oxford University Press, 1989).

90. Andersen, *Sentence*, 18–19.

91. Ibid., 94–95. He does, however, ultimately include all *hinnēh* clauses under the notion of "surprise clause."

92. Ibid., 96.

93. August Dillmann, *Die Genesis*, 6th ed. (Leipzig: S. Hirzel, 1892), 251.

94. As reported in Driver, *Introduction*, 15. For a detailed discussion, see Dillmann, *Genesis*, 246, 251.

95. Due to the common ambiguity in Biblical Hebrew with respect to identifying the pronoun's antecedent, it is conceivable that these *wĕhinnēh* clauses represent the thoughts of the midwife. Tamar is the more important character, however, and at least the second *wĕhinnēh* clause presumably sets up the naming scene in verse 29, which undoubtedly belongs to Tamar.

96. Berlin, *Poetics and Interpretation of Biblical Narrative*, 93.

97. The repetition is not fully redundant. Just because Amnon is lying down in verse 6 does not mean he will be lying down some hours later when Tamar finally arrives in verse 8. The "repetition" also builds suspense as the reader sees Amnon's immensely consequential scheme, conceived in verse 5, gradually come to pass.

98. I admit that the verse as it stands is a bit abrupt, but one must again reckon with the composite nature of the passage. Israel Knohl (*The Sanctuary of Silence: The Priestly Torah and the Holiness School* [Minneapolis, Minn.: Fortress Press, 1995], 96–97) has argued that a long stretch of JE narrative has just ended (25:5); the scenario now under consideration is an expansion by HS (the Holiness School) designed to promote Phinehas and to provide an etiology for the war against the Midianites. This invented scene may place us abruptly at the tent of meeting (though this may be justified by Num. 1:1), but a smoother transition would have required more invasive editing: an insertion *within* JE, probably at verse 5, explaining how Moses called the "judges" of Israel to meet him at the tent. HS apparently preferred the more economical solution.

99. There is one remaining, albeit outlandish, possibility, namely, one might assign point of view to the animals themselves. The donkey and the lion, after all, are the last two grammatical subjects mentioned in the narrative. Though one might object that animals cannot have point of view attributed to them, one should recall Balaam's donkey, who saves the wayward prophet's life by turning aside before the angel of God. In fact, in that story narration recounts three times how "the donkey saw the angel of the Lord" (*wattēreʾ hāʾātôn ʾet malʾak yhwh*, Num. 22:23, 25, 27), using exactly the same language that describes human sight. Unfortunately for this disobedient prophet, his donkey cannot save him from the lion (1 Kings 13:24, 28). The donkey, as though conspiring with fate against the prophet, does not flee from the deadly predator. And neither it nor the corpse is devoured by the lion, who, having slain the prophet, stands peacefully next to victim and co-conspirator. Having accomplished their mission, these animals have no reason for standing there except to be the spectacle bearing witness to the prophet's bizarre if divinely orchestrated end. So as these men come upon this carnivalesque scene, these animals-turned-divine-agents, according to this interpretation, already behold them in their own gaze. Perhaps, then, the representation of the animals' point of view is meant to contribute to this story's topsy-turvy, unsettling quality.

5. Biblical Time and Epic Time

1. Benedict Anderson, *Imagined Communities: Reflections on the Origin and Spread of Nationalism*, rev. ed. (London: Verso, 1991), 25–26; subsequent references are given parenthetically.

2. See Walter Benjamin, "Theses on the Philosophy of History," in his *Illuminations* (New York: Schocken Books, 1968), 253–64. Benjamin opposes "homogeneous, empty time" to "Messianic time," a complicated notion which Anderson glosses as "a simultaneity of past and future in an instantaneous present" (24).

3. Auerbach, *Mimesis*, 74; emphasis added. Anderson (*Imagined Communities*, 24) considers this medieval apprehension of time as a near equivalent of Benjamin's "Messianic time."

4. Elizabeth Deeds Ermarth, *Realism and Consensus in the English Novel: Time, Space and Narrative*, rev. ed. (Edinburgh: Edinburgh University Press, 1998); subsequent references are given parenthetically.

5. Auerbach, *Mimesis*, 74.

6. Thaddeus Zielinski, "Die Behandlung Gleichzeitiger Ereignisse im Antiken Epos," *Philologus Supplement* 8 (1899-1901): 405-49; subsequent references are given parenthetically. Richardson (*Homeric Narrator*, 90-95) misleadingly suggests that scholars have discovered numerous counterexamples to Zielinski's law, which is thus apparently in need of refinement, but the examples he produces are unconvincing. Indeed, he himself concedes that "even in these exceptional cases there is no noticeable reversal in time." Tilman Krischer (*Formale Konventionen der homerischen Epik* [Munich: C. H. Beck'sche Verlagsbuchhandlung, 1971], 91-129) does make an important contribution by further clarifying the principles underlying Zielinski's law, but this will not concern me here since it does not affect my thesis.

7. In light of the connection Anderson draws between simultaneity in the novel and the idea of the nation, it is worth noting that Meir Sternberg points to the complexity of the human social world as the requisite "stage" for simultaneous events in the Bible ("Time and Space in Biblical (Hi)story Telling: The Grand Chronology," in *The Book and the Text: The Bible and Literary Theory*, ed. Regina Schwartz [Cambridge, Mass: Basil Blackwell, 1990], 97). One might even argue that biblical narrative concerns itself with its own "imagined community," namely, "the children of Israel." See Ilana Pardes, *The Biography of Ancient Israel: National Narratives in the Bible* (Berkeley: University of California Press, 2000).

8. Zielinski, "Die Behandlung Gleichzeitiger Ereignisse im Antiken Epos," 411.

9. Ibid., 413.

10. Ibid., 420-22.

11. One might liken the scene's configuration to figure and ground rather than foreground and background.

12. Zielinski, "Die Behandlung Gleichzeitiger Ereignisse im Antiken Epos," 427-28.

13. Ibid., 432-33.

14. Ibid., 437-38.

15. Shemaryahu Talmon, "The Presentation of Synchroneity and Simultaneity in Biblical Narrative," in *Literary Studies*, 112-33; subsequent references are given parenthetically. Others have also returned to the problem of simultaneity. Taking Talmon as his starting point, Burke O. Long ("Framing Repetitions in Biblical Historiography," *JBL* 106 [1987]: 385-99) seeks, in his own words, to "advance the discussion further [by relating] resumptive repetitions to some broader aspects of synchronic narrative theory" (387). For my purpose his study makes no substantive advance on Talmon's work. Sternberg ("Time and Space," esp. 96-123), conversely, criticizes Talmon's study for being reductive (143 n. 12). He analyzes the various narratological means — *other* than resumptive repetition — for effecting simultaneity, as well as the mimetic and poetic motives for doing so. Sternberg's analysis thus focuses on a different set of issues than the present study. For while I, too, adopt a critical stance toward Talmon, I do so by making needed discriminations *within* his account of resumptive repetitions.

16. Talmon quotes the definition in H. M. Wiener, *The Composition of Judges II 11 to 1 Kings II 46* (Leipzig: Hinrichs, 1929), 2; he also refers to Curt Kuhl, "Die 'Wiederaufnahme'—ein literarkritisches Prinzip?" *ZAW* 64 (1952): 1-11.

17. LXX reads "and [that] all Israel loved him" (*kai pas Israēl ēgapa auton*). Driver, for one, accepts the Greek variant (*Notes on . . . the Books of Samuel*, 155). See also P. Kyle McCarter, Jr., *1 Samuel*, AB 8 (Garden, City, N.Y.: Doubleday, 1980), 320-21.

18. One might also read verse 28b as part of Saul's perception: "Saul . . . knew that [*kî*] . . . and that Michal loved him [*ûmîkal . . . ʾāhēbathû*]." After all, Saul's growing fear of David in verse 29 follows from his perception of David's favor with God in verse 28, which, in turn, represents his interpretation of David's uncanny accomplishment of seemingly impossible feats in verses 21–27. In this context verse 28b quite plausibly reiterates Saul's awareness of his daughter's feelings for David, of which he was informed in verse 20b, providing one more reason for his growing fear of and enmity toward David. In this case verse 28b does not constitute a resumptive repetition of verse 20 in any sense, for it is no longer a narrative event but a thought within Saul's mind. Driver (*Notes on . . . the Books of Samuel,* 155) implicitly agrees with my reading of the syntax in MT verse 28b. Reading with LXX in verse 28b—"and all Israel loved him" (*kai pas Israēl ēgapa auton*) —he retroverts the Greek into "and that all Israel loved him" (*wĕkî kol-yiśrāʾēl ʾōhēb ʾōtô*), supplying a subordinate conjunction—cf. MT *kî* and LXX *hoti* in verse 28a—absent in LXX as well as in MT but implied, I suggest, in both.

19. This construction could also signal a pluperfect, but the following verse, recounting with the consecutive Saul's growing fear of David, clearly continues the main narrative sequence which has run without interruption in verses 20–28a, making it difficult to read verse 28b with a pluperfect sense.

20. I omit verse 3 as an insertion of E into what is otherwise J, though this does not affect the present analysis one way or the other. See, more recently, Friedman, *Hidden Book in the Bible,* 119–20.

21. Depending on the layout of Pharaoh's palace, one might imagine that the sound of Joseph's first emotional outburst traveled more or less directly to Pharaoh's house. But how likely is it that Pharaoh heard and comprehended Joseph's subsequent explanations in Hebrew (cf. 42:23)? Perhaps one can accept even this bit of virtuosic eavesdropping as a literary conceit—consider the ambiguity of *qôl* ("voice" or "sound" or even "report") —tolerated for its dramatic effect. But note that this rumor, reported as direct discourse (*lēʾmōr*), refers to Joseph in the third person—"Joseph's brothers have come" (v. 16) —suggesting the secondhand report of a third party.

22. Reading with LXX: *tetaragmenē enthen kai enthen* (Heb. *nāmôg hālōm wahālōm*). See Driver, *Notes on . . . the Books of Samuel,* 109.

23. Reading with 4QSamᵃ and LXX (*kai epeskepsato*): *wayyipqōd.* See Driver, *Notes on . . . the Books of Samuel,* 33; and McCarter, *1 Samuel,* 80.

24. See Hendel's discussion of this passage in "Hebrew Verbal System," 166. I differ from his analysis only in taking the consecutive, *wayyōʾmer* (2:23), as a habitual with incipient force, that is, as the beginning of a habitual sequence: "And he began to say . . ." Eli's sons' repeated refusals to take heed of his warnings, after all, presuppose a series of disregarded rebukes. This use of the consecutive resembles that in 2:21 (*wayyipqōd*), except that there the verb marks the start of an iterated sequence, one that has a definite number of repetitions.

25. I cannot address this noteworthy fact here, but I hope to devote a future study to narrative perspective as such, in which I will account for the differences between biblical and Homeric "pseudosimultaneity." It will entail making Zielinski's law more precise: Homer's desultory alternations between scenes follow certain stipulations that avoid creating any sense of perspective. For now I might mention Krischer's important analysis of Homer's "branching" (*Verzweigung*) technique: he begins with a single scene, in which two narrative threads are explicitly

announced; the scene then branches into these, which in turn, observing Zielinski's law, take place one after the other (*Formale Konventionen*, 103–21). Thus, in *Il* 24.112-19 Zeus commands Thetis to instruct Achilles to surrender Hector's corpse, informing her that he himself will send Iris to tell Priam to recover his son's body. Thetis immediately does so (120–40), and only afterward does Zeus summon Iris (141–58). One result of this technique is that there is no sense of perspective or depth between these two narrative threads since it places them in single file. Biblical narrative, however, uses what Krischer calls a "converging" (*Vereinigung*) technique. This convergence of originally independent narrative situations creates perspective.

26. Robert Alter, *The David Story: A Translation with Commentary of 1 and 2 Samuel* (New York: Norton, 1999), 189. His own translation of this clause reads: "And meanwhile the Philistines were battling against Israel." As he points out, Rashi had already correctly interpreted this passage: "As when a person says, 'Let us return to the previous subject'" (189).

27. Regarding the anterior construction, viz., the pluperfect, see Zevit, *Anterior Construction*.

28. I concede that Mount Gilboa, the site of Saul's defeat, lies considerably to the north of Aphek, so it may stand to reason that the messenger's trip took longer than three days. Conversely, David and his men, unaware of the Amalekite attack, presumably made no particular effort to rush home, whereas this lone survivor, fearing for his life and anxious to deliver the news of Saul and Jonathan's fate to David, likely made a quicker trip of it, suggested as well by his disheveled appearance in 1:2. However, even assuming that one should take "three days" more or less literally (rather than as a rough approximation), other details remain unclear. For instance, one knows that David has been in Ziklag for three days, but how long did it take him to get there after killing the Amalekites? Here the narrative simply does not spell out the story's chronology in all its details, though I would suggest that its carefully matched three-day periods generally indicate how key events line up with each other.

29. This clause seems in need of emendation. One could have a flashback to Absalom here, but then one would not expect the consecutive, which seems to continue rather than turn back upon the narrative, but something like what one finds in verse 37: "And Absalom had fled" (*wĕʾabšālôm bāraḥ*). For several plausible solutions to this problem, see Driver, *Notes on . . . the Books of Samuel*, 303–304.

30. Again, even if one did assign verse 37:26 to J, it would still be the pluperfect of verse 39:1, not its repetitive echo of the earlier verse, that would effect the resumption of Joseph's story.

31. See Talmon, "Presentation of Synchroneity and Simultaneity," 123. In the final version of Genesis, Joseph only spends about twenty years in Egypt before meeting his brothers again: he arrives at the age of seventeen (37:2); is thirty years old when he appears before Pharaoh (41:46); and meets his brothers only after famine has set in seven years later. While J in and of itself does not provide a detailed chronology, one suspects that Ibn Ezra's observation would still hold true of this source considered by itself.

32. See Zielinski, "Die Behandlung Gleichzeitiger Ereignisse im Antiken Epos," 416, 426 and note.

33. Though one cannot locate Ziklag precisely, note that from this base David claims to attack the Negeb (27:10), while in actuality he attacks settlements "on the way to Shur and till Egypt" (27:8).

34. Driver, *Notes on . . . the Books of Samuel*, 213–14.

35. Subjective time corresponds to what the philosopher J. M. E. McTaggart calls the A series ("The Unreality of Time" [1908]); in 1915 Russell analogously speaks of "mental time" ("On the Experience of Time," 212).

36. Objective time corresponds to McTaggart's B series, Russell's "physical time."

37. Regarding the use of dates in history, see Banfield, "Grammar and Memory," 47–48. Talmon similarly comments on the importance of dates in the Books of Kings (112). For a general discussion of temporal markers in biblical narrative, see Brian Peckham, "History and Time," in *Ki Baruch Hu*, ed. Robert Chazan, William W. Hallo, and Lawrence H. Schiffman (Winona Lake, Ind.: Eisenbrauns, 1999), 295–314.

38. Egbert Bakker has an analogous dichotomy in mind when he opposes a conception of the past "that *excludes* the present" to one that "*includes* the present," namely, "the past in myth and epic tradition" ("Storytelling in the Future," 13), but his use of grammatical theory is vague and misleading.

39. A modern *literary* analogue of memory might be Camus's *L'Etranger*, not because of its first-person narrator but rather its celebrated use of the *passé composé*. Sartre, commenting on Camus's use of this tense, suggests: "It was in order to emphasize the isolation of each sentence unit that M. Camus chose to tell his story in the present perfect tense" ("Camus' 'The Outsider'," in *Literary Essays* [New York: Philosophical Library, 1957], 38). Just as each individual epic event is narrated by and thus located from the perspective of the singer, so here a "passive . . . consciousness" (37), viz. the "Outsider's mind" (36), "records all the facts" (37), each "atom of time" (39). The *passé simple*, conversely, is, as Sartre notes in anticipation of Barthes, "the tense of continuity" (38). As an interesting counterpart to Camus's novel, one might mention Proust's *Recherche*, a first-person novel that begins with the *passé composé*: "Longtemps je me suis couché de bonne heure"—a sentence discussed, not coincidentally, by Sartre apropos of *L'Etranger*. Unlike Camus's narrator Mersault, however, Proust's Marcel, more historian than storyteller, quickly recedes from the text in the act of writing as the narration turns to the *imparfait* and the *passé simple*. Proust's "search" (*recherche*)—the root meaning, one might recall, of "history"—transforms memory into history.

40. Frye, *Anatomy of Criticism*, 246; bracketed material added.

41. Barthes, *Camera Lucida*, 91.

42. Banfield, however, revises Barthes's account, arguing that the tense of the photograph is, in fact, the imperfect of memory ("L'Imparfait de l'Objectif: The Imperfect of the Object Glass," *Camera Obscura* 24 [1990]: 65–87).

43. Barthes, *Camera Lucida*, 64.

44. Ibid, 96. Barthes's "absolute past" may also refer to the photograph's apparent temporal aspect, its "pose," as he puts it. For the aorist is often defined as a "punctive" rather than "durative" or "progressive" verb form, as a "still shot," if you will. Conversely, the *imparfait* functions alternately as an iterative and progressive past. This would explain Barthes's identification of the photograph with history. For if the aorist, the tense of history, has the aspect of the photograph, the imperfect, the tense of memory, has a progressive aspect seemingly incompatible with the photograph, at least at first glance.

45. Benveniste, "Correlations of Tense," 210.

46. Barthes, *Camera Lucida*, 64.

47. Russell, "Experience of Time," 220; see also 226–27. In the latter passage Russell also allows for acquaintance with (subjective knowledge of) succession between immediately adjacent events, so that a restricted type of succession can enter "mental time." I will return to this point later.

In defining his B series, McTaggart, unlike Russell, considers only the relations earlier than and later than. McTaggart's series, however, both comprise a set of temporal positions, not the set of multiple events that occupy each of those positions. And if two events may be simultaneous, it makes little sense to describe two points of time in the same way. Either they are nonidentical (one is earlier than the other) or they are identical (they are a single point, not two simultaneous points).

48. Talmon, "Presentation of Synchroneity and Simultaneity," 112.

49. Barthes, "The Discourse of History," *Comparative Criticism: A Yearbook*, ed. E. S. Shaffer, 3 (1981): 9. Barthes's cursory reference to the problem of time in historical discourse, however, reveals that he has not fully apprehended it. For he illustrates the temporal "zig-zag" with the example of Herodotus, "who turns back to the ancestors of a newcomer, and then returns to his point of departure to proceed a little further—and then starts the whole process all over again with the next newcomer" (9). In fact, as Zielinski points out, Homer uses this very procedure in his frequent flashbacks ("The poet uses [*die zurückgreifenden Methode*] when new persons appear, in order to share characteristic details from their past" ["Die Behandlung Gleichzeitiger Ereignisse im Antiken Epos," 441]) without disturbing the narrative's "Einplanigkeit," since he (like Herodotus) reaches back beyond the temporal frame of the primary narrative and thereby avoids narrating parallel (i.e., simultaneous) narrative sequences. At least in this respect, then, Herodotus merely follows the practice of his great predecessor.

50. Zielinski, "Die Behandlung Gleichzeitiger Ereignisse im Antiken Epos," 414.

51. Russell, *Theory of Knowledge*, 171.

52. Banfield, "Grammar and Memory," 48; emphasis added.

53. Theodore M. Andersson relatedly observes of Homeric space: "The *Odyssey* also shares with the *Iliad* an indifference toward the location of places relative to one another" (*Early Epic Scenery: Homer, Virgil, and the Medieval Legacy* [Ithaca, N.Y.: Cornell University Press, 1976], 42).

54. In principle retrospective simultaneity could take the form of indirect speech using the pluperfect, but it functions in a structurally analogous way, and so I will not consider it here.

55. See Muraoka, "Review of Niccacci," 190; and Driver, *Treatise*, 195–211. In terms of general linguistic theory, the perfect behaves here as a "relative tense"; see, more recently Hendel, "Hebrew Verbal System," 158–63.

56. Recall that according to Russell immediate succession falls within the domain of subjective time.

57. Auerbach, *Mimesis*, 12; emphasis added.

58. Ibid., 12–13; emphasis added.

59. See Zielinski, "Die Behandlung Gleichzeitiger Ereignisse im Antiken Epos," 448–49.

60. When Odysseus tells his hosts how he arrived at their island, he repeats information Homer has already provided, but he does so in a most economical fashion.

61. Presumably any language lacking a pluperfect verbal form still possesses the innate means to generate the force of a pluperfect, just as English, although lacking a proper future tense, can nonetheless speak of the future. Bearing in

mind, however, that Homer's *Kunstsprache* never served as the vernacular of any actual linguistic community, it is instructive that his tradition could develop such a rich artistic medium and yet never bother to develop a fully realized pluperfect.

62. Chantraine, *Grammaire Homérique*, §297; emphasis added.

63. Ibid., §271; he proffers *Od* 18.5 and *Il* 1.484, 1.606, and 2.513 as examples. See also §278 on the similar use of the aorist participle, for which he adduces *Il* 1.356, 9.216, 16.473–74, and 17.334.

64. I translate the following passages from Homer myself in order to indicate the possible tense values.

65. Even if one takes it as a pluperfect, it conveys immediate succession, which, as I noted earlier, Russell ("Experience of Time," 226–27) classifies as mental time.

66. Auerbach, *Mimesis*, 7; emphasis added. Irene de Jong ("Eurykleia and Odysseus' Scar") and Theodore M. Andersson (*Early Epic Scenery*, 50–52) argue against Auerbach's reading of this passage. Andersson, in particular, sees this as evidence of Homeric "background." Both base their argument on the claim that the digression in question actually describes Eurikleia's memories. As Auerbach already noted, however, the digression takes the form of an extended subordinate clause, which precludes this alternate reading.

67. Bakker independently provides a similar reading of Auerbach's notion of Homeric foreground: "When we perceive pictures and verbalize that perception, what we focus on at any one moment is by definition 'foreground'; the detail is in sharp focus at a particular moment: that of perception and of speech, the present. And as such it is foreground, even when it is background in terms of the picture that is scanned and conceived of as a static object" ("Mimesis as Performance: Re-reading Auerbach's First Chapter," *Poetics Today* 20 [1999]: 24).

68. Parker, *Pre-Biblical Narrative Tradition*, 228.

69. See Zielinkski, "Die Behandlung Gleichzeitiger Ereignisse im Antiken Epos," 409–11.

70. Blanchot, "The Narrative Voice," 135.

71. See Marcel Detienne, "The Memory of the Poet," in *The Masters of Truth in Archaic Greece* (New York: Zone Books, 1996), 39–52.

72. See Richard P. Martin, *The Language of Heroes: Speech and Performance in the Iliad* (Ithaca, N.Y.: Cornell University Press, 1989), esp. 77–88, and the conclusion, which he entitles "The Poet as Hero" (231–39).

73. Regarding the interpretation of this colophon, see Jack M. Sasson, "Literary Criticism, Folklore Scholarship, and Ugaritic Literature," in *Ugarit in Retrospect: Fifty Years of Ugarit and Ugaritic*, ed. Gordon Douglas Young (Winona Lake, Ind.: Eisenbrauns, 1981), 90–93. Colophonic "signatures," although uncommon, occur in Mesopotamian texts as well (e.g., *Atrahasis*). See Dalley, *Myths from Mesopotamia*, 35 and 38 n. 47.

74. Regarding Ilimilku's possible role as author, see Nicolas Wyatt, "Ilimilku's Ideological Programme: Ugaritic Royal Propaganda, and a Biblical Postscript," *UF* 29 (1997): 775–96; and Marjo C. A. Korpel, "Exegesis in the Work of Ilimilku of Ugarit," *OS* 40 (1998): 86–111.

75. Cross suggests an alternate translation of this line: "master singer, ʾAtn Prln" ("Prose and Poetry in the Mythic and Epic Texts from Ugarit," 1; see also Michael David Coogan's translation in *Stories from Ancient Canaan* [Philadelphia: Westminster, 1978], 115). But this seems a tendentious attempt to support Lord's theory that Homer dictated his epics to a scribe. In order to justify his translation

of *lmd*, Cross appeals to 1 Chron. 25:7—"trained in singing" *mĕlummĕdê-šîr*—in effect interpreting the Ugaritic term as an ellipsis of the full phrase. Surely one cannot supply the crucial missing term *šîr* on the basis of this post-exilic attestation. To the extent that it sheds light on the Ugaritic at all, it suggests that Ilimilku's training under Attenu may have included instruction in singing the poem.

76. Regarding Ilimilku's possible significance as a religious figure, see Nicolas Wyatt, "The Religion of Ugarit: An Overview," in *Handbook of Ugaritic Studies*, ed. Wilfred G. E. Watson and Nicolas Wyatt (Leiden, Holland: Brill, 1999), 551–53. Even if one ascribes these roles to "Attenu the diviner," they still help indicate the text's official religious pedigree.

77. Friedman, *Who Wrote the Bible?*, 150–60, 217–33.

78. The Law, typically reported by Moses as the quoted words of God—e.g., Lev. 1:1–2, "And the Lord spoke to [Moses] . . . 'Speak to the children of Israel' "— derives its authority from God and from his authorized human mediator, hence the designation the Book of the Law *of Moses*. The narratives in which these laws are embedded, however, are ascribed to no one.

79. Apropos of this passage, see the apt commentary by Halpern, *First Historians*, 84–85.

80. The language of 5:22 emphasizes that Sisera's flight took place only after the defeat of his army: "Then [*'āz*] beat the horse's hoofs."

81. Barthes, *Writing Degree Zero*, 30.

82. See Krischer, *Formale Konventionen*, 9–10, 91–129.

83. Zielinski, "Die Behandlung Gleichzeitiger Ereignisse im Antiken Epos," 408.

84. Perry, "The Early Greek Capacity for Viewing Things Separately," 403–27; subsequent references are given parenthetically.

85. Hugh Kenner, *The Stoic Comedians: Flaubert, Joyce, and Beckett* (Berkeley: University of California Press, 1974), 31.

86. Viktor Shklovsky, "Sterne's *Tristram Shandy:* Stylistic Commentary," in *Russian Formalist Criticism*, ed. Lemon and Reis, 31.

87. Ibid.

88. Ibid., 30–31.

6. The Art of Biblical Narrative as Technique

1. Cassuto, "Biblical and Canaanite Literature," 18.

2. Ibid., 17.

3. See, e.g., Susan Niditch, *Chaos to Cosmos* (Chico, Calif.: Scholars Press, 1984); idem, *Folklore and the Hebrew Bible* (Minneapolis, Minn.: Fortress Press, 1993); idem, *Oral World and Written Word;* idem, ed., *Text and Tradition*.

4. Niditch, "Oral Register in the Biblical Libretto: Towards a Biblical Poetic," *Oral Tradition* 10 (1995): 388–89.

5. Alter, *Biblical Narrative*, 47.

6. Bynum, "Samson as a Biblical φὴρ ὀρεσκῷος," in *Text and Tradition*, ed. Niditch, 59.

7. It bears noting that Niditch adduces "repetition," "formulas," and "conventionalized patterns" (type-scenes) as evidence of "oral register" in the Bible. I believe my arguments regarding technique can be extended to the former devices as well, but I will not do so here.

8. Shklovsky, "Art as Technique," in *Russian Formalist Criticism*, ed. Lemon and Reis, 3–24.

9. Ibid., 12.

10. Shklovsky, "Sterne's *Tristram Shandy*," 30–31. Regarding Shklovsky's important notion, one must distinguish between two analogous but distinct classes of aesthetic phenomena. In his study of *Tristram Shandy*, which was originally published in 1921, Shklovsky speaks of "violating form," what I will call "formal defamiliarization." It has to do with art's self-referential character, and so it is not surprising that it arises in the course of a reading of Sterne's novel. However, his earlier definition, dating to 1917, describes what one might call "referential defamiliarization": "[A]rt exists that one may recover the sensation of life; it exists to make one feel things, to make the stone *stony*" ("Art as Technique," 12). Here he focuses on "things" (both concrete and abstract) and "sensation" found in life rather than art. In suggesting a link between writing and defamiliarization, I speak only of the "formal" variety. While oral traditions are by definition formally conservative, it seems reasonable to suppose that they can defamiliarize objects of perception. It is worth noting, however, that Homeric similes describe the unfamiliar (the world of the legendary past) in terms of the familiar (the known world of the present). See Mark Edwards, *Homer: Poet of the* Iliad (Baltimore, Md.: Johns Hopkins University Press, 1987), 102–10.

11. Benjamin, "The Storyteller," in *Illuminations*, 84, 93.

12. M. Parry, *Making of Homeric Verse*, 424–25. His master's thesis, "A Comparative Study of Diction as One of the Elements of Style in Early Greek Epic Poetry," was written at the University of California, Berkeley, in 1923.

13. M. Parry, *Making of Homeric Verse*, 6. His dissertation, "L'Épithète traditionelle dans Homère: Essai sur un problème de style homérique," was written at the University of Paris and subsequently published (Paris: Société Editrice Les Belles Lettres, 1928).

14. Shklovsky, "Art as Technique," 7. He makes a strong empirical claim that one might challenge, but I am less concerned here with the correctness of this or that claim than with his general train of thought.

15. Ibid., 7; emphasis added.

16. So Albert Lord, e.g., in his famous synthesis of the oral-formulaic theory: "He is not a conscious iconoclast, but a traditional creative artist. His traditional style also has individuality, and it is possible to distinguish the songs of one singer from those of another" (*Singer of Tales*, 5). His appeal to the "iconoclast" seems to be a searching nod toward the notion of defamiliarization. Johannes Th. Kakrides, in his apology for the "neo-analytical method," argues that while the unitarians "see only the imagination of a single man creating the Iliad and the Odyssey out of nothing . . . our analysis reveals a poet, a truly great poet, who unhesitatingly borrows from his model's rich material." This leads him to conclude:

> I believe that the poet's personality, as it emerges objectively from the study of his work, is just what we should expect from a Greek classic. He does not ignore the old tradition, nor does he imitate it blindly, but he uses the material bequeathed to him and assimilates it in order to create something new. His genius is thus presented to us as creating freely and at the same time tied to the age-old tradition of Greek epic poetry. (*Homeric Researches* [Lund, Sweden: Gleerup, 1949], 9–10)

Finally, James I. Armstrong, trying to recuperate a "literary" Homer, asserts:

"Specifically I shall be concerned to show that at one of the most traditional and fixed points in his poetic style, i.e. the extended traditional formula, the poet can create within the circumscription of the traditional a vitality which one might call an individuality of style" ("The Arming Motif in the *Iliad*," *American Journal of Philology* 79 [1958]: 339).

17. Shklovsky, "Art as Technique," 8.

18. Ibid., 9.

19. It is no coincidence that Shklovsky opposes the defamiliarizing "poetic" language of literature to the language of folklore, which he relates instead to "practical" or "prosaic" language: "[T]here are two aspects of imagery: imagery as a practical means of thinking . . . and imagery as a means of reinforcing an impression. . . . But poetic imagery only externally resembles either the *stock imagery of fables and ballads* or thinking in images. . . . Poetic imagery is but one of the devices of poetic language. Prose imagery is a means of abstraction" (8–9; emphasis added). Thus, Potebnya's rejected theory (viz. art as thinking in images) rings most true for Shklovsky precisely in the realm of folklore: "[T]he least self-contradictory part of Potebnya's theory is his treatment of the fable" (13).

20. Ibid., 12.

21. Benjamin, "The Storyteller," 83–84.

22. Shklovsky, "Art as Technique," 11.

23. Ibid., 12. This is an entry from Tolstoy's *Diary,* dated February 29, 1897.

24. Shklovsky, "Art as Technique," 12.

25. Benjamin, "The Storyteller," 92–93; no source for the Valéry quotation is provided.

26. Ibid., 93.

27. Ibid., 87.

28. I avoid the terms *oral* and *written* because I view writing as a necessary but insufficient condition for the shift from the traditional to the post-traditional. Writing may proceed for a time as a type of transcription of what is still a fundamentally traditional craft. Leskov (Benjamin's storyteller) would seem to be one example.

29. I suspect that the iterative nature of Homer's oral tradition and its resultant "familiarity" is related to what John Miles Foley has referred to as "traditional referentiality." See his studies *Homer's Traditional Art* (University Park: Pennsylvania State University Press, 1999), and *Immanent Art: From Structure to Meaning in Traditional Oral Epic* (Bloomington: Indiana University Press, 1991).

30. Walter Arend, *Die typischen Scenen bei Homer* (Berlin: Weidmannsche Buchhandlung, 1933), 24.

31. M. Parry, "On Typical Scenes in Homer" (1936), in *Making of Homeric Verse*, 404–407; subsequent references are given parenthetically. For a survey of type-scene analyses, see Mark Edwards, "Homer and Oral Tradition: The Type-Scene," *Oral Tradition* 7 (1992): 284–330.

32. Arend, *Die typischen Scenen bei Homer*, 26. Parry's translation, 405; all subsequent translations are Parry's. To my mind, however, Arend's idea of a narrative *eidos*, what amounts to a type of narratological essentialism, conveys a certain truth. One could link it to various remarks Auerbach makes apropos of Homeric characterization:

Abraham's actions are explained not only by what is happening to him at the moment, nor yet only by his character (as Achilles' actions by his courage and his pride, and Odysseus' by his versatility and foresightedness), but by his previous history. . . . Such a problematic psychological situation as this is impossible for any of the Homeric heroes, whose destiny is clearly defined and who wake every morning as if it were the first day of their lives: their emotions though strong, are simple and find expression instantly. (*Mimesis*, 12; see also 17)

In Arend's study, however, Greek insight into the essential precedes a certain style of presentation as its cause ("And therefore this type of *journey by land* can and must recur whenever a like happening comes up"), whereas in Auerbach's study the inverse holds true. Perhaps one should revise Arend's theory by stating that the narrative *eidos* is related to but not necessarily the cause of Homer's type-scenes.

33. Arend, *Die typischen Scenen bei Homer*, 27; Parry, 405.

34. Bernard Fenik, *Typical Battle Scenes in the* Iliad: *Studies in the Narrative Techniques of Homeric Battle Description* (Wiesbaden, Ger.: Franz Steiner, 1968), 204; emphasis added.

35. The following discussion is loosely based on Armstrong, "The Arming Motif in the *Iliad*." As noted earlier, however, Armstrong attempts to recuperate Homer as a literary artist. He frames his argument as a revision of a certain reception of Parry's theories (Lord's synthesis had not yet been published).

It has been strongly and persuasively argued that Homer and his fellow poets in the post-Mycenaean Greek world recited principally at great festal gatherings. Under such conditions recitation might well be less a process of impromptu versification. Rather preparation, including reflection, selection, and meditation would be possible prior to recitation. This view of the circumstances of performance, though not absolutely necessary, makes sense, I think, if one is to construct an hypothesis of composition in harmony with the literary quality of the *Iliad*. (339)

By "literary quality" he apparently refers to "a subtlety in the use of formula beyond a traditional style of mechanical improvisation."

The technique of verse-making is, I believe, an oral technique, but poetry of such high quality leads me to believe also that Homer worked and reworked his poems, perhaps over a very long period of time, devoting even a lifetime to the shape of certain scenes and the *Iliad* as a whole. Consequently, we may imagine that Homer could mold his poem where he so wished in a manner not entirely unrelated to that of the writing poet. (340)

In other words, he all but equates "quality" and "subtlety" with "writing," opposing it to the "oral," whose style is that of "mechanical improvisation." He fails to consider whether an oral traditional art can possess its own nonliterary quality. In fact, Homer surely "worked and reworked his poems" as part of that same process by which he mastered his *Kunstsprache*. Just as the formula evolved over time, so the *extended* formula, the type-scene, no doubt evolved over time as well, thus explaining its subtlety and quality. The quality thus cultivated in these poems, however, is not that literary quality of defamiliarization but the traditional one of familiarity.

36. Fenik, *Typical Battle Scenes in the* Iliad, 204.

37. Krischer, *Formale Konventionen,* 15; see also 75–84. Subsequent references are given parenthetically.

38. One could argue that such omitted elements are optional to begin with, or that this larger level of composition allows a bit more flexibility than type-scenes, which do not generally omit expected elements.

39. Shklovsky, "Art as Technique," 12.

40. Ibid., 9.

41. In certain respects form criticism anticipated Alter's application of type-scene analysis to biblical narrative. Thus, as early as 1901 Hermann Gunkel, one of the pioneers of form criticism, was already commenting on certain narrative "variants" in the Bible:

> If any one proposes to study this history he will do well to begin with the variants. It is the characteristic of legend as well as of oral tradition that it exists in the form of variants. Each one, however faithful it may be, and especially every particular group and every new age, tells somewhat differently the story transmitted to it. The most important variants in Genesis are the two stories of Ishmael (xvi.; xxi. 8ff.), and next the legend of the danger to the patriarch's wife, which is handed down to us in three versions (xii. 13ff.; xxvi. 7ff.), and then the associated legend of the treaty at Beersheba, likewise in three versions. (*The Legends of Genesis* [New York: Schocken Books, 1964], 99)

Note, however, his focus on historical development as opposed to interpretation. Here mention should be made of James Muilenburg ("Form Criticism and Beyond," *JBL* 88 [1969], 1–18), who urged less emphasis on the typical and more on the meaning of the particulars of each instantiation of the underlying form.

42. Robert C. Culley, *Studies in the Structure of Hebrew Narrative* (Philadelphia, Pa.: Fortress Press, 1976).

43. Alter, *Biblical Narrative,* 50; subsequent references are given parenthetically.

44. The "modifications" Alter makes to the Homeric type-scene are the epic's *detailed* descriptions of the *quotidian* versus the Bible's *spare* treatment of the *portentous.* As such, these do not mitigate the analogy drawn between the use of type-scenes by the two narrative traditions.

45. Cf. Armstrong's comments in note 35.

46. The following discussion draws upon Alter's article "How Convention Helps Us Read: The Case of the Bible's Annunciation Type-Scene," *Prooftexts* 3 (1983): 115–30; subsequent references are given parenthetically.

47. *Midrash Rabbah,* 3d ed. (London: Soncino Press, 1983), 1.312.

48. Structuralists, too, have sometimes spoken of "deep structure" in their analyses. However, unlike its precise technical meaning in generative linguistics, structuralists have employed it in a loose metaphorical sense to differentiate between underlying binary structures and their "surface" manifestations, a type of form–content dichotomy.

49. Here the analogy with generative grammar breaks down. Transformations are given to the native speaker as part of the grammar of the language and thus are used, like language in general, without linguistic self-consciousness; hence they cannot be discovered through mere introspection. The biblical writers, conversely, inherit the tradition but invent the transformations themselves.

50. Throughout this section I will use the "classical" source-critical analysis in S. R. Driver, *Introduction*, 15–16; see also Friedman, *Hidden Book in the Bible*, 398.

51. Armstrong leaves this out of his analysis, observing that "the panoply of the goddess is distinguished; it is a special arming" ("The Arming Motif in the *Iliad*," 342 n. 11).

52. Achilles' arming is similarly distinguished when he puts on "the gifts of the god, that Hephaistos wrought him with much toil [*kame teuchōn*]" (19.368).

53. She throws the aegis "across her shoulders" (5.738) just as in the four arming scenes, discussed earlier, where the hero slings his sword "across his shoulders" (3.334, 11.29, 16.135, 19.372). The description of her "helm with its four sheets / and two horns" is identical to that of Agamemnon's (5.743 = 11.41).

54. I am ignoring the negligible switch from *hoisin* (5.747) to *toisin* (8.391).

55. If one assigns 11:30 to J, one finds a comparable "parenthesis" separating this report of Sarah's barrenness and the rest of the type-scene. It highlights the many years the aging couple must endure before receiving their promised son.

56. Since Genesis 20 belongs to E, I will not take it into account here as part of J's interruption of the type-scene.

57. He borrows the concept from Boris Tomashevsky, who defines as "free" those motifs in a narrative "which may be omitted without disturbing the whole causal-chronological course of events," as opposed to "bound" motifs, "which cannot be omitted" ("Thematics," in *Russian Formalist Criticism*, ed. Lemon and Reis, 68).

58. One should recall Auerbach's related comment on the Homeric flashback: "To the word scar (v. 393) there is first attached a *relative clause . . .* which enlarges into a voluminous syntactical parenthesis . . . until, with verse 467 ("The old woman now touched it . . ."), the scene which had been broken off is resumed" (*Mimesis*, 7; emphasis added). In the previous chapter I observed, with respect to this passage, that it was the absence of the pluperfect, in addition to the relative clause, that circumvented any sense of temporal perspective.

59. Driver and Friedman differ widely in their source-critical analyses of Genesis 30, but the verses crucial to my argument here are almost certainly E: Driver assigns vv. 1–3a to E, Friedman vv. 1b–3; looking ahead, while Friedman assigns vv. 22–23 to E, Driver excepts v. 22b$_\beta$ (!) as J.

60. Armstrong omits it from his study with the remark: "The arming is tailored to its importance which is in a sense ephemeral; it has no consequences. Once armed, Teucer fades out of the action" ("The Arming Motif in the *Iliad*," 342 n. 11).

61. Parker, *Pre-Biblical Narrative Tradition*, 104; subsequent references are given parenthetically. See also Ronald S. Hendel, *The Epic of the Patriarch: The Jacob Cycle and the Narrative Traditions of Canaan and Israel* (Cambridge, Mass.: Harvard University Press, 1987), 35–67.

62. For a discussion of some of these subsections, see Parker, *Pre-Biblical Narrative Tradition*, 52–54.

63. Note that Parker appeals to "the comparative evidence for stories with similar beginnings and endings and with some similar scenes and episodes, *always in the same order*" (*Pre-Biblical Narrative Tradition*, 163; emphasis added).

64. I similarly disregard the lack of a "departure" in Aqhat, which one does find in Kirta. The arrival of Baal (or his messenger) to Kirta was presumably narrated in the missing lines at the end of 1.17.1. Since this visit is a relatively minor event, as opposed to Kirta's banquet, the corresponding departure is apparently passed over in silence, but this in no way disturbs the narrative flow.

65. Within the context of biblical narrative, it seems preferable to interpret Abraham's type-scene as a departure from an established Israelite convention rather than as an archaic survival of an earlier convention.

66. Alter, "Convention," 124–26.

67. Krischer, "Unhomeric Scene-Patterns in Vergil," *Papers of the Liverpool Latin Seminar* 2 (1979): 143; subsequent references are given parenthetically. Krischer doesn't explicitly address the question of writing in relation to Virgil's practice, emphasizing instead certain Virgilian, and thus post-Homeric, values: the importance of Fate and, above all, of *pietas.* He does take for granted, however, that Virgil is a "writer" (148) whose audience is made up of "readers" (146, 147, 151, 152). Furthermore, his 1971 study of Homer, *Formale Konventionen*, explicitly and ingeniously addresses the relation of Homer's compositional techniques to oral improvisation. Thus, he was no doubt aware of the importance of writing for Virgil's "unhomeric" art.

68. Edwards, "Homer and Oral Tradition: The Type-Scene," 289.

69. Parry, *Making of Homeric Verse*, 451–52.

70. Michael Nagler, *Spontaneity and Tradition: A Study in the Oral Art of Homer* (Berkeley: University of California Press, 1974), 202.

71. Woolf, "Modern Fiction," 150.

72. Quoted in Benjamin, "The Storyteller," 92.

73. Parry, *Making of Homeric Verse*, 6.

74. Ibid., 425.

75. Benjamin, "The Storyteller," 93.

76. Barthes, *Writing Degree Zero*, 17.

77. Quoted in Martin, *Language of Heroes*, xiii.

7. Conclusion

1. Von Rad, *Problem of the Hexateuch*, 170.

2. Cassuto, "Biblical and Canaanite Literature," 18.

3. Cassuto, "Israelite Epic," 81; for his reconstruction, see 80–97.

4. Talmon, "The Comparative Method in Biblical Interpretation," 46.

5. Alter, *Biblical Narrative*, 25.

6. Greenstein, "Between Ugaritic Epic and Biblical Narrative."

7. See Bakhtin, "Epic and Novel," 3; and Benjamin, "The Storyteller," 87.

8. See Watt, *The Rise of the Novel*, 295; and Banfield, *Unspeakable Sentences*, 273.

9. For a survey of the history of scholarship on biblical religion and the methodological issues involved, see P. D. Miller, "Israelite Religion," in *The Hebrew Bible and Its Modern Interpreters,* ed. Douglas A. Knight and Gene M. Tucker (Philadelphia, Pa.: Fortress Press, 1985), 201–37.

10. Peter Machinist, "The Question of Distinctiveness in Ancient Israel: An Essay," in *Ah, Assyria . . . : Studies in Assyrian History and Ancient Near Eastern Historiography Presented to Hayim Tadmor,* ed. Mordechai Cogan and Israel Eph'al (Jerusalem: Magnes Press, 1991), 201.

11. Ibid., 197.

12. Ibid., 200.

13. See, e.g., Susan Ackerman, *Under Every Green Tree: Popular Religion in Sixth-Century Judah* (Atlanta, Ga.: Scholars Press, 1992); and Susan Niditch, *Ancient Israelite Religion* (New York: Oxford University Press, 1997).

14. For Foucault's place in the French philosophical tradition, see Jean-

Claude Milner, "Lacan and the Ideal of Science," in *Lacan and the Human Sciences,* ed. Alexandre Leupin (Lincoln: University of Nebraska Press, 1991), 27–42; see esp. 29–31. Thomas Kuhn's notion of a "paradigm shift" is a related if overused concept.

15. Milner succinctly glosses "episteme" as "the system of production of statements that is characteristic of a certain discourse configuration" ("Lacan," 41 n. 3).

16. Michel Foucault, *The Order of Things: An Archaeology of the Human Sciences* (New York: Random House, 1971), xxi–xxii; subsequent references are given parenthetically.

17. Milner, "Lacan," 30.

18. Machinist, "Distinctiveness," 200; emphasis added.

19. I have borrowed the phrase "Galilean science" from Milner's reading of Koyré's work on the history of science (see "Lacan," 29).

20. Friedman similarly observes of the distinction between "pagan" and Israelite religion: "In recent years this dichotomy has been criticized and revised so that the distinction between nature and history [as the defining domain of deity] is not so simply drawn as in the past. The essential distinction between the deities nonetheless holds true" (*The Disappearance of God: A Divine Mystery* [Boston: Little, Brown, 1995], 291 n. 14).

21. Miller, "Israelite Religion," 202. In Wright's own words: "For [the Christian] the unique, the discontinuous, the extraordinary nature of the Old Testament can only be explained as the dramatic, purposeful intervention of God, who here was inaugurating a special revelation of himself, one which culminated in Christ" (*The Old Testament Against Its Environment* [London: SCM Press, 1950], 73).

22. Miller, "Israelite Religion," 203.

23. Halpern, "'Brisker Pipes than Poetry': The Development of Israelite Monotheism," in *Judaic Perspectives on Ancient Israel,* ed. Jacob Neusner, Baruch A. Levine, and Ernest S. Frerichs (Philadelphia, Pa.: Fortress Press, 1987), 84. As Halpern points out, Julius Wellhausen had long ago anticipated this point: "Moab, Ammon, and Edom, Israel's nearest kinsfolk and neighbours, were monotheists in precisely the same sense in which Israel itself was" (*Prolegomena to the History of Israel* [New York: Meridian Books, 1957], 440).

24. Machinist, "Distinctiveness," 197; emphasis added.

25. Karl Jasper locates this age from 800 to 200 B.C.E., during which period "thinking is the object of itself" (quoted in Halpern, "'Brisker Pipes than Poetry,'" 88). Inasmuch as this formulation already assumes a thinking that involves objects rather than other subjects (i.e., a dualism), one may need to look further back in time in order to locate the crucial, underlying epistemic break.

26. Yehezkel Kaufmann, *The Religion of Israel: From Its Beginnings to the Babylonian Exile* (Chicago: University of Chicago Press, 1960), 7; see also 9–11.

27. Ibid., 29. As Israel Knohl has convincingly argued ("Between Voice and Silence: The Relationship between Prayer and Temple Cult," *JBL* 15 [1996]: 17–30), the Priestly Torah knows of magical rituals, but these manipulate the miasma of sin and guilt, a quasi-physical hypostasis, and do not attempt to influence God's will.

28. Kaufmann, *Religion of Israel,* 60. See also Tikva Frymer-Kensky, *In the Wake of the Goddesses: Women, Culture and the Biblical Transformation of Pagan Myth* (New York: Free Press, 1992), 83–99.

29. "'Brisker Pipes than Poetry,'" 81; discussing Kaufman, *Religion of Israel,* 29.

30. Halpern may have something similar in mind when he states: "[T]his man-

ifold reality must be repudiated as different from yet pointing to the underlying causal force, YHWH" ("'Brisker Pipes than Poetry,'" 96).

31. Halpern suggests that "the notion . . . that YHWH was the god who indisputably mastered the cosmos" is "the premise from which Kaufmann's specific criteria ultimately flow" ("'Brisker Pipes than Poetry,'" 81). One must specify, however, that in so doing YHWH transcends the cosmos and comes to exist on a nonmaterial plane.

32. Simone Pétrement, for instance, traces its origins in Western philosophy specifically to Pythagoras ("Dualism in Philosophy and Religion," in *Dictionary of the History of Ideas*, ed. Philip P. Wiener [New York: Scribner, 1973], 2:38a–44a). See also A. A. Long, ed., *The Cambridge Companion to Early Greek Philosophy* (Cambridge: Cambridge University Press, 1999).

33. Henri and H. A. Frankfort, "Myth and Reality," in *The Intellectual Adventure of Ancient Man: An Essay on Speculative Thought in the Ancient Near East* (Chicago: University of Chicago Press, 1977), 4.

34. Ibid., 11.

35. Wilson, "Egypt: The Function of the State," in *The Intellectual Adventure of Ancient Man*, 62.

36. Ibid., 63.

37. Ibid., 66. See also Jan Assmann, *The Search for God in Ancient Egypt* (Ithaca, N.Y.: Cornell University Press, 2001), 53–82.

38. Henri and H. A. Frankfort, "The Emancipation of Thought from Myth," in *The Intellectual Adventure of Ancient Man*, 363. See also Thorkild Jacobsen, *The Treasures of Darkness: A History of Mesopotamian Religion* (New Haven, Conn.: Yale University Press, 1976), 5–17; von Soden, *Ancient Orient*, 177–84; Jean Bottéro, *Mesopotamia: Writing, Reasoning, and the Gods* (Chicago: University of Chicago Press, 1992), 211–17; Jean Bottéro, Clarisse Herrenschmidt, and Jean-Pierre Vernant, *Ancestor of the West: Writing, Reasoning, and Religion in Mesopotamia, Elam, and Greece* (Chicago: University of Chicago Press, 2000), 54–56.

39. Henri and H. A. Frankfort, "Emancipation of Thought," 367.

40. Ibid., 369.

41. Ibid., 363.

42. Machinist, "Distinctiveness," 199–200. Cf. Kaufman, *Religion of Israel*, 60.

43. Carlos A. Benito, "Enki and Ninmah" and "Enki and the World Order" (Ph.D. diss., University of Pennsylvania, 1969).

44. Kaufmann, *Religion of Israel*, 29.

45. Similarly, while El is not a nature god, neither is he transcendent. Rather, he is in a sort of semiretirement, much like Ea in *Enuma Elish*. He has real (if rarely wielded) authority over the other gods—consider, for instance, his intervention in the Baal cycle's final battle between Baal and Mot (1.6.6.22–35)—but he in no way transcends the plane of the very real struggles between his "children"; witness the parental loss he feels as he mourns over Baal's death (1.5.6.11–25). Finally, that El dreams of Baal's eventual return to life indicates that in Ugaritic thought the divine realm, no less than the human, is subject, in turn, to external forces (Fate?) whose workings can only be partially and occasionally divined.

46. This view is controversial but firmly established as a plausible position. In fact, Kaufmann's *Religion of Israel* presented an early and formidable criticism of Wellhausen's classic formulation of the documentary hypothesis. Of the many relevant studies published since, I will simply mention Moshe Weinfeld's programmatic

remarks in "Julius Wellhausen's Understanding of the Law of Ancient Israel and Its Fallacies" (in Hebrew), *Shnaton* 4 (1980): 62–93.

47. More precisely, in *Enuma Elish* the primordial waters—apparently fresh spring water and salt seawater—are themselves gods, and it is the "mingling" of these divine elements that generates the rest of the gods and the world. See Jacobsen, *Treasures of Darkness*, 167–91.

48. Kaufmann, *Religion of Israel*, 68.

49. Ibid.

50. Hebrew *ʾēd* would seem to derive from Akkadian *edû*, meaning flood. While Speiser reads the cognate as "an underground swell, a common motif in Akkadian literary compositions" (*Genesis*, 16), John Skinner reads it as "the annual overflow of a river" (*A Critical and Exegetical Commentary on Genesis*, 2d ed. [Edinburgh: T & T Clark, 1930], 55). If one turns to Gen. 13:10 (J), one finds that the Jordan plain was "watered before the Lord's destruction of Sodom and Gomorrah, like the garden [*gan*] of the Lord, like the land of Egypt till you come to Zoar." This parallel between the Garden of Eden and Egypt favors *ʾēd* as an annual river overflow, modeled after that of the Nile, so crucial to Egyptian agriculture. Such gentle and dependable flooding is preferable to rain since the latter will arbitrarily fall short of or exceed that golden idyllic mean, as is spectacularly the case a few chapters later in Genesis. A benevolent nature's irrigation system, it provides an appropriate water source for Eden, God's personal garden.

51. If J's creation seems to lack the cosmic scope of P's, one would do well to remember that "earth and heaven" (2:4b), as a merism, most likely signifies the totality of the physical world, namely, earth, heaven, and everything in between. J's creation is no less universal than P's.

52. Kaufmann, *Religion of Israel*, 67–69.

53. Ibid., 29.

54. Ibid., 60; emphasis added.

55. See Moshe Weinfeld, "God the Creator in Gen. 1 and in the Prophecy of Second Isaiah" (in Hebrew), *Tarbits* 37 (1968): 105–32. For Deutero-Isaiah's place in the history of monotheism, see Halpern, "'Brisker Pipes than Poetry,'" 99–100.

56. Enkidu's initiation into culture in *Gilgamesh* must be understood in terms of this myth.

57. Humankind is partially responsible for its own creation. See Robert Kawashima, "*Homo Faber* in J's Primeval History," *ZAW*, forthcoming.

58. See Knohl, *Sanctuary of Silence*, 128–37.

59. Friedman, *Disappearance of God*, 98.

60. Kaufmann, *Religion of Israel*, 24–31 and 67–69.

61. Halpern, "'Brisker Pipes than Poetry,'" 85–86.

62. For a further discussion of the significance of homonymy and synonymy, see Jean-Claude Milner, *Les Noms Indistincts* (Paris: Éditions du Seuil, 1983), 51–61.

63. Ronald S. Hendel, "Of Demigods and the Deluge: Toward an Interpretation of Genesis 6:1–4," *JBL* 106 (1987): 14.

64. Kaufmann, *Religion of Israel*, 68–69.

65. Contra Halpern's understanding of the difference between *ʾĕlōhîm* and *hāʾĕlōhîm* ("'Brisker Pipes than Poetry,'" 85).

66. For a further discussion, see Kawashima, "*Homo Faber* in J's Primeval History."

67. Friedman, *Disappearance of God*, 7–29.

68. Note that these mythic events take place in the east (*miqqedem*), first in

Eden "in the east" (2:8), then to "the east of Eden" (3:24; cf. 4:16), where "the east" carries with it the suggestion of "antiquity," the "dawn" of humanity, so to speak. Only here, as we approach the age of Abraham, do we find humans moving westward toward history: "And it was as they traveled from the east" (*miqqedem*, 11:2).

69. I follow Hendel ("Demigods and the Deluge," 15 n. 10) in translating *yādôn* as "be strong." Note again the classificatory use of "the human" (*bāʾādām*) with the definite article.

70. See Tryggve N. D. Mettinger, *No Graven Image? Israelite Aniconism in Its Ancient Near Eastern Context* (Stockholm, Sweden: Almqvist & Wiksell, 1995); idem, "Israelite Aniconism: Developments and Origins," in *The Image and the Book: Iconic Cults, Aniconism, and the Rise of Book Religion in Israel and the Ancient Near East,* ed. Karel van der Toorn (Louvain, Belgium: Peeters, 1997), 173–204.

71. Ronald S. Hendel, "Aniconism and Anthropomorphism in Ancient Israel," in *The Image and the Book,* ed. van der Toorn, 206.

72. Hendel's comparison of Israelite aniconism with analogous developments in Mesopotamian and Egyptian religion brings this point into focus. If Mesopotamian texts also entail speculation as to the nature of Marduk's body, their solution — which Hendel refers to as "transcendent anthropomorphism" ("Aniconism and Anthropomorphism," 206–209), namely, describing the god's body in hyperbolic terms — only causes the human observer to gaze that much more indulgently upon his sublime body. Even Egyptian theology, which abstracted the divine to a remarkable extent (210–12), did not reject iconism as such; the sun, however abstract a representation of the divine, is eminently material and, unlike the divine wind of Genesis 1, visible.

73. Ibid., 220. Hendel points to Gen. 32:31; Exod. 33:20; Judg. 6:22–23; 13:22; Isa. 6:5.

74. Howard Eilberg-Schwartz, *God's Phallus and Other Problems for Men and Monotheism* (Boston: Beacon Press, 1994), 60.

75. Hendel, "Aniconism," 222–23 n. 68.

76. Henri Frankfort, *Kingship and the Gods: A Study of Ancient Near Eastern Religion as the Integration of Society and Nature* (Chicago: University of Chicago Press, 1978), 342–43. Elsewhere, the Frankforts similarly remark: "We also find there a new and utter lack of *eudaimonia,* of harmony — whether with the world of reason or with the world of perception" ("Emancipation of Thought," 371).

77. Thus, in the Frankforts' essay "The Emancipation of Thought from Myth" they comment on the "freedom" found through Israelite religion: "In the Old Testament we find man possessed of a new freedom and of a new burden of responsibility. . . . [N]omadic freedom can be bought only at a price; for whoever rejects the complexities and mutual dependencies of agricultural society not only gains freedom but also loses the bond with the phenomenal world" (370–71, 372).

78. Louis Althusser, *The Spectre of Hegel: Early Writings,* ed. François Matheron and trans. G. M. Goshgarian (London: Verso, 1997), 137.

79. Chomsky once observed that one cannot paraphrase "my leg" as "the leg that I have." This is because body parts are "inalienable," whereas objects "that I have" came into my possession at a certain point in time and could presumably leave my possession at some later time. The law, too, seems to distinguish between inalienable and alienable property: one cannot sell parts of one's body (as a recent online auction scandal demonstrated), one's freedom ("unalienable," according to the Declaration of Independence), and so forth.

80. Barthes, *Writing Degree Zero,* 32–33; emphasis added. My thanks to Ann Banfield for pointing out the implicit Althusserian argument in this passage. I should mention that while Barthes goes on to speak of the novel and its preterite as "mythological objects," he has a different sense of "myth" in mind.

81. I discuss this at greater length in "The Priestly Tent and the Problem of Divine Transcendence" (paper presented at the annual meeting of the Society of Biblical Literature, Atlanta, Ga., November 2003). Milner, summarizing Koyré, makes a similar distinction between empiricity-contingency and eternity-necessity, with regard to science. An empirical statement must meet two conditions: "(1) the state of things it refers to should be directly or indirectly representable in space and time; (2) it should be possible to think of the state of things it refers to as different from what it is." Modern science constitutes itself as such precisely by directing its statements to the empirical and contingent: "Throughout a long philosophical tradition, the system of stars and planets embodied what never changes: they were an image of eternity. But astronomy becomes a modern science as soon as the system of stars and planets is conceived as something that could be different from what it is without contradicting either logical necessity or metaphysical necessity" ("Lacan," 34). History, like science, refers itself to the empirical in this double sense. While condition (1) corresponds to the empirically observable nature of history as opposed to the necessarily private character of memory, condition (2) corresponds to the contingency of history versus the necessity of myth.

82. Regarding this "sacred time" of myth, see Mircea Eliade, *The Sacred and the Profane: The Nature of Religion* (San Diego, Calif.: Harcourt Brace, 1959), 68–113.

83. As the expression of a will, history, at least in the biblical view, is susceptible to interpretation. Thus, as Yosef Hayim Yerushalmi aptly remarks: "If Herodotus was the father of history, the fathers of meaning in history were the Jews" (*Zakhor: Jewish History and Jewish Memory* [New York: Schocken Books, 1989], 8). Albrektson (*History and the Gods*) has unconvincingly attributed the same sense of history to the ancient Near East in general. In fact, these other traditions, while aware of what I would call historical events, do not apprehend them as empirical, temporal, contingent occurrences. Thus, *Enuma Elish,* while registering the ascendance of Babylon, conceives of this historical development in mythic terms, projecting this recent event into the primordial past, namely, the time of creation.

84. The Mesha stele similarly attributes historical events to the will of Chemosh—in language, I might add, strikingly similar to biblical prose narrative. This leads Halpern (rightly, I think) to attribute "monotheism" to Moab ("'Brisker Pipes than Poetry,'" 84); perhaps Moab, too, made an epistemic break with the "pagan," monistic view of the world.

85. The relevant passages are Deut 33:3; Judg. 5:4–5; Hab 3:3, 7; and Ps 68:8–9. For a discussion of the evidence, see P. Kyle McCarter, Jr., "The Origins of Israelite Religion," in *The Rise of Ancient Israel,* ed. Hershel Shanks (Washington, D.C.: Biblical Archaeological Society, 1992), 118–41.

86. Relatedly, I have recently analyzed the priestly land grant as a "quasi-mythical" construction, a type of historical autochthony ("The Jubilee Year and the Return of Cosmic Purity," *Catholic Biblical Quarterly* 65 [2003]: 370–89, esp. 379–83). It is also worth noting here that the concept of possession itself becomes an object of theological reflection through a number of freighted and nearly synonymous terms: "possession" (*yĕruššâ*), "inheritance" or "portion" (*naḥălâ*), and "holding" (*ʾăḥuzzâ*). Not coincidentally, such an understanding of possession (in

contrast to its mythic counterpart) could accommodate the idea of exile. For some of the issues involved, see Gerhard von Rad, *Old Testament Theology* (New York: Harper & Row, 1962), 1:296–305.

87. One should recall here Auerbach's remarks on the conception of time underlying figural interpretation: "The horizontal, that is the temporal and causal, connection of occurrences is dissolved; the here and now is no longer a mere link in an earthly chain of events, it is simultaneously something which has always been, and which will be fulfilled in the future; and strictly, in the eyes of God, it is something eternal, something omni-temporal, something already consummated in the realm of fragmentary earthly event" (*Mimesis*, 74). The notion of *figura*, in other words, reintroduces into history a type of mythic necessity or eternity. Correspondingly, the medieval descendant of Yahweh effectively comes to embrace the universe in a Christian version of monism: "[T]he mentality of classical antiquity . . . down to the very structure of . . . its literary language . . . became superfluous as soon as earthly relations of place, time, and cause had ceased to matter, as soon as a vertical connection, ascending from all that happens, *converging in God,* alone became significant" (74; emphasis added).

88. One might relate this claim to Amos Funkenstein's suggestive observation regarding Israel's historical consciousness:

> Very few ancient societies confessed to their fairly recent origins, but the ancient Israelites, and so to a measure the Greeks (and Romans), admitted it. Both suffered, each in his way, from an acute historical sense of youth. The origins of Israel took place *in* history, indeed in recent history.
>
> In and of itself, such a consciousness of being a relatively young nation must have been a burden rather than an asset, a blemish that made their own community inferior to others of an older pedigree. True nobility is recognized by its old vintage. . . .
>
> But the blemish was turned into a virtue. True, Israel is much younger than most nations, and much smaller. Yet this circumstance is amply compensated for by the fact that God has chosen this particular nation. . . . Historical consciousness and the Israelite version of monotheism went, from the outset, hand in hand. (*Perceptions of Jewish History* [Berkeley: University of California Press, 1993], 52)

In fact, it may have been in large part Israel's consciousness of its youth that led to its historical consciousness. It forced Israel to imagine a world in its absence, before its inception, to see the world, in other words, as comprising a set of contingent realities, *not* an eternal order of necessary metaphysical entities.

89. Note as well the historical dimension established by the form of the covenant: the prelude gives a brief account of the relevant past events leading to the covenant's enactment; the postlude's list of blessings and curses speaks of possible futures.

90. Nahum Sarna, *Exploring Exodus: The Origins of Biblical Israel* (New York: Schocken Books, 1986), 140; subsequent references are given parenthetically.

91. Henri and H. A. Frankfort, "Emancipation of Thought," 370. In calling this idea a "myth," they seem to have in mind the particularism it attributes to an otherwise transcendent being. Calling the will of God a myth in this sense does not contradict my own argument.

92. Walter Eichrodt, *Man in the Old Testament* (London: SCM Press, 1951), 9.

93. Ibid., 13.

94. Wright, *Old Testament Against Its Environment,* 58.

95. Thus, when Marduk decides to create humans, he decrees: "He shall be charged with the service of the gods / That they might be at ease!" (*ANET,* 68).

96. For example, in his study of biblical prose prayer Moshe Greenberg cogently argues that it is the sincerity of one's interior "self" (*nepeš*) or "heart" (*lēb*), not properly fulfilled (magic) ritual, which leads to effective prayer (*Biblical Prose Prayer,* 47-51). Inasmuch as the will of God and the Israelite subject constitute each other in a demythologized confrontation, one thinks of Althusser's contention that authority (ideology, God, etc.) and the individual subject constitute each other in a speech-act, a second-person "hail," which he calls "interpellation"—not unlike divine apodictic law in the Bible (see "Ideology and Ideological State Apparatuses (Notes Towards an Investigation)," in *Lenin and Philosophy and Other Essays* [New York: Monthly Review Press, 1971], 170-77). In fact, Althusser himself refers to Moses and the Ten Commandments:

> God thus defines himself as the Subject *par excellence,* he who is through himself and for himself ('I am that I am'), and he who interpellates his subject, the individual subjected to him by his very interpellation, i.e. the individual named Moses. And Moses, interpellated-called by his Name, having recognized that it "really" was he who was called by God, recognizes that he is a subject, a subject *of* God, a subject subjected to God, *a subject through the Subject and subjected to the Subject.* The proof: he obeys him, and makes his people obey God's Commandments. (179)

97. Jack Goody and Ian Watt, "The Consequences of Literacy," in *Literacy in Traditional Societies,* ed. Jack Goody (Cambridge: Cambridge University Press, 1968), 27-68; subsequent references are given parenthetically.

98. With respect to this increased emphasis on the individual, Goody and Watt—the latter also wrote *The Rise of the Novel*—proffer the novel as a representative aesthetic product of literate culture: "[T]he novel, which . . . purports to portray the inner as well as the outer life of individuals in the real world, has replaced the collective representations of myth and epic" (62-63). They even suggest an affinity between the novel and the Platonic dialogues in order to emphasize the literate character of Greek thought. The striking linguistic and literary affinities between the novel and biblical narrative should by now need no further comment.

99. I. J. Gelb, *A Study of Writing: A Discussion of the General Principles Governing the Use and Evolution of Writing,* rev. ed. (Chicago: University of Chicago Press, 1963), 166. "The old Hebrew writing," he explains, "like other West Semitic systems, used only syllabic signs beginning with a consonant and ending in any vowel" (166). His definitions, however, may need some revision. For instance, if the alphabet, defined as a correspondence between individual signs and sounds, constitutes an advance in phonetic writing, alphabetic spelling is not yet as a result entirely phonetic (Banfield, *Unspeakable Sentences,* 243-53). A full syllabary is, in fact, at least as phonetic as—if more complex than—an alphabet.

100. Ugaritic represents an interesting middle ground between the Hebrew alphabet and a full-blown cuneiform syllabary.

101. That the great civilizations of Egypt and Mesopotamia lacked this particular

technological innovation may help explain why their venerable literary traditions did not match the achievement of their rather obscure younger neighbor, Israel.

102. In chapter 5 ("Attitudes to Writing in the Hebrew Bible") of her *Oral World and Written Word*, Niditch observes that the "magical and memorial aspects of writing in an oral world . . . are richly represented in the writings of the Hebrew Bible" (79). Although in chapter 6 ("The Literate End of the Continuum") she acknowledges the literate end of attitudes toward writing she nevertheless concludes (tautologically, in my opinion): "[E]ven in the passages at the literate end of the continuum are nuances of orality, a reminder of the oral context that frames the use of writing" (98).

103. The NRSV renders *wayyiktōb* more ambiguously as "and he listed," though the meaning of the verb *kātab* seems indisputable. At any rate, the fixture of these names in written form seems to be logically demanded by the story, since they round up these elders in verse 16—unless, that is, one assumes the activation of an oral tradition or of an oral-mnemonic technique, which seems unlikely for a purely incidental list of names intended for onetime use.

104. See Foley, *Homer's Oral Traditional Art*, 1–5.

105. On the question of Israelite literacy, including additional references, see Niditch, *Oral World and Written Word*, 39–59.

106. Goody and Watt, "Consequences of Literacy," 42.

107. See Goody, introduction to *Literacy in Traditional Societies*, 1–5.

108. My discussion relies in large part on two works by Banfield: "*Écriture*, Narration and the Grammar of French" and "*L'Écriture Et Le Non-Dit,*" *diacritics* 21, no. 4 (winter 1991): 21–31.

109. See, e.g., Barthes, *Writing Degree Zero*, 19–20; subsequent references are given parenthetically.

110. In fact, it is likely present—at least *in potentia*—in all languages, which is to say it is a feature of universal grammar.

111. Foucault, *The Order of Things*, 299–300.

112. Milner, echoing Foucault, links literature more generally to the triumph of modern science, of which philology, the first modern linguistics, is one realization:

> there should be a history of literature in the same way that there is a history of madness or a history of sexuality. If such a history were constituted, it would appear that literature is essentially modern. It has of course several distinctive features: it has something to do with the relevance of style; it has something to do with the primacy of the novel over the other literary forms, and so on. But essentially, it has something to do with the letter [the formalism of modern science] and the modern universe. ("Lacan," 39)

In such a universe "what literature adds is precisely the insistent belief that life would be unbearable if something existing *in* the universe did not exceed the letter" (39). In other words, literature, like the so-called human sciences, is "an illusory solace in the face of a painful truth" (38) that modern science reveals.

113. Von Rad, "Historical Writing in Ancient Israel," 204.

114. Von Rad, "Form-Critical Problem of the Hexateuch," 68.

115. Cross, "Epic Traditions of Early Israel," 29.

116. If "salvation" carries Christian connotations, "redemption" has roots in ancient Semitic law.

117. Foucault, *The Order of Things*, 300.

BIBLIOGRAPHY

Ackerman, Susan. *Under Every Green Tree: Popular Religion in Sixth-Century Judah.* Atlanta, Ga.: Scholars Press, 1992.

Aitken, Kenneth T. "Oral Formulaic Composition and Theme in the Aqhat Narrative." *UF* 21 (1989): 1–16.

———. "Word Pairs and Tradition in an Ugaritic Tale." *UF* 21 (1989): 17–38.

Albrektson, Bertil. *History and the Gods: An Essay on the Idea of Historical Events as Divine Manifestations in the Ancient Near East and Israel.* Lund, Sweden: Gleerup, 1967.

Allen, Thomas W., ed. *Homeri Opera.* Vols. 3–4, *Odyssea.* 2d ed. Oxford: Oxford University Press, 1917–19.

Alonso-Schökel, L. "Erzählkunst im Buche der Richter." *Bib* 42 (1961): 143–72.

———. "Nota estilística sobre la partícula הנה." *Bib* 37 (1956): 74–80.

Alter, Robert. *The Art of Biblical Narrative.* New York: Basic Books, 1981.

———. *The Art of Biblical Poetry.* New York: Basic Books, 1985.

———. *The David Story: A Translation with Commentary of 1 and 2 Samuel.* New York: Norton, 1999.

———. *Genesis: Translation and Commentary.* New York: Norton, 1996.

———. "How Convention Helps Us Read: The Case of the Bible's Annunciation Type-Scene." *Prooftexts* 3 (1983): 115–30.

———. "Imagining History in the Bible." In *History and . . . : History within the Human Sciences,* edited by R. Cohen and M. Roth, 53–72. Charlottesville: University of Virginia Press, 1995.

———. *The Pleasures of Reading in an Ideological Age.* New York: Simon and Schuster, 1989.

———. "A Response to Critics." *JSOT* 27 (1983): 113–17.

———. "Samson Without Folklore." In *Text and Tradition,* ed. Niditch, 47–56.

———. *The World of Biblical Literature.* New York: Basic Books, 1992.

Althusser, Louis. *Essays on Ideology.* London: Verso, 1984.

———. *Lenin and Philosophy and Other Essays.* New York: Monthly Review Press, 1971.

———. *The Spectre of Hegel: Early Writings.* Edited by François Matheron and translated by G. M. Goshgarian. London: Verso, 1997.

Andersen, Francis I. "Moabite Syntax." *Orientalia* 35 (1966): 81–120.

———. *The Sentence in Biblical Hebrew.* The Hague, Neth.: Mouton, 1974.

Anderson, Benedict. *Imagined Communities: Reflections on the Origin and Spread of Nationalism.* Rev. ed. London: Verso, 1991.

Andersson, Theodore M. *Early Epic Scenery: Homer, Virgil, and the Medieval Legacy.* Ithaca, N.Y.: Cornell University Press, 1976.

Arend, Walter. *Die typischen Scenen bei Homer.* Berlin: Weidmannsche Buchhandlung, 1933.

Armstrong, James I. "The Arming Motif in the *Iliad.*" *American Journal of Philology* 79 (1958): 337–54.

Assmann, Jan. *The Search for God in Ancient Egypt.* Translated by David Lorton. Ithaca, N.Y.: Cornell University Press, 2001.

Auerbach, Erich. *Mimesis: The Representation of Reality in Western Literature.* Translated by Willard Trask. Princeton, N.J.: Princeton University Press, 1953.

Bakhtin, M. M. *The Dialogic Imagination: Four Essays.* Edited by Michael Holquist and translated by Caryl Emerson and Michael Holquist. Austin: University of Texas Press, 1981.

Bakker, Egbert J. "Mimesis as Performance: Rereading Auerbach's First Chapter." *Poetics Today* 20 (1999): 11–26.

———. "Storytelling in the Future: Truth, Time, and Tense in Homeric Epic." In *Written Voices, Spoken Signs: Tradition, Performance, and the Epic Text,* edited by Egbert Bakker and Ahuvia Kahane, 11–36. Cambridge, Mass.: Harvard University Press, 1997.

———. "The Study of Homeric Discourse." In *A New Companion to Homer,* edited by Ian Morris and Barry Powell, 284–304. Leiden, Holland: Brill, 1997.

Bal, Mieke. *Narratology: Introduction to the Theory of Narrative.* Toronto: University of Toronto Press, 1985.

Banfield, Ann. "Describing the Unobserved: Events Grouped Around an Empty Centre." In *The Linguistics of Writing: Arguments between Language and Literature,* edited by Nigel Fabb et al., 265–85. Manchester, Eng.: Manchester University Press, 1987.

———. "*L'Écriture et le Non-Dit.*" *Diacritics* 21, no. 4 (winter 1991): 21–31.

———. "*Écriture,* Narration and the Grammar of French." In *Narrative: From Malory to Motion Pictures,* edited by Jeremy Hawthorn, 1–22. London: Edward Arnold, 1985.

———. "The Formal Coherence of Represented Speech and Thought." *PTL* 3 (1978): 289–314.

———. "Grammar and Memory." In *Interdisciplinary Approaches to Language: Essays in Honor of S.-Y. Kuroda,* edited by Carol Georgopoulos and Roberta Ishihara, 39–50. Dordrecht, Holland: Kluwer, 1991.

———. "L'Imparfait de l'Objectif: The Imperfect of the Object Glass." *Camera Obscura* 24 (1990): 65–87.

———. "Linguistic Competence and Literary Theory." In *Essays on Aesthetics: Perspectives on the Work of Monroe C. Beardsley,* edited by John Fisher, 201–34. Philadelphia, Pa.: Temple University Press, 1983.

———. "The Name of the Subject: The 'il'?" *Yale French Studies* 93 (1998): 133–74.

———. "Narrative Style and the Grammar of Direct and Indirect Speech." *Foundations of Language* 10 (1973): 1–39.

———. "The Nature of Evidence in a Falsifiable Literary Theory." In *The Concept of Style,* edited by Berel Lang, 183–210. Philadelphia: University of Pennsylvania Press, 1979.

———. *The Phantom Table: Woolf, Fry, Russell and the Epistemology of Modernism.* Cambridge: Cambridge University Press, 2000.

———. Review of *Transparent Minds,* by Dorrit Cohn. *Journal of Aesthetics and Art Criticism* 37 (1979): 208–11.

———. *Unspeakable Sentences: Narration and Representation in the Language of Fiction.* Boston: Routledge and Kegan Paul, 1982.

Bar-Efrat, Shimon. *Narrative Art in the Bible.* Sheffield, Eng.: Almond Press, 1989.

Barthes, Roland. *Camera Lucida: Reflections on Photography.* Translated by Richard Howard. New York: Hill and Wang, 1981.

———. *La Chambre Claire: Note sur la Photographie.* Paris: Éditions de l'Étoile, Gallimard, Le Seuil, 1980.

———. "The Death of the Author." In *The Rustle of Language,* translated by Richard Howard, 49–55. Berkeley: University of California Press, 1989.

———. *Le Degré Zéro de l'Écriture.* Paris: Éditions du Seuil, 1953.

———. "The Discourse of History." *Comparative Criticism: A Yearbook* 3 (1981): 3–20.

———. "The Reality Effect." In *French Literary Theory Today: A Reader,* edited by Tzvetan Todorov, 11–17. Cambridge: Cambridge University Press, 1982.

———. "The Struggle with the Angel." In *Image Music Text,* translated by Stephen Heath, 125–41. New York: Hill and Wang, 1977.

———. *Writing Degree Zero.* Translated by Annette Lavers and Colin Smith. New York: Noonday Press, 1968.

Basset, Louis. "L'Augment et la Distinction Discours/Récit dans *L'Iliade* et *L'Odyssée.*" In *Études Homériques,* 9–16. Lyon: Maison de l'Orient Méditerranéen, 1989.

Ben-David, Abba. *Biblical Hebrew and Mishnaic Hebrew* (in Hebrew). 2 vols. Tel Aviv: Dvir, 1967–71.

Benito, Carlos Alfredo. "Enki and Ninmah" and "Enki and the World Order." Ph.D. diss., University of Pennsylvania, 1969.

Benjamin, Walter. *Illuminations.* Translated by Harry Zohn. New York: Schocken Books, 1968.

Benveniste, Emile. *Problèmes de linguistique générale.* Paris: Éditions Gallimard, 1966.

———. *Problems of General Linguistics.* Translated by Mary Elizabeth Meek. Coral Gables, Fla.: University of Miami Press, 1971.

Bergen, Robert D., ed. *Biblical Hebrew and Discourse Linguistics.* Winona Lake, Ind.: Eisenbrauns, 1994.

Berlin, Adele. *The Dynamics of Biblical Parallelism.* Bloomington: Indiana University Press, 1985.

———. *Poetics and Interpretation of Biblical Narrative.* Sheffield, Eng.: Almond Press, 1983.

Blanchot, Maurice. *The Gaze of Orpheus and Other Literary Essays.* Edited by P. Adams Sitney and translated by Lydia Davis. Barrytown, N.Y.: Station Hill Press, 1981.

———. "La Voix narrative (le 'il', le neutre)." In *L'Entretien Infini,* 556–67. Paris: Éditions Gallimard, 1969.

Blau, Joshua. "Adverbia als psychologische und grammatische Subjekte/Praedikate im Bibelhebräisch." *VT* 9 (1959): 130–37.

———. *A Grammar of Biblical Hebrew.* Wiesbaden, Ger.: Otto Harrassowitz, 1976.

———. "*Marginalia Semitica* III." *IOS* 7 (1977): 23–27.

———. Review of *Biblical Hebrew and Mishnaic Hebrew,* by Abba Ben-David (in Hebrew). *Kiryat Sefer* 29 (1953): 26–35; 44 (1968–69): 29–35; 46 (1970–71): 424–28.

Blenkinsopp, Joseph. *Ezra-Nehemiah.* Philadelphia, Pa.: Westminster Press, 1988.

Bloom, Allan. "An Interpretation of Plato's *Ion.*" In *The Roots of Political Philosophy: Ten Forgotten Socratic Dialogues,* edited by Thomas L. Pangle, 371–95. Ithaca, N.Y.: Cornell University Press, 1987.

———, trans. "Plato's *Ion.*" In *The Roots of Political Philosophy,* ed. Pangle, 356–70.

Bodine, Walter R., ed. *Discourse Analysis of Biblical Literature: What It Is and What It Offers*. Atlanta, Ga.: Scholars Press, 1995.

—, ed. *Linguistics and Biblical Hebrew*. Winona Lake, Ind.: Eisenbrauns, 1992.

Boling, Robert G. *Judges*. AB, 6A. Garden City, N.Y.: Doubleday, 1975.

Bottéro, Jean. *Mesopotamia: Writing, Reasoning, and the Gods*. Translated by Zainab Bahrani and Marc van de Mieroop. Chicago: University of Chicago Press, 1992.

Bottéro, Jean, Clarisse Herrenschmidt, and Jean-Pierre Vernant. *Ancestor of the West: Writing, Reasoning, and Religion in Mesopotamia, Elam, and Greece*. Chicago: University of Chicago Press, 2000.

Bresnan, Joan. "On Complementizers: Towards a Syntactic Theory of Complement Types." *Foundations of Language* 6 (1970): 297-321.

Bronzwaer, W. J. M. "A Hypothesis Concerning Deictic Time Adverbs in Narrative Structure." *Journal of Literary Semantics* 4 (1975): 53-72.

—. *Tense in the Novel: An Investigation of Some Potentialities of Linguistic Criticism*. Groningen, Neth.: Wolters-Noordhoff, 1970.

Brooke-Rose, Christine. "Narrating Without a Narrator." *Times Literary Supplement*, 31 December 1999, 12-13.

Brown, F., S. R. Driver, and C. A. Briggs. *A Hebrew and English Lexicon of the Old Testament*. Oxford: Clarendon Press, 1907.

Brunot, Ferdinand. *La Pensée et la Langue*. 3d ed. Paris: Masson, 1936.

Burnet, John. *Platonis Opera*. Vols. 3-4. Oxford: Oxford University Press, 1902-1903.

Burney, C. F. *The Book of Judges with Introduction and Notes*. London: Rivingtons, 1930; New York: Ktav, 1970.

Bynum, David E. "Samson as a Biblical φὴρ ὀρεσκῷος." In *Text and Tradition*, ed. Niditch, 57-73.

Bywater, Ingram, trans. "Aristotle's *Poetics*." In *The Rhetoric and The Poetics of Aristotle*, 219-66. New York: Random House, 1954.

Cassuto, Umberto. *Biblical and Oriental Studies*. Vol. 2, *Bible and Ancient Oriental Texts*. Translated by Israel Abrahams. Jerusalem: Magnes Press, 1975.

Chantraine, Pierre. *Grammaire Homérique: Tome II, Syntaxe*. Paris: Librairie C. Klincksieck, 1958.

Chatman, Seymour. *Coming to Terms: The Rhetoric of Narrative in Fiction and Film*. Ithaca, N.Y.: Cornell University Press, 1990.

—. *Story and Discourse*. Ithaca, N.Y.: Cornell University Press, 1978.

Chomsky, Noam. *Aspects of the Theory of Syntax*. Cambridge, Mass.: MIT Press, 1965.

—. *Cartesian Linguistics: A Chapter in the History of Rationalist Thought*. Lanham, Md.: University Press of America, 1966.

—. "Conditions on Transformations." In *A Festschrift for Morris Halle*, edited by S. Anderson and P. Kiparsky, 232-86. New York: Holt, Rinehart and Winston, 1975.

—. *Language and Mind*. New York: Harcourt, Brace & World, 1968.

—. *Syntactic Structures*. The Hague, Neth.: Mouton, 1957.

Cohn, Dorrit. *Transparent Minds: Narrative Modes for Presenting Consciousness in Fiction*. Princeton, N.J.: Princeton University Press, 1978.

Comrie, Bernard. *Tense*. Cambridge: Cambridge University Press, 1985.

Conroy, Charles. "Hebrew Epic: Historical Notes and Critical Reflections." *Bib* 61 (1980): 1-30.

Coogan, Michael David, ed. and trans. *Stories from Ancient Canaan*. Philadelphia, Pa.: Westminster Press, 1978.

Cross, Frank Moore. *Canaanite Myth and Hebrew Epic: Essays in the History of the Religion of Israel.* Cambridge, Mass.: Harvard University Press, 1973.

————. "The Epic Traditions of Early Israel: Epic Narrative and the Reconstruction of Early Israelite Institutions." In *The Poet and the Historian,* ed. Friedman, 13–39.

————. "Prose and Poetry in the Mythic and Epic Texts from Ugarit." *HTR* 67 (1974): 1–15.

Cross, Frank Moore, and David Noel Freedman. *Studies in Ancient Yahwistic Poetry.* Missoula, Mont.: Scholars Press, 1975.

Culley, Robert C. "Introduction." *Semeia* 5 (1976): 1–33.

————. *Oral Formulaic Language in the Biblical Psalms.* Toronto: University of Toronto Press, 1967.

————. *Studies in the Structure of Hebrew Narrative.* Missoula, Mont.: Scholars Press / Philadelphia, Pa.: Fortress Press, 1976.

————. *Themes and Variations: A Study of Action in Biblical Narrative.* Atlanta, Ga.: Scholars Press, 1992.

Dalley, Stephanie, trans. *Myths from Mesopotamia: Creation, the Flood, Gilgamesh and Others.* Oxford: Oxford University Press, 1989.

Damrosch, David. *The Narrative Covenant: Transformations of Genre in the Growth of Biblical Literature.* San Francisco: Harper & Row, 1987.

Detienne, Marcel. *The Masters of Truth in Archaic Greece.* New York: Zone Books, 1996.

Dillmann, August. *Die Genesis.* 6th ed. Leipzig: S. Hirzel, 1892.

Dillon, George L., and Frederick Kirchhoff. "On the Form and Function of Free Indirect Style." *PTL* 1 (1976): 431–40.

Driver, S. R. *Introduction to the Literature of the Old Testament.* Rev. ed. New York: Scribner, 1910.

————. *Notes on the Hebrew Text and the Topography of the Books of Samuel.* 2d ed. Oxford: Clarendon Press, 1913.

————. *A Treatise on the Use of the Tenses in Hebrew and Some Other Syntactical Questions.* 3d ed. Oxford: Clarendon Press, 1892.

Edwards, Mark W. "Homer and Oral Tradition: The Type-Scene." *Oral Tradition* 7 (1992): 284–330.

————. *Homer: Poet of the* Iliad. Baltimore, Md.: Johns Hopkins University Press, 1987.

Eichrodt, Walther. *Man in the Old Testament.* London: SCM Press, 1951.

Eilberg-Schwartz, Howard. *God's Phallus and Other Problems for Men and Monotheism.* Boston: Beacon Press, 1994.

Eliade, Mircea. *The Myth of the Eternal Return: or, Cosmos and History.* Princeton, N.J.: Princeton University Press, 1954.

————. *The Sacred and the Profane: The Nature of Religion.* San Diego, Calif.: Harcourt Brace, 1959.

Ermarth, Elizabeth Deeds. *Realism and Consensus in the English Novel: Time, Space and Narrative.* Edinburgh: Edinburgh University Press, 1998.

Fenik, Bernard. *Typical Battle Scenes in the* Iliad: *Studies in the Narrative Techniques of Homeric Battle Description.* Wiesbaden, Ger.: Franz Steiner, 1968.

Flaubert, Gustave. *L'Éducation sentimentale.* Paris: Garnier Frères, 1964.

————. *Madame Bovary.* Paris: Garnier Frères, 1971.

Fludernik, Monika. *The Fictions of Language and the Languages of Fiction: The Linguistic Representation of Speech and Consciousness.* London: Routledge, 1993.

Fokkelman, J. P. *Narrative Art in Genesis: Specimens of Stylistic and Structural Analysis.* Assen, Neth.: Van Gorcum, 1975.

Foley, John Miles. *Homer's Traditional Art.* University Park: Pennsylvania State University Press, 1999.

———. *Immanent Art: From Structure to Meaning in Traditional Oral Epic.* Bloomington: Indiana University Press, 1991.

———. *The Theory of Oral Composition: History and Methodology.* Bloomington: Indiana University Press, 1988.

Forster, E. M. *Aspects of the Novel.* New York: Harcourt Brace & World, 1927.

Foucault, Michel. *The Archaeology of Knowledge* and *The Discourse on Language.* Translated by A. M. Sheridan Smith. New York: Pantheon Books, 1982.

———. *Essential Works of Foucault, 1954–1984.* Vol. 2, *Aesthetics, Method, and Epistemology.* Edited by James D. Faubion and translated by Robert Hurley. New York: New Press, 1998.

———. *The Order of Things: An Archaeology of the Human Sciences.* New York: Vintage Books, 1973.

Frankfort, Henri. *Kingship and the Gods: A Study of Ancient Near Eastern Religion as the Integration of Society and Nature.* Chicago: University of Chicago Press, 1978.

Frankfort, Henri, and H. A. Frankfort. "The Emancipation of Thought from Myth." In Henri Frankfort et al., *The Intellectual Adventure of Ancient Man,* 363–88.

———. "Myth and Reality." In Henri Frankfort et al., *The Intellectual Adventure of Ancient Man,* 3–27.

Frankfort, Henri, H. A. Frankfort, John A. Wilson, Thorkild Jacobsen, and William A. Irwin. *The Intellectual Adventure of Ancient Man: An Essay on Speculative Thought in the Ancient Near East.* Chicago: University of Chicago Press, 1977.

Frei, Hans. *The Eclipse of Biblical Narrative: A Study in Eighteenth and Nineteenth Century Hermeneutics.* New Haven, Conn.: Yale University Press, 1974.

Friedman, Richard Elliott. "The Deuteronomistic School." In *Fortunate the Eyes That See: Essays in Honor of David Noel Freedman in Celebration of His Seventieth Birthday,* edited by Astrid B. Beck et al., 70–80. Grand Rapids, Mich.: Eerdmans, 1995.

———. *The Disappearance of God: A Divine Mystery.* Boston: Little, Brown, 1995.

———. *The Hidden Book in the Bible.* San Francisco: HarperCollins, 1998.

———. *Who Wrote the Bible?* New York: Summit Books, 1987.

———, ed. *The Poet and the Historian: Essays in Literary and Historical Biblical Criticism.* Chico, Calif.: Scholars Press, 1983.

Frye, Northrop. *Anatomy of Criticism: Four Essays.* Princeton, N.J.: Princeton University Press, 1957.

Frymer-Kensky, Tikva. *In the Wake of the Goddesses: Women, Culture and the Biblical Transformation of Pagan Myth.* New York: Free Press, 1992.

Funkenstein, Amos. *Perceptions of Jewish History.* Berkeley: University of California Press, 1993.

Garr, Randall. *Dialect-Geography of Syria-Palestine.* Philadelphia: University of Pennsylvania Press, 1985.

Gelb, I. J. *A Study of Writing: A Discussion of the General Principles Governing the Use and Evolution of Writing.* Rev ed. Chicago: University of Chicago Press, 1963.

Geller, Stephen. *Parallelism in Early Biblical Poetry.* Missoula, Mont.: Scholars Press, 1979.

Genette, Gérard. *Fiction & Diction*. Translated by Catherine Porter. Ithaca, N.Y.: Cornell University Press, 1993.

———. *Narrative Discourse: An Essay in Method*. Translated by Jane E. Lewin. Ithaca, N.Y.: Cornell University Press, 1980.

———. *Narrative Discourse Revisited*. Translated by Jane E. Lewin. Ithaca, N.Y.: Cornell University Press, 1988.

Gerleman, Gerlis. "The Song of Deborah in the Light of Stylistics." *VT* 1 (1951): 168–80.

Gesenius, Wilhelm. *Gesenius' Hebrew Grammar*. Edited by E. Kautzsch and translated by A. E. Cowley. 2d ed. Oxford: Clarendon Press, 1910.

Givón, Talmy. "The Drift from VSO to SVO in Biblical Hebrew: The Pragmatics of Tense-Aspects." In *Mechanisms of Syntactic Change*, edited by Charles N. Li, 181–254. Austin: University of Texas Press, 1977.

———. "Verb Complements and Relative Clauses: A Diachronic Case Study in Biblical Hebrew." *Afroasiatic Linguistics* 1, no. 4 (1974): 1–22.

Goldfajn, Tal. *Word Order and Time in Biblical Hebrew Narrative*. Oxford: Oxford University Press, 1998.

Goody, Jack. "Introduction." In *Literacy in Traditional Societies*, ed. Goody, 1–26.

———, ed. *Literacy in Traditional Societies*. Cambridge: Cambridge University Press, 1968.

Goody, Jack, and Ian Watt. "The Consequences of Literacy." In *Literacy in Traditional Societies*, ed. Goody, 27–68.

Greenberg, Moshe. *Biblical Prose Prayer as a Window to the Popular Religion of Ancient Israel*. Berkeley: University of California Press, 1983.

———. *Understanding Exodus*. New York: Behrman House, 1969.

Greenstein, Edward L. "Autobiographies in Ancient Western Asia." In *Civilizations of the Ancient Near East*, vol. 4, edited by Jack M. Sasson, 2421–32. New York: Scribner, 1996.

———. "Between Ugaritic Epic and Biblical Narrative: The Role of Direct Discourse." Paper presented at the annual meeting of the Society of Biblical Literature, Washington, D.C., November 1993.

———. "On a New Grammar of Ugaritic." *IOS* 18 (1998): 397–420.

———. "On the Canaanite Background of Biblical Prose Narrative" (in Hebrew). Forthcoming.

———. "On the Genesis of Biblical Prose Narrative." *Prooftexts* 8 (1988): 347–54.

———. "Prefixed Preterite." *Hebrew Studies* 29 (1988): 7–17.

Greimas, A.-J. *Structural Semantics: An Attempt at a Method*. Translated by Daniele McDowell, Ronald Schleifer, and Alan Velie. Lincoln: University of Nebraska Press, 1983.

Gresseth, Gerald K. "The Gilgamesh Epic and Homer." *Classical Journal* 70 (1975): 1–18.

Gunkel, Hermann. *The Legends of Genesis*. Translated by W. H. Carruth. New York: Schocken Books, 1964.

Gunn, David M. "The 'Battle Report': Oral or Scribal Convention?" *JBL* 93 (1974): 513–18.

———. "Narrative Patterns and Oral Tradition in Judges and Samuel." *VT* 24 (1974): 286–317.

Habel, Norman C. "The Narrative Art of Job: Applying the Principles of Robert Alter." *JSOT* 27 (1983): 101–111.

Hainsworth, Bryan. *The Iliad: A Commentary.* Vol. 3, Books 9-12. Cambridge: Cambridge University Press, 1993.

Hainsworth, J. B. *The Idea of Epic.* Berkeley: University of California Press, 1991.

Halpern, Baruch. "'Brisker Pipes than Poetry': The Development of Israelite Monotheism." In *Judaic Perspectives on Ancient Israel,* edited by Jacob Neusner, Baruch A. Levine, and Ernest S. Frerichs, 77-115. Philadelphia, Pa.: Fortress Press, 1987.

————. "Doctrine by Misadventure: Between the Israelite Source and the Biblical Historian." In *The Poet and the Historian,* ed. Friedman, 41-73.

————. *The Emergence of Israel in Canaan.* Chico, Calif.: Scholars Press, 1983.

————. *The First Historians: The Hebrew Bible and History.* University Park, Pa.: Pennsylvania State University Press, 1996.

————. "The Resourceful Israelite Historian: The Song of Deborah and Israelite Historiography." *HTR* 76 (1983): 379-401.

Hamburger, Käte. *The Logic of Literature.* Translated by Marilynn J. Rose. 2d rev. ed. Bloomington: Indiana University Press, 1993.

————. "Noch einmal: Vom Erzählen. Versuch einer Antwort und Klärung." *Euphorion* 59 (1965): 46-71.

Hanson, Kristin, and Paul Kiparsky. "The Nature of Verse and Its Consequences for the Mixed Form." In *Prosimetrum: Crosscultural Perspectives on Narrative in Prose and Verse,* edited by Joseph Harris and Karl Reichl, 17-44. Rochester, N.Y.: D. S. Brewer, 1997.

Hartman, Geoffrey. "The Struggle for the Text." In *Midrash and Literature,* edited by Geoffrey H. Hartman and Sanford Budick, 3-18. New Haven, Conn.: Yale University Press, 1986.

Havelock, Eric. *Preface to Plato.* Cambridge, Mass.: Harvard University Press, 1963.

Hendel, Ronald S. "Aniconism and Anthropomorphism in Ancient Israel." In *The Image and the Book: Iconic Cults, Aniconism, and the Rise of Book Religion in Israel and the Ancient Near East,* ed. van der Toorn, 205-28.

————. *The Epic of the Patriarch: The Jacob Cycle and the Narrative Traditions of Canaan and Israel.* Cambridge, Mass.: Harvard University Press, 1987.

————. "In the Margins of the Hebrew Verbal System: Situation, Tense, Aspect, Mood." *ZAH* 9 (1996): 152-81.

————. "Of Demigods and the Deluge: Toward an Interpretation of Genesis 6:1-4." *JBL* 106 (1987): 13-26.

————. "Sibilants and *šibbōlet* (Judges 12:6)." *BASOR* 301 (1996): 69-75.

Hess, Richard S. *Amarna Personal Names.* Winona Lake, Ind.: Eisenbrauns, 1993.

Hintikka, Jaakko. *Time and Necessity: Studies in Aristotle's Theory of Modality.* Oxford: Clarendon Press, 1973.

Huffmon, Herbert Bardwell. *Amorite Personal Names in the Mari Texts: A Structural and Lexical Study.* Baltimore, Md.: Johns Hopkins University Press, 1965.

Jackendoff, Ray S. *Semantic Interpretation in Generative Grammar.* Cambridge, Mass.: MIT Press, 1972.

Jacobs, Roderick A., and Peter S. Rosenbaum. *English Transformational Grammar.* Waltham, Mass.: Blaisdell, 1968.

Jacobsen, Thorkild. *The Treasures of Darkness: A History of Mesopotamian Religion.* New Haven, Conn.: Yale University Press, 1976.

James, Henry. *The Art of the Novel: Critical Prefaces.* Boston: Northeastern University Press, 1984.

Jobling, David. "Robert Alter's *The Art of Biblical Narrative.*" *JSOT* 27 (1983): 87–99.

de Jong, Irene J. F. "Eurykleia and Odysseus' Scar: *Odyssey* 19.393–466." *Classical Quarterly* 35 (1985): 517–18.

———. *Narrators and Focalizers: The Presentation of the Story in the* Iliad. Amsterdam: Grüner, 1987.

Joosten, Jan. "The Indicative System of the Biblical Hebrew Verb and Its Literary Exploitation." In *Narrative Syntax and the Hebrew Bible: Papers of the Tilburg Conference 1996,* edited by Ellen van Wolde, 51–71. Leiden, Holland: Brill, 1997.

Josipovici, Gabriel. *The Book of God: A Response to the Bible.* New Haven, Conn.: Yale University Press, 1988.

Joüon, Paul, and Takamitsu Muraoka. *A Grammar of Biblical Hebrew.* Rome: Pontifical Biblical Institute, 1991.

Joyce, James. *Dubliners.* Harmondsworth, Eng.: Penguin Books, 1968.

———. *Ulysses.* New York: Random House, 1961.

Kakrides, Johannes Th. *Homeric Researches.* Lund, Sweden: Gleerup, 1949.

Katsumura, Hiroya. "Zur Funktion von *hinneh* und *wᵉhinnēh* in der biblischen Erzählung." *Annual of the Japanese Biblical Institute* 13 (1987): 3–21.

Kaufmann, Yehezkel. *The Religion of Israel: From Its Beginnings to the Babylonian Exile.* Translated and edited by Moshe Greenberg. New York: Schocken Books, 1972.

Kawashima, Robert S. "*Homo Faber* in J's Primeval History." Forthcoming.

———. "The Jubilee Year and the Return of Cosmic Purity." *CBQ* 65 (2003): 370–89.

———. "The Priestly Tent and the Problem of Divine Transcendence." Paper presented at the annual meeting of the Society of Biblical Literature, Atlanta, Ga., November 2003.

Kelber, Werner H. *The Oral and the Written Gospel: The Hermeneutics of Speaking and Writing in the Synoptic Tradition, Mark, Paul, and Q.* Philadelphia, Pa.: Fortress Press, 1983.

Kenner, Hugh. *The Stoic Comedians: Flaubert, Joyce, and Beckett.* Berkeley: University of California Press, 1974.

Kermode, Frank. *The Art of Telling: Essays on Fiction.* Cambridge: Harvard University Press, 1983.

———. *The Genesis of Secrecy: On the Interpretation of Narrative.* Cambridge, Mass.: Harvard University Press, 1979.

Kirk, G. S., J. E. Raven, and M. Schofield. *The Presocratic Philosophers: A Critical History with a Selection of Texts.* 2d ed. Cambridge: Cambridge University Press, 1983.

Kittay, Jeffrey, and Wlad Godzich. *The Emergence of Prose: An Essay in Prosaics.* Minneapolis: University of Minnesota Press, 1987.

Knohl, Israel. "Between Voice and Silence: The Relationship between Prayer and Temple Cult." *JBL* 15 (1996): 17–30.

———. *The Sanctuary of Silence: The Priestly Torah and the Holiness School.* Minneapolis, Minn.: Fortress Press, 1995.

Kogut, Simcha. "On the Meaning and Syntactical Status of הנה in Biblical Hebrew." *Scripta Hierosolymitana* 31 (1986): 133–54.

Kojève, Alexandre. *Introduction to the Reading of Hegel.* Assembled by Raymond Queneau, edited by Allan Bloom, and translated by James H. Nichols, Jr. Ithaca, N.Y.: Cornell University Press, 1980.

Korpel, Marjo C. A. "Exegesis in the Work of Ilimilku of Ugarit." *OS* 40 (1998): 86-111.

Koyré, Alexandre. *From the Closed World to the Infinite Universe.* Baltimore, Md.: Johns Hopkins University Press, 1968.

Krischer, Tilman. *Formale Konventionen der homerischen Epik.* Munich: C. H. Beck'sche Verlagsbuchhandlung, 1971.

———. "Unhomeric Scene-Patterns in Vergil." *Papers of the Liverpool Latin Seminar* 2 (1979): 143-54.

Kugel, James. *The Idea of Biblical Poetry.* New Haven, Conn.: Yale University Press, 1981.

Kuhl, Curt. "Die 'Wiederaufnahme'–ein literarkritisches Prinzip?" *ZAW* 64 (1952): 1-11.

Kuroda, S.-Y. *The 'Whole of the Doughnut: Syntax and Its Boundaries.* Ghent: E. Story-Scientia P.V.B.A., 1979.

Labuschagne, C. J. "The Emphasizing Particle *gam* and Its Connotations." In *Studia Biblica et Semitica,* 193-203. Wageningen, Neth.: H. Veenman en Zonen, 1966.

———. "The Particles הן and הנה." *OS* 18 (1973): 1-15.

Lacan, Jacques. *The Four Fundamental Concepts of Psycho-Analysis.* Edited by Jacques-Alain Miller and translated by Alan Sheridan. New York: Norton, 1978.

Lambdin, Thomas O. *Introduction to Biblical Hebrew.* New York: Scribner, 1971.

Lattimore, Richmond, trans. *The Iliad of Homer.* Chicago: University of Chicago Press, 1951.

———, trans. *The Odyssey of Homer.* New York: Harper & Row, 1967.

Le Bidois, George, and Robert Le Bidois. *Syntaxe du français moderne.* Paris: Picard, 1936.

Lemon, Lee T., and Marion J. Reis, eds. and trans. *Russian Formalist Criticism: Four Essays.* Lincoln: University of Nebraska Press, 1965.

Lévy-Bruhl, Lucien. *Primitive Mentality.* Translated by Lilian A. Clare. 1923. Reprint, Boston: Beacon Press, 1966.

Loewenstamm, Samuel E. "The Quaking of Nature at the Appearance of God" (in Hebrew). In *Oz le-David: D. Ben-Gurion Jubilee Volume.* Jerusalem: Kiryat Sefer, 1964.

Long, A.A., ed. *The Cambridge Companion to Early Greek Philosophy.* Cambridge: Cambridge University Press, 1999.

Long, Burke O. "Framing Repetitions in Biblical Historiography." *JBL* 106 (1987): 385-99.

———. "Reports of Visions among the Prophets." *JBL* 95 (1976): 353-65.

Longacre, Robert E. "Discourse Perspective on the Hebrew Verb: Affirmation and Restatement." In *Linguistics and Biblical Hebrew,* ed. Bodine, 177-89.

Lord, Albert B. *Epic Singers and Oral Tradition.* Ithaca, N.Y.: Cornell University Press, 1991.

———. "Memory, Meaning, and Myth in Homer and Other Oral Epic Traditions." In *Oralità: Cultura, Letteratura, Discorso,* edited by Bruno Gentili and Giuseppe Paioni, 37-67. Rome: Edizioni dell'Ateneo, 1985.

———. *The Singer of Tales.* Cambridge, Mass.: Harvard University Press, 1960.

MacDonald, J. "Israelite Spoken Hebrew." *BibOr* 32 (1975): 162-75.

MacHale, Brian. "Free Indirect Discourse: A Survey of Recent Accounts." *PTL* 3 (1978): 249-87.

————. "Unspeakable Sentences, Unnatural Acts. Linguistics and Poetics Revisited." *Poetics Today* 4, no. 1 (1983): 17–45.

Machinist, Peter. "The Question of Distinctiveness in Ancient Israel: An Essay." In *Ah, Assyria . . . : Studies in Assyrian History and Ancient Near Eastern Historiography Presented to Hayim Tadmor,* edited by Mordechai Cogan and Israel Eph'al, 196–212. Jerusalem: Magnes Press, 1991.

Martin, Richard P. *The Language of Heroes: Speech and Performance in the* Iliad. Ithaca, N.Y.: Cornell University Press, 1989.

McCarter, P. Kyle, Jr. *1 Samuel,* AB 8. Garden City, N.Y.: Doubleday, 1980.

————. "The Origins of Israelite Religion." In *The Rise of Ancient Israel,* edited by Hershel Shanks, 118–41. Washington, D.C.: Biblical Archaeological Society, 1992.

McCarthy, Dennis J. "The Uses of *wᵉhinnêh* in Biblical Hebrew." *Bib* 61 (1980): 330–42.

McTaggart, J. M. E. "The Unreality of Time." In *The Philosophy of Time,* edited by Robin Le Poidevin and Murray MacBeath, 23–34. Oxford: Oxford University Press, 1993.

Mettinger, Tryggve N. D. "Israelite Aniconism: Developments and Origins." In *The Image and the Book,* ed. van der Toorn, 173–204.

————. *No Graven Image? Israelite Aniconism in Its Ancient Near Eastern Context.* Stockholm, Sweden: Almqvist & Wiksell, 1995.

Miller, Cynthia L. "The Pragmatics of *waw* as a Discourse Marker in Biblical Hebrew Dialogue." *ZAH* 12 (1999): 165–91.

————. *The Representation of Speech in Biblical Hebrew Narrative: A Linguistic Analysis.* Atlanta, Ga.: Scholars Press, 1996.

Miller, Patrick D. "Israelite Religion." In *The Hebrew Bible and Its Modern Interpreters,* edited by Douglas A. Knight and Gene M. Tucker, 201–37. Philadelphia, Pa.: Fortress Press, 1985.

————. *The Religion of Ancient Israel.* Louisville, Ky.: Westminister John Knox Press, 2000.

Milner, Jean-Claude. *De la syntaxe à l'interprétation: quantités, insultes, exclamations.* Paris: Éditions du Seuil, 1978.

————. *For the Love of Language.* Translated by Ann Banfield. New York: St. Martin's Press, 1990.

————. "Lacan and the Ideal of Science." In *Lacan and the Human Sciences,* edited by Alexandre Leupin, 27–42. Lincoln: University of Nebraska Press, 1991.

————. *Les Noms Indistincts.* Paris: Éditions du Seuil, 1983.

Momigliano, Arnaldo. "Biblical Studies and Classical Studies: Simple Reflections Upon Historical Method." In *Essays on Ancient and Modern Judaism,* 3–9. Chicago: University of Chicago Press, 1994.

Monro, David B., and Thomas W. Allen, eds. *Homeri Opera.* Vols. 1–2, *Iliadis.* 3d ed. Oxford: Oxford University Press, 1920.

Morin, Yves-Charles. "On the Two French Subjectless Verbs *Voici* and *Voilà.*" *Language* 61 (1985): 777–820.

Mowinckel, Sigmund. "Hat es ein israelitisches Nationalepos gegeben?" *ZAW* 53 (1935): 130–53.

Muffs, Jochanan. *Love and Joy: Law, Language and Religion in Ancient Israel.* New York: JTS, 1992.

Muilenburg, James. "Form Criticism and Beyond." *JBL* 88 (1969): 1–18.

Muraoka, Takamitsu. *Emphatic Words and Structures in Biblical Hebrew.* Jerusalem: Magnes Press, 1985.

———. Review of *Sintassi del verbo ebraico nella prosa biblica classica,* by Alviero Niccacci. *Abr Nahrain* 27 (1989): 187–193.

Myers, Jacob M. *Ezra-Nehemiah.* AB 14. Garden City, N.Y.: Doubleday, 1965.

Nagler, Michael. *Spontaneity and Tradition: A Study in the Oral Art of Homer.* Berkeley: University of California Press, 1974.

Nagy, Gregory. *The Best of the Achaeans.* Baltimore, Md.: Johns Hopkins University Press, 1979.

———. *Comparative Studies in Greek and Indic Meter.* Cambridge, Mass.: Harvard University Press, 1974.

———. *Homeric Questions.* Austin: University of Texas Press, 1996.

Neef, Heinz-Dieter. "Deboraerzählung und Deboralied: Beobachtungen zum Verhältnis von Jdc. IV und V." *VT* 44 (1994): 47–59.

Niccacci, Alviero. "The Stele of Mesha and the Bible: Verbal System and Narrativity." *Orientalia* 63 (1994): 226–48.

———. *Syntax of the Verb in Classical Hebrew Prose.* Translated by W. G. E. Watson. Sheffield, Eng.: JSOT Press, 1990.

Niditch, Susan. *Ancient Israelite Religion.* New York: Oxford University Press, 1997.

———. *Chaos to Cosmos: Studies in Biblical Patterns of Creations.* Chico, Calif.: Scholars Press, 1984.

———. *Folklore and the Hebrew Bible.* Minneapolis, Minn.: Fortress Press, 1993.

———. "Oral Register in the Biblical Libretto: Towards a Biblical Poetic." *Oral Tradition* 10 (1995): 387–408.

———. *Oral World and Written Word: Ancient Israelite Literature.* Louisville, Ky.: Westminster John Knox Press, 1996.

———, ed. *Text and Tradition: The Hebrew Bible and Folklore.* Atlanta, Ga.: Scholars Press, 1990.

Noth, Martin. *The Deuteronomistic History.* Sheffield, Eng.: JSOT Press, 1981.

———. *Die israelitischen Personennamen im Rahmen der gemeinsemitischen Namengebung.* Stuttgart: Kohlhammer, 1928.

Oberhuber, K. "Zur Syntax des Richterbuches: Der Einfache Nominalsatz und die Sog. Nominale Apposition." *VT* 3 (1953): 5–10.

Pardes, Ilana. *The Biography of Ancient Israel: National Narratives in the Bible.* Berkeley: University of California Press, 2000.

———. *Countertraditions in the Bible: A Feminist Approach.* Cambridge, Mass.: Harvard University Press, 1992.

Parker, Simon B. *The Pre-Biblical Narrative Tradition: Essays on the Ugaritic Poems Keret and Aqhat.* Atlanta, Ga.: Scholars Press, 1989.

———. *Stories in Scripture and Inscriptions: Comparative Studies on Narratives in Northwest Semitic Inscriptions and the Hebrew Bible.* Oxford: Oxford University Press, 1997.

———, ed. *Ugaritic Narrative Poetry.* Atlanta, Ga.: Scholars Press, 1997.

Parry, Adam M. *The Language of Achilles and Other Papers.* Oxford: Oxford University Press, 1989.

Parry, Milman. *The Making of Homeric Verse: The Collected Papers of Milman Parry.* Edited by Adam Parry. Oxford: Oxford University Press, 1971.

Peckham, Brian. "History and Time." In *Ki Baruch Hu: Ancient Near Eastern, Biblical, and Judaic Studies in Honor of Baruch A. Levine,* edited by Robert Chazan,

William W. Hallo, and Lawrence H. Schiffman, 295–314. Winona Lake, Ind.: Eisenbrauns, 1999.

Perry, Ben. "The Early Greek Capacity for Viewing Things Separately." *Transactions of the American Philological Association* 68 (1937): 403–27.

Pétrement, Simone. "Dualism in Philosophy and Religion." In *Dictionary of the History of Ideas: Studies of Selected Pivotal Ideas,* vol. 2, edited by Philip P. Wiener, 38a–44a. New York: Scribner, 1973.

Polotsky, Hans Jakob. "A Note on the Sequential Verb-Form in Ramesside Egyptian and in Biblical Hebrew." In *Pharaonic Egypt: The Bible and Christianity,* edited by Sarah Israelit Groll, 157–61. Jerusalem: Magnes Press, 1985.

Polzin, Robert. *David and the Deuteronomist: A Literary Study of the Deuteronomic History.* Bloomington: Indiana University Press, 1993.

Pritchard, James B. *Ancient Near Eastern Texts Relating to the Old Testament.* 3d ed. Princeton, N.J.: Princeton University Press, 1969.

Propp, Vladimir. *The Morphology of the Folk Tale.* 2d ed. Translated by Lawrence Scott. Austin: University of Texas Press, 1968.

Proust, Marcel. *Against Sainte-Beuve and Other Essays.* Translated by John Sturrock. New York: Penguin, 1988.

———. *In Search of Lost Time.* 6 vols. Translated by C. K. Scott Moncrieff and Terence Kilmartin and revised by D. J. Enright. New York: Modern Library, 1992.

Quang Phuc Dong. "Phrases anglaises sans sujet grammatical apparent." *Langages* 14 (1969): 44–51.

Radford, Andrew. *Transformational Syntax: A Student's Guide to Chomsky's Extended Standard Theory.* Cambridge: Cambridge University Press, 1981.

Rainey, A. F. "The Ancient Hebrew Prefix Conjugation in the Light of Amarnah Canaanite." *Hebrew Studies* 27 (1986): 4–19.

———. "Further Remarks on the Hebrew Verbal System." *Hebrew Studies* 29 (1988): 35–42.

Reichenbach, Hans. *Elements of Symbolic Logic.* New York: Free Press, 1947.

Rendsburg, Gary. *Diglossia in Ancient Hebrew.* New Haven, Conn.: American Oriental Society, 1990.

Richardson, Scott. *The Homeric Narrator.* Nashville, Tenn.: Vanderbilt University Press, 1990.

Richter, Wolfgang. *Grundlagen einer althebräischen Grammatik.* 3 vols. St. Ottilien, Ger.: EOS, 1978–80.

———. "Traum und Traumdeutung im AT: Ihre Form und Verwendung." *Biblische Zeitschrift,* n.s., 7 (1963): 202–20.

Robertson, D. A. *Linguistic Evidence in Dating Early Hebrew Poetry.* Missoula, Mont.: Scholars Press, 1972.

Russell, Bertrand. *An Inquiry into Meaning and Truth.* London: George Allen & Unwin, 1980.

———. *Mysticism and Logic.* Garden City, N.Y.: Doubleday, Anchor Books, n.d.

———. "On the Experience of Time." *The Monist* 25 (1915): 212–33.

———. *The Philosophy of Logical Atomism.* LaSalle, Ill.: Open Court, 1985.

———. *Problems of Philosophy.* Oxford: Oxford University Press, 1959.

———. *Theory of Knowledge: The 1913 Manuscript.* London: George Allen & Unwin, 1984.

Saenz-Badillos, Angel. *A History of the Hebrew Language.* Translated by John Elwolde. Cambridge: Cambridge University Press, 1993.

Sarna, Nahum. *Exploring Exodus: The Origins of Biblical Israel.* New York: Schocken Books, 1986.

———. *Understanding Genesis.* New York: Schocken Books, 1970.

Sartre, Jean-Paul. "Camus' 'The Outsider'." In *Literary Essays,* 24–41. New York: Philosophical Library, 1957.

Sasson, Jack M. "Literary Criticism, Folklore Scholarship, and Ugaritic Literature." In *Ugarit in Retrospect: Fifty Years of Ugarit and Ugaritic,* edited by Gordon Douglas Young, 81–98. Winona Lake, Ind.: Eisenbrauns, 1981.

Schein, Seth L. *The Mortal Hero: An Introduction to Homer's* Iliad. Berkeley: University of California Press, 1984.

Schneidau, Herbert N. *Sacred Discontent: The Bible and Western Tradition.* Baton Rouge, La.: Louisiana State University Press, 1976.

Schneider, Wolfgang. *Grammatik des Biblischen Hebräisch.* 5th ed. Munich: Claudius, 1982.

Seeligman, I. L. "Menschlisches Heldentum und göttliche Hilfe: Die doppelte Kausalität im alttestamentlichen Geschichtsdenken." *Theologische Zeitschrift* 19 (1963): 385–411.

Segert, Stanislav. *A Basic Grammar of the Ugaritic Language: With Selected Texts and Glossary.* Berkeley: University of California Press, 1984.

Shklovsky, Viktor. "Art as Technique." In *Russian Formalist Criticism,* ed. Lemon and Reis, 3–24.

———. "Sterne's *Tristram Shandy:* Stylistic Commentary." In *Russian Formalist Criticism,* ed. Lemon and Reis, 25–57.

———. *Theory of Prose.* Translated by Benjamin Sher. Elmwood Park, Ill.: Dalkey Archive Press, 1990.

Sivan, Daniel. *Grammar of the Ugaritic Language.* Leiden, Holland: Brill, 1997.

———. *A Grammar of Ugaritic* (in Hebrew). Jerusalem: Bialik Institute, 1993.

Skinner, John. *A Critical and Exegetical Commentary on Genesis.* 2d ed. Edinburgh: T & T Clark, 1930.

Slatkin, Laura M. *The Power of Thetis: Allusion and Interpretation in the* Iliad. Berkeley: University of California Press, 1991.

Smith, Mark S. *Origin and Development of the* Waw-*Consecutive: Northwest Semitic Evidence from Ugarit to Qumran.* Atlanta, Ga.: Scholars Press, 1991.

Speiser, E. A. *Genesis.* AB 1. Garden City, N.Y.: Doubleday, 1964.

Stamm, Johann Jakob. *Beiträge zur Hebräischen und altorientalischen Namenkunde.* Göttingen, Ger.: Vandenhoeck & Ruprecht, 1980.

Steiner, Peter. *Russian Formalism: A Metapoetics.* Ithaca, N.Y. Cornell University Press, 1984.

Sternberg, Meir. *The Poetics of Biblical Narrative: Ideological Literature and the Drama of Reading.* Bloomington: Indiana University Press, 1985.

———. "Time and Space in Biblical (Hi)story Telling: The Grand Chronology." In *The Book and the Text: The Bible and Literary Theory,* edited by Regina Schwartz, 81–145. Cambridge, Mass: Basil Blackwell, 1990.

Talmon, Shemaryahu. "Bridegroom of Blood" (in Hebrew). *Eretz Israel* 3 (1954): 93–95.

———. *Literary Studies in the Hebrew Bible: Form and Content.* Jerusalem: Magness Press, 1993.

Talstra, Eep. "Text Grammar and Hebrew Bible. I: Elements of a Theory." *BibOr* 35 (1978): 169–74.

———. "Text Grammar and Hebrew Bible. II: Syntax and Semantics." *BibOr* 39 (1982): 26–38.

Tomashevsky, Boris. "Thematics." In *Russian Formalist Criticism,* ed. Lemon and Reis, 61–95.

Toolan, Michael J. *Narrative: A Critical Linguistic Introduction.* London: Routledge, 1988.

van der Merwe, C. H. J. *The Old Hebrew Particle "gam": A Syntactic-semantic Description of "gam" in Gn–2Kg.* St. Ottilien, Ger.: EOS, 1990.

———. "The Old Hebrew 'Particles' אך and רק (in Genesis to 2 Kings)." In *Text, Methode und Grammatik: Wolfgang Richter zum 65. Geburtstag,* edited by W. Gross, H. Irsigler, and T. Siedl, 297–311. St. Ottilien, Ger.: EOS, 1991.

van der Merwe, C. H. J., Jackie A. Naudé, and Jan H. Kroeze. *A Biblical Hebrew Reference Grammar.* Sheffield, Eng.: Sheffield Academic Press, 1999.

van der Toorn, Karel, ed. *The Image and the Book: Iconic Cults, Aniconism, and the Rise of Book Religion in Israel and the Ancient Near East.* Louvain, Belgium: Peeters, 1997.

Van Seters, John. *Abraham in History and Tradition.* New Haven, Conn.: Yale University Press, 1975.

———. "The Conquest of Sihon's Kingdom: A Literary Examination." *JBL* 91 (1972): 182–97.

———. *In Search of History: Historiography in the Ancient World and the Origins of Biblical History.* New Haven, Conn.: Yale University Press, 1983.

Vernant, Jean-Pierre. *Myth and Thought among the Greeks.* London: Routledge and Kegan Paul, 1983.

von Rad, Gerhard. *Old Testament Theology.* 2 vols. Translated by D. M. G. Stalker. New York: Harper & Row, 1962–65.

———. *The Problem of the Hexateuch and Other Essays.* Translated by E. W. Trueman Dicken. Edinburgh: Oliver & Boyd, 1966.

———. *Studies in Deuteronomy.* Translated by David Stalker. London: SCM Press, 1953.

von Soden, Wolfram. *The Ancient Orient: An Introduction to the Study of the Ancient Near East.* Grand Rapids, Mich.: Eerdmans, 1994.

Waltisberg, Michael. "Zum Alter der Sprache des Deboraliedes Ri 5." *ZAH* 12 (1999): 218–32.

Waltke, Bruce, and M. O'Connor. *An Introduction to Biblical Hebrew Syntax.* Winona Lake, Ind.: Eisenbrauns, 1990.

Washburn, David L. "Chomsky's Separation of Syntax and Semantics." *Hebrew Studies* 35 (1994): 27–46.

Watt, Ian. *The Rise of the Novel: Studies in Defoe, Richardson, and Fielding.* Berkeley: University of California Press, 1965.

Weinfeld, Moshe. "Divine Intervention in War in Ancient Israel and in the Ancient Near East." In *History, Historiography and Interpretation: Studies in Biblical and Cuneiform Literatures,* edited by H. Tadmor and M. Weinfeld, 121–47. Jerusalem: Magnes Press, 1983.

———. "God the Creator in Genesis 1 and in the Prophecy of Second Isaiah" (in Hebrew). *Tarbits* 37 (1968): 105–32.

———. "Julius Wellhausen's Understanding of the Law of Ancient Israel and Its Fallacies" (in Hebrew). *Shnaton* 4 (1980): 62–93.

Weinrich, Harald. *Tempus: Besprochene und erzählte Welt.* 3d ed. Stuttgart: W. Kohlhammer, 1977.

———. "Tempusprobleme eines Leitartikels." *Euphorion* 60 (1966): 263-72.

Weiss, Meir. "Einiges über die Bauformen des Erzählens in der Bibel." *VT* 13 (1961): 456-75.

Wellek, René, and Austin Warren. *Theory of Literature.* 3d ed. New York: Harcourt, Brace & World, 1956.

Wellhausen, Julius. *Prolegomena to the History of Israel.* New York: Meridian Books, 1957.

West, Martin, ed. *Hesiod: Theogony.* Oxford: Oxford University Press, 1966.

———, ed. *Hesiod: Works and Days.* Oxford: Oxford University Press, 1978.

White, Hayden. *The Content of the Form: Narrative Discourse and Historical Representation.* Baltimore, Md.: Johns Hopkins University Press, 1987.

———. *Metahistory: The Historical Imagination in Nineteenth-Century Europe.* Baltimore, Md.: Johns Hopkins University Press, 1973.

———. *Tropics of Discourse: Essays in Cultural Criticism.* Baltimore, Md.: Johns Hopkins University Press, 1978.

Whitman, Cedric H. *Homer and the Heroic Tradition.* Cambridge, Mass.: Harvard University Press, 1958.

Whybray, R. N. "On Robert Alter's *The Art of Biblical Narrative.*" *JSOT* 27 (1983): 75-86.

Wiener, H. M. *The Composition of Judges II 11 to 1 Kings II 46.* Leipzig: Hinrichs, 1929.

Wilson, John A. "Egypt: The Function of the State." In Henri Frankfort et al., *The Intellectual Adventure of Ancient Man,* 62-92.

Woolf, Virginia. "Modern Fiction." In *The Common Reader,* 150-58. New York: Harcourt, Brace, 1925.

———. *Mrs. Dalloway.* San Diego, Calif.: Harcourt Brace Jovanovich, 1953.

———. "Mrs. Dalloway in Bond Street." In *The Complete Shorter Fiction of Virginia Woolf,* edited by Susan Dick, 152-59. 2d ed. San Diego, Calif.: Harcourt Brace Jovanovich, 1989.

———. *Orlando.* San Diego, Calif.: Harcourt Brace, 1956.

———. *To the Lighthouse.* San Diego, Calif.: Harcourt Brace Jovanovich, 1955.

———. *The Years.* New York: Harcourt Brace Jovanovich, 1965.

Wright, G. Ernest. *The Old Testament Against Its Environment.* London: SCM Press, 1950.

Wyatt, Nicolas. "Ilimilku's Ideological Programme: Ugaritic Royal Propaganda, and a Biblical Postscript." *UF* 29 (1997): 775-96.

———. "The Religion of Ugarit: An Overview." In *Handbook of Ugaritic Studies,* edited by Wilfred G. E. Watson and Nicolas Wyatt, 529-85. Leiden, Holland: Brill, 1999.

Yerushalmi, Yosef Hayim. *Zakhor: Jewish History and Jewish Memory.* New York: Schocken Books, 1989.

Zakovitch, Yair. "Sisseras Tod." *ZAW* 93 (1981): 364-74.

Zevit, Ziony. *The Anterior Construction in Classical Hebrew.* Atlanta, Ga.: Scholars Press, 1998.

Zewi, Tamar. "The Particles הנה and והנה in Biblical Hebrew." *Hebrew Studies* 37 (1996): 21-37.

Zielinski, Thaddeus. "Die Behandlung Gleichzeitiger Ereignisse im Antiken Epos." *Philologus Supplement* 8 (1899-1901): 405-49.

INDEX

Abraham (Abram), 118-19, 150, 178, 179, 185, 208-209
Absalom, 142-43, 150, 249n.29
Achilles, 71-72, 132-33, 144, 150, 171-76, 180, 186, 258n.52
Achish, 144-46
adjectives (classifiant and evaluative), 46
adverbials: *ʾak* as, 49-51; *gam* as, 48; infinitive absolute construction as, 53, 233n.48; speaker-oriented adverbials, 53, 231n.36
Aeneid (Virgil), 162-63
Agamemnon, 131-32, 171-76, 186
aharê, 242n.35
Ajax, 131-32
ʾak, 49-52, 56, 232nn.38,40
Albrektson, Bertil, 264n.83
alienation, 208
Alter, Robert: biblical narrative study of, 8; on conventions, 162-63, 186; on discourse, 112, 218n.40; on free motif, 180; on literary understanding of the Bible, 191; on modern fiction and biblical prose, 8, 9; on speech, 235n.69; on style, 63, 216n.20; on temporal relations, 142; on transition from oral to written, 18; on type-scenes, 175-76, 177, 178, 257n.41
Althusser, Louis, 207, 208, 263n.78, 264n.80, 266n.96
Ammon, 196, 197
Amnon, 142-43, 246n.97
Andersen, Francis I.: criticism of, 122; on "first event clause," 118; on *hinnēh*, 96, 97, 114-15, 117, 240n.16
Anderson, Benedict, 125-28, 142, 247n.7
aniconism, 206, 263n.72
animals (in oral tradition), 27, 224n.31, 246n.99
annunciation type-scenes, 177; of Danel, 183-85; of Hannah, 182; of Rachel, 182; of Rebekah, 181; of Sarah, 178, 179

anthropomorphization of God, 202, 205, 206, 263n.72
aorist: in Homer, 104, 152-53; perfect compared to, 61; as primary narrative tense, 72; in speech, 37, 235n.69; temporal relations and, 37-39, 41, 152, 237n.94; tense of the photograph, 147, 250n.44
Aqhat, 185
Arad Inscription, 237n.85
Aramaic, 4
archaeology of knowledge, 193-96, 197
Arend, Walter, 169-70, 176, 255n.32
aristeiai ("excellence"), 175
Aristotle, 32, 33
arming scenes, 171-75, 180, 258n.52; of Athena, 178-79, 181, 183; of Teucer, 182-83, 258n.60
Armstrong, James I., 254n.16, 256n.35
Asher, tribe of, 21
Asherah, 185
asyndeton, 65, 86
Athena, 132, 178-79, 181, 183
Atrahasis, 113
ʿattâ ("now"), 44-45, 57-58, 63, 85, 230n.27
audience, 3, 4, 219n.48
Auerbach, Erich: on Bible and Homer, 7-8, 16; on biblical realization of character, 150-51; on externalized characters, 76; on Homeric flashbacks, 258n.58; on Jewish concept of God, 190; on temporal relations, 125-26, 144, 153-54, 265n.87
authorial intrusions, 51, 55, 64, 86, 229n.27
Axial Age, 197

Baal, 184, 209
Baal, 155-56, 110
Babylon, 209
Babylonian traditions, 203
background, influence of, 150-51
Bakhtin, M. M., 36, 69, 70, 72
Bakker, Egbert J., 237n.93, 250n.37

ABOUT THE AUTHOR

Robert S. Kawashima was awarded the doctorate in comparative literature from the University of California, Berkeley, where he also taught for two years as a Faculty Fellow. He is currently Dorot Assistant Professor / Faculty Fellow at New York University's Skirball Department of Hebrew and Judaic Studies.